BIRDS

Readings from
SCIENTIFIC AMERICAN

BIRDS

With Introductions by
Barry W. Wilson
University of California, Davis

W. H. Freeman and Company
San Francisco

Most of the SCIENTIFIC AMERICAN articles in *Birds* are available as separate Offprints. For a complete list of articles now available as Offprints, write to W. H. Freeman and Company, 660 Market Street, San Francisco, California 94104.

Library of Congress Cataloging in Publication Data

Main entry under title:

Birds.

Includes bibliographies and index.
1. Birds—Addresses, essays, lectures.
I. Wilson, Barry W., 1931–
II. Scientific American.
QL672.B57   598.2   79–26134
ISBN 0–7167–1206–7
ISBN 0–7167–1207–5 pbk.

Printed in the United States of America

9 8 7 6 5 4 3 2

PREFACE

This book contains 25 of the more than 40 *Scientific American* articles about birds published since 1948. The articles are grouped into seven sections, each covering a different aspect of the life of birds and their relationship with humans. There are articles on the general features of birds and their distribution (Section I), how birds fly (Section II), and how they find their way (Section III). Several articles discuss the evolution of birds (Section IV). Others deal with behavior (Section V) and with physiology and song (Section VI). The last section concerns the human impact on birds (Section VII). Included at the back of the book are references to various books on birds, a brief list of ornithological journals, and a list of all *Scientific American* articles on birds that are not reprinted here.

Why are birds so popular among scientists and the general public? Virtually every aspect of their lives has come under scrutiny since at least the time of Aristotle. Perhaps it is because they are one of the most visible and beautiful parts of our living landscape. Who has not paused to listen to the cries of gulls or watch a formation of geese sweep across the sky?

Birds and humans share the same planet, but they lead very different lives. Birds are specialists—small, feathered, winged animals with specific adaptations that have given them access to the sky, the sea, and the land. Even though they are capable of complicated individual and group activities, approaching what some call intelligence, their behavior often seems stereotyped, much of it determined by unlearned responses programmed into their genes. In contrast, we are generalists—large, unspecialized mammals whose "specialty" is not a matter of external body design; we are capable of transmitting learned behavior from generation to generation, accomplishing in a few thousand years with oral and written history what it might take eons for evolution to bring about through genetic change.

The gulf between birds and people is wide; they are strangers, neither fully comprehending the other. We can only imagine with Canadian zoologist N. J. Berrill what it would be like to be a bird: ". . . to be alive more intensely than any other living creature. . . . Birds live in a world that is always in the present, mostly full of joy . . . with little memory of the past and no real anticipation of what is yet to come—intensely conscious of sight and sound, strongly swayed by joy and anger and sometimes petrified by ecstasy or fear."

The formal study of birds has been going on for a long time both for its own sake and for the insights it gives into the ways of nature. The avian egg and embryo were described by Aristotle (384–322 B.C.); Roman nobles maintained elaborate zoos with exotic birds. Frederick II (A.D. 1194–1250) of Germany wrote a treatise about falconry and the raising of birds in the Middle Ages—a treatise based upon observations rather than the superstitions of his day. Today, birds are valued as experimental animals in studies of reproduction, development, behavior, hormones, nutrition, inherited abnormalities, and cancer, as well as being important in ecological and agricultural research.

Biological research has become so complicated that much of it has become the province of the professional scientist with access to elaborate and expensive equipment. Fortunately, avian biology is one field of science in which amateurs can make lasting contributions. Careful studies by dedicated amateurs have added much to our knowledge of the numbers, distributions, and life histories of birds. The breeding of birds in captivity has been a special province of the amateur; reproductive colonies of many endangered species of birds have been established by their efforts.

Many people just enjoy watching birds. There are at least 10 million active bird watchers in the United States. Armed with binoculars and cameras, they stalk the feathered residents of field, forest, and shore. Bird watchers who live on major paths of migration have the opportunity to observe more than a hundred different species over the course of a year.

The day when comedians were guaranteed a laugh by making fun of bird watchers and their bird books is past. Societies dedicated to birds and other wildlife have become major forces in shaping public policy concerning land use. A photograph of a turn-of-the-century belle wearing egret feathers in her hat is occasionally used by the National Audubon Society to remind readers of the campaign waged by the society for legislation to prevent egrets and other birds from being decimated for the demands of fashion. Bank clerk, housewife, or professor, people who like and study birds have had a dramatic impact on conservation.

I do not know whether some birds watch people in the same way that people watch birds, but many wild birds have adapted to our ways. They make their homes in gardens, farms, and cities, often to the dismay of the human inhabitants. Pigeons, blackbirds, robins, starlings, sparrows, gulls, and many other birds successfully live with and exploit us.

Much of my research is done in the laboratory, where I work as a specialist with my students and colleagues, studying the development of birds and applying our knowledge to agriculture and human health. Each spring I am fortunate to get a chance to be a generalist, when I help teach an introductory course called "Birds, Man and the Environment." I enjoy this opportunity to expand my horizons as a teacher, a biologist, and a person. Some of the material in the introductions to the sections of this book are drawn from my lectures. I hope some of the enthusiasm of the students who take and who help teach this course is communicated in this book. I am grateful to C. R. Grau, W. W. Weathers, U. K. Abbott, and R. E. Burger of the University of California, Davis, L. Swan of San Francisco State University, and to J. R. Blanchard, Emeritus Librarian of the University of California at Davis, for their critical reading of the manuscript; to the staff of W. H. Freeman and Company, in particular Dick Johnson and Gunder Hefta; and to the staff of Scientific American, Inc., for the opportunity to prepare this collection. I am most grateful to my wife, Joyce Wilson, for her assistance in preparing the index to the articles and introductions.

This book was designed for the general nonscience reader, bird watcher, or aviculturist interested in learning more about birds. It should also be useful as supplemental reading material and as a basis for discussions in college biology courses. Whatever may be your reason for reading this book, I hope that you enjoy it and that it stimulates you to look further into the lives of the birds that share our yards, farms, woods, lakes, mountains, and skies.

October 1979   Barry W. Wilson

CONTENTS

Note on cross-references to SCIENTIFIC AMERICAN *articles:* Articles included in this book are referred to by title and page number; articles not included in this book but available as Offprints are referred to by title and offprint number; articles not included in this book and not available as Offprints are referred to by title and date of publication.

BIRDS

I

DIVERSITY OF BIRDS

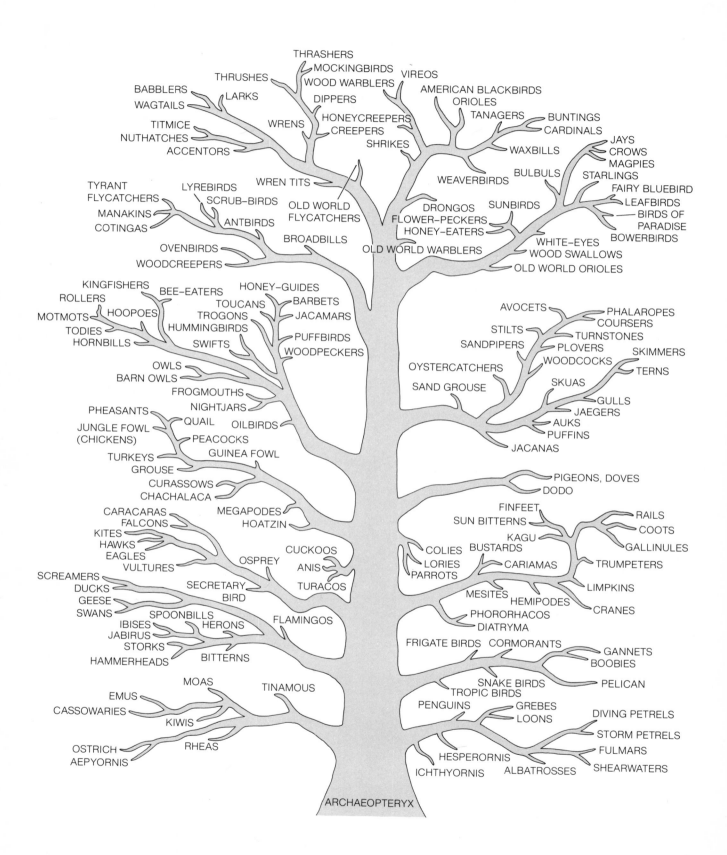

Figure 1. Possible evolutionary relationships of birds. [After J. C. Welty, *The Life of Birds*, Saunders, Philadelphia, 1975.]

DIVERSITY AND DISTRIBUTION OF BIRDS I

INTRODUCTION

Birds are one of the most distinctive groups of animals. Zoologists consider them different enough from other vertebrates to place them in their own class, on a par with reptiles, mammals, and amphibians. Their feathers, a unique feature, and their wings and hard-shelled eggs readily set them apart from other animals. They are also remarkably diverse in their appearance, making them, like butterflies, attractive to people who enjoy collecting things. The life lists of bird watchers—records of the species they have seen—are world-wide symbols of the avid amateur naturalist.

The major features and distribution of birds are the subjects of the two articles in this section, both written by Carl Welty, a distinguished avian biologist. The first article ("Birds as Flying Machines") discusses the major adaptations of birds and how their general body plan is tailored to the stringent demands of flight.

Today, most avian scientists (including Welty in *The Life of Birds*) agree that there are approximately 8,700 different species of birds—that is, about 8,700 distinctive kinds of birds that do not ordinarily interbreed. These are placed into about 170 families, which are themselves combined into 27 orders. Authorities differ on the exact number of species in each genera. All agree that more than 5,000 of the species are songbirds and that 315–339 of the rest are parrots. There are 147 species of swans, geese, and ducks and one species of ostrich. (The colorful *World Atlas of Birds*, edited by Peter Scott, and the textbook *Fundamentals of Ornithology*, by Josselyn Van Tyne and Andrew J. Berger, are two recent books that contain detailed listings of the orders and families of birds.) The relationships between the many kinds of birds are pictorially represented in Figure 1.

How many birds are there? The late British ornithologist James Fisher estimated that the world population exceeds 100 billion birds, approximately 25 times the number of human beings. Accurate figures exist for only a very few species. Oceanic birds may be the most populous; many island breeding colonies of petrels, shearwaters, fulmars, dovekies, and puffins exceed a million birds. A single flock of Slender-billed Shearwaters off Australia was estimated at 150 million birds. Ten million cormorants and boobies nest on a few islands off the coast of Peru. The populations of some endangered species are very low in number . Fewer than 30 California Condors live the year round in a small mountainous region above Los Angeles, and approximately 400 Kirtland's Warblers spend the breeding season in the Jack Pine forests of north-central Michigan and winter in the Bahamas. Each year, newspapers record the migration of the few dozen remaining Whooping Cranes as they fly from their summer home on a lake in Canada to their winter habitat in coastal Texas.

The most numerous wild bird in the United States today may be the Red-winged Blackbird. This was once believed to be true of the Passenger Pigeon;

4

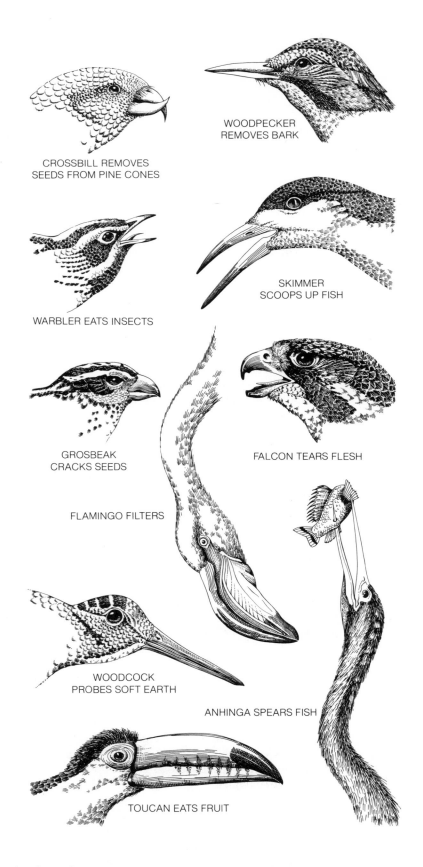

CROSSBILL REMOVES
SEEDS FROM PINE CONES

WOODPECKER
REMOVES BARK

WARBLER EATS INSECTS

SKIMMER
SCOOPS UP FISH

GROSBEAK
CRACKS SEEDS

FALCON TEARS FLESH

FLAMINGO FILTERS

WOODCOCK
PROBES SOFT EARTH

ANHINGA SPEARS FISH

TOUCAN EATS FRUIT

Figure 2. Examples of specializations of beaks and bills. Crossbills remove seeds from pine cones. Warblers catch insects. Grosbeaks crack seeds. Woodcocks probe for their food in soft earth. Toucans eat tropical fruits. Woodpeckers seek insects beneath the bark of trees. Skimmers scoop up fish while flying low over the water with their lower mandible cleaving the surface. Falcons tear the flesh of their prey. Anhingas spear fish with their sharp beak. Flamingos filter their food from the bottom waters of lakes and swamps.

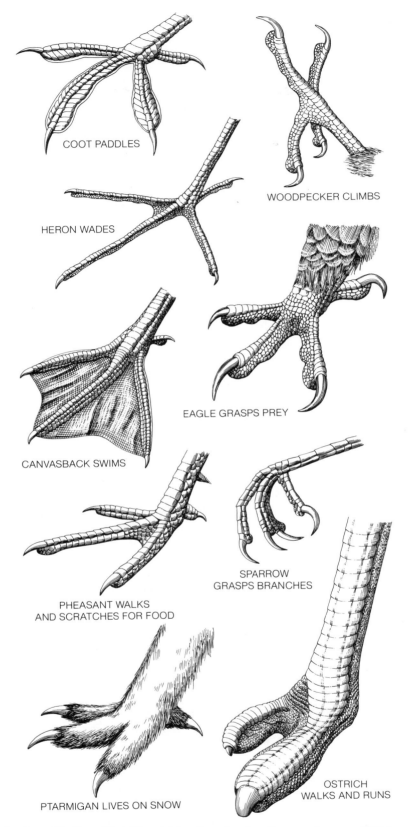

COOT PADDLES

WOODPECKER CLIMBS

HERON WADES

EAGLE GRASPS PREY

CANVASBACK SWIMS

PHEASANT WALKS
AND SCRATCHES FOR FOOD

SPARROW
GRASPS BRANCHES

PTARMIGAN LIVES ON SNOW

OSTRICH
WALKS AND RUNS

Figure 3. Examples of specializations of feet. The ostrich walks on two toes; it can run in excess of 50 kilometers (about 30 miles) per hour. Coots have lobed toes; ducks have webbing between their toes. The heron wades in water; its long toes distribute its weight so that it does not sink in the mud. The eagle grasps its prey with sharp talons. Woodpeckers climb trees with two toes in front and two behind. The pheasant scratches with three toes in front and one behind. Perching birds like the sparrow have feet especially adapted to grasping branches. Ptarmigans have feathers on their feet that help them walk in the snow.

136 million of these birds were estimated to have nested in an 850-square-mile area (2,200 square kilometers) in central Wisconsin in 1871. Audubon calculated that more than a billion Passenger Pigeons occupied a roost near Louisville, Kentucky, in 1813! Today there are none. The last known Passenger Pigeon died in captivity in 1914. The species was destroyed by humans—by hunting, by loss of habitat, and possibly by disease.

People are becoming the most imporant of the many factors that determine the numbers and distribution of birds. Almost 100 species of birds have become extinct since the Industrial Revolution began 300 years ago and human populations soared. Over 150 species are currently considered endangered, rare, or depleted by the International Union for Conservation of Nature and Natural Resources.

How long do birds live? Relatively speaking, the larger the bird, the longer its life span. Some birds live almost as long as people. Owls, eagles, and pelicans have survived to more than 50–60 years of age in captivity. Chickens and pigeons may live more than 30 years. Like other animals, birds are not apt to reach their maximum life expectancy in the wild. For example, in England, the average life expectancy of an intensively hunted game bird, the mallard, is only 11 months. Young birds have the highest death rates, even among species not hunted. David Lack, the late British ornithologist, estimated that only 25 percent or less of eggs laid result in young that live long enough to breed. Predators account for most of the mortality, but disease, bad weather, and accidents also take their toll.

A nesting pair of birds is biologically capable of raising many young in a season. If there were no factors controlling their reproductive potential, their fertility would soon result in an incredible number of birds. If, for example, one pair of mallards produced eight offspring that each survived to produce eight more offspring, and so forth, then within 16 years their descendants would exceed 300 billion, more than the total number of birds on this planet.

The major factors that affect population levels are: (1) fertility, (2) food supply, (3) habitat, (4) diseases, (3) weather, (4) predators, (5) nesting sites, and (6) parasites. These factors are not always the same for every species. For example, the number of nesting sites available for woodpeckers will establish an upper limit to their reproductivity. Conversely, the epidemics of botulism that periodically strike flocks of migrating ducks, geese, and swans may significantly reduce their numbers.

Charles Darwin used the harsh fact that more animals are born than survive as one of the bases for proposing a process he called "natural selection." Those that live to reproduce pass on to their offspring the genes that helped them to survive. An often-used example is the egg of the murre. The egg of this common sea bird is wider on one end than it is on the other, so that it rolls in a very small circle. Murres nest on narrow ledges of sea cliffs, and some believe that the shape of the egg helps keep it from rolling off to smash on the rocks below. Birds that lay rounder eggs that roll too far would be unlikely to pass on their genes to future generations.

Each species' life style, anatomy, and physiology is suited to the microenvironment in which it lives. The major external adaptations of birds—their beaks and bills, feet and wings—help to determine the *ecological niche* of each species (see Figs. 2, 3, and 4.): the flexible bill of the flamingo, the position of the toes of the woodpecker, the broad wings of the vulture are adaptations that suit the birds in these groups to their particualr ways of making a living, thus enabling them to avoid competition with closely related species.

The physical features of the landscape (topography and drainage, soil and water) and the climate (temperature range and annual precipitation) determine the kinds of plants that will grow in a region. Together, these constitute the habitat: the prairie, tropical rain forest, or riverbank in which specific animals live. It is convenient to think of the habitat as the address of an animal and its ecological niche as its occupation.

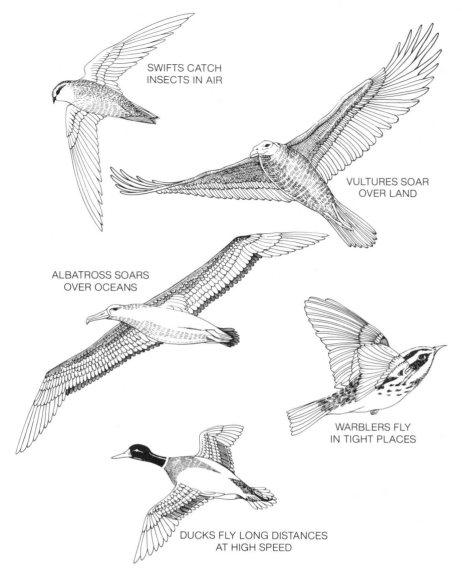

SWIFTS CATCH
INSECTS IN AIR

VULTURES SOAR
OVER LAND

ALBATROSS SOARS
OVER OCEANS

WARBLERS FLY
IN TIGHT PLACES

DUCKS FLY LONG DISTANCES
AT HIGH SPEED

Figure 4. Examples of specializations of wings. Fast fliers like swifts often have swept-back wings. Oceanic soaring birds like albatrosses have long, thin wings. Vultures, hawks, and eagles, which soar in thermals over land, have broad, slotted wings. Small forest birds like warblers have short stubby wings that help them maneuver in cluttered places. Ducks may fly 800 kilometers (approximately 500 miles) at better than 80 kilometers (50 miles) per hour.

The more we study natural systems, the more we learn that one of the important differences between natural ecosystems and those modified to suit human needs is that man simplifies and nature complicates. Man drastically alters the evolution of a region by severely reducing the possible number of ecological niches. A tree farm has fewer species of plants and animals living in it than did the forest it replaced.

The web of life in a forest is so intricate that a disaster befalling any single species of plant or animal need not mean disaster to all. The artificial systems that we manage in order to provide food, fiber, and timber lack the finely tuned checks and balances of the natural ecosystems. The native plants of the Great Plains of the United States and Canada have extensive root systems that enable them to survive periodic dry spells. The wheat that replaced these plants did not. When dry years came—and they often do on the Great Plains—the "monocultures" of wheat died, and, rootless, the land and the fortunes of those that farmed it blew away.

One might imagine that birds can escape the consequences of habitat destruction by flying somewhere else, but this is often not the case, particularily for migratory species, whose paths have become fixed over millions of years. Our ability to destroy habitats is outdistancing the ability of birds to escape. The Central Valley of California, where I live, once afforded hundreds of square miles of wetlands in the spring and fall that served as landing sites for millions of waterfowl during their migrations between northern Canada and the warmer regions of the western United States, Mexico, and Central America. Drainage of the swamps has produced one of the major agricultural regions of the world, but, at the same time, the much reduced wetlands provide food for far fewer ducks and geese than the flocks that darkened the sky a century ago. Those birds did not go someplace else; they perished of starvation, significantly reducing the future breeding population of waterfowl.

The second article by Carl Welty ("The Geography of Birds") tells about the distribution of birds on Earth and how changes in geography and climate have been an impetus to the evolution of the different birds we see today. Also discussed are the conditions that promote dispersal of species, how competition within a species for limited resources favors an increase in the range of a bird, and how competition between species tends to drive them apart into narrower, noncompetitive ranges.

REFERENCES

Scott, P. *The World Atlas of Birds*. Random House, New York, 1974.

Van Tyne, J., and A. J. Berger. *Fundamentals of Ornithology* (2nd ed.). Wiley, New York, 1976.

Welty, J. C. *The Life of Birds* (2nd ed.). Saunders, Philadelphia, 1975.

Birds as Flying Machines

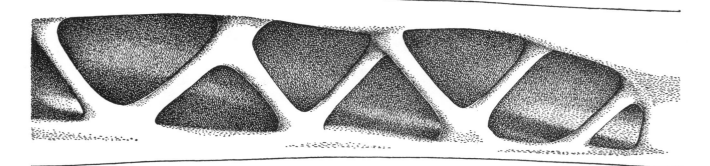

by Carl Welty
March 1955

A sequel to the article on the aerodynamics of birds in the April, 1952, issue of Scientific American. Among the remarkable adaptations birds have made to life in the air are high power and light weight.

The great struggle in most animals' lives is to avoid change. A chickadee clinging to a piece of suet on a bitter winter day is doing its unconscious best to maintain its internal status quo. Physiological constancy is the first biological commandment. An animal must eternally strive to keep itself warm, moist and supplied with oxygen, sugar, protein, salts, vitamins and the like, often within precise limits. Too great a change in its internal economy means death.

The spectacular flying performances of birds—spanning oceans, deserts and whole continents—tend to obscure the more important fact that the ability to fly confers on them a remarkably useful mechanism to preserve their internal stability, or homeostasis. Through flight birds can search out the external conditions and substances they need to keep their internal fires burning clean and steady. A bird's wide search for specific foods and habitats makes sense only when considered in the light of this persistent, urgent need for constancy.

The power of flight opens up to birds an enormous gaseous ocean, the atmosphere, and a means of quick, direct access to almost any spot on earth. They can eat in almost any "restaurant"; they have an almost infinite choice of sites to build their homes. As a result birds are, numerically at least, the most successful vertebrates on earth. They number roughly 25,000 species and subspecies, as compared with 15,000 mammals and 15,000 fishes.

At first glance birds appear to be quite variable. They differ considerably in size, body proportions, color, song and ability to fly. But a deeper look shows that they are far more uniform than, say, mammals. The largest living bird, a 125-pound ostrich, is about 20,000 times heavier than the smallest bird, a hummingbird weighing only one tenth of an ounce. However, the largest mammal, a 200,000-pound blue whale, weighs some 22 million times as much as the smallest mammal, the one-seventh-ounce masked shrew. Mammals, in other words, vary in mass more than a thousand times as much as birds. In body architecture, the comparative uniformity of birds is even more striking. Mammals may be as fat as a walrus or as slim as a weasel, furry as a musk ox or hairless as a desert rat, long as a whale or short as a mole. They may be built to swim, crawl, burrow, run or climb. But the design of nearly all species of birds is tailored to and dictated by one pre-eminent activity—flying. Their structure, outside and inside, constitutes a solution to the problems imposed by flight. Their uniformity has been thrust on them by the drastic demands that determine the design of any flying machine. Birds simply dare not deviate widely from sound aerodynamic design. Nature liquidates deviationists much more consistently and drastically than does any totalitarian dictator.

Birds were able to become flying machines largely through the evolutionary gifts of feathers, wings, hollow bones, warm-bloodedness, a remarkable system of respiration, a strong, large heart and powerful breast muscles. These adaptations all boil down to the two prime requirements for any flying machine: high power and low weight. Birds have thrown all excess baggage overboard. To keep their weight low and feathers dry they forego the luxury of sweat glands. They have even reduced

INTERNAL STRUCTURE of the metacarpal bone of a vulture's wing is shown in this drawing of a longitudinal section. The braces within the bone are almost identical in geometry with those of the Warren truss commonly used as a steel structural member.

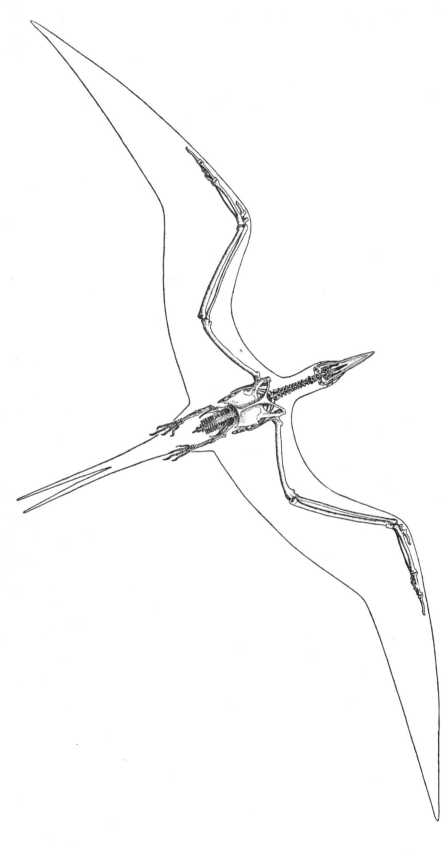

their reproductive organs to a minimum. The female has only one ovary, and during the nonbreeding season the sex organs of both males and females atrophy. T. H. Bissonette, the well-known investigator of birds and photoperiodicity, found that in starlings the organs weigh 1,500 times as much during the breeding season as during the rest of the year.

As early as 1679 the Italian physicist Giovanni Borelli, in his *De motu animalium*, noted some of the weight-saving features of bird anatomy: ". . . the body of a Bird is disproportionately lighter than that of man or of any quadruped . . . since the bones of birds are porous, hollowed out to extreme thinness like the roots of the feathers, and the shoulder bones, ribs and wing bones are of little substance; the breast and abdomen contain large cavities filled with air; while the feathers and the down are of exceeding lightness."

The skeleton of a pigeon accounts for only 4.4 per cent of its total body weight, whereas in a comparable mammal such as a white rat it amounts to 5.6 per cent. This in spite of the fact that the bird must have larger and stronger breast bones for the muscles powering its wings and larger pelvic bones to support its locomotion on two legs. The ornithologist Robert Cushman Murphy has reported that the skeleton of a frigate bird with a seven-foot wingspread weighed only four ounces, which was less than the weight of its feathers!

Although a bird's skeleton is extremely light, it is also very strong and elastic—necessary characteristics in an air frame subjected to the great and sudden stresses of aerial acrobatics. This combination of lightness and strength depends mainly on the evolution of hollow, thin bones coupled with a considerable fusion of bones which ordinarily are separate in other vertebrates. The bones of a bird's sacrum and hip girdle, for example, are molded together into a thin, tube-like structure—strong but phenomenally light. Its hollow finger bones are fused together, and in large soaring birds some of these bones have internal trusslike supports, very like the struts inside airplane wings. Similar struts sometimes are seen in the hollow larger bones of the wings and legs.

To "trim ship" further, birds have evolved heads which are very light in proportion to the rest of the body. This has been accomplished through the simple device of eliminating teeth and the accompanying heavy jaws and jaw muscles. A pigeon's skull weighs about

FRIGATE BIRD has a seven-foot wing span, but its skeleton weighs only four ounces. This is less than the weight of its feathers. The skeleton is shown against the outline of the bird.

one sixth as much, proportionately, as that of a rat; its skull represents only one fifth of 1 per cent of its total body weight. In birds the function of the teeth has been taken over largely by the gizzard, located near the bird's center of gravity. The thin, hollow bones of a bird's skull have a remarkably strong re-

inforced construction [*see photograph on page 12*]. Elliott Coues, the 19th-century U. S. ornithologist, referred to the beautifully adapted avian skull as a "poem in bone."

The long, lizard-like tail that birds inherited from their reptilian ancestors has been reduced to a small plate of bone

AIR SACS connected to the lungs of a pigeon not only lighten the bird but also add to the efficiency of its respiration and cooling. The lungs are indicated by the two dark areas in the center. Two of the air sacs are within the large bones of the bird's upper "arm."

at the end of the vertebrae. The ribs of a bird are elegantly long, flat, thin and jointed; they allow extensive movement for breathing and flying, yet are light and strong. Each rib overlaps its neighbor—an arrangement which gives the kind of resilient strength achieved by a woven splint basket.

Feathers, the bird's most distinctive and remarkable acquisition, are magnificently adapted for fanning the air, for insulation against the weather and for reduction of weight. It has been claimed that for their weight they are stronger than any wing structure devised by man. Their flexibility allows the broad trailing edge of each large wing-feather to bend upward with each downstroke of the wing. This produces the equivalent of pitch in a propeller blade, so that each wingbeat provides both lift and forward propulsion. When a bird is landing or taking off, its strong wingbeats separate the large primary wing feathers at their tips, thus forming wing-slots which help prevent stalling. It seems remarkable that man took so long to learn some of the fundamentals of airplane design which even the lowliest English sparrow demonstrates to perfection [see "Bird Aerodynamics," by John H. Storer, *beginning on page 32*].

Besides all this, feathers cloak birds with an extraordinarily effective insulation—so effective that they can live in parts of the Antarctic too cold for any other animal.

The streamlining of birds of course is the envy of all aircraft designers. The bird's awkwardly angular body is trimmed with a set of large quill, or contour, feathers which shape it to the utmost in sleekness. A bird has no ear lobes sticking out of its head. It commonly retracts its "landing gear" (legs) while in flight. As a result birds are far and away the fastest creatures on our planet. The smoothly streamlined peregrine falcon is reputed to dive on its prey at speeds up to 180 miles per hour. (Some rapid fliers have baffles in their nostrils to protect their lungs and air sacs from excessive air pressures.) Even in the water, birds are among the swiftest of animals: Murphy once timed an Antarctic penguin swimming under water at an estimated speed of about 22 miles per hour.

A basic law of chemistry holds that the velocity of any chemical reaction roughly doubles with each rise of 10 degrees centigrade in temperature. In nature the race often goes to the metabolically swift. And birds have evolved the highest operating temperatures of all animals. Man, with his conservative 98.6

degrees Fahrenheit, is a metabolic slow-poke compared with sparrows (107 degrees) or some thrushes (113 degrees). Birds burn their metabolic candles at both ends, and as a result live short but intense lives. The average wild songbird survives less than two years.

Behind this high temperature in birds lie some interesting circulatory and respiratory refinements. Birds, like mammals, have a four-chambered heart which allows a double circulation, that is, the blood makes a side trip through the lungs for purification before it is circulated through the body again. A bird's heart is large, powerful and rapid-beating [see table of comparisons on page 13]. In both mammals and birds the heart rate, and the size of the heart in proportion to the total body, increases as the animals get smaller. But the increases seem significantly greater in birds than in mammals. Any man with a weak heart knows that climbing stairs puts a heavy strain on his pumping system. Birds do a lot of "climbing," and their circulatory systems are built for it.

The blood of birds is not significantly richer in hemoglobin than that of mammals. The pigeon and the mallard have about 15 grams of hemoglobin per 100 cubic centimeters of blood—the same as man. However, the concentration of sugar in their blood averages about twice as high as in mammals. And their blood pressure, as one would expect, also is somewhat higher: in the pigeon it averages 145 millimeters of mercury; in the chicken, 180 millimeters; in the rat, 106 millimeters; in man, 120 millimeters.

In addition to conventional lungs, birds possess an accessory system of five or more pairs of air sacs, connected with the lungs, that ramify widely throughout the body. Branches of these sacs extend into the hollow bones, sometimes even into the small toe bones. The air-sac system not only contributes to the birds' lightness of weight but also supplements the lungs as a supercharger (adding to the efficiency of respiration) and serves as a cooling system for the birds' speedy, hot metabolism. It has been estimated that a flying pigeon uses one fourth of its air intake for breathing and three fourths for cooling.

The lungs of man constitute about 5 per cent of his body volume; the respiratory system of a duck, in contrast, makes up 20 per cent of the body volume (2 per cent lungs and 18 per cent air sacs). The anatomical connections of the lungs and air sacs in birds seem to provide a one-way traffic of air through most of the system, bringing in a constant stream of unmixed fresh air, whereas in the lungs

of mammals stale air is mixed inefficiently with the fresh. It seems odd that natural selection has never produced a stale air outlet for animals. The air sacs of birds apparently approach this ideal more closely than any other vertebrate adaptation.

Even in the foods they select to feed their engines birds conserve weight. They burn "high-octane gasoline." Their foods are rich in caloric energy—seeds, fruits, worms, insects, rodents, fish and so on. They eat no low-calorie foods such as leaves or grass; a wood-burning engine has no place in a flying machine. Furthermore, the food birds eat is burned quickly and efficiently. Fruit fed to a young cedar waxwing passes through its digestive tract in an average time of 27 minutes. A thrush that is fed blackberries will excrete the seeds 45

minutes later. Young bluejays take between 55 and 105 minutes to pass food through their bodies. Moreover, birds utilize a greater portion of the food they eat than do mammals. A three-weeks-old stork, eating a pound of food (fish, frogs and other animals), gains about a third of a pound in weight. This 33 per cent utilization of food compares roughly with an average figure of about 10 per cent in a growing mammal.

The breast muscles of a bird are the engine that drives its propellers or wings. In a strong flier, such as the pigeon, these muscles may account for as much as one half the total body weight. On the other hand, some species—e.g., the albatross—fly largely on updrafts of air, as a glider does. In such birds the breast muscles are greatly re-

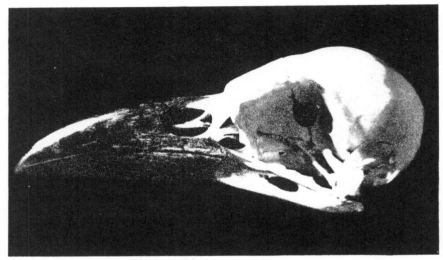

SKULL OF A CROW achieves the desirable aerodynamic result of making the bird light in the head. Heavy jaws are sacrificed. Their work is largely taken over by the gizzard.

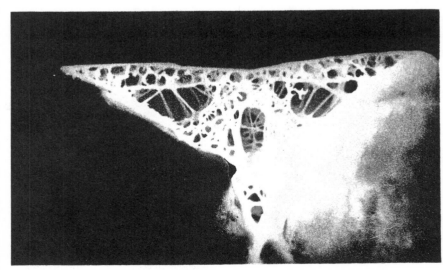

FRONTAL BONE in the skull of a crow is cut through to show its hollow and braced internal construction. The skull of the bird accounts for less than 1 per cent of its total weight.

HEART	PERCENT OF BODY WEIGHT	HEART BEATS PER MINUTE
FROG	.57	22
MAN	.42	72
PIGEON	1.71	135
CANARY	1.68	514
HUMMINGBIRD	2.37	615

HEART WEIGHT and pulse rate are compared for a number of animals. The hearts of birds are relatively large for body size.

duced, and there are well-developed wing tendons and ligaments which enable the bird to hold its wings in the soaring position with little or no effort.

A bird may have strong breast muscles and still be incapable of sustained flight because of an inadequate blood supply to these muscles. This condition is shown in the color of the muscles; that is the explanation of the "white meat" of the chicken and the turkey—their breast muscles have so few blood vessels that they cannot get far off the ground. The dark meat of their legs, on the other hand, indicates a good blood supply and an ability to run a considerable distance without tiring.

After a ruffed grouse has been flushed four times in rapid succession, its breast muscles become so fatigued that it can be picked up by hand. The blood supply is simply inadequate to bring in fuel and carry away waste products fast enough. Xenophon's *Anabasis* relates the capture of bustards in exactly this manner: "But as for the Bustards, anyone can catch them by starting them up quickly; for they fly only a short distance like the partridge and soon tire. And their flesh was very sweet."

In birds the active phase of the breathing cycle is not in inhaling but exhaling. Their wing strokes compress the rib case to expel the air. Thus instead of "running out of breath" birds "fly into breath."

Probably the fastest metabolizing vertebrate on earth is the tiny Allen's hummingbird [see "The Metabolism of Hummingbirds," by Oliver P. Pearson; SCIENTIFIC AMERICAN, January, 1953]. While hovering it consumes about 80 cubic centimeters of oxygen per gram of body weight per hour. Even at rest its metabolic rate is more than 50 times as fast as man's. Interestingly enough, the hovering hummingbird uses energy at about the same proportionate rate as a hovering helicopter. This does not mean that man has equalled nature in the efficiency of energy yield from fuel. To hover the hummingbird requires a great deal more energy, because of the aerodynamic inefficiency of its small wings and its very high loss of energy as dissipated heat. The tiny wings of a hummingbird impose on the bird an almost incredible expenditure of effort. Its breast muscles are estimated to be approximately four times as large, proportionately, as those of a pigeon. This great muscle burden is one price a hummingbird pays for being small.

A more obvious index of the efficiency of bird's fuel consumption is the high mileage of the golden plover. In the fall the plover fattens itself on bayberries in Labrador and then strikes off across the open ocean on a nonstop flight of 2,400 miles to South America. It arrives there weighing some two ounces less than it did on its departure. This is the equivalent of flying a 1,000-pound airplane 20 miles on a pint of gasoline rather than the usual gallon. Man still has far to go to approach such efficiency.

2 The Geography of Birds

by Carl Welty
July 1957

Although they are free to fly wherever they please, few birds are cosmopolitan. After 150 million years of evolution in a constantly changing environment, most species are confined to provincial abodes

When birds took to the air, some 150 million years before the Wright brothers, they had a highway to every possible habitat on the earth's surface. Today they are at home in the polar regions and the tropics, in forest and desert, on mountain and prairie and on the ocean and its islands. Yet when one considers the superb mobility of birds and the eons of time they have had to populate the globe, it is surprising how few cosmopolitan species there are. Some shore and sea birds—sandpipers and plovers, petrels and gulls—are fairly world-wide in distribution. The barn owls, kingfishers, hawks and acrobatic swallows are at home on every continent. Ravens have inherited the earth except, for some obscure reason, South America. But what we mostly see, especially in land

BROWN PELICAN is restricted in range by its feeding habits. It must be able to see the swimming fish it seizes in plunging dives. The turbidity of the Atlantic at the mouth of the Amazon [see *map on page 18*] bars it from that region and the waters farther to the south. This and all the other photographs that accompany this article were provided by the National Auubon Society.

birds, is a picture of curiously limited and seemingly haphazard distribution.

Why are the birds of England and Japan more alike, though 7,000 miles apart, than the birds of Africa and Madagascar, separated by a mere 250 miles? Why does South America have more than 400 species of hummingbird and Africa, with quite similar habitats, not a single one? Why have the finches, found on even the most isolated oceanic islands, not found their way to Australia? Why does the North American turkey, Benjamin Franklin's nominee for our national bird, occur nowhere else in the world? How explain the even more circumscribed range of the wirebird plover, unique to the little island of Saint Helena; or the confinement of a species of Ecuadorian hummingbird to the slopes of the volcano Chimborazo at an elevation of 16,000 feet; or the perilous distinction of the 161 remaining Laysan teal that inhabit the tiniest range of all, the shores of a marshy lagoon, one square mile in area, on the tiny Hawaiian island of Laysan?

The main scheme of the world distribution of birds was laid out by Alfred Russel Wallace in his monumental *Geographic Distribution of Animals,* published in 1876. His six great zoogeographic regions today provide a useful way to sort out the distribution of species, as shown in the map on the next two pages. But this still does not explain how the birds came to be distributed as they are. As a Darwinian intensely aware of the dynamic nature of evolution, Wallace could have told us that we must seek our answer in the interplay of two great dynamic agents: the perpetually changing environment and the unending evolution of the birds.

A restless world of heaving earthquakes, wandering shorelines, shifting climate and changing coats of vegetation can scarcely be expected to have sedentary tenants. A species' range is not likely to stand firm before the chilling, grinding advance of a glacier. We dig up the bones of large ostrich-like birds in the U.S.S.R. and the U. S. The fossils around Paris tell us this was once the home of now pan-tropical trogons and parrots. Ancient guano deposits in Peru show how the native pelican shifted from place to place during prehistoric times.

But birds are not mere passive creatures of these forces. The very geological and climatic changes that move and isolate existing species provide the mechanism of natural selection through which new species evolve. The families

PIGMENTATION AND SIZE of bird species are correlated with climate. British chickadee (*upper right*) is more heavily pigmented than Siberian chickadee (*upper left*). Hairy woodpecker of Canada (*lower left*) is larger than the same species in Costa Rica (*lower right*).

of modern birds, though established as late as the Miocene, have still had enough time to undergo many profound genetic changes. These in interaction with the changing environment have played their part, too, in distributing species around the globe. The migratory birds that summer in the temperate latitudes and winter in the tropics must have evolved during the comparatively recent millennia in which the world developed its present climatic system. But evolution does not always provide for maintenance and extension of range. The Ascension man-of-war bird, for instance, is a splendid sea-flyer, yet cannot venture far from land. Its oil-producing preen gland has become so small that it cannot alight on the ocean without becoming waterlogged, and it is endangered if caught too far from shore by a heavy rain.

Wallace's map, then, is a single frame from a motion picture, a moment arrested in a long history. To understand how it came about requires the accounting of many factors. Principal among these are the arrangement of the earth's land and sea masses, the circulation systems of the oceans and of the atmosphere, climate, the availability of plant life and the competition of animal life. By considering what each element contributes to the picture alone and in concert with others we can begin to reconstruct the history that lies behind the present geography of birds.

Let us consider first the accidents of geography. It is obvious that land masses are barriers to the spread of sea birds and that the seas are barriers to land birds. This leads straight to the explanation of why South American birds are so different from those of North America: It is because the two continents were so long separated by a sea before the Isthmus of Panama was thrust up. Conversely the fact that many North American birds are closely related to Asiatic species clearly means that their ancestors must have come over "from the old country" when the Bering Strait was a land bridge.

We can see the same processes going on today. As Ernst Mayr of Harvard University has observed, the geologically active regions are also regions of active species-making. The tributaries of the Amazon have cut the forest bordering the river into great "islands," each of which has isolated its distinct but related species of birds. The geologically recent building of the Andes split apart numerous populations of tropi-

cal birds in Colombia and Ecuador. They have evolved into new species, with those on the Pacific side of the range having their nearest relatives across the peaks in the Amazon basin. Just as mountains may isolate species, so mountain passes can provide bridges to join them. The ornithologist Frank Chapman described one pass where the tropical zone reaches nearly up to the saddle. Here we can actually see a large reservoir of species ready to spill over into a new and enlarged range the moment a saddle sinks, or the life zones rise, a few hundred feet.

Once a species surmounts a barrier, it may invade and colonize an enormously larger range with explosive speed, as did the starlings here or the skylarks in New Zealand. About 20 years ago the Old World cattle egret somehow made its way to South America, where it prospered mightily. Now it has reached the United States and is already consolidating its invasion by breeding.

The winds set up by the circulation system of the atmosphere have played the decisive part in distributing some species. For birds as for planes the flight west across the Atlantic in the teeth of the prevailing westerlies is more difficult than the reverse trip. Only five species of wild European land birds have been taken alive in North America; in Great Britain, with but one tenth the coastline, there have been recorded 14 American land species, not to mention 25 aquatic. On the island of South Georgia in the Antarctic are two endemic species, a pipit and a teal, whose nearest relatives live 1,000 miles due west to windward, on the tip of Tierra del Fuego. The islands of the Caribbean are to the leeward of the late summer cyclones of the north equatorial Atlantic; hence they have received as guests from the eastern Atlantic one species each of the tropic bird, frigate bird and booby.

The circulation system of the oceans is important in the distribution of birds not only because it helps or hinders their locomotion but for its effects on climate and food resources. The royal tern, a warm-water species, is bottled up in the Pacific within 30 degrees of latitude, between the cool south-flowing California Current and the chilly north-flowing Peru Current. But in the Atlantic, thanks to the warm Gulf Stream and Brazil Current, its range covers 70 degrees of latitude, from Florida to Argentina. The shoemaker petrel, on the other hand, is tied to cold surface waters and is sand-

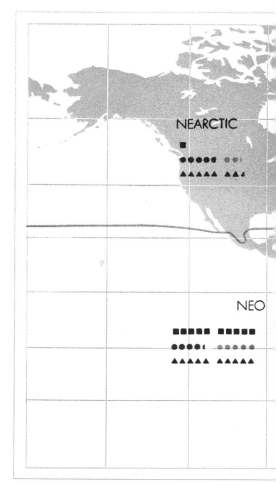

■   1 PECULIAR FAMILY

●   25 GENERA (● PECULIAR GENERA)

▲   100 SPECIES

wiched in between the Antarctic pack ice and the Equatorial and Brazil currents. The 12-degree surface-water isotherm marks the northern limit of both the snow petrel and its chief food, the opossum shrimp.

Sea birds in general, unlike land birds, are more abundant in the cooler latitudes because the circumpolar waters are more fertile than the equatorial. Where cool upwelling currents bring nitrates, phosphates and other essential minerals upward into the sunlight, marine plants and consequently fish life abound. Hence the flying multitudes that follow the cold Peru Current, while the warm Sargasso Sea remains a silent watery desert.

The dependence of certain birds on the prevailing ocean currents is dramatically demonstrated on those occasions when nature experiments with the circulation of the oceans. Once about every

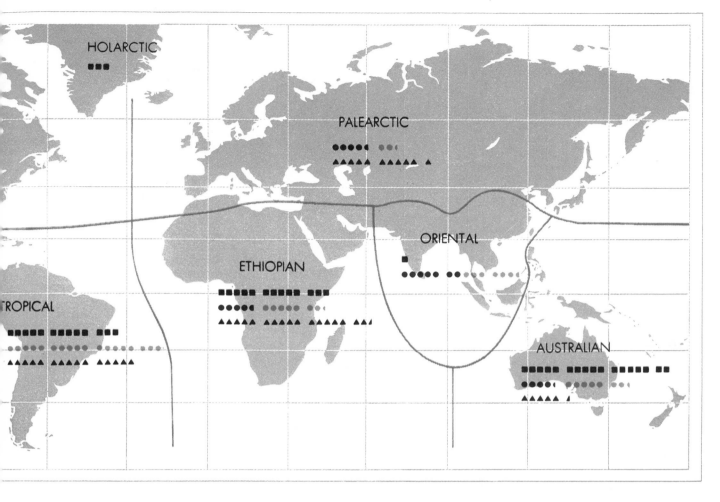

DISTRIBUTION OF BIRDS is mapped in the six zoogeographic regions proposed by Alfred Russel Wallace in 1876. The black squares tally the families "peculiar" to each region, but not all of the families in it. The black and gray circles together tally all the genera in each region; the black triangles, all the species. The Holarctic, comprising the two northern regions, has only three families peculiar to it. The contrast with tropical regions indicates that the latter have been the principal recent evolutionary center for birds.

seven years "El Niño," the warm equatorial countercurrent off Colombia and Ecuador, swings south, head-on into the Peru Current. In 1925 El Niño shifted its course so strongly that it warmed the littoral waters as far south as Arica, Chile, with these catastrophic effects: the Peru Current plankton died; the normal fish population died or fled and was replaced by warm-water species; hundreds of thousands of cormorants, boobies and pelicans perished or succumbed to disease; tropical sea birds moved down the coast, supplanting the sick and dying guano birds.

The distribution of sea birds, as has been indicated, runs counter to the major pattern of land-bird distribution. Some 85 per cent of all living species occur in the tropics, becoming progressively less abundant toward the poles. The major factor in these statistics is undoubtedly climate. Birds have special physiological problems of high body-temperature, rapid breathing and water conservation; all of these, to say nothing of food needs, are more readily solved in a warm, moist climate. This reflects the fact that more of the earth was tropical, humid and perpetually verdant in the Miocene and early Pliocene, when the birds were evolving. So today we find 1,780 species of birds breeding in Ecuador, 195 in New York State, 56 in Greenland and 3 in Antarctica.

The intimate and long-standing relationship between climate and bird distribution is reflected in the contrasting anatomy and physiology of warm- and cold-climate birds. The response of bird evolution to change of environment is so direct and systematic that it can be expressed in a series of biological rules. For example, species of birds living in colder climates will be larger than related species in warmer climates. This rule, which also holds for mammals, clearly results from natural selection in favor of the physiological advantage involved. Birds with larger bodies have relatively less surface through which to lose heat, a large bird being in essence the same as two or three small birds huddled together to keep warm. Birds in colder regions also have relatively shorter beaks, legs and wings from which to radiate body heat. According to another rule, the birds in the cooler part of a species' range will lay more eggs per clutch than those in the warmer. Egg counts by David Lack, the British ornithologist, show the European robin laying an average of 6.2 eggs per clutch in Scandinavia, 4.9 in Spain and 3.5 in the Canary Islands. Despite the short Scandinavian summer, birds can raise large broods of young because of the abundance of insect food and the long daylight hours. For less obviously adap-

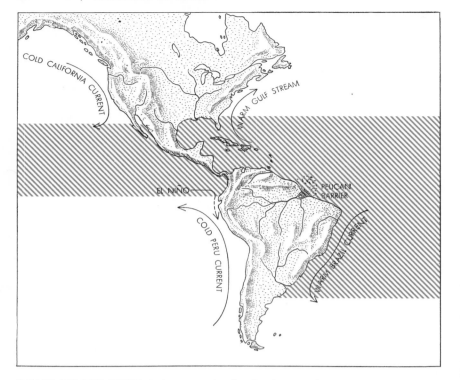

OCEAN TEMPERATURE is important in the distribution of oceanic birds. The warm-water zone (*colored area*) of the Atlantic is wider than that of the Pacific; the currents in the two oceans account for the contrast. Caption on page 14 explains "pelican barrier."

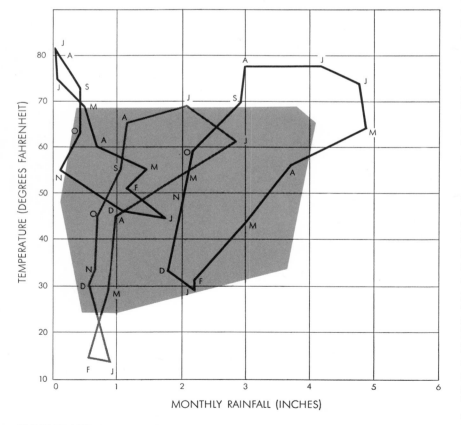

CLIMOGRAPH charts monthly rainfall and temperature. The colored area is the optimum climograph for the European partridge. The black lines give the data for California (*left*) and Missouri, where this bird fails; the gray line describes Montana, where it succeeds.

tive reasons, birds and mammals in the tropics have more of the dark pigment melanin than their relatives in cooler climates. Where tropical birds have brighter and more metallic hues, those in the polar regions tend toward white.

The high correlation of range and climate in some species is clearly demonstrated when the climate changes. As is well known, the mean annual temperature of the Northern Hemisphere has been gradually rising during recent decades. It is equally common knowledge that many southern birds, like the cardinal, egret and mockingbird, have been slowly coming northward. In Sweden 50 years ago the hooded crow was a harbinger of spring; today it is a common winter resident. In Finland 262 bird species were known before 1885; now there are 298, the new ones coming mostly from southern Europe and the Mediterranean.

The principle of climatic distribution has been put to practical use in game management. Before a game species is transplanted to a new habitat a climograph, a chart combining temperature and humidity factors [*see illustration at bottom of this page*], is drawn up for its natural range and compared with that of its proposed home. Where the two match fairly closely, there is at least a chance that the transplant will take hold.

The concentration of bird species in the tropics is correlated with food supply as well as with climate. Since green plants supply the first step in the animal food chain, it follows that the verdure of the tropics offers more of all kinds of sustenance than other regions. Conversely it is clear that insect-eating birds must migrate southward from freezing temperatures when winter comes.

The connection between food supply and range is clearly indicated in cases of adaptation to special diets. Woodpeckers will scarcely seek wood-boring insects on steppes or prairies. Nectar-feeding hummingbirds must have long-season flower resources; some species are bound by the shape of their bills to particular flowering plants. The beaks of crossbills are peculiarly adapted to secure a diet of conifer seeds. The white booby specializes in the catching of flying fish; its breeding islands must accordingly lie in waters where they abound. Such narrow dependency is, of course, an invitation to extinction. When a natural catastrophe all but wiped out the eelgrass along the Atlantic coast of the U. S. in 1931-33, one of the many casualties was the sea brant that fed upon it; the numbers of this goose were reduced by 80 per cent. Such a fate is not likely to overtake the wide-ranging South American kelp gull. Its diet includes fish, marine invertebrates and shellfish, the eggs and young of other birds, carrion, offal—in fact, almost anything.

The ranges of some species are fixed by adaptations to other aspects of their environment that may seem less compelling than food. For nesting sites Scott's oriole in the American Southwest is apparently dependent on the drooping dead leaves of the yucca; the European reed warbler, on beds of freshwater reeds; the palm swift, on the hanging fronds of the fan palm. The Tristan Island penguins depend upon the indigenous tussock grass to protect them from the elements and predatory gulls, and they reciprocally fertilize it with their droppings. The Bigua cormorant of Tierra del Fuego and the red-footed booby of Little Cayman in the Caribbean present a contrasting picture. They are tree-top nesters; sometimes they nest in such dense colonies that their guano kills the trees, compelling them to move on to new ones.

A force that seems always to promote the expansion of range and the wider dispersal of a species is the competition of other birds of the same species. Overpopulation—or the shortage of food, which is the other side of the same coin—gives a dramatic demonstration of its power in the occasional mass movements of a species, known as "invasions" or "irruptions." The snowy owl's repeated southward irruptions into the U. S. are known to coincide with the ebb years in the population cycle of the Canadian lemming. Siberian nutcrackers have invaded Germany 15 times between 1896 and 1933, each time when the pine-seed crop failed at home. Pallas's sand grouse has many times in years of drought burst out of its native steppes northeast of the Caspian Sea and swept in enormous numbers across Europe as far as Britain and Ireland. In the great invasion of 1888 the British Parliament, hoping to naturalize the bird, passed a special act for its protection, but four years later there was not a single grouse to be seen in all England. In these irruptions we see a momentary surmounting of normal barriers through the build-up of dispersal pressure from behind. They provide a mechanism for sampling new ranges, though they rarely succeed in establishing permanent new homes for the species.

Competition within a species promotes the extension of range more com-

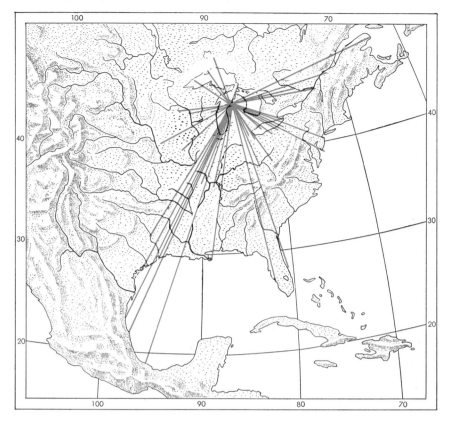

DISTANCES FLOWN by herring gulls, banded and released in the Great Lakes region, are charted here. Most of the birds recaptured at the most distant points were found to be yearlings. Dispersal tendency in young birds relieves population pressure on natal areas.

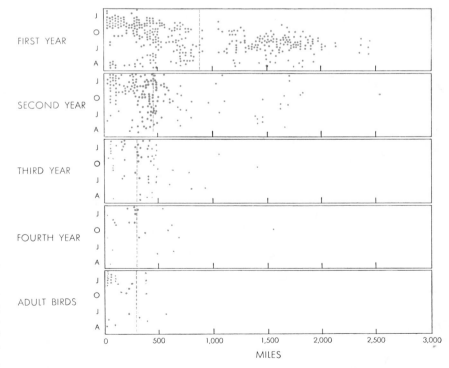

DISPERSAL TENDENCY of yearling herring gulls is indicated by this chart based upon recapture of 773 out of 23,434 nestlings banded in New Brunswick. The chart shows the age, the season of the year and the distance from home to the place of recapture of each bird. The mean distance traveled by the birds in each age group is indicated by the broken line.

SKYLARK, the common, field-nesting bird celebrated in Shelley's ode, was transplanted from Europe to New Zealand and has prospered there.

RING-NECKED PHEASANT, familiar to U. S. sportsmen, is an import, a hybrid of British and Chinese species.

CALIFORNIA CONDOR is nearly extinct. A carrion eater, it requires a wide range of undisturbed wilderness to sustain its life.

TURKEY is a genus peculiar to North America. Domesticated varieties now abound, but the wild bird is very nearly extinct.

monly through what seems to be an inborn tendency in the young of all species to strike out and explore the world in all directions. Every new generation puts some added strain on the traditional habitat for food, territory and nesting sites, and the younger birds find themselves in unequal competition with the entrenched older ones. The wanderlust of first-year birds is the adaptive device by which natural selection has met this contingency. In Switzerland the banding of young barn owls showed that in years

of high nestling productivity 57 to 68 per cent of them dispersed 50 kilometers or more from their natal nests; in years of normal productivity the percentage was only 37. Similar results were found by Alfred Gross in the banding of 23,434 herring gulls on Kent Island in the Canadian province of New Brunswick between 1934 and 1938. Of the 3 per cent recovered at points distant from Kent Island more than half were less than a year old and the great majority of these were captured

hundreds of miles from their birthplace.

Seasonal migration is quite a different thing, but it also undoubtedly encourages the extension of range. Long-distance migrants are in a better position to discover new habitats, and they are naturally more tolerant of diversity in the environment. In the mountains of Colombia such winter visitors from North America as the yellow-billed cuckoo, the rose-breasted grosbeak and the yellow, blackburnian and mourning

CATTLE EGRET, from Africa, is established in South America and is invading U.S.

WHOOPING CRANE is another nearly extinct American genus; some 30 survive.

warbler have been observed ranging freely throughout the temperate, subtropical and tropical life-zones, whereas the permanent residents are more rigidly confined within zonal boundaries.

Competition between species, in contrast to the dispersal force of intraspecific competition, tends to confine species to narrower ranges. Lack observes that if two species of the same genus have the same diet, they rarely live in the same habitat. Competition be-

tween related species thus promotes the concentration of each in a slightly different locality. In this country the black-capped chickadee is without close relatives and ranges widely over forests and marshes. But in Europe this same bird must compete with eight other titmouse species and so breeds only in swampy thickets, leaving all its other possible habitats for relatives to enjoy.

The same sort of mutual accommodation is found even among unrelated species. The amateur naturalist T. E. Musselman tells of a late-spring freeze that killed several thousand bluebird eggs in the nesting boxes he had set up around Quincy, Ill. The birds laid substitute clutches, but this caused their incubation to coincide with the arrival of the house wrens from the south. In the ensuing competition for nesting sites the wrens destroyed many bluebird eggs. It may have been precisely to avoid such disastrous competition that natural selection had advanced the first nesting of the bluebird, thus permitting both species to occupy the same range.

Sometimes interspecific relations are even more accommodating. In Germany the stock dove depends upon the black woodpecker to furnish it with nest holes. Small, defenseless birds have been known to build their nests in the margins of hawk and eagle nests, thereby securing the protection of their landlords against other predators.

On the other hand, it must be conceded that birds are not always so cooperative with one another. On Muskeget Island, off the coast of Maine, there used to be great colonies of terns. These were supplanted around 1940 by colonies of laughing gulls. Now the laughing gulls are being displaced by the more aggressive herring gulls. In rural areas of the U. S. the aggressive English sparrow has driven the cliff swallow from its former haunts under the eaves of barns and farmhouses.

Predators may close a habitat to a species, especially if they prevent it from breeding. In tropical forests many open-nesting species, like the pigeons, have been virtually eliminated by nest-robbing monkeys. Nesting ducks suffer heavy losses of eggs and young wherever there is an abundance of crows. Such predation may not be an unmixed curse; if the marauding crows did not force the ducks to stagger their egg-laying, their usually synchronized nesting would expose them to wholesale calamity in late-spring freezes.

The biological force that has had the harshest impact and most far-reaching effect on the geography of birds is man.

In a few cases his cultural interference with the natural environment has encouraged the spread of a species, like the robin, barn swallow or chimney swift. The spread of the barn owl through the state of New York has been attributed to mechanical refrigeration and the resulting abandonment of old icehouses. But in the main man has been a force for restriction and extermination. The classic instruments of his predation have been the ax, the plow, the cow, fire and the gun. To which the modern era has added water pollution, insecticides and herbicides. Cats and rats have been known to depopulate oceanic islands of their birds, completely extinguishing a half-dozen species at a time. That byword for an extinct species, the flightless, ground-nesting dodo, was sent on its way by the pigs introduced onto the island of Mauritius.

Occasionally civilized man has tried to atone for his ecological misdeeds by importing foreign species. Alas, as with the English sparrow and the starling, only the less desirable species seem to take hold. The worst failures have been his experiments with the bird life of oceanic islands. There used to be about 40 passerine (perching) species on the Hawaiian Islands; more than half have been driven out by the hundred or more foreign species that have been imported there. Mayr says that more kinds of birds have become extinct on the islands of the Pacific than in all the rest of the world put together.

HERRING GULL, shown here in adult plumage, is a wide-ranging bird, familiar in inland regions as well as on coasts of U. S.

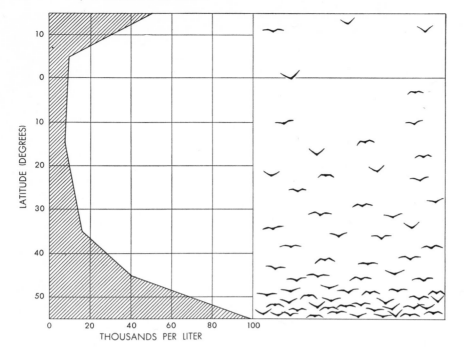

DISTRIBUTION OF SEA BIRDS in Southern Hemisphere, roughly indicated at right, shows significant correlation with the concentration of plankton in ocean waters, indicated by the crosshatched area at left. Plankton provides food for fish on which the birds depend.

Even without man, of course, the bright tapestry of bird geography will continue to be alternately torn and mended by the wearing and restorative forces of nature. But since man has willy-nilly taken a hand in the process, we must hope he will acquire the wisdom to provide refuge for the most threatened species before they too go the way of the dodo.

II

FLIGHT

II   FLIGHT

INTRODUCTION

ail to thee blithe spirit! Bird thou never wert . . . ," said Shelley in "Ode to a Skylark." Flight has always been thought of as a transcendental experience, a moment of ecstasy and joy. Gravity weighs heavily upon us ground dwellers, and we seek ways to be free of its clutches.

Mankind was the fifth animal to take to the air and become capable of flying long distances. Insects were first, 300 million years ago, and they are still the most common flying animal. Insects are probably the most successful fliers. Their exoskeleton readily adapts to form wings, and their small size gives them a surface-to-volume ratio favorable for flight. The pterosaurs were next, followed by birds and bats (see Fig. 1).

Pterosaurs were flying reptiles that became extinct 80–100 million years ago, during a time when many reptile groups perished. Some think of them as evolutionary failures, consigned to the scrap heap of history. But their existence spanned 50–60 million years of the fossil record, a creditable showing in any animals's flight log. Pterosaurs were designed like sailplanes, with membranous wings supported by a single elongated finger. They ranged greatly in size, some species being as small as a sparrow and others, like Pteranodon, having a body the size of a swan and an immense wingspread of about 7 meters (23 feet). The breast bones of pterosaurs were small, suggesting that they did not have large flight muscles. Perhaps they were cliff dwellers, gliding down to the sea to catch fish and then soaring back to their nests on the ledges.

Bats are the only group of mammals capable of powered flight. Their membranous wings are supported by several fingers, the hind limbs, and , in some, the tail. Many bats are small, but fruit bats have wingspans up to 1.5 meters (5 feet). Most are nocturnal, finding their way by a sensitive sonar (a system of echolocation using high-pitched sounds not audible to the human ear). The Oilbird of South America lives in dark caves and uses a similar system, but with audible sounds, to find its way in and out on its flights to find its favorite food of palmnuts.

Some animals possess winglike structures that enable them to glide, although they are not capable of true sustained flight. These include various fish, frogs, and reptiles. Draco, the so-called flying dragon, is a lizard of Southeast Asia about 8 inches long; it has a flattened body and winglike membranous extensions of skin attached to the last six or seven ribs. The animal glides from tree to tree and has been seen executing a full roll during courtship.

The wing of a bird is designed to fit its life style, be it a speed demon like a swallow, a land-soaring sailplane like a condor, or a ground dweller like the pheasant. Mycologist and avian scientist D. B. O. Savile has designated the most common wing designs (see Fig. 2):

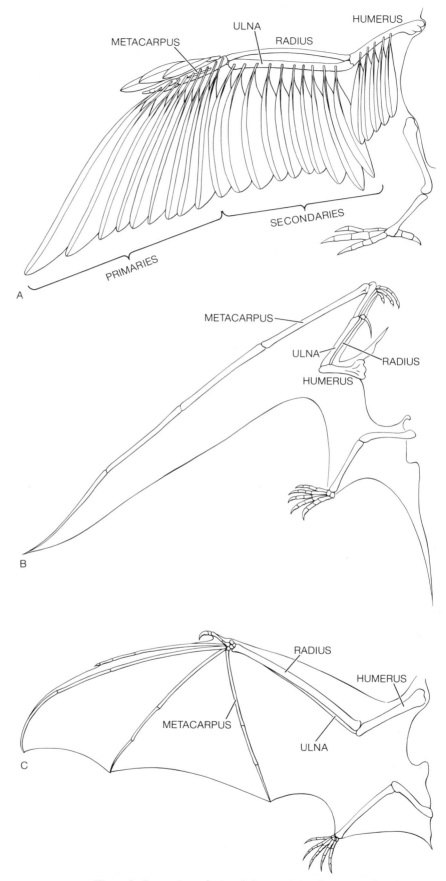

Figure 1. Comparison of wing skeletons. A. Duck. B. Pterodactyl. C. Bat.

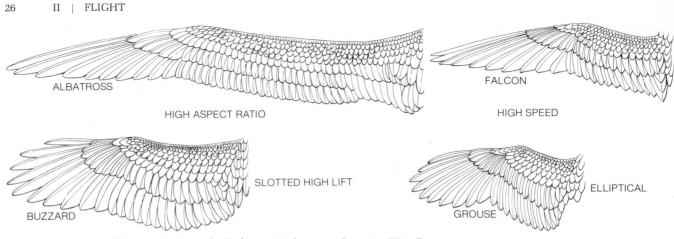

ALBATROSS
HIGH ASPECT RATIO

FALCON
HIGH SPEED

BUZZARD
SLOTTED HIGH LIFT

GROUSE
ELLIPTICAL

Figure 2. Wing types. [After D. B. O. Savile, "Adaptive Evolution in the Avian Wing," *Evolution* 11:212–224, 1957.]

1. *Elliptical wing.* Birds that live in the forest and on the ground, such as gallinaceous birds, doves, woodpeckers, and perching birds have short, wide wings with many slots (variable spaces between the primary feathers.) Such a design confers high manueverability and rapid takeoffs.

2. *High-speed wing.* Long, relatively slim wings without slots are found in birds that feed in the air, like swifts, or make long migrations, like terns. This wing is better suited to fast, level flight than to fast takeoffs and maneuvering in close quarters.

3. *High-aspect-ratio wing.* Soaring sea birds, like the albatrosses and shearwaters, very long, slim wings designed for high-speed gliding in strong, steady winds.

4. *Slotted high-lift wing.* Birds that soar over the land, such as condors, vultures, hawks, and owls, have long, wide wings with many slots. The design combines maneuverability with efficient gliding, enabling the birds to circle in small updrafts of warm air that occur over land.

TABLE 1   WING AREA AND WEIGHTS OF SELECTED BIRDS.

Species	Weight (grams)	Wing area (cm²)	Wing area/weight (cm²/gram)
HUMMINGBIRD	3.0	12.4	4.2
HOUSE WREN	11.0	48.4	4.4
CHICKADEE	12.5	76.0	6.1
BARN SWALLOW	17.0	118.5	7.0
CHIMNEY SWIFT	17.3	104.0	6.0
SONG SPARROW	22.0	86.5	3.9
LEACH'S PETREL	26.5	251.0	9.5
PURPLE MARTIN	43.0	185.5	4.3
REDWINGED BLACKBIRD	70.0	245.0	3.5
STARLING	84.0	190.3	2.2
MOURNING DOVE	130.0	357.0	2.4
PIED-BILLED GREBE	343.5	291.0	0.8
BARN OWL	505.0	1,683.0	3.4
COMMON CROW	552.0	1,344.0	2.4
HERRING GULL	850.0	2,006.0	2.4
PEREGRINE FALCON	1,222.5	1,342.0	1.1
MALLARD	1,408.0	1,029.0	0.7
GREAT BLUE HERON	1,905.0	4,436.0	2.3
COMMON LOON	2,425.0	1,358.0	0.6
GOLDEN EAGLE	4,664.0	6,520.0	1.4
CANADA GOOSE	5,662.0	2,820.0	0.5
MUTE SWAN	11,602	6,808.0	0.6

Source: After E. L. Poole, "Wings and wing areas in North American birds," *Auk* **55**:511–517, 1938.

Figure 3. Powered flight. *A.* Flight cycle of duck. Primary feathers are bent into miniature propellors on the downstroke, twist open on the upstroke, still providing some propulsion, and then snap back, ready for a new cycle. *B.* Hovering flight of hummingbirds. The wings of hummingbirds move back and forth when they hover in midair. [Duck cycle after E. M. Queeny and R. E. Bishop. *Prairie Wings.* Ducks Unlimited, Inc., New York, 1946. Hummingbird cycle after W. Scheithauer. *Hummingbirds.* T. Y. Crowell, New York, 1967.]

The first article on this section, by John H. Storer ("Bird Aerodynamics"), presents some of the aeronautical principles governing the flight of birds and airplanes. It explains how the relatively immobile inner part of the wing provides lift and the propellorlike action of the outer part and the primary feathers drives the bird through the air (see Fig. 3).

If ordinary birds are sailplanes with feathered propellors at their wingtips, then hummingbirds are helicopters. These remarkable creatures can fly straight up, hover, and even fly backward! Their wings are structurally different from those of other birds; they are almost rigid, moving little at the wrist and elbow, but rotating freely at the shoulder joint. The wings move forward and downward, backward and upward during hovering, describing a figure eight, as if the tiny bird were sculling through the air (see Fig. 3).

The relationship of wing area to weight is an important aeronautical factor, and its range in birds is a lesson in the kind of mathematics practiced by nature. Table 1 lists the wing areas and weights of several birds. The heavier birds tend to have relatively less surface area per unit weight than the lighter birds. Put another way, the smaller the bird, the relatively larger is its wing area compared to its weight. One interpretation is that the larger birds are approaching an upper limit in size. They cannot get much bigger without giving up the luxury of a large wing. However, this assumes there is an arithmetic relation between surface area and weight. The data in the table tell a different story if the relationship that applies is geometric rather than arithmetic. The fact that doubling the surface area of a cube triples (not doubles) its volume predicts that birds with twice the wing area will be approximately three times the weight if size is the only important consideration. Mathematically, this means that a bird's wing area would equal its weight to the 2/3 power as a first approximation. A plot of the data supports this prediction; the area-to-weight curve of most birds conforms closely to a line depicting weight to the 2/3 power (see Fig. 4).

Interestingly, birds whose area-to-weight ratios lie below the 2/3 power curve, such as hummingbirds, loons, and geese, soar poorly, and those that lie above the line, such as herons or eagles, soar well. It is as if evolution has acted by producing small modifications in the relative growth of the wings and bodies of birds, shifting the relative surface areas of their wings to one side or another of the 2/3 power curve, depending upon their ecological niche.

C. J. Pennycuick ("The Soaring Flight of Vultures") studies soaring by doing it himself, tracking vultures with a glider. His article compares the soaring abilities, aeronautical designs, and styles of living of two kinds of vultures, those that hunt intensively over a restricted region, and those that follow

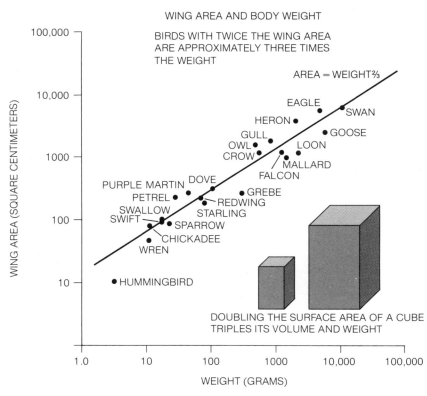

WING AREA AND BODY WEIGHT

Figure 4. **Wing area and body weight. The surface area of the wings of a bird is approximately equal to its weight to the two-thirds power.**

the large herds of herbivores, such as the wildebeest, zebra, and Thomson's gazelle, that migrate over the plains of East Africa. He finds that such factors as the ratio of wing area to weight (expressed as its inverse: wing loading) are important in establishing the different ecological niches of the several vultures.

The last article in the section, by Vance A. Tucker ("The Energetics of Bird Flight"), brings the bird to the scientist instead of the other way round. It describes how he studies the energy cost of flight by measuring the metabolism of birds trained to fly in a wind tunnel while wearing gas masks. His analysis of the caloric cost of flight indicates that it is an economical mode of transportation. In a sense, the cost of becoming airborne is offset by the savings of energy gained by gliding and soaring. When a runner stops running, he stops; but when a bird stops flapping, its forward motion continues. (The designs of the first airplanes were based on models of gliders whose wing areas were large compared to their weight. Modern supersonic airplanes have relatively small wings; they sacrifice gliding ability for speed and streamlining.)

The article also discusses how the size of a bird influences its energy needs. The small size of many birds has much to do with their high rates of metabolism. Small animals have high surface-to-volume ratios and tend to radiate away much of the heat they produce. Small birds must eat frequently in order to get enough food to maintain a high body temperature.

Ever since Leonardo da Vinci developed his ideas of flight by watching birds and making models of them, aeronautics has benefited from the study of bird flight. One way to understand flight better is for you to fly something yourself. Kites, model airplanes, and hang gliders all have their proponents. Perhaps the simplest of model systems is the paper airplane. Its popularity is attested to by the number that appear in the wastebaskets of the offices of America everyday and by the almost 12,000 entries to the "1st International Paper Airplane Competition," sponsored by *Scientific American* in 1967. The announcement for the competition is reproduced in Figure 5.

[*Scientific American Calls For Entries: Can It Be
There's A Paper Plane Which Makes The SST 30 Years Obsolete?*]

1st International Paper Airplane Competition

SCIENTIFIC AMERICAN primarily concerns itself with what Man is up to these days, and our readership is known for travelling more than that of any other magazine. So it is little wonder we have spent considerable time studying the two designs for the supersonic SST airplane recently announced by Boeing and Lockheed. (See Fig. 1 and Fig. 2.)

Soon we'll all be flying around in thin air at Mach 2.7, i.e., from New York to London in 150 minutes. Quite a prospect!

FIG. 1: Lockheed SST.

FIG 2: Boeing SST.

Still, at the close of our inquiry there remained this nagging thought: Hadn't we seen these designs somewhere before?

Of course. Paper airplanes. Fig. 3 and Fig. 4 illustrate only the more classical paper plane designs, in use since the 1920's or so, having a minimum performance capability of 15 feet and four seconds.*

We do not mean to question the men at Boeing and Lockheed, or their use of traditional forms. But it seems

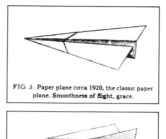

FIG. 3: Paper plane circa 1920, the classic paper plane. Smoothness of flight, grace.

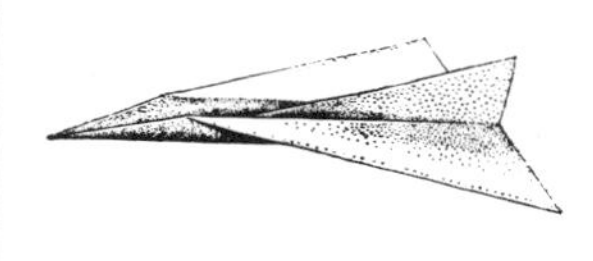

FIG. 4: First developed among paper airplane designers in the 1930's. Known for spectacular darting motions. Note hooked nose.

to us unjust that several million paper plane designers around the world are not also given their due, a credit which if it had been extended some years ago would have saved the pros quite some straining at the drawing boards.

Well anyway, with design having caught up with itself, we can now postulate that there is, right now, flying down some hallway or out of some moviehouse balcony in Brooklyn, the aircraft which will make the SST 30 years obsolete. No?

Consider this: Never since Leonardo da Vinci, the Patron Saint of paper airplanes, has such a wealth of flight research and experimentation remained untouched by cross-disciplinary study and publication. Paper airplane design has become one of those secret pleasures performed behind closed doors. Everybody does it,

but nobody knows what anyone else has learned.

Many's the time we've spied a virtuoso paper plane turn the corner of the office hallway, or suddenly rise up over the desk, or on one occasion

FIG. 5: Drawn from memory, this plane was last seen in 12th floor stairwell at 415 Madison Ave. Do you know its designer? Where is he?

we'll never forget, veer first down the stairs to the left, and suddenly to the right, staying aloft 12 seconds in all. (See Fig. 5.)

But who is its designer? Is he a Board Chairman or a stock boy? And what has he done lately?

All right then. In the interests of filling this information gap, and in light of the possibility that the future of aeronautics may now be flying in a paper plane, we are hereby calling for entries to the 1st International Paper Airplane Competition.

*(In paper plane circles, of course, a *better* time is a *longer* time. If a plane can stay aloft, floating on the air as it were, for 15 seconds, *that* is a virtue, as indeed it was for the Bros. Wright. One would assume that today's commercial designers, who seek planes to get from here to there and *down* as quickly as possible, would not have been much interested in the study of paper planes, or the Bros. Wright. In light of the illustrations, our assumption appears to be wrong.)

RULES

1. Scientific American has created The Leonardo (see Fig. 6) to be winner's trophy in each of these four categories:
a) duration aloft,
b) distance flown,
c) aerobatics, and
d) Origami.
2. A silver Leonardo will go to winners not involved professionally in air travel, and a titanium Leonardo (the metal being used in the SST) to professional entrants, that is, people employed in the air travel

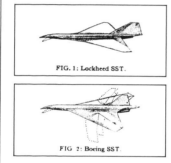

FIG. 6: The Leonardo.

business, people who build non-paper airplanes, and people who subscribe to Scientific American, because they fly so much.
3. Please feel at liberty to rip out this page, fold it, and use it as your official entry. If you find newsprint is not suitable to your particular design, however, use your own paper of any size or description. (Rag content and water marks will not have any bearing on the final decision.) Or, send for your free Official Entry Form Pad—reprints of this ad, padded, which you can stand on your desk, or hang near it, and with which you and your associates can make literally dozens of Official Entries.
4. You may enter as often as you like, being sure to include your *name*, *address*, *employer*, if any,

and the *classes* in which you would like your entry to qualify.
5. Send your entry to us, somehow, at this address: Scientific American, Leonardo Trophy Competition, 415 Madison Ave., New York 10017, postmarked by January 16, 1967. On January 21 all entries will be test-flown down our hallways by a panel of distinguished judges whose identity we'll announce at a later date (so as to not influence anyone's design).
6. Except that we will publish scale drawings of the winning designs, all other rights to same remain reserved to the designer. We, however, will do our bit towards assuring immediate production.

Thank you.

Figure 5. Advertisement for the 1st International Paper Airplane Competition.

THE MYSTERY GLIDER

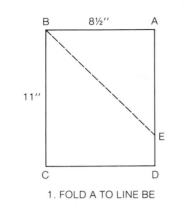

1. FOLD A TO LINE BE

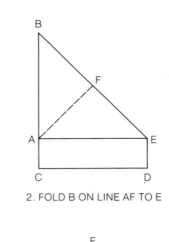

2. FOLD B ON LINE AF TO E

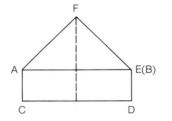

3. CREASE ON THE CENTER
   LINE AND REOPEN

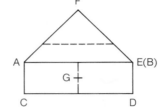

4. FOLD F BACK ON
   CENTER LINE TO G

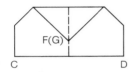

5. FOLD ON CENTER LINE

6. FOLD WINGS DOWN ON
   BOTH SIDES

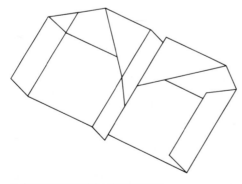

7. SPREAD WINGS HORIZONTAL.
   FOLD UP STABILIZERS AT ENDS OF WINGS.

Figure 6. Instructions for constructing the "Mystery Glider," an endurance flier.

The best paper airplane I know was never entered in the competition; it appeared as a "mystery plane" in the announcement. I remember constructing it when I was a youngster during World War II. Its ratio of surface area to volume is higher than that of the classic pointed-nose model and gives it much lift. Students like myself regaled their teachers with its ability to stay aloft for long periods. Perhaps we learned of it through a security leak from some secret project.

Here, possibly for the first time in print, are the instructions for building this paragon of fliers, (see Fig. 6). Use it for simple experiments of flight. Vary the surface area of the wings; cut flaps into the rear of the wings to make the plane turn or loop; observe what happens when you remove the vertical stabilizers from the tips of the wings.

More designs may be found in *The Great International Paper Airplane Book*, by J. Mander, G. Dippel, and H. Gossage. It is dedicated to " . . . Capt. Fear God Bascomb, out of New Bedford, Massachusetts, who brought the first known pad of lined 8½" × 11" paper from China on May 1, 1743. It may well be said of Capt. Bascomb that without him, the paper airplane as we know it would not have been possible."

REFERENCES

Mander, J., G. Dippel, and H. Gossage. *The Great International Paper Airplane Book.* Simon and Schuster, New York, 1967.
Saville, D. B. O. "Adaptive Evolution in the Avian Wing." *Evolution* 11:212–224, 1957.

3   Bird Aerodynamics

by John H. Storer
April 1952

*It is even more like that of the airplane than is
generally assumed. A bird does not fly through the air
as a man swims through the water; it employs the
airfoil and the propeller*

THE flight of birds has always excited man's envy and wonder. At first sight the process looks simple enough: a bird seems to lift and drive itself forward by beating its wings against the air in much the same way as a swimmer propels himself through water by flapping his arms. When men first tried to fly, they built their flying machines ("ornithopters") on this principle, with mechanical wings that flapped. But the machines never got off the ground.

For this is not at all the way birds fly. Paradoxically it was the development of the modern propeller plane that finally taught us how birds fly—not the other way around. A bird is actually a living airplane. It flies by the same aerodynamical principles as a plane and uses much of the same mechanical equipment—wings, propellers, steering gear, even slots and flaps for help in taking off and landing.

The slow-motion camera shows that a bird does not push itself along by beating its wings back against the air. On the downstroke the wings move forward, not backward. And when the bird lifts its wings for the next stroke, it does not lose altitude, as might be expected, but sails on steadily on a level course. The easiest way to understand its flight is to consider first how an airplane flies.

The air, like any fluid, has weight, and it presses against every surface of anything submerged in it—downward from above, upward from below and inward from all sides. At sea level the air presses on all surfaces with a force of 14.7 pounds per square inch. The air therefore will supply the force to support flight, provided the flying object can somehow reduce the pressure on its upper surface to less than the lifting pressure, and decrease the pressure against its front surface or increase that from behind. Birds and airplanes do this by means of properly shaped wings and propellers which they manipulate to drive themselves forward at a certain required angle and speed.

We can study the aerodynamical problems involved by blowing a stream of smoke, which makes the air currents visible, against an obstruction in a wind tunnel. When the smoke stream hits the obstruction, it does not flow smoothly around the surface and close up again immediately behind it. Instead, it breaks up and is deflected away from the obstruction so that the air no longer presses against the object's sides with the same force. Moreover, the air stream does not close up again until it has moved some distance past the obstruction, so the pressure on the rear surface of the obstacle also is reduced. There remains a disproportionate pressure on the front surface of the obstacle: what would be known as "drag" if the object instead of the air stream were moving.

Now suppose we place in the air stream an object so shaped that it fills in the spaces that were left vacant when the air was deflected by the first obstruction. The air flows smoothly around this new object, and the pressure is more nearly even on all sides. Drag is reduced. We have "streamlined" the obstacle. By altering this shape just a little, we can change the relative pressures on its different surfaces. Let us flatten the bottom surface slightly, reducing the downward deflection of the air stream. Now the upward pressure of air against the bottom surface is more nearly normal, while the downward pressure on the top surface remains subnormal as before. Presto! We have more pressure from below than from above. If the streamlined model is light enough, the moving air will lift it. We have the beginning of a wing.

If the front edge of this embryo wing is tilted upward just a little so that the air strikes the bottom surface more directly, the lifting force on the wing is increased. The more the wing is tilted, the more lift it will give—up to a certain point. As the angle of tilt approaches the vertical, the pressure against the bottom surface begins to push the wing backward rather than upward. Eventually,

if a plane's wing is tilted too much, the lifting force vanishes, the drag is so great that it stops the plane, and we have what is known as a "stall." The plane must regain the proper angle and speed or it will crash.

In the air a pilot controls the lifting power of his plane both by tilt and by speed: the more speed, the more lift. In taking off or landing, however, he must rely mainly on tilt: to get enough lifting force he must hold his wing at the greatest possible angle against the air, up to the point of stalling. The angle to which he can tilt the wing without stalling can be increased by placing a very small auxiliary wing in front of or behind the main wing. The "slot" formed between the main wing and the small auxiliary airfoil increases the speed of the air flow over the wing and so maintains its lifting power, even after it has passed the normal stalling point.

Once we have a streamlined wing, the next step necessary for flying is to move it through the air fast enough to generate lift. This we accomplish by equipping the machine with propellers, which are actually another set of wings, whose "lift" is exerted forward rather than upward. For mechanical reasons the blades of a propeller function better with a shape and angle slightly different from those of the wings, but the principle on which they work is just the same.

So we have, basically, a single mechanism which, placed in one position, holds an airplane up, and in another, drives it forward. Now we can look at a bird's anatomy and find exactly the same mechanism used in just the same two ways.

THE WING of a bird consists of two parts, which have two very different functions. It is divided into an inner half, operated from the shoulder joint, and an outer half, which is moved separately by a "wrist" midway along the wing. The inner half of the wing is devoted almost exclusively to giving lift. It is held rather rigidly at a slight angle, sloping like the wing of a plane. It also

RING-BILLED GULL has a long, narrow wing characteristic of birds that do much gliding over water. The anatomy of the wing is shown at the top of page 36. Birds that do little gliding have shorter and broader wings.

BROWN PELICAN is another gliding bird. The feathers at the tip of its left wing are turned up by a current of air. When the wing beats down during active flight, this same effect occurs and pushes the bird forward.

has the streamlined shape of a plane's wing: its upper feathers are arched to make a curved surface.

At the front edge of the wrist, where the inner and outer wings join, is a small group of feathers called the alula. This is the bird's auxiliary airfoil for help in taking off and landing. The bird can raise the alula to form a slot between that structure and the main wing. Without the alula a bird cannot take off or land successfully.

But where is the propeller? Astonishing as it may seem, every bird has a pair of them, though where they might be is certainly far from obvious. They can be seen in action best in a slow-motion picture of a bird in flight. During the downward beat of the wings the primary feathers at the wing tips stand out almost at right angles to the rest of the wing and to the line of flight. These feathers are the propellers. They take on this twisted form for only a split second during each wing beat. But this ability to change their shape and position is the key to bird flight. Throughout the entire wing beat they are constantly changing their shape, adjusting automatically to air pressure and the changing requirements of the wing as it moves up and down.

This automatic adjustment is made possible by special features of the feather design. The front vane of a wing-tip feather (on the forward side of the quill) is much narrower than the rear vane. Out of this difference comes the force that twists the feather into the shape of a propeller. As the wing beats downward against the air, the greater pressure against the wide rear vane of each of these feathers twists that vane upward until the feather takes on the proper shape and angle to function as a propeller. The degree and shape of its twist is controlled largely by the design of the quill, which is rigid at its base but flattened and flexible toward the end.

With their specialized design the primary feathers are beautifully adapted to meet the varied demands of bird flight. An airplane's propeller rotates around a pivot in one direction; the bird's propeller, in contrast, oscillates rapidly down and up, and it must automatically adapt its shape, position, angle and speed to the changing requirements of the moment. The feathers are not fastened immovably to the bone of the wing but are held by a broad flexible membrane, which allows considerable freedom of movement to each feather. While the bird is flying easily, only the tips of the feathers twist to become propellers. But if the bird is in a hurry and beats its wings more strongly against the air, the whole outer section of the wing, from the wrist out, may be twisted by the greater pressure into one big propeller.

The path of the propeller on the

FLYING egret shows the different functions of the inner and outer halves of a bird wing. In the first two pictures the wings are moving downward. In the third the inner half rises ahead of the outer to maintain lift.

LANDING American egret demonstrates the use of feathers in its alulas and wing tips to maintain balance and control. The alula is a small bunch of feathers on the leading edge of the wing. By opening slots with these feathers and those of the wing tips, the bird can control its lift while losing flying speed.

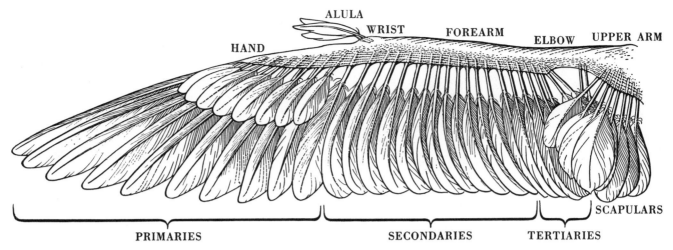

ALULA
WRIST
FOREARM
ELBOW
UPPER ARM
HAND

SCAPULARS

PRIMARIES   SECONDARIES   TERTIARIES

ANATOMY of a herring gull's wing reflects the different functions of its inner and outer halves. The inner half of the wing, from the shoulder to the wrist, is adapted primarily to lift; the outer half, from the wrist to the wing tip, to control and propulsion. Only the principal feathers of the wing are shown in this illustration.

downstroke is downward and forward; on the upstroke, upward and backward. The amount of forward and backward motion varies with the bird's wingbeat. When the bird beats its wings fast, as in taking off, the increased pressure drives the wing tips forward on a more nearly horizontal path; in leisurely flight the movement is more nearly vertical. The inner wing, by maintaining the proper angle, supports the bird's weight through the entire wing beat. This angle is constantly adjusted to maintain a steady lifting force.

In free flight the bird's powerful breast muscles sweep the whole wing up and down from the shoulder. The inner wing does not actually need to move, but it acts as a handle to move the propeller and gives the latter greater speed and power. I have a slow-motion movie of a low-flying white heron skimming some bushes so closely that it did not have room to make a full downward wing beat. The bird held the inner half of each wing extended horizontally and beat the outer half up and down from the wrist. To move the propeller fast enough without the help of the breast muscles must have required great effort. But this flight demonstrated perfectly the true function of each half of the wing. The inner half was the wing of a living airplane, lifting the bird. The outer half was the propeller, driving it forward.

Like an airplane, a bird has special equipment for steering and balancing. It steers by turning its tail, up, down or sidewise. (It can also spread the tail wide to give added lifting surface when needed.) The bird balances itself by means of its wings; if it tips to one side, it can restore itself to an even keel by increasing the lift of that wing, either by beating more strongly with it or by changing its angle.

OF ALL the powers of birds in the air probably none has caused more wonder than their soaring ability. To see a bird rise in the air and sail on motionless wings into the distance until at last it disappears from sight gives one a sense of magic. We now know how it is done, but it is still difficult to realize what is happening as we watch it.

Actually the bird is coasting downhill in relation to the flow of air. It rises because it is riding a rising current of air which is ascending faster than the bird is sinking in the current.

Ascending air currents on which birds can soar or glide arise from two different kinds of situations. One is an obstruction, such as an ocean wave, a shore line or a hillside, which deflects the wind upward. It is common to see a pelican or albatross sailing over the water on motionless wings just above the crest of a moving wave, or a gull hanging motionless against a wind current that rises over a headland, or a hawk soaring on the air current that sweeps up a mountainside.

The second type of rising current is heated air, known as a thermal. A field warmed by the sun heats the air above it, causing it to expand and rise. If the field is surrounded by a cooler forest, the heated pocket of air may rise in the form of a great bubble or of a column. Everyone has seen birds soaring in wide circles over land; usually they are coasting around the periphery of a rising air column. Over the ocean, when the water warms colder air above it, the air rises in a whole group of columns, packed together like the cells of a honeycomb. If the wind then freshens, it may blow the columns over until they lie horizontally on the water. The flat-lying columns of air may rotate around their axes, each in the opposite direction from its neighbor. This has been demonstrated in the laboratory by blowing smoke-filled air over a warmed surface at increasing speed, corresponding to an increase in the wind over the ocean. If you put your two fists together and rotate them, the right clockwise and the left counterclockwise, you will see that the two

	MILES PER HOUR
Great Blue Heron [cruising]	18-29
Great Blue Heron [pressed]	36
Canada Goose [easy flight]	20
Canada Goose [pressed by plane]	45-60
Mallard [pressed by plane]	55-60
Duck Hawk [pressed by plane]	175-180
Pheasant [average top speed]	60
Woodcock	5-13
Ruby-throated Hummingbird [easy flight]	45-55
Barn Swallow	20-46
Crow	25-60
Sharp-shinned Hawk	16-60
Osprey	20-80

FLYING SPEEDS of 13 species of birds are listed in this table. The conditions under which the observations were made are in parentheses.

inner faces of the fists rise together. Just so two adjoining air cells rotating in opposite directions will push up between them a ridge of rising air. Birds can glide in a straight line along such a ridge.

At the Woods Hole Oceanographic Institution Alfred H. Woodcock studied the soaring of sea gulls at different seasons. During the summer, when the air is warmer than the water, gulls seldom do any soaring. But they do a great deal of it in the fall, when the water is warmer than the air and produces many updrafts. The gull's movements may clearly mark the outlines of the rising air columns. When the wind is relatively light, under 16 miles an hour, the gulls soar in spirals, showing that the columns are standing upright. But as the wind freshens and tilts over the columns, the birds' soaring patterns begin to change; when the wind speed reaches 24 miles per hour, all the gulls soar in straight lines. The spectacle is all but incredible, with the birds sailing into the strong wind on motionless wings and gaining altitude as they go, until they disappear in the distance. I watched it once, and it is a never-to-be-forgotten sight.

How fast do birds fly? A great deal of nonsense has been uttered on this subject. The measurement of a bird's speed capabilities is a very uncertain and tricky thing. The wind, the angle of the bird's flight, whether it is being pressed—these factors and many others affect its speed.

The cruising and top speeds of some common birds are listed in the table at the bottom of the opposite page. Birds vary greatly, of course, in their speed requirements and possibilities. The pheasant and grouse, which have short wings adapted to maneuvering in underbrush, must fly with a rapid wing beat and considerable speed to stay in the air. The same is true of ducks, which do not need large wings because they have an easy landing field on the water. Herons, on the other hand, must be able to land slowly to protect their long, slender legs, which they use for wading to find food. Their big, cumbersome wings are suited for slow landing, but they produce so much friction and drag in the air that herons cannot fly very fast.

As the table shows, 60 miles an hour is fast for a bird, and the fastest known species, the duck hawk, does not exceed 175 to 180 miles per hour. These speeds, of course, are far slower than the speeds of modern planes. They involve very different problems in aerodynamics, and different streamline designs. But some of them do approach the speed of the early planes, and it is interesting to see how closely the designs produced by nature approach the best results of the human engineer.

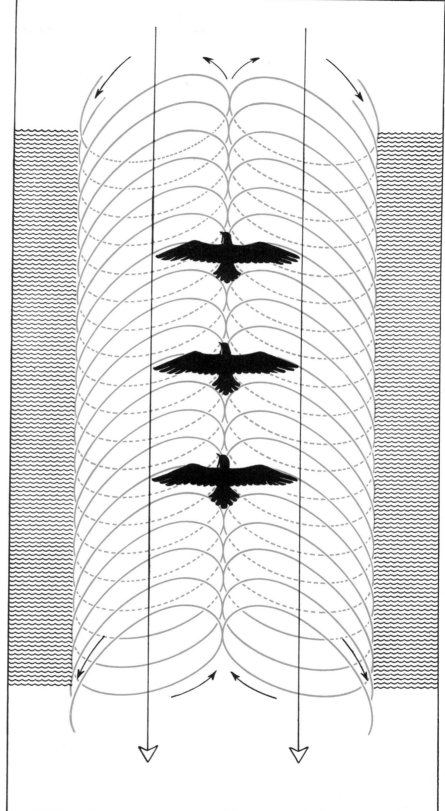

SEA BIRDS sometimes soar against a prevailing wind (*vertical arrows*) by riding an updraft between two counter-rotating cylinders of air. These cylinders result from the fact that when the sea is warmer than the air, many vertical columns of warm air rise from the surface of the water. If the wind freshens, the columns lie parallel to the surface. Birds are not drawn to scale.

4

The Soaring Flight of Vultures

by C. J. Pennycuick
December 1973

The six common vultures of East Africa can make a round trip of as much as 200 kilometers by skillfully riding updrafts. How they do so is examined with the aid of a powered glider

To watch a vulture soar effortlessly overhead for hours at a time is to become convinced that these birds are among the most skillful of fliers. Yet there are occasions when vultures cannot fly at all. Early in the morning on the East African plains one quite often meets little groups of vultures that had gathered at some small find the night before and then slept where they happened to be when night fell. If the birds are pursued, they take off, but they do not fly far before they land again. If they are forced to take off several times in rapid succession, they quickly become exhausted and can be caught by hand. Two of the commonest East African vultures, Rüppell's griffon (*Gyps rüppellii*) and the white-backed vulture (*Gyps africanus*), can easily be caught this way. Later in the morning, say after about 9:00 A.M., the technique sometimes still works on a vulture that is heavily gorged with food. More often the bird will fly straight ahead for a short distance, then turn sharply and at the same time start climbing. After turning in a few irregular narrow circles and intermittently flapping its wings, the vulture settles down to gliding in steady circles. It then continues to climb without flapping its wings and drifts downwind as it circles.

The reason these vultures have such difficulty flying under their own muscle power is that they are too big. There is a relation between the power required to fly, the power available from the muscles and the body weight that sets an upper limit to the weight of animals able to fly by muscle power. The larger vultures, storks and pelicans are quite near this limit and would barely be able to stay airborne were it not for their ability to extract energy from the atmosphere and use it for their locomotion.

The flight path of a bird that is gliding along at a steady speed (that is, not flap-ping its wings) is invariably inclined downward. The gliding bird therefore has a vertical downward component of velocity, called the "sinking speed." If the air through which the bird is flying happens to be rising at a speed greater than the sinking speed, the bird is carried up with it and acquires potential energy it can use later to glide through air that is not rising. Any system of maneuvers whose effect is to produce this result by taking advantage of some atmospheric process constitutes a method of soaring.

Soaring techniques can be classified according to the atmospheric process responsible for the rising air, or "lift" [*see illustration on page 41*]. The existence of lift in sufficient quantities, however, satisfies only part of the requirement for a successful soaring technique. Sufficient information must also be available to the bird to enable it to locate the lift and, having found it, to carry out the correct maneuvers to make use of it. If the bird executes the wrong maneuver, it will usually lose the lift.

A soaring bird can work with several different kinds of lift, for example slope lift, in which the air rises when a wind encounters a slope; thermal lift, in which columns or bubbles of air rise when heated from below by warm ground, and wave lift, in which the air rises in the course of undulatory motion downwind of an obstacle. The correct procedure for a bird using slope lift is for the bird to tack to and fro, remaining above the windward slope. If the lift happens to be due to a thermal, however, the bird must change over to circling, drifting downwind with the thermal instead of remaining over the slope. Wave lift, on the other hand, remains stationary with respect to the ground, and it must be worked in the same way as slope lift, except that there is no slope to indicate where the

lift is. Inexperienced glider pilots often mistake wave lift for thermal; they circle in it and as a result drift downwind into the downgoing part of the wave. This error is apt to lead to a rapid and embarrassing descent *aux vaches*, as French pilots say. Present indications are that many, if not all, birds make the same mistake when they encounter wave lift.

Soaring birds are not the easiest birds to study, partly because the bird watcher, traditionally equipped with binoculars and rubber boots, cannot match their mobility and tends to lose track of them, and partly because one can never tell from the ground what kind of air movements a bird is soaring in. There is a limit to what one can deduce from even the most meticulously detailed ground observation, and in fact not a great deal of progress has been made with this approach since E. H. Hankin's classic book *Animal Flight* appeared in 1913.

Entirely new opportunities have been opened up with the advent in recent years of practical powered gliders. I have been extremely fortunate in having the use of one of the best of these, the Schleicher ASK-14, which was generously put at my disposal by Anglia Television and Okapia Film. The ASK-14 was developed from the well-known K-6E sailplane, and it is powered by a 26-horsepower engine. Because of its highly efficient aerodynamic design, the aircraft takes off and climbs in a lively manner with the aid of this tiny power plant. The engine is normally run for five or 10 minutes after takeoff until a thermal has been found, after which the engine is switched off and the propeller is feathered. The aircraft then becomes an excellent soaring glider, and the flight can be extended, usually for several hours, without further recourse to the engine. If the thermals should fail, or if the pilot gets too low over some unsuitable place, the engine can be restarted to extract him from the difficulty.

I have flown the ASK-14 mainly over the Serengeti National Park in northern Tanzania and neighboring areas of Tanzania and Kenya. This area enjoys good soaring weather throughout most of the year, and it is frequented by a remarkable variety of species of soaring birds. Many of the birds are common enough to be encountered during nearly every flight.

The common soaring birds of East Africa soar mainly in slope lift and thermals. Slope lift is, of course, useful only in the hillier areas and at comparatively low altitudes, and so in general thermals are the most important source of lift. When vultures are taking off from the ground, one can see at once that they are using some definite structure in the atmosphere rather than the randomly distributed kind of energy characteristic of turbulent air. As soon as one vulture is climbing successfully it is quickly joined by others (and often by other kinds of birds as well), until soon a group of birds forms, all circling around a common axis. This axis marks the "core" of a thermal, which at low altitudes is generally a vortex of the "dust devil," or columnar, type. "Dust devil" refers to the fact that over dry ground vigorous thermals of this type are often visible as

whirling columns of dust. Higher up vortex-ring thermals may form, and the tops of many thermals of either type are marked by cumulus clouds. As far as the soaring bird or pilot is concerned, either type of thermal can be considered a circular patch of lift that drifts along with the wind. The appropriate soaring maneuver is to fly in steady circles of as small a radius as possible, in order to stay as close as possible to the middle of the core, where the lift is strongest.

A bird's ability to use thermals, either for staying airborne or for traveling cross-country, depends on its gliding performance. This is most often expressed in terms of its "glide polar," which is a graph of sinking speed plotted against forward speed. The glide polar for a glider can be measured directly. The same type of graph for a gliding bird can be produced by estimating the differences in horizontal and vertical speed between a glider with a known polar and the bird. In this way the glide polars of the ASK-14 and the white-backed vulture have been compared.

In a straight glide the glider can travel much faster than the vulture at a given gliding angle. This is owing partly to the glider's superior aerodynamic efficiency and partly to its higher wing loading (the ratio of weight to wing area). On the other hand, when the glide polar is translated into circling flight, the effect of the vulture's lower wing loading is that it

can turn in much smaller circles at a similar rate of sink. This means that in a narrow thermal the bird can center its circle in the strongest part of the core, whereas the glider is obliged to fly in the weaker lift around the outside. Thus the vulture can often outclimb the glider, particularly at low altitude and early in the day, when the thermals tend to be weak and narrow, even though its sinking speed in straight flight is much the same. On one occasion, on a day of exceptionally narrow thermals, I was outclimbed by a tawny eagle (which has a still lower wing loading than the white-backed vulture), even though I had my engine running while the eagle was only gliding.

Many birds of prey are adapted primarily to using thermals as a means of remaining airborne in order to look out for food below. The African martial eagle (*Polemaetus bellicosus*), which preys on other birds, uses thermals in much the same way that smaller eagles and hawks use a rocky crag or a telephone pole. When foraging, it climbs by circling in a thermal to some modest height, usually from 300 to 600 meters above the ground, and then glides slowly along with its head pointing down, looking out for prey below.

Vultures use much the same technique in searching for carrion, but their tactics are based on the need to arrive promptly on the scene whenever and wherever a

POWERED GLIDER, its engine off and its propeller feathered, soars in rising air over the Serengeti National Park in northern Tanzania, accompanied by a pair of vultures that utilize the same lift to gain altitude effortlessly. The glider is a Schleicher ASK-14.

dead animal happens to turn up. By alternately climbing in thermals and gliding straight in different directions, they patrol over likely areas, usually between 200 and 500 meters above the ground. Starting from a height of, say, 300 meters, a vulture can reach any point on the ground within a radius of about 4.5 kilometers within six minutes. Points nearer at hand can be reached more quickly in a fast, steep dive; the steeper the angle is, the faster the vulture can glide. The mammalian scavengers, mainly the spotted hyena (*Crocuta crocuta*), react like the vultures to signs of activity in the distance (including descending vultures), but they have to work much harder to get to the site and have lower maximum speeds. Thus the vultures, although they cannot drive off the hyenas in a direct confrontation, can still compete with them effectively through their advantage in arriving quickly at an unpredictable source of food.

The African vultures have evolved two different approaches to the strategy of searching for food. One is to learn the geography of a home range and search it very thoroughly. In areas where game is scarce no other approach is possible. One of the special features of the East African fauna, however, is the existence of large populations of migratory ungulates, and this opens up another niche for scavengers adapted to take advantage of it. In the Serengeti, for instance, hundreds of thousands of wildebeest make an annual migration around a circuit some 500 kilometers in length, and comparable populations of zebras and Thomson's gazelles make similar migrations [see "A Grazing Ecosystem in the Serengeti," by Richard H. V. Bell; SCIENTIFIC AMERICAN, July, 1971].

To a sedentary scavenger the arrival of the migratory herds represents a temporary superabundance of potential food, but the herds move somewhat erratically and are apt to move out of reach as suddenly as they came. A scavenger that is adapted primarily to feeding on migratory game must dispense with a fixed home range and follow the migrating herds wherever they go. Thus it cannot learn the ground as thoroughly as a sedentary scavenger.

It seems that among the four large species of East African vultures two are basically sedentary and two are itinerant. This was postulated several years ago by Hans Kruuk, on the basis of differences in the behavior of the birds at the carcasses on which they were feeding. The two sedentary species, the lappet-faced vulture (*Torgos tracheliotus*) and the white-headed vulture (*Trigonoceps occipitalis*), never gather in large numbers; it is rare to see more than eight of the former and two of the latter at the same gathering. The two species manage to arrive first at carcasses much more often than their relatively small numbers would lead one to expect, indicating that these sedentary birds pursue a "thorough search" strategy. In contrast, the itinerant Rüppell's griffon and its fellow member of the genus *Gyps*, the white-backed vulture, often gather in the hundreds at a large carcass, but in spite of their numbers they do not usually arrive first. It would be an exaggeration to say that they never find their own food, but they seem to rely more heavily on following carnivorous mammals or other vultures and less on searching directly by themselves. Unlike the other two species, they never fight in the air. They seem to have no territorial behavior whatever, although they do squabble a good deal when they are actually feeding.

In the air the difference in behavior is evident even from a powered aircraft. Once the thermals are under way lappet-faced vultures and white-headed vultures may be met almost anywhere, usually in pairs, but the griffons concentrate over the migratory herds (particularly the wildebeest), often in spectacular numbers. When griffons are encountered away from concentrations of game, they are usually traveling steadily cross-country, commuting between their feeding area, which is changeable, and their nesting area, which is necessarily fixed. Because the two areas may be widely separated, the griffons have to be able to use thermals for cross-country travel as well as for staying aloft while foraging.

The bird that travels the farthest is Rüppell's griffon, which nests in colonies on cliffs. This habit, in which it differs from the white-backed vulture (a tree-nester), is most probably a reflection of

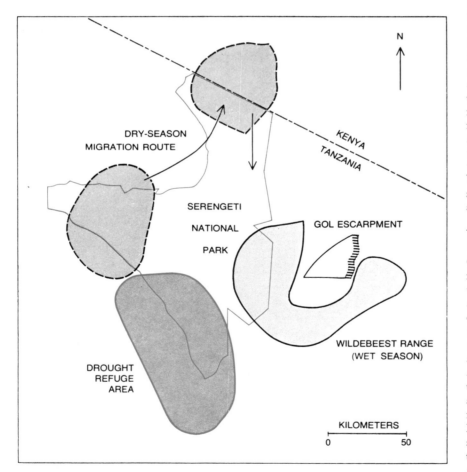

NESTING GROUND of the Rüppell's griffons that frequent the Serengeti National Park is the Gol Escarpment (*right*), a zone convenient to the grazing area preferred by wildebeest in the wet season when the griffons are raising their nestlings (*light color*). An unseasonable drought, however, will move the wildebeest to the west (*dark color*), forcing the griffons to travel 100 kilometers in each direction to get food for the nestlings. In the dry season, during the annual wildebeest migration (*gray zones*), the griffons follow them.

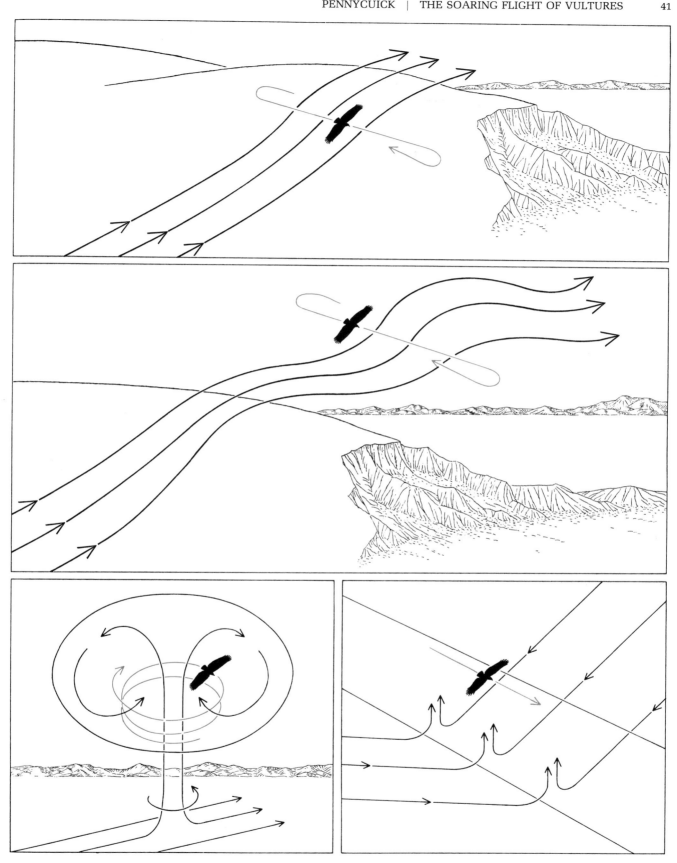

FOUR KINDS OF LIFT are exploited by different patterns of flight. Where air movement uphill provides "slope lift" (*top*), bird or sailplane should tack back and forth, heading sufficiently into the wind to stay within the same zone of rising air. The same pattern of flight is used to exploit "wave lift" on the leeward side of a slope (*middle*). To exploit a "thermal" (*bottom left*) the soarer travels downwind with the rising air column, circling within the thermal. When two air masses converge (*bottom right*), producing a line of "frontal lift," the soarer can either tack back and forth or set off in one direction and travel the entire length of the line.

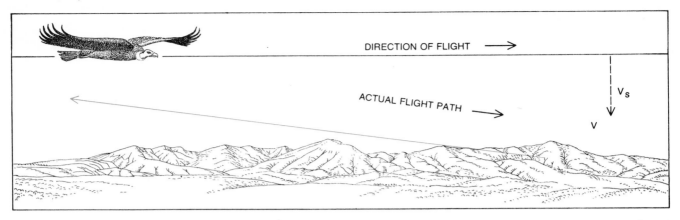

DIRECTION OF FLIGHT ⟶

ACTUAL FLIGHT PATH ⟶

V_s

V

GLIDING BIRD in still air loses altitude at a "sinking speed" (V_s) while traveling forward at a "flight speed" (V); the ratio V/V_s is the bird's "glide ratio" and is equal to the distance traveled forward per unit of altitude lost. If the air, instead of being still, rises faster than the bird sinks, the bird will not lose but gain altitude and acquire potential energy proportional to the altitude gained.

the fact that, being mainly a bird of the more arid country to the north, it is near the edge of its range in the Serengeti. The only suitable cliffs in the Serengeti area are outside the national park along the eastern escarpment of the Gol Mountains, and here some 500 or so pairs of Rüppell's griffons nest. Their breeding season is so timed that they normally raise their young during the period from February to May. This is the rainy season, during which the main migratory ungulate populations are usually on the Serengeti and Salei plains, within easy reach of the nesting cliffs. It often hap-

pens, however, that the rains are interrupted by dry spells, and wildebeest and zebras are then forced to move away to the south and the west. That may oblige the griffons to travel 100 kilometers or more each way to get food for their young, which have to be fed daily by one parent or the other.

By following vultures on cross-country flights I have found that in good soaring weather, which usually prevails when the plains are dry, they can keep up average cross-country speeds of some 45 kilometers (28 miles) per hour. Thus they must travel two or three hours each

way between the nesting cliffs and the dry-weather areas. In windy weather the vultures take off and start slope soaring along the cliffs at the first light. The prevailing winds are easterly, and by moving from slope to slope the vultures can make their way westward across the hills to the edge of the Serengeti Plain. There they have to wait for convection to begin (usually between 8:00 and 9:00 A.M.) before they can drift farther downwind across the plains by circling in the first weak thermals.

The best soaring hours of the day are usually between 11:00 A.M. and 4:00

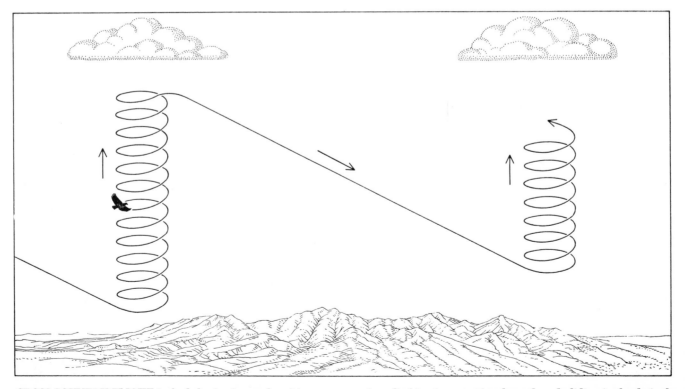

CROSS-COUNTRY FLIGHT is the behavior imposed on itinerant vultures such as Rüppell's griffon by the movements of prey. It re-quires climbing in successive thermals and gliding in the desired direction. In nesting season 200-kilometer flights are common.

P.M., when in dry weather frequent thermals provide rates of climb typically between two and four meters per second over an altitude range from very near the ground (say 1,600 meters above sea level) up to cloudbase (which is normally about 3,500 meters above sea level). A climb from the bottom to the top of this range usually takes 10 minutes or so, after which the bird can glide off straight in the direction it wants to go.

The speed on the straight glides is typically between 70 and 85 kilometers (45 and 55 miles) per hour. At these speeds the glide ratio is about 10 : 1, that is, the bird loses one meter of height for every 10 it travels forward. If it encountered no vertical motion in the air at all, it could glide some 18 kilometers in, say, 15 minutes before the need for another thermal became urgent. The total time needed to travel this distance, including the time for the climb, would be about 25 minutes, equivalent to an average cross-country speed of 43 kilometers per hour. In practice the vultures do not generally use the full altitude range available to them; they usually leave a thermal at between 2,500 and 3,000 meters above sea level. Moreover, they flatten their gliding angle considerably by slowing down as they fly through thermals and speeding up in between. On one occasion a Rüppell's griffon I was accompanying in the glider flew for 32 kilometers without circling by using this tactic and managed to lose only 520 meters of altitude—an achieved glide ratio of better than 60 : 1!

The griffon vultures' ability to forage at a distance of 100 kilometers from the nest gives them another competitive advantage over their formidable competitor the spotted hyena. Hyena pups are confined to a den for the first few months of their life, so that when the game concentrations are not in the immediate vicinity, the mother may have to travel many kilometers to get food, periodically coming back to suckle the young. A hyena's foraging radius cannot be reliably estimated, but it is certainly much less than that of a griffon vulture, because of the hyena's lower speed and the greater effort that travel on foot requires.

The biggest advantage low wing loading gives a bird is the ability to soar early in the day, when the first thermals are usually feeble dust devils, both narrow and weak. This advantage is important to foraging vultures: the earlier they become airborne in the morning, the better are their chances of getting pickings from the remains of animals that have

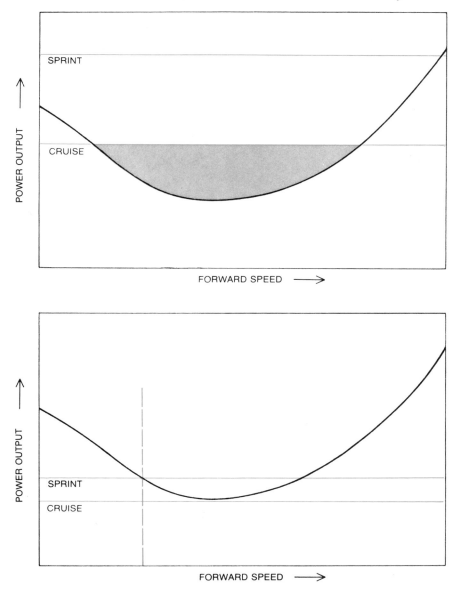

POWER REQUIRED FOR FLIGHT is less at moderate speeds (*trough of "u"*) and greater at hovering (*left*) and high (*right*) speeds. For a bird of medium size, such as a pigeon (*top*), continuously available muscle power (*lower line*) is enough for protracted flight over a wide range of speeds (*shaded area*) and sprint power (*upper line*) allows jump takeoffs. For a big bird such as a vulture (*bottom*) continuously available muscle power is not enough to allow protracted flight at any speed. The big bird must run, or dive from a high perch, to reach minimum flying speed (*broken vertical line*) and then use sprint power to remain airborne long enough to reach lift and begin relatively exertionless soaring flight.

died or been killed by predators during the night. In the heat of the day the thermals are broader and stronger, and the advantage in rate of climb to be had from a very low wing loading becomes insignificant; the beneficial effect on cross-country speed is more than offset by the loss of speed on the straight glides. To some extent birds achieve the best of both worlds, because they can reduce their wing area for fast flight. Even so the cross-country speeds they can achieve are modest compared with those of man-made gliders.

When the wing loadings of various birds are plotted against their mass on a double-logarithmic scale, the different vulture species segregate into two groups [see bottom illustration on next page]. The sedentary lappet-faced vultures and white-headed vultures have low wing loadings; they are specialized for being able to stay airborne in the weakest possible thermals. The griffons, being cross-country fliers, have compromised by having somewhat higher wing loadings.

Not much is known about the ecology

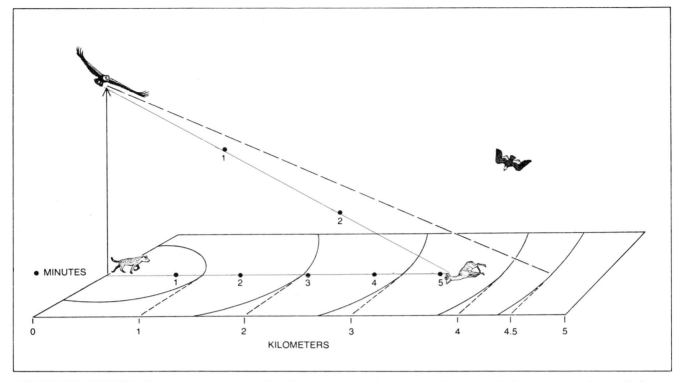

0   1   2   3   4   4.5   5
KILOMETERS

VULTURES' ADVANTAGE over scavenging quadrupeds when prey is sighted lies in being able to reach the carrion first. In this example the descent of a vulture in the distance (*right*) attracts the attention of a hyena and a lappet-faced vulture (*left*) to a carcass some 3.5 kilometers away. The vulture, targeting in at 70 kilometers per hour, reaches the carrion in three minutes, whereas the hyena, running at 40 kilometers per hour, needs 4.25 minutes to cover the same distance. A vulture flying 300 meters above the ground, as in this example, can reach any point 4.5 kilometers away in only six minutes and can get to closer points proportionately faster.

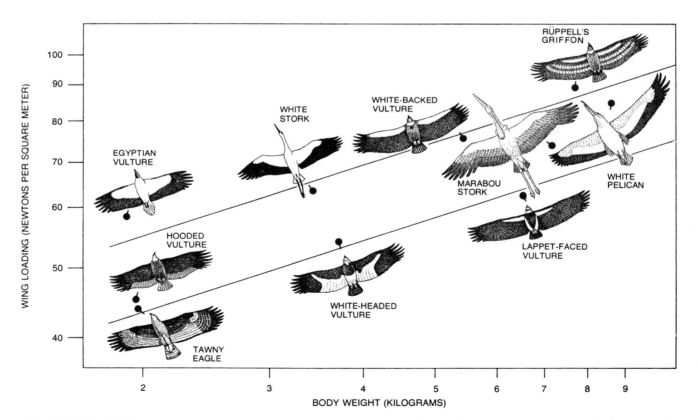

TEN SOARING BIRDS observed in East Africa fall mainly into two groups: five birds with a relatively heavy wing loading (*upper diagonal*) and four with a relatively light wing loading (*lower diagonal*). The wing loading of the 10th bird, the marabou stork, is intermediate on this double-logarithmic plot. The more lightly loaded birds, able to soar in thermals too small and weak for use by the others, hunt intensively over relatively small territories. The heavily loaded birds instead often fly cross-country for food.

of the two species of small vultures: the Egyptian vulture and the hooded vulture. Both frequent human habitations and garbage dumps, which the larger species do not. They also gather around dead animals and predator kills, and they tend to remain, picking up small scraps, after the bigger vultures have left. The Egyptian vulture's wing loading agrees with that of the high-loading group. The bird also resembles Rüppell's griffon in being a cliff-nester, although it does not form colonies. The hooded vulture, which falls in the low-loading group, sometimes gathers at carcasses in large numbers, but it is a solitary tree-nester.

Even in strong convection currents neither a bird nor a man-made glider can afford simply to glide along in one direction, relying on chance to bring it to the next thermal. All too often the ground is reached before a thermal is found. Thermals are mostly invisible, except for vigorous dust devils, but it is possible to increase the chance of encountering one by flying under a growing cumulus cloud or over a ground feature that looks likely to warm up differentially in the heat of the sun. A glider pilot's skill largely reflects his ability to notice such things, which in turn is based on his knowledge of atmospheric processes. Vultures and eagles are very good at finding the best lift, and they appear to make use of the visible signs in the same way the glider pilot does. For example, a common phenomenon in East Africa is the alignment of thermals into "streets" that are marked by lines of cumulus clouds. Here the thermals can be so close together that a bird or a glider pilot can fly from one to another, without circling and without losing height, for as much as 80 kilometers. Vultures regularly fly along thermal streets, and they will go out of their way to do so.

Vultures will also join other birds (or gliders) that are already climbing in a thermal, and often quite a large group will gather in this way. There is no "flock," however, in the sense of a continuing group. When the individual birds have gained enough height for their immediate needs, they leave the thermal separately in different directions, and the group disperses.

An entirely different kind of behavior is seen in the European white stork (*Ciconia ciconia*). This species is the longest-distance cross-country flier of them all, and it relies almost entirely on thermal soaring to make its annual migration between northern Europe and the southern half of Africa. On the wing

loading diagram it falls in the high-loading group. In some years many hundreds of these birds spend the northern winter in East Africa rather than pressing on farther south. There they can often be seen traveling about in search of the best feeding areas.

The white storks rely on coordinated social behavior to increase their chance of finding thermals. It is rare to see one of these birds flying by itself; usually there are at least 20 of them together, and big flocks numbering several hundred individuals are common. When the storks are between thermals, they press on in the direction they want to go regardless of the appearance of the sky ahead. They will make detours to avoid rain showers but not to follow thermal streets or to fly under active-looking cumulus clouds. The members of the flock spread out laterally into a loose formation, and they fly steadily along on parallel headings. As soon as one part of the flock happens to fly into a thermal, the birds in that part start rising with respect to the rest. The others then alter their headings to converge on those birds that are rising fastest. Soon all the storks are concentrated in a spiraling column in the strongest part of the thermal, each of them constantly adjusting the position of its circle by reference to the relative rates of climb of its neighbors. At the top of the thermal all the birds leave together and once again spread out in their lift-searching formation. The net effect of this behavior is to increase the probability of finding thermals by searching a path 200 or 300 meters wide.

White storks tend to spend more time at the relatively high altitudes near cloudbase than vultures. The thinner air at high altitudes has much the same effect on performance as an increase of wing loading, and it increases cross-country speed provided that the thermals are large and strong. Glider pilots often continue their climb up into a cumulus cloud, but successful use of this tactic calls for a compass and at least one gyroscopic instrument. It is not quite clear whether storks can make an extended climb in cloud. They do enter cumulus clouds from the bottom, but on some occasions (and perhaps always) they stop circling just after they have entered the cloud and fly straight, skimming half in and half out of cloudbase, until they come out at the edge.

One of the most interesting species of East African soaring birds is the marabou stork (*Leptoptilos crumeniferus*). Marabous spend much of their time dabbling about in marshes and shallow water like other storks, but in addition they

are partial to carrion, and they search for it like vultures. Their flight resembles that of white storks in some ways; for example, they sometimes travel in flocks. There is the curious difference, however, that although the marabous' formation on the straight glides is held just as steadily as the white storks', the marabou flock tends to spread out along the direction of travel rather than laterally. This behavior suggests that the marabous depend less than white storks on flock behavior for finding thermals. Supporting this notion is the fact that marabous often soar individually, like vultures, and will follow thermal streets.

The use of the flock as a thermal-searching unit is most highly developed in the white pelican (*Pelecanus onocrotalus*). On the interthermal glides the members of a pelican flock, which again may number several hundred individuals, spread out in an extended echelon, or multiple-V, formation, making a continuous line with no gaps. When the birds are circling, the entire flock turns in formation, so that from a distance one sees a periodic flash of white as they all catch the sun together. Pelican flocks travel in this way between the different lakes of the East African Rift Valley system.

The primary source of energy in soaring flight is of course that extracted from the motion of the atmosphere. For soaring birds, however, there is always some metabolic expense as well. The wings of the bird are not mechanically locked in the horizontal position but have to be held there by the pectoral muscles. All soaring birds, whatever their evolutionary origins, have a subdivided pectoralis muscle, and it appears that one division is a tonic muscle adapted for the function of sustaining tension. The metabolic cost of running this muscle is somewhat conjectural, but it is certainly much less than that needed for flapping flight. In small birds the actual saving is not very great, because the basal metabolism is large compared with the power needed for flight. In large birds the metabolic rate is relatively much less, and so a greater proportion of the total power can be saved by soaring. Some small birds, notably swifts, do soar, but soaring as the primary means of locomotion is chiefly characteristic of large species, most of which would have limited powers of flight without it. Like man, soaring birds extend their powers of locomotion by using a source of energy external to their own bodies; they are perhaps the only other group of animals that do so.

5

The Energetics of Bird Flight

by Vance A. Tucker
May 1969

The metabolism of gulls and parakeets is measured during ascending, descending and level flight in the wind tunnel. The results show how flying birds can husband their "fuel."

How hard must a bird work to fly? The speed and endurance of birds in flight have always challenged the curiosity of students of animal physiology. Even the smallest birds not only stay in the air for hours but also travel without stopping for hundreds or even thousands of miles at speeds well above those attained by all but the fastest ground animals. In my laboratory at Duke University I have been examining how birds accomplish these feats by measuring the power expenditure of budgerigars (the common parakeet) and laughing gulls flying at various speeds and attitudes in a wind tunnel. These are the only birds for which direct information is available, and they are among the few birds for which there are any such data at all.

The speed and endurance that make bird flight so interesting also make measurements of the energetic cost of flight difficult to obtain. Many methods for estimating the cost of free or hovering flight have been used, including aerodynamic calculations, measurements of weight loss during flight, studies of the washout rates of radioactive compounds and studies of the rate of oxygen consumption. The last method is more accurate than the others, which depend on more or less tenuous assumptions. All these techniques, however, have a common failing when applied to free-flying birds: they do not allow experimental manipulation of the speed, duration and direction of a bird's flight so that such factors can be related to metabolic data.

This is precisely the advantage of the wind-tunnel method. At the beginning of an experimental run a budgerigar or a gull is placed in the test chamber of the wind tunnel so that the bird flies into the stream of air [*see illustration at right*]. In this way the bird can be made to fly as rapidly in relation to the air as it does in natural flight, while remaining stationary from the observer's point of view. The bird's flight in the wind tunnel can be likened to the progress of a sailboat heading into a strong tide; although water moves rapidly past the boat's hull, to someone on the shore the boat may seem to be standing still. The experimenter can select the speed of the bird's flight by controlling the air velocity. He can also set the duration of the flight and determine whether the bird is flying on a level path or on an ascending or descending one.

To simulate ascending flight the tunnel is tilted so that its forward end points upward. A downward tilt creates the conditions of descending flight. Ideally the aerodynamic and gravitational forces on a stationary object in a wind tunnel are exactly the same as if the object were moving through still air. This is why I refer to a bird as ascending or descending when the wind tunnel is tilted, even though the bird's actual position does not change.

While flying, the bird wears a clear plastic mask over its head to collect exhaled gases. An elastic band around the back of the bird's head holds the mask in place, and a vacuum pump draws the exhalations down a flexible plastic tube to gas analyzers so that the rate at which the bird obtains energy from fats and carbohydrates can be measured. Oxygen consumption and carbon dioxide production are determined by measuring the concentration of these gases in the air entering and leaving the mask, and also by metering the total flow rate of air through the mask. In addition to providing gases for the analyzers the vacuum pump system draws fresh air in through the back of the mask.

The budgerigar was chosen for the experiments because it is tame, is readily available in pet stores and is a steady flier. (An early attempt to work with a sparrow failed when the bird, instead of flying on a level path, tried to escape and dived and turned inside the wind tunnel.) A small bird such as the budgerigar, which weighs 30 to 40 grams, was the only one that could be accommodated in the wind tunnel available at the time, a nine-foot-long affair with a somewhat cramped test chamber. When I

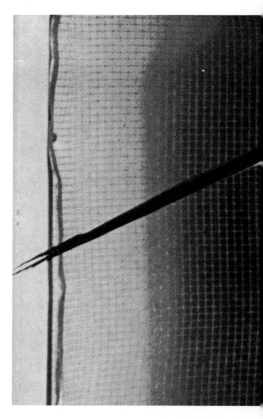

LAUGHING GULL flying in the experimental chamber of a wind tunnel wears a

sought to study a larger bird, I chose the laughing gull, which weighs 300 to 400 grams; it happened that one of my colleagues had a number of gulls at hand for other work. To accommodate them I had a larger tunnel built.

Training birds to fly in a wind tunnel is a lengthy process. My basic approach is simply to punish the bird mildly if it does not fly and reward it if it does. The punishment is an electric shock (detectable by humans but not painful) administered when the bird lands on the floor of the tunnel. The reward is the presentation of a perch on which the bird can rest after a successful flight. As the bird learns to control its movements in the confines of the test section and improves in physical condition, it will fly for steadily lengthening periods before it will risk a shock. In fact, gulls can be trained to fly in the wind tunnel without the use of electric shock; they will fly when nudged with a stick. After several weeks of training both budgerigars and gulls had reasonable endurance, even when they wore masks. They could fly at least twice as long as a typical half-hour experimental period without stopping. One herring gull flapped and glided almost continuously in the wind tunnel for 10 hours!

Once trained, both the budgerigars and the gulls "liked" to fly in the sense that they flew voluntarily as soon as the tunnel was turned on. During the training period, however, the budgerigars cleverly frustrated the observer. One bird avoided both flying and being shocked by hanging on to every protuberance in the test section. As these were discovered and removed, the bird finally learned to hold on to the electric grid with one foot to avoid completing the circuit. Another bird accomplished the same thing by rolling over on its back on the floor and keeping both feet in the air. When the birds could fly well in the tunnel, they were trained to wear the transparent mask.

Whether in wind tunnels or in natural flight gulls and budgerigars, like other animals, obtain power for sustained work from reactions that combine oxygen from the air with fats, carbohydrates and proteins to produce carbon dioxide, nitrogenous wastes, water and usable energy. Of these sources fat, many investigators have concluded, probably provides most of the power for flight. Fat is certainly the best source of fuel in terms of weight. Gram for gram it contains almost as much energy as gasoline, more than twice as much energy

as protein and eight times more energy than stored carbohydrate.

My research confirms that fat is the main source of energy in bird flight. When fats are burned in a calorimeter, they yield .7 milliliter of carbon dioxide and 4.7 calories for each milliliter of oxygen consumed. The experimental birds exhibited almost exactly the same exchange rates: the ratio of carbon dioxide exhaled to oxygen consumed by budgerigars and gulls was always between 1 : 0.7 and 1 : 0.8 during sustained flights. Animals normally do not use protein for fuel, and if the birds had been metabolizing carbohydrate, they would have consumed and produced equal quantities of oxygen and carbon dioxide. It can be calculated that more than 70 percent of the energy for flight came from fat metabolism, and that 4.8 calories of energy are released for each milliliter of oxygen consumed. This caloric equivalent of oxygen consumption offers a convenient way to determine the power expenditure of flight at different speeds and angles of ascent and descent.

The wind-tunnel experiments show that there is no simple answer to the question of how hard a bird works to fly. The power expenditures of the budgeri-

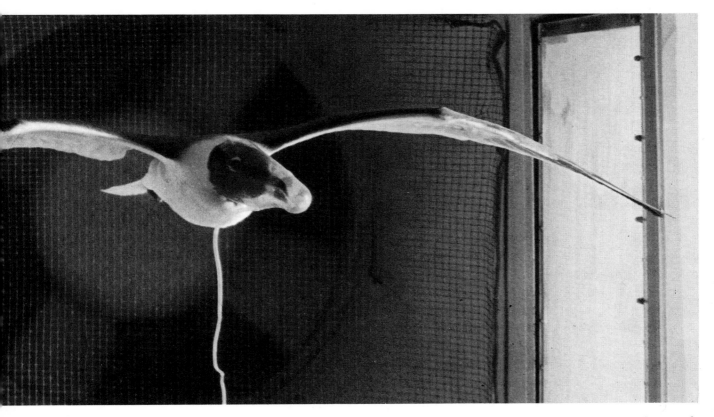

plastic mask that captures its exhalations. A pump draws gases through tube to analyzers so that the gull's rate of fat and carbohydrate metabolism can be measured. Because the bird flies into the airstream it appears to stand still. In the rear is the tunnel's fan.

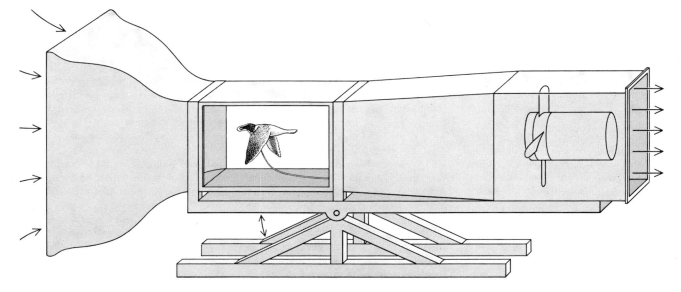

WIND TUNNEL designed for author's experiments can hold a flying laughing gull or other large birds. The 25-foot device can be tilted eight degrees to simulate ascending or descending flight. Speeds above 40 miles per hour can be achieved in the tunnel.

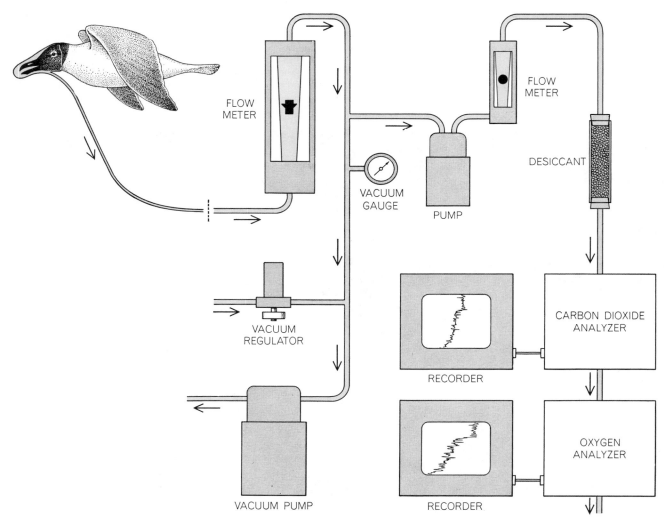

FLOW METER

FLOW METER

VACUUM GAUGE

PUMP

DESICCANT

VACUUM REGULATOR

RECORDER

CARBON DIOXIDE ANALYZER

VACUUM PUMP

RECORDER

OXYGEN ANALYZER

ANALYZING EQUIPMENT measures the carbon dioxide and oxygen exchange rates of a bird as it ascends, descends or flies a level course in the wind tunnel. The energy costs of the different kinds of flight can be calculated from the exchange rates. A vacuum pump draws gases from the mask while a smaller pump samples the flow continuously for the analyzers. Desiccant absorbs water vapor.

gar were markedly dependent on flight speed and angles of ascent and descent. For example, in level flight a budgerigar flying at 12 miles per hour expends energy at a rate of 152 calories per gram hour (the number of calories needed to move each gram of body weight at a given speed for one hour). As the bird's flight speed increases to 22 m.p.h. its power expenditure declines to a low point of 105 calories per gram hour. At higher speeds the power expenditure rises, reaching a high point of 165 calories per gram hour at 30 m.p.h.

When the budgerigar climbs at an angle of five degrees, its power expenditure is 140 calories per gram hour at 15 m.p.h. and rises slowly with flight speed to a maximum of 170 calories per gram hour at 26 m.p.h. When the bird is descending at an angle of five degrees, its power expenditure drops precipitously as its flight speed increases from 12 to 22 m.p.h. [see illustration on next page].

In evaluating the performance of the gull it should be noted that the animal was in some respects noticeably hindered by the mask. Its top sustained speed of 28 m.p.h. increased by almost 15 percent when the mask was removed. Moreover, the masked gull usually flew with its beak open, which wild gulls seldom do. This may mean that the bird was working unusually hard, or that the mask induced panting by interfering with the airflow that normally cools the beak.

Nonetheless, the wind-tunnel results are similar to the bird's performance in nature. The range of speeds at which the gull flew most economically in the tunnel (19 m.p.h. for endurance, 28 m.p.h. for distance) was about the same as the usual range of airspeeds for free-flying gulls. Laughing gulls have been tracked at 29 m.p.h. by a double-theodolite system. Radar tracking of ring-billed gulls and herring gulls respectively yielded mean airspeeds of 23 and 25 m.p.h. It should also be mentioned that the gull would not fly on an ascending path in the tunnel for more than a few minutes. This behavior, however, is not unusual in nature, where gulls prefer to gain altitude by soaring rather than flapping.

In level flight the power expenditure of the laughing gull, in contrast to that of the budgerigar, remains quite constant. It stays between 50 and 60 calories per gram hour whether the bird flies at 15 or 29 m.p.h. Both birds can expend power at much the same multiple of the basal, or resting, metabolic rate. The multiple is 13 to 20 for the budgerigar and 11 to 14 for the gull. Some mammals can do as well, but only for a short time. For example, a well-trained human athlete can expend power for a few minutes at 15 to 20 times his basal rate.

Power requirements in the wind tunnel obviously are related to the speed and angle of flight. This fact suggests that a bird in its natural environment could save energy by flying in such a way that minimal demands would be made on its metabolic resources. It is interesting to consider the various flight requirements a bird may encounter and how the animal could meet them with the lowest possible expenditure of energy.

A bird might, for instance, need to stay aloft for as long as possible, as

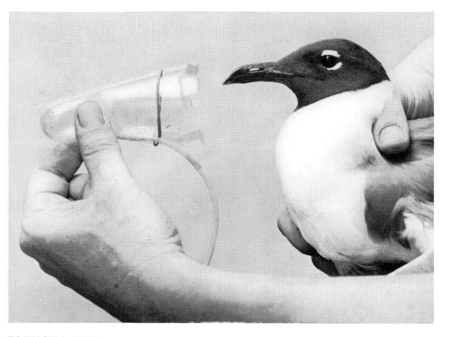

TO MASK A GULL the experimenter waits for a moment when the bird has stopped moving its head and then slips the mask over its beak. A rubber band secures mask to bird's head.

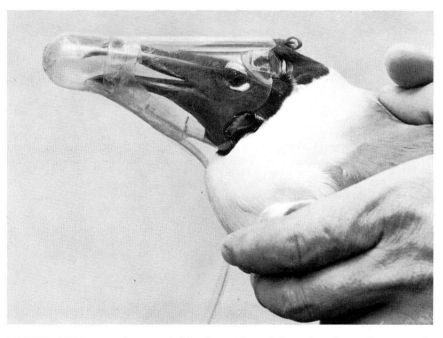

MASKED GULL, somewhat impeded by the weight and drag of mask, can fly at a steady top speed of 28 m.p.h. Without the mask the bird can increase its speed to 32 m.p.h.

in the case of a gull searching for food over the water. Here the bird might maintain a constant altitude and fly at a speed where power requirements would be at a minimum. This speed is 19 m.p.h. for the laughing gull and 22 m.p.h. for the budgerigar. At 22 m.p.h. a budgerigar consumes 1.1 percent of its body weight each hour as fuel when it metabolizes fat, and the gull uses half this proportion at 19 m.p.h. Since some birds can accumulate fat until it comprises half of their total body weight, they should have enough fuel to fly nonstop for tens of hours. Their precise endurance, however, is hard to estimate because not all the fat is available for fuel. Furthermore, the power requirements of flight probably decrease as the bird uses up its fuel supply and becomes lighter.

A migrating bird such as a budgerigar might also need to cover the maximum possible distance with a given amount of fuel. This would be accomplished at the speed where the ratio of power expenditure to flight speed is smallest. Budgerigars travel most economically at 22 to 26 m.p.h., at which speeds they consume .05 percent of their body weight in fat for each mile traveled. The laughing gull travels most economically at 28 m.p.h. and consumes only .024 percent of its body weight in fat for each mile traveled. These figures confirm that some birds can fly 2,000 miles without feeding. Indeed, the golden plover migrates 2,100 miles without food from Alaska to the Hawaiian Islands, and other land birds fly without food from the northeastern U.S. to Bermuda, and from Africa across the Sahara and the Mediterranean to Europe.

It is not surprising that both the budgerigar and the laughing gull have about the same speeds for maximum endurance and range in spite of the tenfold difference in their weight. In nature both are exposed to the vagaries of the ambient wind, and both must fly faster than ordinary wind speeds if they are to reach their destination against a head wind. In fact, the airspeed of almost all migratory birds, large or small, is more than 20 m.p.h.

Birds may also save energy during ascending or descending flight by seeking the speed where the ratio between the rate of climb and power expenditure is highest. To determine this point for budgerigars I used data from experiments where the wind tunnel was tilted at five degrees to simulate ascending or descending flight conditions. The rates of climb or descent were calculated by multiplying each bird's airspeed by .087, the number of feet its altitude changed (in effect) for each foot traveled forward. Finally these data were compared with the records of each animal's energy expenditure during the flight. I concluded that both ascending and descending flight were most economical at the speed where budgerigars have their maximum range: 26 m.p.h.

Thus far I have discussed the economics of avian flight but have not mentioned its efficiency. Whereas flight economics involves the fuel costs of flying for various lengths of time and various distances, efficiency measures the relation between power input (power expenditure) and power output. The efficiency of a machine expresses the power output of the machine as a percentage of the power input. It shows how much of the energy put into the machine appears as useful work.

Several kinds of efficiency can be calculated, including the relation between total input and total output. In the case of the budgerigar, however, it is revealing to consider another kind of efficiency: the relation between the changes in power output that occur when the bird departs from level flight to ascend or descend and the accompanying changes in power expenditure or input. This approach makes it possible to compare the bird's efficiency with that of other animals. It also leads to a hypothesis that may explain why some birds swoop in flight instead of pursuing a level course.

Power output is the product of the speed of the bird and the thrust force it exerts. The bird also expends energy to create a lift force, but this force is essentially constant as the tunnel is tilted to represent ascending and descending flight. Therefore when the bird ascends from its level flight path at a given speed, its power output increases over power output in level flight solely because of changes in thrust, and when it descends,

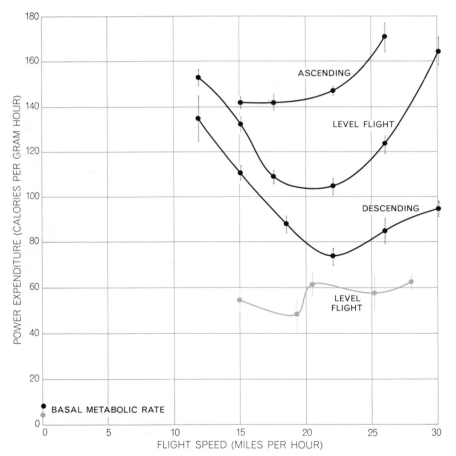

ENERGETIC COST OF FLIGHT for gulls and budgerigars is plotted. The steep curves represent a budgerigar's power expenditure in three kinds of flight. The gull produces a curve only for level flight (*color*) because it will not ascend in the tunnel and it behaves so erratically during descending flight that no valid data can be taken. When flying, budgerigars and gulls expend energy at 11 to 20 times the rate at which they metabolize while at rest.

its power output decreases for the same reason. This increase or decrease in power output exactly equals the rate at which a bird would gain or lose potential energy if it actually changed altitude.

Once the power output changes have been derived, calculations of efficiency can be completed by using the measured increases or decreases in power expenditure for climbing or descending at a particular speed. For an ascending budgerigar the efficiency is more than 50 percent at the lowest speed of 12 m.p.h. The efficiency then drops to between 15 and 18 percent as the speed reaches and exceeds 17 m.p.h. Efficiency during descent is more constant, changing from 14 to 24 percent between speeds of 12 and 30 m.p.h. At 17 and 27 m.p.h. the efficiency of ascent and descent are equal.

Since the efficiencies for ascent describe a bird working to increase thrust, they are comparable to efficiencies for increased work rates in other animals walking up inclines or pulling loads. Appropriate measurements under these conditions are available for men, dogs and horses. All have efficiencies between 30 and 35 percent (that is, the change in power output is 30 to 35 percent of the change in power input). The budgerigar over most of its range of flight speeds is about half as efficient as these animals, but at low flight speeds it is more efficient.

High efficiency for increasing thrust at low speed is consistent with the fact that in nature budgerigars often feed on the ground. Since the budgerigar must take off from the ground, it must simultaneously accelerate and gain altitude. (If it took off from a tree it would already have altitude and would need only to accelerate.) Because of the efficiency with which the bird utilizes energy at low speeds it can both get into the air and reach cruising speed at a cost that is little more than that of slow and level flight.

The reader should not conclude at this point that a bird gains altitude most economically at low speeds. I have already mentioned that the best speed for climbing is 26 m.p.h. Slow flight for the budgerigar is a costly process, but as long as the bird must fly slowly it might as well go up. The extra cost is small. At speeds above 17 m.p.h. the efficiency of ascent has dropped, but so has the total cost of flight. As a result the bird gains altitude with increasing economy as it approaches its optimum climbing and cruising speed of 26 m.p.h.

These studies of the budgerigar's effi-

ASCENDING FLIGHT can be simulated in the wind tunnel by raising the front end. To "climb" at a given speed the budgerigar increases thrust while lift remains almost constant.

DESCENDING FLIGHT is simulated when the tunnel is tipped downward. As the bird "climbs" or "falls," aerodynamic and gravitational forces are identical with those in nature.

ciency suggest that the swooping flight of some finches and woodpeckers and the slowly undulating flight of migratory birds (which may ascend and descend as much as 20,000 feet during long journeys) may represent an energy-saving stratagem. When the efficiencies of ascending and descending flight are the same at a particular speed, as they are for the budgerigar at 17 and again at 27 m.p.h., the extra power expenditure during ascent is just equal to the saving during descent. Thus the bird could climb to a given altitude and descend at no extra cost over level flight for the same length of time.

It follows that if the efficiency of ascent is greater than the efficiency of descent, the bird can actually save energy by flying in a swooping or undulating path. In fact, the lower the efficiency of descent, the more energy the bird saves. Since the efficiency of descent for the budgerigar is always less than 25 percent, one can speculate that if this bird could ascend (that is, increase its thrust) at cruising speeds with efficiencies as high as the 30 to 35 percent values for man, the dog and the horse, it could save energy by flying in a swooping pattern. One would predict, however, that in nature the budgerigar cruises on a straight path because in actuality the

efficiency for ascent is less than the efficiency for descent between speeds of 17 and 27 m.p.h.

How does flight compare as a form of locomotion with walking or running, or with the flight of aircraft? Two points of comparison are speed and endurance. In these respects birds are clearly superior to ground animals. Even small birds fly for hours at speeds in excess of 20 m.p.h., and larger birds such as ducks can cruise at 40 to 50 m.p.h. A few large ground animals such as antelopes, the ostrich and the cheetah can attain these higher speeds, but none can maintain them for long. I have mentioned that some birds are able to fly without feeding for tens of hours and for 1,000 miles or more. No walking or running animal can equal these feats, which in terms of endurance are respectable even for aircraft.

Another point of comparison is the energetic cost of transport, measured in units of calories required to transport a gram of body weight one kilometer. These units have the advantage that, whatever the size of an animal, they indicate the cost of moving a given mass a given distance. For example, the cost of transport for a flying bee is about the same as the cost for a running rat weigh-

ing 3,000 times as much. Thus when 300 grams are moved one kilometer, either in the form of a swarm of 3,000 bees or a single rat, the caloric cost is the same.

When measured in this way, the cost of transport for various swimming, walking, running and flying animals generally goes down as body weight goes up. A fruit fly, for instance, expends more energy to move each unit of its weight a given distance than a locust does [*see illustration on page 53*]. When walking, **running and flying animals are compared** with one another, however, flying animals prove to be much more economical than ground ones. A walking or running mammal expends 10 to 15 times more energy to cover a given distance than a bird of the same size does. It is no wonder that small mammals do not undertake long seasonal migrations! Some birds can even travel more economically than some machines. For example, a pigeon flies more economically than a light plane. Moreover, a Canada goose may be able to perform better than a jet transport.

Although the wind-tunnel experiments yield interesting information about metabolism and flight, it must be remembered that these experiments reproduce only certain aspects of natural flight conditions, never their entire rich variety. In addition, the experiments introduce some unnatural conditions. Although the aerodynamic forces in the test chamber ideally are the same as those in still air, the flow of air in the tunnel is more or less turbulent, and the walls of the test chamber may interfere with the flow of air around the bird. The effect of these distortions can be hard to determine. Relatively small amounts of turbulence, for instance, can improve the aerodynamic performance of model birds and model airplane wings, but extreme turbulence increases the power expenditure of flying budgerigars. Furthermore, a bird flying in a tunnel and wearing a mask has limited room to maneuver, and its shape, weight and weight distribution differ from those of a free-flying bird.

Even if one could be certain that a bird flying in a wind tunnel utilized energy at exactly the same rate as a bird flying through still air, there is a degree of uncertainty in any estimate of the cost of flight in the natural environment. This is particularly true of long migratory flights. The air in which a free bird flies is not still but moves in a complex manner. It is heated at the surface of the earth, rises and is replaced by descending air. Superimposed on these thermal currents are wind currents that flow hor-

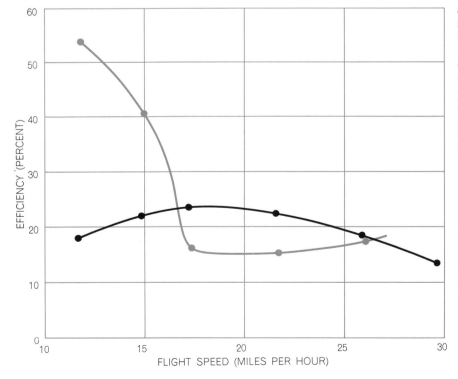

EFFICIENCY OF FLIGHT varies at different speeds for the budgerigar. At 17 m.p.h. and again at 27 m.p.h. the efficiencies of ascending (*colored curve*) and descending flight are equal to each other, indicating that at these points swooping costs no more than level flight.

izontally over flat surfaces but develop vertical components when they encounter other wind currents or surface features such as trees and hills. Such drafts and currents are strong enough to influence the power expenditures of flying birds. Since most birds fly at airspeeds of 20 to 30 m.p.h., even everyday winds could change their ground speed by 50 percent.

Vertical currents can be strong enough to hold a bird aloft, as is demonstrated by birds soaring in thermals, over ridges or over ships at sea. Even in the absence of vertical currents birds are accelerated upward or downward by changes in either the speed or the direction of the wind. The albatross in particular is reputed to remain aloft indefinitely without flapping its wings by moving through wind-velocity gradients over the sea. Changes in horizontal wind velocities large enough to influence bird flight in this way are ubiquitous on windy days. They occur with gusts of wind, in the wake of surface features such as trees and in the wind boundary layers above the surface of the land and the sea.

I have commented here only on the energetics of avian flight, but I have also used the wind tunnel to investigate other aspects of flight physiology: respiratory mechanics, water and heat budgets and responses to simulated high altitudes. In addition the wind tunnel is useful for aerodynamic investigations. In this connection my colleagues and I have studied the flapping flight and the gliding flight of vultures and hawks. Over the next few years we hope to use our wind tunnel to investigate other areas of avian biology.

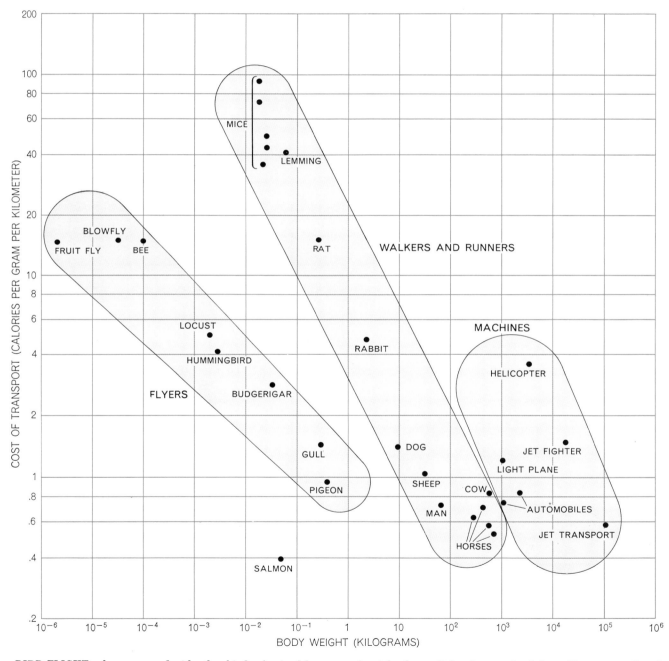

BIRD FLIGHT, when compared with other kinds of animal locomotion, generally is more economical than walking or running. Large flying birds can even travel farther for each calorie per unit of weight than a light plane or jet fighter. The young salmon's performance shows, however, that a fish can travel more economically than gulls, pigeons, horses or any other kind of animal.

III

MIGRATION AND NAVIGATION

III MIGRATION AND NAVIGATION

INTRODUCTION

More than one-third of the species of birds in the world, and a majority of the birds of North America and Europe, migrate; that is, they undertake seasonal mass movements over long distances, breeding well to the north of their wintering grounds. Some seasonal journeys are too short to call migrations, like the hike of a Mountain Quail down a California mountain side. Others may be as long as that of the Bobolink—a North American bird the size of a large sparrow—which flies from Canada to Argentina, a distance of 10,000 to 12,000 kilometers (6,000 to 7,000 miles).

It is difficult to generalize about migration. Flying enables birds to move readily from place to place in their search for optimum living conditions, and the time, place, and relationships between manner of their movements are not simple. Many birds of the Northern Hemisphere summer in the north and winter in the south. Large numbers of waterfowl and sea birds breed on the Arctic tundra during the few weeks of its short summer. Food is plentiful there, and predators are few.

Some birds, such as the Cardinal, Blue Jay, and Mockingbird are year-round residents of the conterminous United States. Others, like the Oldsquaw, Tree Sparrow, and Ross' Goose, are winter visitors that nest farther north. Still others breed here and then fly south to winter feeding grounds in Mexico and Central and South America. Examples are vireos, warblers, kingbirds, and swallows. There are also passage migrants, birds that winter south of and summer to the north of the temperate regions, such as the Solitary Sandpiper and many species of waterfowl.

"Migration is the greatest adventure in the life of a bird, the greatest risk it must take," says Roger Toey Peterson. Of the 500 million birds that fly south from Europe and Asia to Africa, it is estimated that nearly one-third do not return. Many die in storms, some are eaten by predators, and many more starve to death.

Major routes of migration connect North America and South America, Eurasia and Africa, and Eurasia and Southeast Asia and Australia. Although there is some overlap, each intercontinental route is separated from the others by oceans, mountains, or deserts. Figure 1 shows some routes taken by birds that migrate between North and South America.

Migrations usually occur over fronts hundreds of kilometers or more across. However, geographical features restrict some migratory pathways to a few miles in width. For example, hawks and eagles follow the ridges of mountain ranges, where wind currents are favorable for soaring. Spectacular flights of these raptors are watched each year from popular lookouts in the Appalachians. White storks in western Europe travel to Africa via the Straits of Gibralter, soaring from great heights over the 10 miles of water to North Africa. Storks from eastern Europe do the same across the narrow Hellespont separating Europe from Asia Minor.

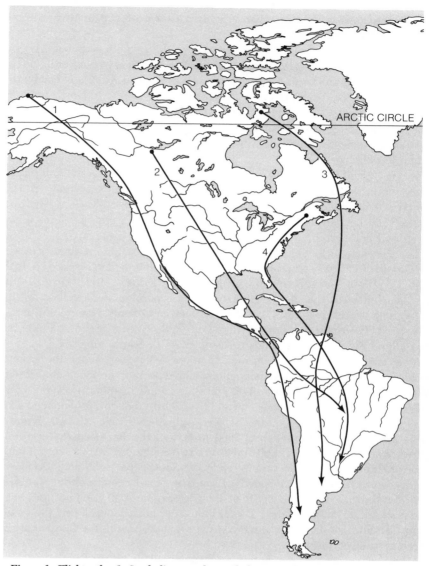

Figure 1. Flightpaths. 1. Sanderling, northern Alaska to southern Argentina. 2. Red-eyed Vireo, Mackenzie River to Mato Grosso. 3. American Golden Plover, Melvile Peninsula to South America via the Atlantic Ocean. 4. Bobolink, Maine to Southern Brazil. [After J. Van Tyne and A. J. Berger, *Fundamentals of Ornithology* (2nd ed.), Wiley, New York, 1976.]

Banding is one way ornithologists have studied migration. Birds are caught, special bands are attached to their legs, and they are then released to continue on their journeys. In the United States, the bands and permits to use them are issued by the U.S. Fish and Wildlife Service. Finders of dead banded birds are requested to return the bands to a central location.

Modern bird banding probably began in 1740, when Johann Leonhard Frisch of Berlin tied strings to the legs of swallows before their autumn migration. Audubon used silver threads to study the nesting habits of phoebes in 1803. Large-scale banding began in 1903 in Rossiten, Germany. Today, over 2,000 people in the United States and Canada alone band approximately 600,000 birds every year. Worldwide, the annual number of birds banded runs into the millions. Only a small proportion of the bands are ever returned. Even so, the information obtained has helped to map routes and establish distances traveled by many birds. Banding has revealed some extraordinary flights of individual birds. For example, Arctic Terns have been found more than 15,000–19,000 kilometers (about 9,000–12,000 miles) from where they were banded. Banding has also shown that some birds may return to the same place year after year. Bob Stewart of Point Reyes Bird Observatory found that one individual Wilson's Warbler returned for at least 7 years to the same breeding site by a stream at the observatory near San Francisco after wintering in Mexico, thousands of kilometers away.

Circuitous routes of migration may reflect the evolutionary history of a species. After breeding in Alaska, the Arctic Warbler crosses the Bering Sea to Siberia and then flies to its wintering ground in tropical Asia; conversely, the Gray-Cheeked Thrush breeds in Asia and then crosses over to North America before flying south to winter in the West Indies and South America. One explanation is that their migrations across the Bering Sea retrace the paths traveled by their ancestors when they left one continent (that of their winter home) to colonize another.

Strong-flying birds, such as swallows, hummingbirds, and American blackbirds, which can feed on the wing or stop to feed while traveling, tend to migrate by day. Many small, secretive birds, like rails, cuckoos, wrens, and vireos, feed by day and migrate at night. Some—for example, shore birds, waterfowl, loons, and auks—migrate both by day and by night.

The first article in this section ("An Oceanic Mass Migration of Birds"), by Timothy C. Williams and Janet M. Williams, tells how radar is used to track migrating birds, revealing much concerning the numbers, altitude, speed, and directions of birds that travel at night. They report on studies done on the millions of small birds that fly to the Caribbean and South America from the East coast. Their observations show how the birds fly a simple compass course that allows the prevailing winds to bring them to South America.

Most birds fly less than 1,500 meters (about 5,000 feet) above the ground or water. However, small numbers of birds have been noted flying at altitudes of 2,400–4,500 meters (8,000–15,000 feet) and some as high as 6,400 meters (21,000 feet) over the ocean. The Yellow-billed Chough (pronounced like "tough"), a relative of the crow, has been sighted in the air over Mt. Everest at an altitude of 8,200 meters (27,000 feet), and the Bar-headed Goose migrates over the Himalayas at altitudes up to 9,100 meters (30,000 feet). (Mammals of similar size would rapidly lose consciousness at such heights.)

Most small birds travel at speeds of less than 50 kilometers (about 30 miles) per hour; hawks may travel at 50–60 kilometers (about 30–40 miles) per hour and ducks at 80–95 kilometers (50–60 miles) per hour. Considering the speed limits for automobile travel, birds compare favorably with the family car for speed of transportation.

Many birds migrate extremely long distances. The Arctic Tern, a real distance champion, breeds on the Arctic tundra in the summer and winters in the Antarctic. It travels from 83 degrees north latitude to 74 degrees south latitude within a single year. The Pacific race of the American Golden Plover is believed to make nonstop flights of 3,200 kilometers (2,000 miles) between the Aleutian islands and Hawaii. The eastern race of the American Golden Plover follows a circular course. In the fall, it flies from northern Canada to Labrador, then goes nonstop to the northern coast of South America and on to Argentina. In the spring, it flies north via Central America and the Mississippi Valley, benefiting from the winds that predominate in the spring and fall.

Some of the shortest seasonal journeys are those of gallinaceous birds. The Bobwhite in northwest Oklahoma and the California Quail in the Sierra Nevada mountains spend summers on the high mountain slopes and winters in the lowlands. They often walk part of the way up and down the mountains traveling in small groups. Although these migrations seldom exceed 40 kilometers (25 miles), the altitudinal change of 1,200 meters (about 4,000 feet) is climatically equivalent to a journey of over 1,600 km (1,000 miles) to the south. A 75-meter (250-foot) change in altitude is roughly equivalent to a journey of 1 degree (69 miles) in latitude.

Although many birds seem to be genetically "locked in" to migrating, others are more variable. The Starling migrates in central Europe, but it does not in Britain. The once-migratory Hooded Crow and Blackbird have become residents of Scandinavia since the region began to have warmer winters (after 1880). The wild canary, or Serin, is a resident bird in the Mediterranean. Within the past century, it has extended its range throughout continental Europe as far as the North Sea and has become migratory in its new territory. A flock of Norwegian Fieldfares (a type of thrush) set up a nonmigratory colony in Greenland after being blown there by a storm in 1937 during a migration flight.

The mechanisms by which birds find their way during migration and while returning ("homing") to the nest after having been removed and transported some distance from it have attracted much attention. Many examples have been recorded of the seemingly incredible ability of birds to home their way over thousands of kilometers of unfamiliar territory. One notable example is the homing behavior of Manx Shearwaters, studied by British ornithologist R. M. Lockley. Female birds removed from their burrows in Wales and transported to Switzerland and Venice returned to their nests in two weeks. Another female transported across the Atlantic Ocean to Boston in a light-tight box returned to her burrow in less than 13 days.

Many mechanisms have been proposed to explain the navigation of birds, including such visual cues as rivers and mountains, use of the sun and stars as compasses, and the ability to sense magnetic fields and polarized light. Stephen T. Emlen ("The Stellar Orientation System of a Migratory Bird") studied migration in the laboratory by making use of the fact that a caged bird tends to restrict its activity to the direction in which it would fly if free to do so. His experiments with Indigo Buntings support the idea that these birds navigate at night using stars as compasses.

In the last article in this section, William T. Keeton ("The Mystery of Pigeon Homing") tackles the problem of how birds that fly during the day navigate. He discusses the evidence that homing pigeons use the sun as a compass and that, in its absence, the birds establish direction by sensing the magnetic field of the earth. Interestingly, neither the day-flying pigeon nor the night-flying bunting could determine their longitude; both seemed to lack the "inner clock" needed for them to compensate for the movements of the sun and stars.

No single factor seems to explain all migrations. Birds, like people, use more than one cue to find out where they are and in what direction they are heading. Some, like ornithologist Bruce Campbell, may be unduly pessimistic: "People say we are getting to know more and more about less and less, and this certainly seems to be true of the . . . study of bird migration, for hardly anyone now is bold enough to say he knows what started birds migrating or how they manage to find their way over thousands of miles of this planet year after year."

6

An Oceanic Mass Migration of Land Birds

by Timothy C. Williams and Janet M. Williams
October 1978

Every fall millions of songbirds and small shorebirds leave the east coast of North America for the Caribbean and South America. Their difficult journey has now been followed with the aid of radar

For about two months after the summer visitors leave the beaches of New England and the Canadian Maritime Provinces those areas experience a far more massive departure that goes unnoticed by most of the remaining inhabitants. More than 100 million birds, most of them fairly small, cross those shores on their annual flight southward over the Atlantic from eastern North America to the Caribbean and South America. A patient observer with a powerful pair of binoculars might see a few of the birds as they traverse the face of a full moon or pass through a beam of light pointed upward at night, but for the most part the participants in the migration cannot be seen directly. With the aid of John M. Teal and John W. Kanwisher of the Woods Hole Oceanographic Institution, Leonard C. Ireland of the Bermuda Biological Station and others we have exploited a network of radars to observe the behavior of the birds. The studies have yielded much information about this remarkable migration and have indicated why some birds succeed at it and others, which seem to be out over the ocean by mistake or misfortune, perish in large numbers.

The birds we have observed by radar along the Atlantic coast during the last week of September and the first half of October are most likely shorebirds (such as sandpipers and plovers) and small songbirds (such as warblers). The vast majority of the birds begin their journey at night, after a cold-front weather system has moved southeast over the coast. If you stand in a quiet area of Cape Cod early of an October evening with a brisk northwest wind at your back, you can hear great numbers of small birds calling to one another as they pass overhead. If you then were to go to any of the three large radar installations on the Cape (Air Force surveillance, air-traffic control or weather radar), you would find the center portion of the screen filled with small bright dots moving in a roughly southeasterly direction.

Such a radar screen represents a map of the area surveyed by the apparatus; north is at the top, and the distance of an object from the radar installation is indicated by concentric range rings at intervals representing about 10 kilometers. The location of any object detected is represented on the screen by a bright dot. The radars to which we had access displayed each object in this way from once to 15 times per minute.

In order to record information from the radar screen we made time-exposure photographs. Any slowly moving object such as a bird would show up in the photograph as a series of small dots or as a streak. By briefly closing and then reopening the shutter toward the end of the time exposure we could ascertain the direction of motion of the bird. By measuring the length of the streak, and therefore the distance traveled, we could (knowing the duration of the time exposure) compute the speed of the bird. The number of birds detected per unit of area served as a basis for estimating the density of migration, which we classified in four categories: no movement, light migration, moderate migration and heavy migration. Most of the radar units could also estimate the altitude of birds from the angle of elevation of the radar beam and the distance of the birds from the radar.

We began our research on these southerly migrations by observing birds as they moved over Cape Cod. Like William H. Drury and Ian C. T. Nisbet of the Massachusetts Audubon Society before us, we were fascinated by the great numbers of birds (up to 12 million per night) that left Cape Cod moving southeast toward the middle of the Atlantic. To determine what happened to these birds we watched from radars on the islands of Bermuda and Antigua. We found that many but not all of the birds continued flying southeast over Bermuda but arrived in the Caribbean flying southwest. Land birds and most shorebirds would have no chance to land during that flight of more than 3,000 kilometers. Moreover, they could not navigate by following coastlines or other landmarks; some other system of guidance was necessary.

The only way we could study the movement of the birds while they were over water was with radars at coastal sites and on islands and ships along the route. These observations had to be made simultaneously with similar radars and under similar conditions. Therefore during the last week of September and the first two weeks of October for six years we enlisted the cooperation of six national governments, four Federal agencies, the Woods Hole Oceanographic Institution and a large number of our friends and students to man as many as nine radar stations along the route of the migration.

The basic patterns of migration that we found appear to involve at least two routes from North America to South America. On one route the birds follow the coast southwest to the vicinity of Florida and then turn southeast to move along the Caribbean islands. The second route involves birds leaving the coast from at least as far north as Nova Scotia and as far south as Virginia, and thereafter moving southeast (a direction of flight observed from ships in all the areas of the Atlantic we studied). We suppose the birds turn in the area of the Sargasso Sea (approximately the southern limit of our observations) as they encounter the northeast trade winds. Aided by those winds, they move in a southwesterly direction over the region occupied by the Caribbean islands.

At all the radar sites we found that the migrations proceeded in waves. Several days would pass with little or no activity, and then for a day or two birds would move in large numbers. The intervals between periods of migratory activity became longer as one moved away from the coast. At coastal sites some movement could almost always be observed at night. At Bermuda we encountered occasional periods without migration, and in the Caribbean several days often passed with no migrants being observed.

By plotting the data obtained by radar on a series of photographs made from weather satellites operated by the National Oceanic and Atmospheric Ad-

ministration (NOAA) one can establish a correlation between migratory activity and the state of the weather. An example is provided by the satellite photographs for October 3 through October 6, 1973 [see illustration on page 64]. On the first day a departure of birds from the North American coast was beginning. A cold front had just moved offshore from Cape Cod to Florida. As the cloud patterns show, the front crossed the shoreline between Cape Cod and Halifax.

Coastal radars recorded heavy movements of birds that night. Birds were moving both along the coast and offshore.

By October 4 the frontal system had become stationary between Bermuda and the coast. Birds observed from a ship penetrated the frontal system all day, moving southeast and reaching the Bermuda area by midafternoon. On October 5 these birds were between Bermuda and the Caribbean. At Bermuda

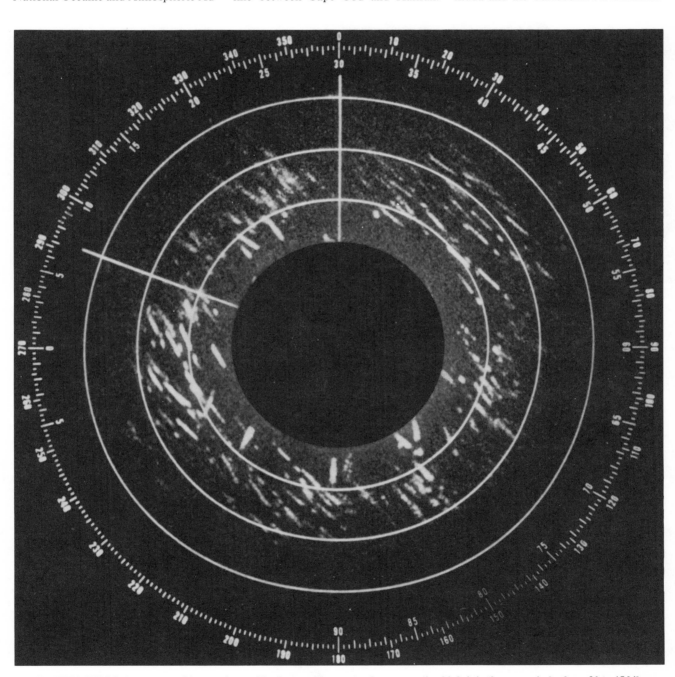

MIGRATING BIRDS show up as white streaks on this photograph of a radar screen on the Caribbean island of Antigua. North is at the top. The white rings represent 10-kilometer intervals from the radar station. The center of the display is blacked out to prevent overexposure of the photograph from ground clutter. The photograph is a five-minute time exposure, in which the largest concentration of streaks representing birds is in the range circles from 20 to 45 kilometers. A dot at the end of a streak, caused by briefly closing the shutter of the camera, shows direction of movement. The white line at the left shows the angle of elevation of the radar beam, which was intersecting a layer of birds at altitudes of from three to six kilometers. Most of the birds were moving southeast; a few were moving southwest.

ATLANTIC MIGRANTS, drawn to a common scale, are portrayed. Included are three shorebirds, the Hudsonian godwit (*a*), the American golden plover (*b*) and the white-rumped sandpiper (*c*), and one **songbird, the blackpoll warbler (*d*). Perhaps half of the migrants are songbirds. An indication of the scale is provided by the warbler, which in life is from 4.5 to 5.5 inches long and weighs less than an ounce.**

the movement had shifted from south-easterly to southerly (possibly reflecting birds moving south from Halifax the previous night). Bird movements at the ship, which was about 400 kilometers behind (northwest of) the weather front, appeared to be scattered in all directions, although the density of birds was scored as being heavy.

On October 6 the wave of migration reached the Caribbean, with heavy movements reported at Antigua during the day and at Barbados during the evening. The total time of flight from North America to Antigua was about 64 hours and to Barbados about 72.

The timing of this migration is typical of the data we have been able to gather. Departures from the coast are triggered by favorable flight conditions behind a cold front. The significant feature of the weather is strong northwest winds, which help the birds to move from the coast to the area of Bermuda in an average of only 18 hours. Radar indicates that few birds land on Bermuda; the great majority of them continue southeast over the island, usually in light and variable winds, until they reach the area of the Sargasso Sea, where they encounter the northeast trade winds that assist them in reaching the Caribbean. This second part of the journey is much slower than the first; the birds appear to fly for about 48 hours between Bermuda and Antigua. The radars at Antigua indicate that, as at Bermuda, few of the birds land; instead most of them seem to continue flying for another 18 hours to reach South America. The total time of nonstop flight over the ocean hence appears to be 86 hours, plus or minus 12.

To the best of our knowledge this migration is the longest (in both time and distance) nonstop flight known for small birds. It also seems to take place at the greatest height above the ground of any bird migration. From radar observations we found that the densest migrations from the North American coast to Bermuda are at an altitude of two kilometers (about 6,500 feet) or somewhat less, although some birds are detected at five kilometers (about 16,000 feet). At Bermuda a different pattern begins. Most birds fly at an altitude of from one to two kilometers. By the time they reach Antigua they are up between three and six kilometers, and on some days the radar showed significant numbers of birds flying over the island at 6.5 kilometers (21,000 feet). Although we made many fewer observations at Barbados and Tobago, it appeared that the birds were by then dropping in altitude, until at Tobago we recorded no birds above 800 meters. Evidently in approaching the South American coast the birds come down gradually in preparation for landing.

Birds at an altitude of six kilometers above Antigua are flying in air at a temperature of zero degrees Celsius, and the air has only about half as much oxygen as air at sea level. The advantage of flying at such heights seems to be that it puts the birds in a region of favorable wind conditions. We plotted the average wind velocity at various altitudes on the days when we detected moderate or heavy migrations at Antigua at an average altitude above 4.2 kilometers. The average direction of bird movement on those days was southeast. Our data for altitudes below four kilometers showed strong east-southeast winds, which were avoided by the high-flying birds.

Physiologically flight at such altitudes is made possible by the distinctive respiratory system of birds. The system embodies a number of adaptations for flight, but in this connection the crucial one is the countercurrent flow of blood and air in the bird's lung. It is the key to the bird's ability to extract oxygen efficiently and so to fly at high altitudes.

Observations made both visually (with the aid of binoculars) and by radar from ships at sea yielded a much clearer picture of how the birds behave during their long flight over the ocean and also indicated what kinds of birds might be making the flight. In order to follow our discussion of these results one needs to be clear about the distinction between a bird's track and its heading. If a bird is flying in a wind, the

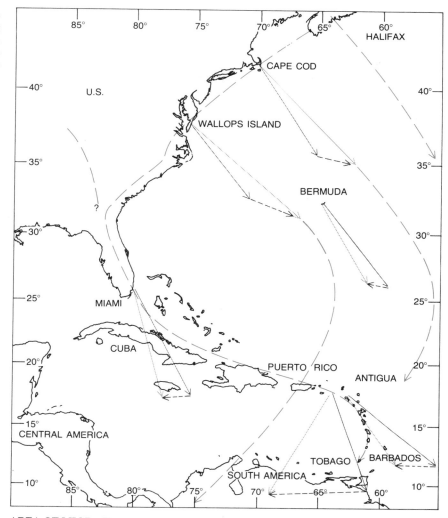

AREA OF MIGRATION from North America to the Caribbean and South America appears based on radar observations from Halifax, Cape Cod, Wallops Island, Bermuda, Miami, Puerto Rico, Antigua, Barbados and Tobago. The broken colored lines indicate two sets of possible migratory routes, one for birds flying along or near the North American coast and the other for birds making most of the trip over the ocean. (The data for Puerto Rico are derived from observations by W. J. Richardson of Environmental Research Associates in Toronto.) The gray lines forming triangles show the relation of the wind to the heading and track of the birds. In each case the broken line shows the direction of the wind (with the relative wind speed indicated by the length of the line), the dark gray line represents the average heading of the birds and the light gray line shows their average track. The birds consistently have a southeasterly heading, but the trade winds that blow from the northeast in the Caribbean create a drift that has the effect of turning the migrating birds toward the southwest as they approach their destination.

movement shown on a radar screen (the track) does not necessarily correspond to the direction in which the bird is orienting its body (the heading). The wind introduces drift, that is, it blows the bird to the downwind side of its heading.

Another factor to be taken into account is the bird's airspeed, which is of course the speed of its flight through the air. Airspeed and heading are calculated from our radar data by means of the direction and speed of the wind as deter-

mined by a weather balloon at the altitude of the bird. In order to distinguish the behavior of birds from their drift caused by the winds we have plotted both track and heading for observations of bird migrations at sea. Following the lead of Ronald P. Larkin of Rockefeller University, who analyzed the first two years of these observations at sea, we have divided all the observations from ships into periods of consistent migratory behavior.

A plot of these data on a map reveals four rather different categories of behavior [*see top illustration on page 66*]. The first category consists of the periods when no significant amount of migration is detected. The second consists of birds with headings from south to southeast and tracks that are southerly. These birds, if they continued the pattern, would be likely to reach South America. The third category consists of groups of birds that appear to be disoriented.

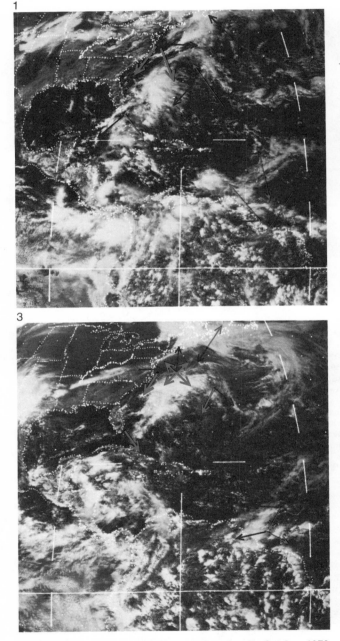
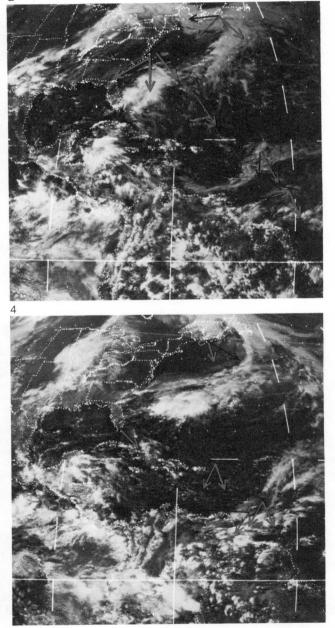

PROGRESS OF MIGRATION during four days in October, 1973, is plotted on weather-satellite photographs made by the National Oceanic and Atmospheric Administration (NOAA). The colored arrows represent the average track of a bird migration, and the thickness of an arrow indicates whether the migration was light, medium or heavy. The black arrows show the wind direction at the altitude of the birds; the longer the arrow, the higher the average wind speed. A migration began October 3 under typical conditions (*1*), after a cold front had just moved offshore from Cape Cod to Florida. The accompanying northwest winds aided the birds. By the next day (*2*) the frontal system was stationary between Bermuda and the coast, and most of the birds had reached Bermuda. Once past Bermuda (*3 and 4*) they encountered the northeast trade winds that shifted them toward their destinations in the Caribbean and South America. The birds were at Barbados by the fourth day after about 72 hours of flight. The total time of nonstop flight over the ocean was about 86 hours.

Their headings are widely scattered, and any net progress of a group is largely attributable to drift caused by the wind. The calculated airspeeds of these birds are generally quite low, less than 20 kilometers per hour. It appears unlikely that any significant proportion of the birds in this category would reach the Caribbean or South America if they persisted in poorly oriented flight at low speed. The last category consists of birds that are apparently trying to move in a direction other than toward the Caribbean.

We could not discern a statistically significant tendency for these four types of behavior to be grouped in any area of the Atlantic we studied. We therefore concluded that some factor other than geography must have been determining the categories of behavior we observed from the ships. If one plots the same data on a diagram of the predominant weather patterns at a given time, a clearer picture emerges.

A typical weather system for which we made such a plot consisted of a low-pressure center or hurricane, a moving cold front, a stationary front and two high-pressure air masses, one subtropical and the other (northwest of the frontal system) representing air that had just moved off the North American continent [see bottom illustration on next page]. The migratory patterns differed according to the weather. In the area around the subtropical high we found only migrants with headings to the south or southeast; they were making effective progress toward the Caribbean. Groups of birds with scattered headings were found only northwest of frontal systems or south and east of low-pressure centers. A common factor in both cases is that the disoriented birds have recently experienced strong offshore winds. It is in these areas also that we found most of the birds with an average airspeed of less than 20 kilometers per hour.

Based on this analysis we can tentatively classify birds observed over the Atlantic as true migrants if they have penetrated the frontal system that initiated their departure and as unsuccessful migrants if they are observed in a high-pressure center northwest of a frontal system or in a low-pressure system. (Some true migrants will occasionally turn up in the second category, usually because the observation was made near the North American coast when the birds had not yet penetrated the frontal system.) It is probable that the unsuccessful migrants are birds that would normally migrate over land but have been blown out to sea.

A heading that is generally southeast is typical of the true migrants, regardless of whether the radar that detects them is coastal, island-based or on a ship. Nevertheless, it is not always easy to identify the true migrants because of the frequent simultaneous occurrence of two or more patterns of migratory behavior, particularly at the large coastal or island-based radars. Therefore at each site we separated groups of birds on the basis of track direction and then computed the average heading of each group. Although the average heading of all migrants at Cape Cod, Wallops Island, Miami and Bermuda was to the southeast, the analysis at Antigua is probably the most important one. There we divided the birds into two groups: those that were moving along the Antilles to the southeast and those that were arriving from the Atlantic moving southwest. In spite of this arbitrary division the average heading of both groups was to the southeast; the difference in track direction was due to the fact that the birds were flying in different wind conditions.

The analysis of headings suggests that a remarkably simple guidance system is adequate for this 3,000-kilometer flight. Once birds leave the coast of North America they maintain a constant compass heading to the southeast until they reach the coast of South America. It apparently is not necessary for them to change this heading; the shift from a southeast track to a southwest one is accomplished for them when they encounter the northeast trade winds in the area of the Sargasso Sea. A substantial body of experimental evidence supports the notion that a bird can establish and maintain a compass heading on the basis of the sun, the stars or the magnetic field of the earth.

Although radar has many advantages

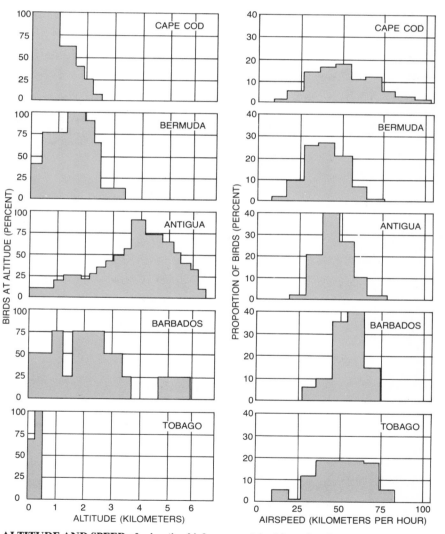

ALTITUDE AND SPEED of migrating birds, as ascertained by radar observations, are charted. The plot of altitude (left) shows the percent of birds found at given altitudes during times of moderate or heavy migration. The average altitude reaches a peak at Antigua and then declines as the birds approach their destination. The plot of airspeed (right) shows the percent of birds detected at each speed. The loss of both the faster and the slower birds between Cape Cod and Antigua suggests that only certain species are adapted to this long migration. The number flying at less than 50 kilometers per hour suggests that many of the birds are small songbirds.

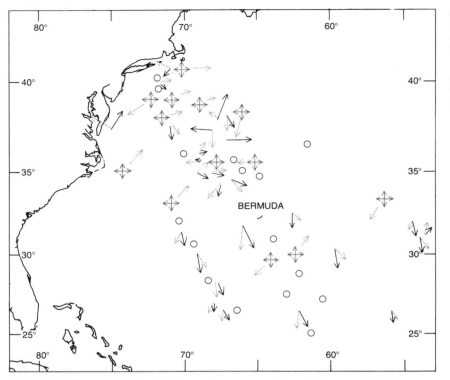

MIGRATORY BEHAVIOR of birds over the ocean was observed by means of shipborne radar. The dark gray arrows indicate the average heading of the birds and, by the length of the arrow, the relative airspeed; the longer the arrow, the higher the average airspeed. The light gray arrows similarly indicate the average track of the birds and their average speed in relation to the ground. The open circles represent areas where no migrating land birds were seen.

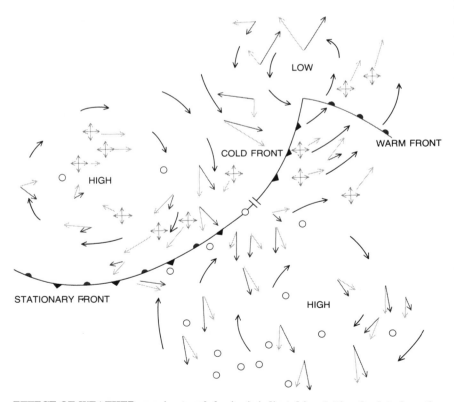

EFFECT OF WEATHER on migratory behavior is indicated by plotting the data from the illustration at the top of the page on a diagram of typical weather conditions. Weather patterns are much more important than geography in influencing the behavior of migrating birds.

for studying the migration of birds, it does not enable us to identify the birds that are detected on the radar screen. We have gone at the question indirectly by determining the airspeed of the 4,600 or more birds we have detected by radar. At coastal sites the range of airspeeds is quite broad, but in the Caribbean it is mainly between 30 and 60 kilometers per hour. Even though airspeed is not a precise means of identifying birds, most of the birds flying at less than 45 kilometers per hour are probably small songbirds. Shorebirds and waterfowl fly faster.

Much better identifications can be made of birds that are seen passing or landing on ships. During the last two years of our shipboard observations Carol P. McClintock of the State University of New York at Buffalo undertook to obtain as many specimens as possible. Since firearms are not allowed on the ships, she resorted to live traps or a slingshot for which green grapes served as the ammunition. Her findings, together with careful observations made with binoculars, reveal that small songbirds were by far the most abundant species seen from ships in all the areas of the Atlantic we investigated.

The variations in the observed distribution of songbirds appeared to reflect behavioral differences rather than physical ones. For example, warblers, sparrows and juncos are about the same size and weight, yet all but one of our observations of sparrows and juncos were confined to the area between the coast and Bermuda, and warblers were seen as far south and east as the ships traveled. We believe many of the birds we have defined as true migrants are warblers, whereas many of the birds seen wandering behind frontal systems or south of low-pressure areas (the unsuccessful migrants) are such species as sparrows and juncos, which do not migrate to the Caribbean or South America.

The Atlantic is not a hospitable place for small songbirds. During storms at sea hundreds or thousands of small birds have been seen flying around a ship, entering cabins and hitting masts or wires. At such times it seemed unlikely that many of the birds could survive for more than a few hours. Our belief that large numbers of these birds perish at sea is supported by reports from oceanographers that bird feathers are often found in the stomachs of deep-sea Atlantic fishes.

Our radar data indicate, however, that such losses arise primarily among birds that lack the behavioral adaptations for flying over the ocean. For the true migrants a relatively simple migratory strategy takes advantage of a surprisingly predictable series of weather conditions along the route. First the migrants wait on the east coast of North America until a strong cold front passes southeast over the coast and out into the Atlantic. This weather pattern not only ensures the birds favorable northwest winds during the first part of their flight but also is a remarkably good indicator of fair weather between the coast and the Sargasso Sea. Tropical storms or hurricanes approaching the North American coast usually halt the southeastward movement of cold fronts. On 93 days or nights we observed moderate or heavy movement of birds along the North American coast or at Bermuda, and on only two of those occasions did we see birds apparently flying into the path of an approaching storm.

Once the migrants have left the coast they have only to fly constantly to the southeast until they reach the Caribbean or South America; their actual track will be first to the southeast to the Sargasso Sea and then, as they encounter the trade winds, southwest until they reach their destination. As soon as they have penetrated the frontal systems near Bermuda their flight will be for the most part under clear skies with either light and variable winds or moderate, steady northeast ones.

The ocean route from Halifax to Antigua is about 2,800 kilometers (47 percent) shorter than a route by way of Florida. Moreover, birds on the ocean route take advantage of both northwest offshore winds and the northeast trade winds as tailwinds, and the route presumably is without predators. The trip does, however, require a degree of exertion that is not matched by any other vertebrate. For a man the metabolic equivalent would be to run four-minute miles for 80 hours. The avian respiratory and muscular systems show many adaptations that make such an output possible. If a blackpoll warbler were burning gasoline instead of its reserves of body fat, it could boast of getting 720,000 miles to the gallon!

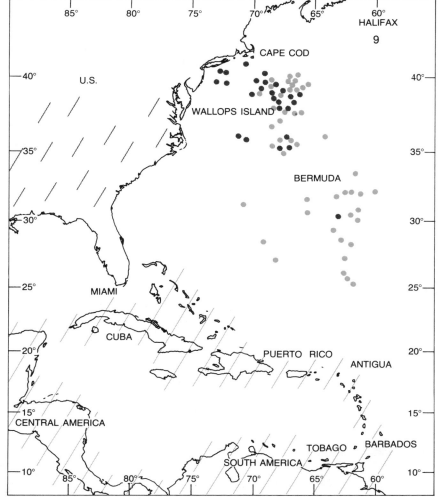

BIRD SIGHTINGS from ships in the western Atlantic reveal a difference between the migratory patterns of small songbirds that winter in the southern U.S. and those that winter in the Caribbean and South America. The first group, represented by gray dots and gray hatching in the wintering area, includes three types of sparrow and the slate-colored junco. The second group includes eight species of wood warbler and is represented by colored dots and hatching. Some species of warbler winter in Central and South America rather than the West Indies.

7

The Stellar-Orientation System of a Migratory Bird

by Stephen T. Emlen
August 1975

When the indigo bunting is put in a planetarium, it exhibits an ability to orient itself by the stars. This, however, can be only one of the cues it uses for long-distance navigation

The blackpoll warbler is a small, inconspicuous songbird that breeds during the summer in the stunted conifer forests of Alaska and northern Canada. When fall approaches, these birds embark on a remarkable migratory journey. They leave the northern forests and fly east-southeast across the North American continent to the Atlantic coast. During this stage of the journey they stop to feed and build up stores of subcutaneous fat that will serve as a vital energy reserve for the next stage. The blackpolls concentrate near the coast of New England and the Maritime Provinces of Canada, waiting for the right weather conditions. Then, as the next high-pressure cell moves in from the west, bringing with it winds from the north or northwest, the blackpolls depart again, this time over the ocean on a nonstop flight that will take them three to five days. They fly over Bermuda, the Antilles and Puerto Rico, stopping only when they make landfall on the northeastern coast of South America. It is a tremendous feat: a nonstop flight of

EXPERIMENTAL ARRANGEMENT in a planetarium for testing the ability of the indigo bunting to orient by the stars is shown. The photograph was made in the Southern Cayuga Atmospherium-Planetarium in Poplar Ridge, N.Y. Projectors are not visible to birds in the cages. Stars at any latitude and longitude, as well as celestial motion, can be projected onto the planetarium dome.

more than 2,400 miles over water by a bird weighing less than 20 grams! Any error in navigation would obviously lead to disastrous results. Any misinterpretation of the weather would also lead to disaster, since a blackpoll that encounters stiff headwinds or a storm has no chance of landing to rest or to find shelter.

The blackpoll warbler is an extreme but not atypical case of birds that migrate south. Fully two-thirds of the species of songbirds that breed in the northern U.S. travel south in the winter. The distances of migration typically range from 600 to 1,800 miles, but each fall some songbirds make one-way trips of up to 4,000 miles. The following spring the birds fly back to their breeding grounds. Year after year the adult birds return with amazing precision to the same several square miles of territory at both their breeding and their wintering grounds.

How do the migrating birds select the appropriate flight directions? Can they determine when they have been blown off course, and can they correct appropriately? How do they know when they have arrived at the latitude of their destination? What is the fate of young birds flying alone on their first migratory trip?

Biologists have long been intrigued by the phenomenon of bird migration, but it is only during the past two decades that significant progress has been made toward answering the fundamental questions about it. Today scientists around the world are focusing their attention on questions of animal navigation. Hundreds of thousands of migrant birds are being individually marked with a leg band so that field investigators can determine their migratory paths by plotting their recapture locations. In the laboratory other workers are testing the ability of birds to detect different potential directional cues and are examining how such cues are used. Ornithologists are tracking "unseen" migrating birds with radar and following individual migrants by attaching small radio transmitters to them.

The results of these various studies have shown that bird navigation is not a simple affair; it is not entirely dependent on any single cue or sensory system. It seems that migrating birds make use of a variety of cues to determine their direction and maintain it in flight. A recent article by my colleague William T. Keeton describes some of the types of cues available and the interplay among them [see "The Mystery of Pigeon Homing," by William T. Keeton, beginning on page 78]. Here I shall concentrate on

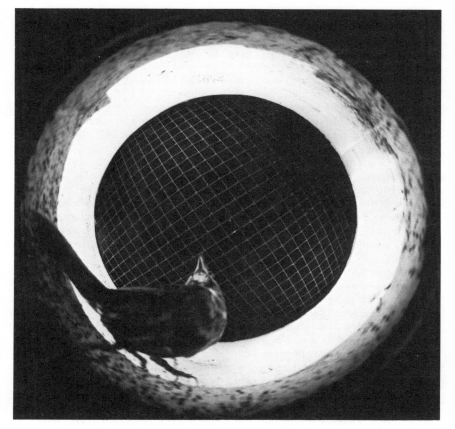

INDIGO BUNTING is shown hopping onto the side of a test cage. The photograph was made by placing a camera with a "fish-eye" lens at the bottom of the cage. Black marks on the white side of the cage are footprints made by the bird. The screen is the top of the cage.

one cue system that has been studied intensively and that appears to be of major importance to night-migrating birds: orientation by the stars. The reader should bear in mind that I am covering only one aspect of how birds navigate. It is only by dissecting out the various aspects and studying them one at a time that an understanding of the full story will ultimately be achieved.

The scientific study of the directional orientation of migratory birds had its breakthrough with the pioneering work of Gustav Kramer, an ornithologist at the Max Planck Institute for Marine Biology at Wilhelmshaven. It had long been known that when migrant songbirds were kept in captivity, they displayed intense activity at night during the periods of their normal spring and fall migration. When Kramer placed songbirds in circular cages during their migratory period, he discovered that they would spontaneously orient their activity in a particular direction. By manipulation of the cues available to the caged birds the determinants of direction finding could be studied. Through this technique migration could be "brought into the laboratory."

In the late 1950's another German ornithologist, E. G. F. Sauer of the University of Freiburg, carried out a long series of experiments with European warblers. It was he who first hypothesized that these warblers determine their migratory direction from the stars in the night sky. Since then much has been learned about star orientation by birds. Numerous species have been examined, and it appears that the ability to orient by the stars is widespread among birds that migrate at night.

For some years I have been studying one night-flying migratory bird, the North American indigo bunting (*Passerina cyanea*). Enough information is now available to piece together a fairly complete picture of how the stellar-orientation system in this species operates. The species breeds throughout the eastern U.S., where the brilliant blue male is a well-known songster. During the fall migration the buntings fly up to 2,000 miles to winter in the Bahamas and in southern Mexico and Central America south to Panama.

When indigo buntings are kept in captivity and exposed to the same pattern of day lengths they would experience in nature, they exhibit intense nocturnal activity in April and May and again in September and October, the times of normal migration. When this restlessness appeared, I tested the birds by placing them individually in circular cages. The cage was constructed of a piece of white blotting paper, rolled and stapled to form a funnel, mounted on a base consisting of an ink pad and topped with either a clear plastic sheet or a hardware cloth screen. A bird inside the cage can see only the sky overhead, since all ground objects are blocked from view.

A bunting in migratory condition stands in one place or turns slowly in a circle, its bill tilted upward and its wings partly spread and quivering rapidly. At frequent intervals the bird hops onto the sloping paper funnel, only to slide back and continue its pointing and quivering. Each hop from the ink pad leaves a black print on the paper. The accumulation of inked footprints provides a simple record of the bird's activity; they can later be counted and analyzed statistically.

In the first stage of my studies I placed the buntings in their funnel cages outdoors on clear, moonless nights. In September and October most of the birds exhibited a distinct preference for jumping toward the southern sector of the

cage, the same direction in which they would have migrated if they could. When the birds are tested in late April and May, however, the preferred direction is to the northeast, the appropriate direction for spring migration.

Since the wall of the test cage completely screens the horizon from view, it seems likely that the buntings are able to determine their migration direction when the only visual cues are those provided by the night sky. This hypothesis was reinforced by the changes observed when the birds were placed outdoors at night under cloudy conditions. As the stars disappeared behind the clouds, the orientation of the birds deteriorated considerably [see lower illustration on opposite page].

In order to test the stellar hypothesis under more rigorous conditions, I took the buntings into a planetarium, an approach also used by Sauer in some of his experiments with European warblers. In September and October, when the birds were exhibiting nocturnal restlessness, I projected the normal fall stars onto the planetarium dome. When the buntings were tested in the funnel cages, they oriented to the south. Birds tested in April and May under a spring sky in the planetarium consistently oriented to the north and northeast. When the North

Star in the artificial sky was shifted to the east or west, the buntings changed their orientation to the new "south" or the new "north," depending on the season of the year. The change in orientation behavior was consistent and predictable. In control experiments I turned off the star projector in the planetarium and exposed the birds to a diffusely illuminated dome. Their behavior paralleled their response to overcast conditions outdoors: the accuracy of their orientation deteriorated considerably.

Since indigo buntings are willing to exhibit meaningful orientation in spite of the confinement of captivity, I was able to further modify the visual cues in the night sky and thus dissect out the detailed workings of the birds' stellar-orientation system. The experiments were designed to answer the following questions: Which stellar cues are important? How are such cues employed? What kind of information does the bird obtain? How accurately does it obtain it?

In theory there are two ways birds could determine direction by the stars. One way would be for the bird to locate a critical star or a group of stars and then guide itself by flying at a particular angle with respect to the star or the group of stars. The absolute position of a star, however, is not constant throughout the night: stars shift from east to west as the result of the rotation of the earth. In order to maintain a given compass direction the bird would have to alter its angle of flight with respect to the selected star in such a way as to compensate for the apparent motion of the star [see top illustration on page 73]. Such a mechanism would be analogous to the sun-compass orientation in which a daytime bird migrant, making use of an internal time sense, correctly compensates for the daily movement of the sun across the sky.

The requirements for a stellar-navigation system are much more demanding than those for a system that depends on the sun for determining compass direction by day. There is only one sun, and it moves at a regular rate, but there are thousands of stars and different stars are visible above the horizon at different times of the night and at different seasons. A nocturnal migrant presumably would need to be able to consistently locate a specific star or a specific group of stars, and that would require it to possess some form of pattern recognition.

In addition the rate of compensation for apparent motion will differ, depending on the star or stars selected. Celestial motion is an apparent motion produced

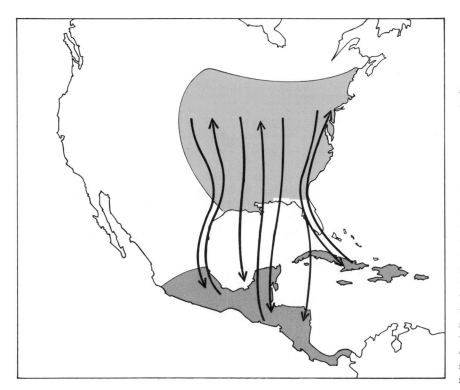

MIGRATION OF INDIGO BUNTINGS proceeds along a broad front. Buntings migrate from their wintering grounds in the Bahamas, southern Mexico and Central America (*gray areas*) in late April and arrive at their breeding grounds in the eastern U.S. (*colored area*) throughout the month of May. They depart for wintering grounds in September and October.

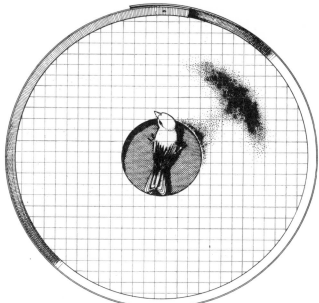

CIRCULAR TEST CAGE for determining the directional preference of an indigo bunting is shown in cross section and in a top view. Funnel portion of the cage is made of white blotting paper.

The bunting stands on an ink pad, and each time it hops onto the sloping funnel wall it leaves black footprints. The bird's view is limited to a 140-degree overhead sector of sky when it hops up.

by the earth's rotation once every 24 hours. All stars move with an angular velocity of 15 degrees per hour, as the sun does. The linear velocity of a star will vary, however, depending on how close it is to the North Star. Stars near the North Star move through a small arc, whereas stars near the celestial equator move through a large one. If a bird were to use star groups in different parts of the sky, it would have to compensate at a different rate for each group. Finally, the direction of compensation depends on whether the guiding stars are in the north or in the south: northern stars would require clockwise compensation, southern stars counterclockwise.

According to the second theoretical model, the bird would use patterns of stars to determine directional reference points. Human beings easily recognize the Big Dipper by the characteristic arrangement of its stars. And by visually extending the line joining the two pointer stars of the Big Dipper, they can readily locate the North Star and hence geographic north. Star patterns such as the Big Dipper also move across the sky, but the shape of each pattern remains constant and each preserves a distinct relation to the North Star.

Since each star bears a fixed geometric relation to other stars, it would be theoretically possible for a bird to determine a directional reference point from any number of star patterns [see middle illustration on page 73]. The major difference between this model and the first one is that a compass direction can be determined from the geometric patterns of the stars independently of an internal time sense, or "biological clock."

I tested these alternative hypotheses in a planetarium by creating an artificial situation in which the astronomical time would be out of phase with a bird's internal time sense. If a time sense is involved in star navigation, then presenting the stars in positions that are advanced or retarded from local time should cause the bird to orient in the wrong direction. On the other hand, there should be no change if the bird relies only on the geometric patterns of the

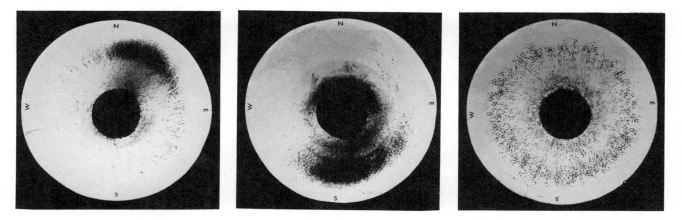

FOOTPRINT RECORDS of male indigo buntings tested in a circular cage placed outdoors under the stars on moonless nights are shown. In the spring the bird typically orients its hopping to the north (left). In the fall its hopping is oriented to the south (middle). When the stars are obscured by clouds, the bunting's activity remains high but orientation of the hopping is random (right).

stars. I tested buntings when the planetarium sky was three, six and 12 hours ahead of local time and when it was three, six and 12 hours behind local time. The results were clear: the birds generally maintained their normal migratory orientation under all these conditions. Apparently indigo buntings do not make use of an internal time sense to orient by the stars but obtain directional information from star patterns, much as human beings do.

I then turned to the question of which star groupings are of particular importance to buntings. Once again the planetarium was an invaluable tool, since one can block from view selected stars, constellations or entire areas of the sky. In a series of experiments I systematically removed and later reinserted portions of the artificial sky. I found that most buntings rely for direction finding on the northern area of the sky that lies within

about 35 degrees of the North Star. The major constellations in this area are the Big Dipper, the Little Dipper, Draco, Cepheus and Cassiopeia. The birds relied on the northern circumpolar stars not only during the spring migrating season when they normally fly north but also during the fall migrating season when they fly south.

An important corollary finding was that there is considerable redundancy in the buntings' recognition of star patterns. The birds are familiar with several star groups, and the removal of one group of stars, say the Big Dipper, often merely forces them to rely on some alternate constellation. Since birds frequently migrate on nights when there is variable cloud cover, such redundancy is obviously adaptive.

Navigation can be regarded as involving a two-step process. Consider a man equipped with a map and a compass. In order to determine how to reach a par-

ticular geographic destination he must first calculate his position on the map with respect to his goal and then use the compass to select the appropriate direction. The navigation problems of a migrating bird can be viewed in the same way, that is, as a "map and compass" process.

Theoretically an accurate knowledge of the absolute positions of the stars coupled with a stable and highly accurate internal time sense could provide enough map-and-compass information for a bird to determine its absolute geographic position. If the bird retains a precise memory of the temporal position of the stars at its destination point, it could in principle select the appropriate direction to the goal from the displacement of the stars in the sky overhead.

The finding that the indigo bunting does not integrate a temporal component with its use of stellar cues implies, however, that the bird does not detect or correct for longitudinal displacement, at least not by celestial cues. Hence star orientation in the indigo bunting appears to be a compass sense that enables the bird to select and maintain a particular direction but does not provide the information that makes it orient to a particular goal.

What, then, does determine how the star compass will be used? The bunting may be able to locate the Big Dipper or other constellations, but why does it use them to orient north or south rather than east or west? And how does the bunting select north in the spring and south in the fall?

The sidereal, or astronomical, day is four minutes shorter than the solar day. Because of this inequality the temporal positions of the stars change with the seasons, with the result that the stellar information available from the fall night sky is quite different from that available from the spring night sky. Does the indigo bunting have a specific northerly directional response to the stellar stimuli in the spring sky and a southerly response to the stellar stimuli in the fall sky?

To test this possibility I captured 15 adult male buntings in their summer breeding territories near Ithaca, N.Y., and divided them into two groups. The weight, fat level and molt status of each bird was recorded weekly until the testing period the following spring.

The control group of eight birds lived in a flight room where the length of the day simulated what they would have normally encountered in nature. An astronomical time clock maintained a day length equivalent to the day length at

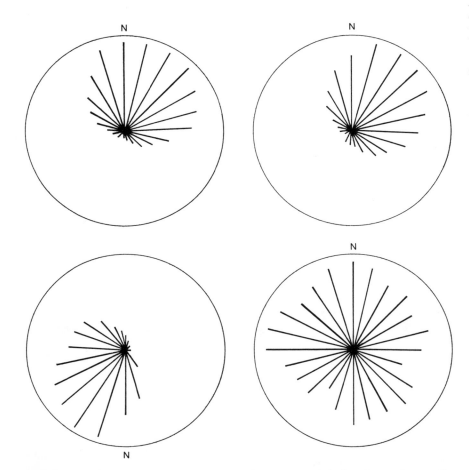

VECTOR DIAGRAMS show the similarity of the orientation of a bunting outdoors under the stars in the spring (*top left*) and under a simulated spring night sky in a planetarium (*top right*). When the planetarium stars were shifted so that the North Star was at the true south, the bird reversed its orientation (*bottom left*). When the stars were turned off and the planetarium was diffusely illuminated, the bunting's orientation became random (*bottom right*). The radius of each circle is equal to the largest amount of activity in any one 15-degree sector, and the vectors for the other 15-degree sectors are proportional to the radius.

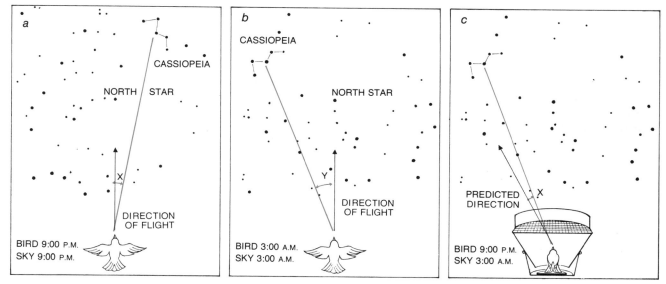

STELLAR-ORIENTATION HYPOTHESIS I proposes that the indigo bunting guides itself by flying at an angle to a particular star or group of stars. Since the positions of the stars change throughout the night, the bird would have to use an internal time sense to compensate for the motion of the stars. For example, a bunting going north at 9:00 P.M. would fly at angle X with respect to a critical star (a). At 3:00 A.M. the bird compensates for the rotation of the stars by flying at angle Y to the critical star (b). According to the hypothesis, when a bunting whose physiological time is at 9:00 P.M. is presented with a 3:00 A.M. star pattern in a planetarium, it should compensate in the wrong direction, that is, it should orient at angle X with respect to the critical star instead of at angle Y (c).

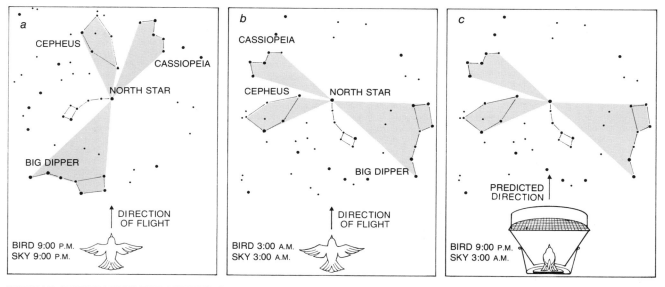

STELLAR-ORIENTATION HYPOTHESIS II states that the bunting obtains directional information from the configuration of the stars. The bird can determine a reference direction such as north from fixed geometric relation of the stars regardless of the time of night (a, b). When the bunting is exposed to a time-shifted sky in a planetarium, there should be no change in its orientation (c).

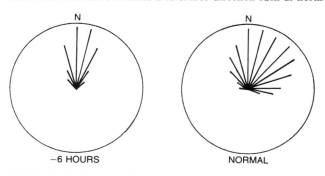
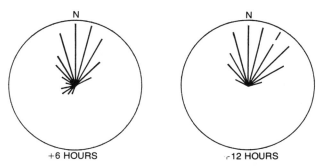

RESULTS OF PLANETARIUM TEST of the two star-navigation hypotheses show that buntings continue to orient correctly regardless of whether planetarium stars are shifted ahead of or behind the bird's normal physiological time. This indicates that the bunting does not incorporate its biological clock in the star-orientation process and obtains only directional information from star patterns.

74

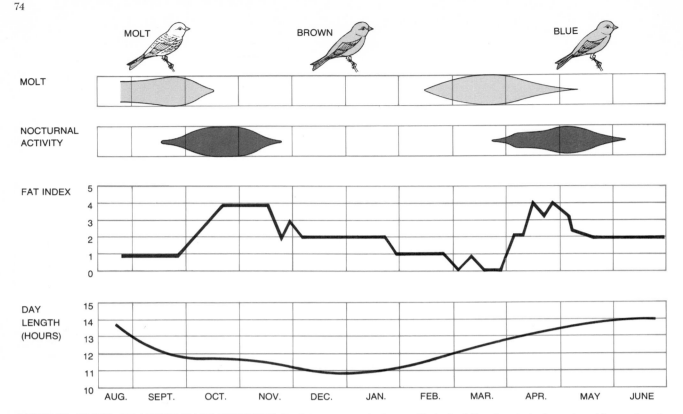

CONTROL GROUP OF ADULT MALE BUNTINGS lived in a flight room where an astronomical time clock maintained the day length equivalent to length at their wintering grounds. The birds molted normally in the fall and again in the spring. After each molt they built up fat reserves and became active at night. In May directional preference of the birds was tested in a planetarium.

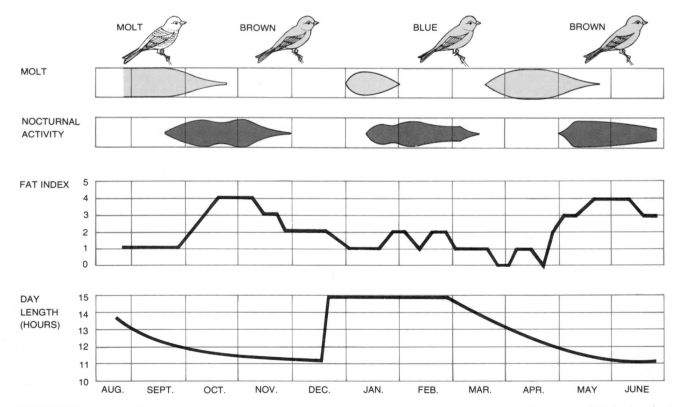

EXPERIMENTAL GROUP OF ADULT BUNTINGS was given an accelerated photoperiod regimen. Beginning in mid-December birds were exposed to the longer day lengths typical of spring. They molted into their blue spring plumage in January. The day lengths were shortened in March, and the birds molted into their brown winter plumage. Their directional orientation was tested in May.

their wintering ground in Guatemala. The male buntings in this group molted normally and acquired their bright blue prenuptial plumage between February and early April. After molting they built up substantial reserves of subcutaneous fat. They became nocturnally restless in April and May.

The experimental group of seven buntings was subjected to the same day-length regime as the control group until mid-December. The birds were then exposed to a spring day length of 15 hours, which caused them to molt into their blue spring plumage in January. Beginning on March 1 the day length was progressively shortened to simulate the day lengths of fall in the buntings' summer breeding territory, and the birds molted out of their blue plumage and into their brown winter coloration. After the molt the buntings built up fat reserves, and nocturnal activity began in May.

The directional preferences of the control group and the experimental group were tested in the planetarium under identical spring night skies. There was a marked dichotomy in the orientation behavior of the two groups. The control group of blue buntings, which were ready for their normal spring migration, oriented to the north and northeast, whereas the experimental group of brown buntings, which were ready for their normal fall migration, oriented to the south.

The results indicate that the physiological state of the indigo bunting affects its migratory orientation. We have already seen that the same northern circumpolar stars are used as the chief stellar reference in both spring and fall. It now appears that the polarity of the migratory orientation—whether it is toward or away from the northern circumpolar stars—is under hormonal control. Recent studies by Albert H. Meier and D. D. Martin of Louisiana State University support this hypothesis. They report being able to reverse the orientation behavior of another nocturnal migrant, the white-throated sparrow, by altering its physiological state with the administration of two hormones, prolactin and corticosterone, which appear to have a synergistic effect in stimulating the birds' migratory activity.

The finding that the physiological state of the indigo bunting affects the direction in which it orients does not, however, fully answer the question of how it chooses a specific direction for its migration. The young of many species of birds migrate independently of the

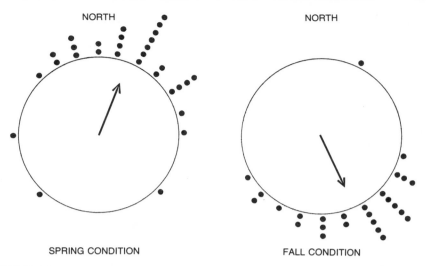

DIFFERENCE IN ORIENTATION of indigo buntings in the control group (*top illustration on opposite page*) and the experimental group (*bottom illustration*) shows that the physiological state of the bunting affects its migratory direction. The control group, which was physiologically in the normal spring migratory condition, oriented to the north-northeast. The experimental group, which was in an induced fall migratory condition, oriented to the south-southeast. The mean vector of the birds in each group is shown by the arrow. The length of the vector represents degree of agreement among the birds in selecting a direction.

adults, setting out on a course they have never traveled before and without the benefit of experienced companions. What causes young, inexperienced birds to select a southerly direction for their first migration? To many investigators the fact that they do so implied that early experience was not important in the development of normal orientation abilities. Some workers even proposed that birds possess a genetically inherited "star map."

Field studies have produced evidence that makes the inherited-star-map hypothesis unlikely. These investigations reveal that there are differences between the navigational abilities of young birds and those of adult birds. When birds of some species, for example the European chaffinch, are captured and displaced from their normal fall migration routes, the adults may correct for the displacement and fly to their regular winter grounds, but young birds on their first migration do not. Prior experience obviously improves the navigational ability of birds.

In my studies adult indigo buntings have always been more accurate and consistent in their orientation than young birds. If very young buntings are prevented from the time of their capture from viewing the normal night sky, aberrant orientation behavior develops. One summer I located numerous nests of indigo buntings near Ithaca, and I carefully removed the young birds when they were between four and 10 days old. The

nestlings were hand-reared in the laboratory, where their visual experience with celestial cues could be controlled. One group of young buntings never saw a point source of light. They lived in a windowless room with diffuse fluorescent lighting until they began depositing migratory fat and exhibiting intense nocturnal activity in September and October. When I tested these birds in the planetarium under a night sky that matched the normal one for the season, they were unable to select a migratory direction. The young birds were highly motivated, jumping with great frequency in the test cages, but the orientation of the jumps was random. They were unable to obtain directional information from the stars.

A second group of young birds was prevented from seeing the sun, but the birds were allowed to view the night sky in a planetarium every other night during August and September. The star projector rotated at a speed of one revolution every 24 hours, thus duplicating the normal pattern of celestial rotation. When these birds began displaying nocturnal activity, they were tested in the planetarium under the same sky as the group of birds that had had no visual experience with the stars. Unlike the inexperienced birds, the buntings that had already been exposed to the night sky were able to orient to the south. In some way the exposure to the stars was of extreme importance for the normal maturation of star-orientation abilities. Finally, a third group of young buntings was exposed to the night sky in the planetarium but with one important difference. I modified the star projector by constructing a special arm that allowed the projector to be rotated around any axis of my choosing. I selected Betelgeuse, a bright star in Orion, as the new polestar around which all other stars rotated. The star patterns and constellations remained unchanged; only their positions and movements with respect to the new axis of rotation were altered.

The young buntings of the third group were exposed to the sky with the Betelgeuse polestar every other night for two months. When they became nocturnally active, they were tested under a normal sky with the North Star at the pole position. The buntings consistently oriented their activity 180 degrees away from Betelgeuse—the appropriate "southerly" direction as defined with respect to the polestar of their early experience [see illustration below].

On the basis of experiments of this kind I have hypothesized that young buntings respond to the apparent rotational motion of stars in the night sky. The stars near the North Star move through much smaller arcs than the stars near the celestial equator, and this enables the young birds to determine a

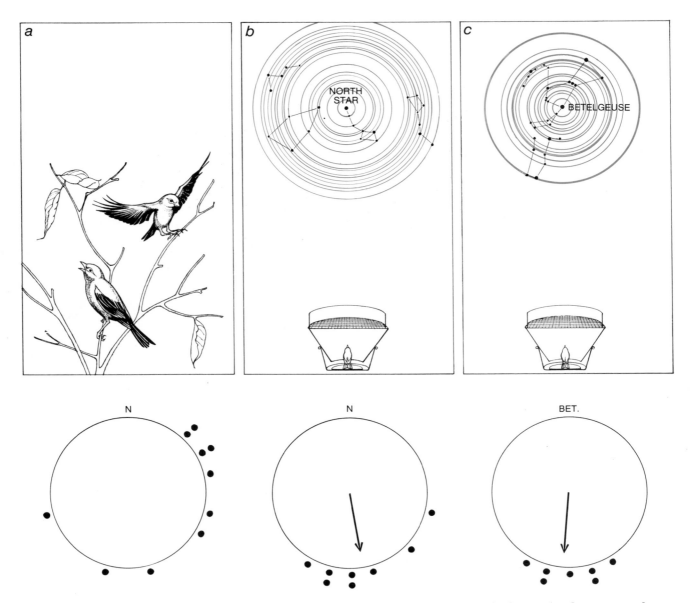

EARLY VISUAL EXPERIENCE of young indigo buntings was found to play an important role in the development of their celestial-orientation abilities. Three groups of nestlings were captured and hand-reared in the laboratory. The first group (a) lived in a windowless room with diffused lighting and never saw a point source of light. In the fall the birds began to display intense nocturnal activity. When they were tested under a stationary night sky in a planetarium, they were unable to select a migratory direction. The second group (b) never saw the sun and was exposed to a night sky in a planetarium every other night for two months. Normal celestial rotation was simulated. When the birds were tested in a planetarium under a normal sky during their fall migratory period, they oriented to the south. The third group (c) also never saw the sun and was exposed to a modified night sky in a planetarium every other night for two months. Betelgeuse, a star in Orion, became the new polestar around which all other stars rotated. When the birds were tested in the fall under a normal night sky, they continued to regard Betelgeuse as the polestar and oriented their activity away from it. The experiment shows that young buntings initially learn the north-south axis from the rotation of stars and that star patterns by themselves are not useful cues to a naïve bunting. Star patterns take on directional meaning only after they have become part of the bird's general orientational framework, the formation of which is influenced, at least in part, by observing the rotation of stars.

north-south directional axis. Individual stars and patterns of stars are of no value for direction finding until their positions with respect to some reference framework have been learned. The axis of the rotation of the stars appears to function as one reference system. Once the stellar information and the rotational have been coupled, however, the bunting can locate the rotational axis from star patterns alone. This is suggested by the finding that adult indigo buntings orient accurately even under stationary planetarium skies. Celestial motion thus becomes a secondary or redundant cue for adult birds.

One cannot help but speculate about the possible selective advantage of a maturation process that makes use of celestial rotation for a directional reference system. One possible explanation lies in the long-term unreliability of the stellar cues themselves. The rotation of the earth can be viewed as being analogous to the spinning of a top. And like most spinning tops, the spinning earth wobbles. This slight wobble, usually described as the precession of the equinoxes, causes the direction of the earth's spin axis to shift. Over a period of 26,000 years the precession of the equinoxes causes the earth's spin axis to trace on the celestial sphere a full circle with a radius of 23.5 degrees. This motion gives rise to marked seasonal and latitudinal changes in the apparent position of stars. The spring stars of the present become the fall stars in 13,000 years, and vice versa. The values of declination also change: as the polar axis moves through its circle Vega becomes the new polestar, and the present North Star shifts to 43 degrees north [see illustration on this page]. Similar changes occur for all stars.

The possible implications of these changes for the star-navigation system of birds are obvious. If birds were to rely on a genetically fixed star map, the rate of genetic change would have to be extremely rapid to allow for the change in position of the stars. A maturation process in birds that involves finding the north-south axis by the rotation of stars, however, minimizes the problem. Of course, several reference cues may play a role, but the axis of celestial rotation is well suited to function as one such reference because that axis is aligned with geographic north-south regardless of which particular stars and patterns of stars are located near the celestial pole.

Experiments in the planetarium have enabled us to learn a great deal about the orientation of night-migrating birds. Young birds develop a north-south reference axis as a result of early exposure to celestial rotation. Then they learn the patterns of stars around the northern celestial pole, which they use in a configurational manner to determine a direction of migration. The precise direction that is selected depends on the hormonal and physiological state of the bird and not on seasonal differences in the position of the stars. The star-orientation process of the indigo bunting is basically one of pattern recognition that does not involve an internal time sense.

The experiments described here are equally important for what they do not explain about migratory orientation. Although the star-orientation process enables a bird to maintain a given course during its migratory trip, as an explanation for the orientation abilities of birds the process by itself is not entirely adequate and not absolutely essential. I say not entirely adequate because the direction-finding system described for the indigo bunting is basically only a star-compass system that enables the bird to select and maintain a given direction. The system does not provide any information about actual geographic location.

The star compass does not tell the bird it has been blown off course to the east or to the west, nor does it tell the bird when it has reached the latitude of its destination. That is because the star-orientation capability I have described still lacks the map component of the map-and-compass hypothesis. It is quite possible that most migrating birds are not at all goal-oriented during the major portion of their migratory flight. Their process of orientation may be fundamentally different from that of homing pigeons and they may only revert to a homing type of process during the very final stages of the migratory flight.

I say not absolutely essential because we now know that migratory birds have numerous directional cues available to them. In addition to the use of the sun and the stars, experiments have shown that songbird migrants can make use of the position of the sunset, the directionality of the winds aloft, the direction of the earth's magnetic field, the presence of topographic landmarks and the activity and the call notes of other birds of the same species as sources of information, enabling them either to select or at least to maintain a given migratory direction.

Birds thus have access to many sources of directional information, and natural selection has favored the development of abilities to make use of them all. Some cues may give more accurate information than others; some may be available throughout the flight, whereas others may be useful only at specific geo-

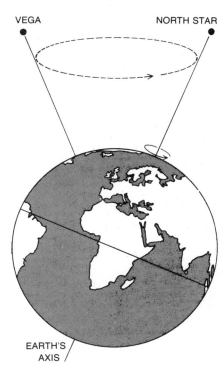

PRECESSION OF EARTH'S AXIS produces change in the apparent position of the stars. In 13,000 years, as the polar axis moves through half of its circle, the star Vega will become the new polestar and the present North Star will shift to 43 degrees north.

graphic locations; some may be available regardless of flight conditions, whereas others may be functional only under optimal meteorological situations.

The realization that birds have multiple cues at their disposal is in itself a finding of major importance. Although I have concentrated here on the star compass, I do not mean to imply that the other cue systems are not important. The discovery of a hierarchy of redundant directional cues makes the search for a single mechanism of migratory orientation obsolete.

The nocturnally migrating bird should be viewed as an animal whose behavior has been shaped by aeons of intensive selection pressure. It is the combination of the bird's skill as a meteorologist and as a navigator that accounts for its successful traversing of thousands of miles of environmentally inappropriate terrain each fall and spring. Although our understanding of the migratory navigation of birds has come a long way since Kramer began the experimental approach some 20 years ago, the total of our knowledge is still not enough to fully explain how an individual bird finds its way between its breeding territory and its wintering grounds.

8

The Mystery of Pigeon Homing

by William T. Keeton
December 1974

*Recent findings have upset previous explanations of
how pigeons find their way home from distant
locations. It appears that they have more than one
compass system for determining direction*

How does a homing pigeon find its way back to its home loft from hundreds of miles away? The answer does not lie in visible landmarks; pigeons taken in covered cages to areas they have never seen before have little trouble finding their way home. Nor does it lie entirely in the bird's ability to determine compass directions from the sun or the earth's magnetic field. Even when a pigeon can determine compass directions, how can it know which way home is? Although the homing prowess of the pigeon has long engaged the curiosity of man, the full story of how the bird navigates still remains a mystery. Nonetheless much has been learned about the pigeon's navigational abilities in the past two decades, particularly in the past six years.

The modern homing pigeon, a de-

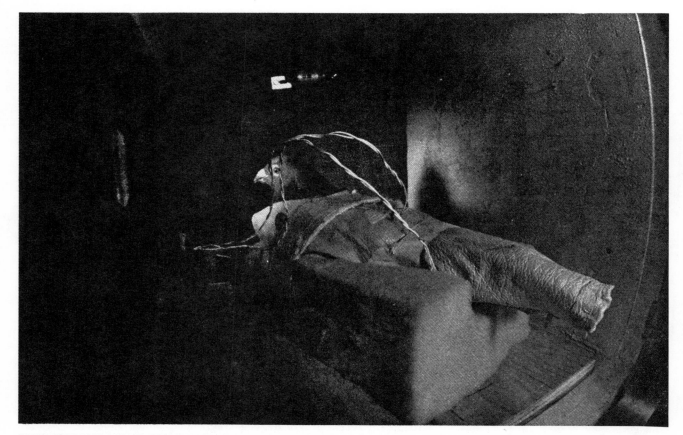

PIGEON IN ISOLATION CHAMBER has been prepared for tests of its unusual sensory capabilities. Two wires go to electrodes on the pigeon that give it a mild electric shock during the test, and two other wires are connected to electrodes that pick up the bird's heartbeat. The pigeon is restrained by a harness to keep it from moving. In a typical experiment the bird receives a shock following a specific stimulus, which might be a change in the strength of an induced magnetic field, a change of air pressure or a change in the plane of polarized light falling on the pigeon's eye. If the bird is able to sense the changes in the stimulus, it begins to anticipate the shock and its heart rate increases at the beginning of the stimulus, which is given at random time intervals. Experiments in the author's laboratory indicate that the pigeon is capable of sensing tiny fluctuations in atmospheric pressure. In addition pigeons, like honeybees, can detect changes in the plane of polarized light. The photograph was made with a camera placed inside the chamber.

scendant of several earlier breeds of pigeons, was developed in Belgium in the middle of the 19th century. Today, in addition to serving as message carriers, homing pigeons are raised for competitive racing. This sport is widespread and very popular in Europe, and has become firmly established in many parts of the U.S. as well. Often several thousand pigeons are entered in a single race. The birds are shipped to a designated point, usually between 100 and 600 miles away, and are then released simultaneously. After the owners of the birds have recorded the arrival times at home, using special devices designed for the purpose, the speed of the individual birds is calculated to determine the winners. Speeds of 50 miles per hour are common; the best pigeons can make it home from 600 miles away in a single day.

The remarkable ability of pigeons to find their way home has been known for at least as long as there has been written history. The armies of the ancient Persians, Assyrians, Egyptians and Phoenicians all sent messages by pigeon from the field. It is known that regular communication via pigeon existed in the days of Julius Caesar. During the siege of Paris in 1870 more than a million messages reached Parisians by means of pigeons that had been smuggled out of the city in balloons. Pigeons did such valuable service in both world wars that monuments in their honor were erected in Brussels and in the French city of Lille. In the U.S. some famous pigeon "heroes" were stuffed and mounted after their death; they are on display at the Army Signal Corps Museum and the National Museum.

In 1949 Gustav Kramer and his students at the Max Planck Institute for Marine Biology at Wilhelmshaven in Germany demonstrated that a pigeon in a circular cage with identical food cups at regular intervals around its periphery could easily be trained always to go to a food cup located in a particular direction, for example the northwest, even though the cage was rotated and the visual landscape around it was changed. They found that the pigeon's ability to determine a direction depended on the bird's being able to see the sun. Under a heavy overcast the bird's choice of food cups became random. If the sun's apparent position was altered by mirrors, the pigeon's choice of food cups was correspondingly altered.

It is obvious that if birds can use the sun as a compass to determine directions, they must be able to compensate for the change in the sun's apparent position during the day. In the Northern Hemi-

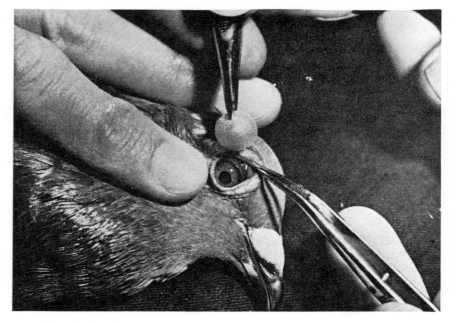

FROSTED CONTACT LENS is placed on a pigeon's eye before a test release. When both of the pigeon's eyes are covered by the lenses, the pigeon is unable to see objects that are more than a few yards away. Control pigeons have clear lenses put on their eyes and are released at the same time from the site. Experiments by Klaus Schmidt-Koenig and H. J. Schlichte of the University of Göttingen, who developed the technique, have demonstrated that pigeons wearing the frosted lenses are able to orient their flight in a homeward direction when they are released at a distant site, and that some pigeons are able to fly back to their home loft. Lenses currently in use are made of a gelatin that dissolves in a few hours.

NIGHT NAVIGATION of pigeons is being studied by Cornell workers. Pigeons with radio transmitters on their back are released and tracked by a radio receiver in the truck. In this time exposure three successive light flashes were used to illuminate the flying pigeon.

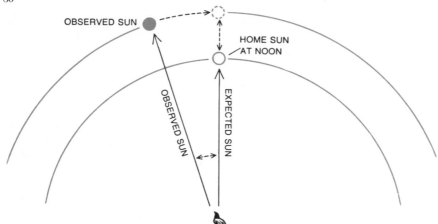

OBSERVED SUN

HOME SUN
AT NOON

OBSERVED SUN

EXPECTED SUN

SUN-ARC HYPOTHESIS was proposed by G. V. T. Matthews of the University of Cambridge in the 1950's to explain how pigeons could obtain from the sun alone all the information required to determine their north-south and east-west displacement from home. For example, if a pigeon were released at noon at an unfamiliar site that is southwest of its home loft, the bird would observe the sun's motion and quickly extrapolate along the sun's arc across the sky to the noon position. It would then compare the sun's noon altitude with the remembered altitude at noon at home. Since the bird is south of home, the sun would be higher at the release site, and the pigeon would know that it has to fly north to make the sun appear lower. In order to determine its east-west displacement the pigeon would compare the position of the sun at the release site with the position the sun should have according to the bird's internal clock. In this instance the bird's clock would inform it that the time at home is noon. The sun at the release site, however, is at an altitude lower than that at noon, so that the bird knows it must fly east. By combining the two displacements, the bird would know that it should start flying to the northeast to get to its home loft.

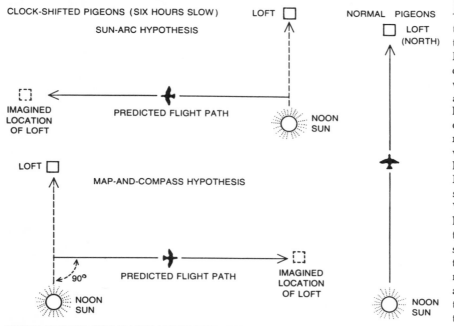

CLOCK-SHIFTED PIGEONS (SIX HOURS SLOW)   LOFT   NORMAL PIGEONS

SUN-ARC HYPOTHESIS   LOFT (NORTH)

IMAGINED LOCATION OF LOFT   PREDICTED FLIGHT PATH   NOON SUN

MAP-AND-COMPASS HYPOTHESIS

LOFT

90°   PREDICTED FLIGHT PATH   IMAGINED LOCATION OF LOFT

NOON SUN   NOON SUN

TESTS OF TWO SUN NAVIGATION HYPOTHESES were made with pigeons whose internal clocks had been shifted six hours slow by altering their day-and-night time periods in the laboratory. According to the sun-arc hypothesis, when the clock-shifted pigeons are taken south of their home loft and released at noon, their internal clock tells them that it is 6:00 A.M. at home. They observe that the sun at the release site is too far along its arc for 6:00 A.M. and that they therefore should fly west (*top left*). The alternative map-and-compass hypothesis suggests that the pigeons know where they are relative to home from some kind of map, and that they use the sun only to get compass direction. Their internal clock says it is 6:00 A.M., and they therefore assume that the sun is in the east. Since the sun is really in the south, they should begin flying east, thinking that this direction is north (*bottom left*). When the experiment was carried out, the clock-shifted pigeons flew east, thereby supporting the map-and-compass hypothesis and contradicting the sun-arc hypothesis. Normal pigeons released at the same site departed in the correct homeward direction (*right*).

sphere the sun rises in the east, moves through south at noon and sets in the west. If a pigeon is to determine a particular direction, it cannot simply select a constant angle relative to the sun. It must change the relative angle by about 15 degrees per hour, which is the average rate of change of the sun's position throughout the day. In short, the bird must have an accurate sense of time, an internal clock, and that clock must somehow be coupled with the position of the sun in the sky if an accurate determination of direction from the sun is to be possible.

In a simple but elegant fashion Kramer demonstrated that birds do indeed compensate for time when they are using the sun as a compass. He trained some birds, in this case starlings, to use the sun to go in a particular direction to get to a food cup. He then substituted a stationary light for the sun. The starlings responded to the light as though it were moving at 15 degrees per hour. Since the light was in fact stationary, the bearing taken by the birds shifted approximately 15 degrees per hour.

Klaus Hoffmann, one of Kramer's students, went an important step further in demonstrating the role of the internal clock in sun-compass orientation. He kept starlings for several days in closed rooms where the artificial lights were turned on six hours after sunrise and turned off six hours after sunset. It is known that the internal clocks of most organisms can be shifted to a new rhythm in this manner; the process is very similar to what is experienced by a human being who flies from the U.S. to Europe in a few hours and then takes several days to adjust to European time. When the starlings whose internal clocks had been shifted six hours slow were tested in a circular cage under the real sun, they selected a bearing 90 degrees to the right of the original training direction. Since their internal clocks were a quarter of a day out of phase with sun time, they made a quarter-circle error in their selection of food cups.

Although Kramer and his colleagues had clearly demonstrated that some birds, including pigeons, can use the sun as a compass, their discovery by itself cannot explain how pigeons home. As I have indicated, homing requires more than a compass. If you were taken hundreds of miles away into unfamiliar territory, given only a magnetic compass and told to start walking toward home, you would not be able to get there. Even though you could determine where north was, you would not know where you were with respect to home, hence such compass information would be nearly useless.

In 1953 G. V. T. Matthews, who was then working at the University of Cambridge, suggested that pigeons get far more information than compass bearings from the sun. He hypothesized that the sun gives them all the information they need to carry out true bicoordinate navigation. Stated briefly, on release at a distant site a pigeon would determine its north-south displacement from home by observing the sun's motion along the arc of its path across the sky, extrapolating to the sun's noon position on that arc, measuring the sun's noon altitude and comparing it with the sun's noon altitude at home (as the bird remembered it). If the sun's noon altitude at the release site was lower than it was at home, the bird would know that it was north of home; if the sun was higher than it was at home, the bird would know that it was south of home. To calculate the east-west displacement the bird would determine local sun time by observation of the sun's position on its arc at the release site and compare the local time with home time as indicated by its internal clock. A local time ahead of home time would indicated the bird was east of home; a local time behind home time would indicated the bird was west of home. Thus, according to Matthews, the bird would determine its north-south displacement from the sun's altitude and its east-west displacement by the time difference; combining these data would indicate the homeward direction [*see top illustration on page 80*].

Matthews' sun-arc hypothesis was a major stimulus to further research on pigeon homing, and it formed the basis for many of the experiments conducted in the following decade. Unfortunately, however, nearly all the results of these experiments contradicted the hypothesis, and investigators actively engaged in research on pigeon homing today no longer regard it as being probable. The evidence against the hypothesis is so extensive that most of it cannot be discussed here. For the moment I shall mention only one kind of experiment to help the reader understand some of the more recent research.

Klaus Schmidt-Koenig, another of Kramer's students, showed in 1958 that when pigeons whose clocks have been artificially shifted are released at a distant site, their initial choice of direction is shifted. Their vanishing bearings (the bearings at which they vanish from the

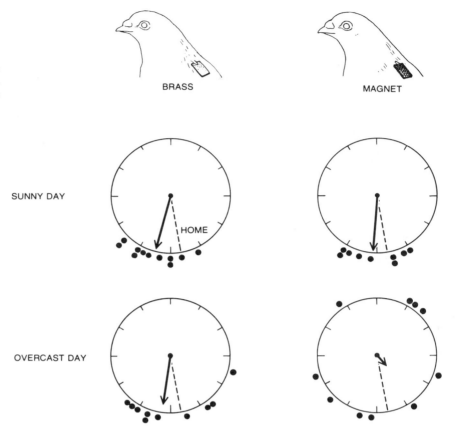

MAGNETIC-FIELD HYPOTHESIS, proposed more than a century ago, had been rejected until recently because earlier experiments failed to show that putting a magnet on a pigeon disorients its homing. Recent tests show, however, that pigeons with bar magnets attached to them are disoriented when they are released at an unfamiliar site under a total overcast but are not disoriented when the sun is visible. Control pigeons with brass bars attached to them show little difference in their mean vanishing bearing under the sun or an overcast. The vanishing bearings of individual pigeons, as determined by an observer with binoculars, are shown by the solid circles. The broken line indicates the true home bearing. The mean vector, or directional tendency, of all the birds in a test group is shown by the arrow. The length of the mean vector is a statistical representation of the degree of agreement among the birds in selecting a direction. Perfect agreement would give a vector length equal to the circle's radius; the more scattered the departing directions, the shorter the vector.

view of an observer using high-power binoculars) deviate from those of normal pigeons by 15 degrees for each hour the birds have been clock-shifted.

Let us examine a test involving clock-shifted pigeons to see whether or not the results agree with what would be predicted by the sun-arc hypothesis. Suppose we shift the birds' internal clock so that it is six hours slow and then release them at noon 100 miles south of their home loft. According to the sun-arc hypothesis, the birds would observe that it is noon at the release site, but their internal clock would tell them it is only 6:00 A.M. at home. They should therefore react as though they were thousands of miles east of home, and they should start flying almost due west. When such an experiment is actually performed,

however, the birds vanish nearly due east, exactly opposite what the sun-arc hypothesis predicts [*see bottom illustration on page 80*].

Is there any way we can make sense of these results? The answer is yes, but to do so we must turn from Matthews' sun-arc hypothesis to an alternative model proposed by Kramer. Kramer emphasized that all the evidence supports the conclusion that pigeons get only compass information from the sun and nothing else. They appear to behave in a manner analogous to a man who uses both a map and a compass, as though they first determine from some kind of map where they are relative to home and in which direction they must fly to get home and then use the sun compass to locate that direction.

Since Kramer could never explain

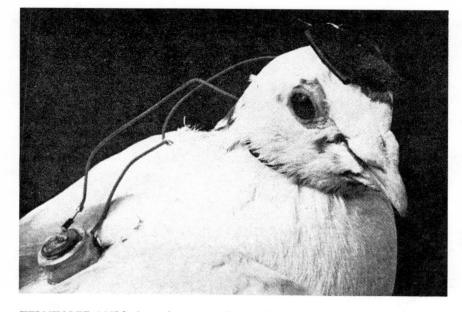

HELMHOLTZ COILS above the pigeon's head and around its neck induce a relatively uniform magnetic field through its head. The coils are powered by a small mercury battery on the bird's back. Direction of the induced field can be reversed simply by reversing the connections of the battery. The strength of the magnetic field can be varied by controlling the amount of current passing through the coils. Battery is exhausted in two or three hours.

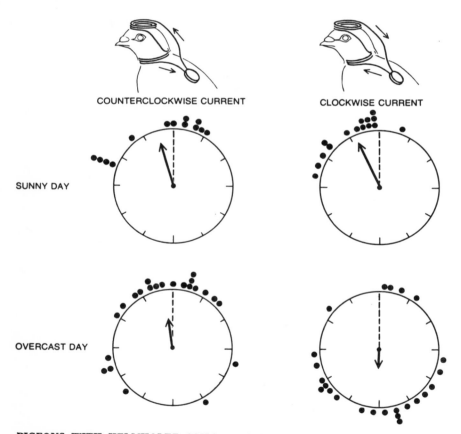

COUNTERCLOCKWISE CURRENT   CLOCKWISE CURRENT

SUNNY DAY

OVERCAST DAY

PIGEONS WITH HELMHOLTZ COILS in which the current flows counterclockwise (south-seeking pole of a compass in the induced magnetic field points up) fly almost directly homeward on both sunny and overcast days. When the current in the coils is made to flow clockwise (north-seeking pole of a compass in the induced magnetic field points up), the pigeons still fly homeward on sunny days, but on overcast days they fly almost 180 degrees away from home. These results were obtained in several experiments conducted by Charles Walcott and Robert Green of the State University of New York at Stony Brook.

what the source of the map information might be, let us for the sake of our example pretend that before we release each pigeon we whisper in its ear, "Home is due north." Now the bird must use its sun compass to locate north. Its internal clock says it is 6:00 A.M., when the sun should be in the east; hence north should be approximately 90 degrees counterclockwise from the sun. Remember, however, that the bird's clock is six hours slow; it is actually noon, when the sun is in the south. Hence the bird's choice of a bearing 90 degrees counterclockwise from the sun sends it east, not north. We can summarize by saying that no matter what combination of directions and clock-shift we use in actual experiments, the results come out consistent with the predictions of Kramer's map-and-compass model and not with Matthews' sun-arc hypothesis.

Because the pigeon's use of the sun compass in orientation was the one thing that was firmly established, there was a tendency in the 1960's for many investigators to assume that the sun is essential for homeward orientation at an unfamiliar release site. Several discrepancies, however, led me and my colleagues at Cornell University to doubt it. First, I knew of numerous instances of fast pigeon races under heavy overcast. Second, our pigeons seemed to perform well under overcast if they had first been made to fly in the vicinity of the home loft in rainy weather. Third, the published evidence that pigeons were disoriented under heavy overcast was not entirely consistent, and fourth, we and others had been able to get pigeons to home at night.

We set out to reexamine the importance of the sun in pigeon navigation. In our most important experiments we too used clock-shifted pigeons. As we expected, when pigeons whose internal clocks had been shifted six hours fast or slow were released under sunny conditions, their vanishing bearings were roughly 90 degrees to the right or left of the vanishing bearings of control pigeons whose internal clocks had not been altered. When the pigeons were released in total overcast, however, the results were quite different: both the clock-shifted birds and the control birds vanished toward home and there was no significant difference in their bearings. This was true even when the release site was completely unfamiliar to the pigeons.

These results led us to several conclusions: (1) Pigeons accustomed to flying in inclement weather are able to orient homeward under total overcast.

Since there is no difference between the bearings of control and clock-shifted birds under such conditions, it is clear they are not able to see the sun through the clouds and hence are no longer using the sun compass. (2) There must be redundancy in the pigeons' navigation system. They use the sun compass when it is available, but they can substitute information from other sources when it is not. (3) The alternative information used in lieu of the sun compass does not require time compensation. (4) The alternative system cannot be pilotage by familiar landmarks, because pigeons can correctly orient themselves homeward under overcast even in distant, unfamiliar territory.

Recognition of the fact that pigeons are able to use alternative cues, depending on the circumstances involved, meant that the results of many older experiments could no longer be accepted at face value. For example, if an experimenter altered cue A while keeping other conditions optimum, and if the pigeons continued to orient well, they may simply have used cue B as an alternative to A. Similarly, if B was altered while everything else was kept at an optimum and the birds oriented well, they may have used A as an alternative to B. In short, we would have been wrong if we had concluded from these experiments that cues A and B are not elements in the pigeons' navigation system. In fact, such experiments show only that neither A nor B alone is essential for proper orientation under the particular test conditions.

This kind of reasoning led us to conduct experiments in which we varied several possible orientational cues simultaneously, on the assumption that if we could interfere with enough of them at the same time we could hope to learn which cues are more important and how they interact with one another.

We chose first to look again at the old idea that birds might obtain directional information from the earth's magnetic field. Although this hypothesis had been known for more than a century, there was no evidence for it and much experimental evidence against it. Nonetheless, it seemed worth reexamining. And it was! When we repeated older experiments of putting bar magnets on pigeons to distort the magnetic field around them, we found, as had others before us, that the birds had no difficulty orienting on sunny days. When the test releases were conducted on totally overcast days, however, the birds carrying

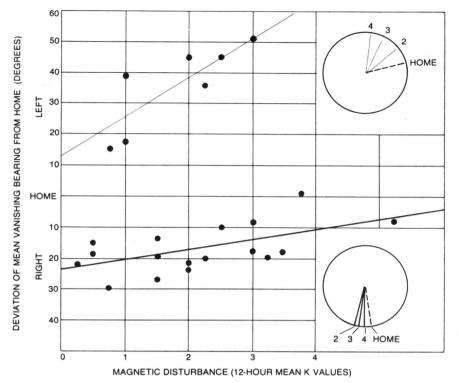

DISTURBANCES OF THE EARTH'S MAGNETIC FIELD caused by solar activity appear to affect a pigeon's initial choice of bearing when it is released at a distant site under sunny conditions. The K-index scale is used to indicate the degree of magnetic activity, ranging from quiet (less than 2) to a major magnetic storm (6 or more). In 1972 a series of releases of Cornell University pigeons from a site 45 miles north of the home lofts revealed that, as the degree of magnetic disturbance increases, the vanishing bearing of the birds steadily shifts to the left as seen by an observer facing homeward (*black curve*). At this release site the shift to the left brought the birds' vanishing bearings closer to the true home bearing, but success in homing was not improved. In another series of tests, pigeons from a different loft were released from a site west of their home. A similar leftward shift of vanishing bearings with increasing magnetic disturbance was found (*colored curve*). In this instance the shift to the left caused the vanishing bearings to recede away from the true home bearing.

magnets usually vanished randomly whereas control birds carrying brass bars of the same size and weight vanished toward home. Several other workers have since repeated these experiments, with the same results.

More recently Charles Walcott of the State University of New York at Stony Brook and his student Robert Green have gone one step further. Instead of working with bar magnets, they put a small Helmholtz coil on the pigeon's head like a cap and another coil around its neck like a collar. Power is supplied from a battery on the bird's back. This device makes it possible to induce a relatively uniform magnetic field through the bird's head. The direction of the induced magnetic field can be made to point up through the bird's head or to point down simply by hooking up the battery to make the current in the coils flow clockwise or counterclockwise. Under sunny conditions Walcott and Green found that the direction of the induced magnetic

field did not affect the pigeon's ability to orient homeward. Under total overcast, however, the direction of the induced magnetic field had a dramatic effect: when the north-seeking pole of a compass in the induced field pointed up, the pigeons flew almost directly away from home, whereas when the south-seeking pole of a compass in the induced field pointed up, the pigeons oriented toward home.

Our results, together with Walcott's, suggest that magnetic information may play a role in the pigeon navigation system. This is consistent with the recent discovery by Friedrich Merkel and Wolfgang Wiltschko of the University of Frankfurt that European robins in circular cages can use magnetic cues to orient themselves in a particular direction. William Southern of Northern Illinois University also has reported that the orientation of ring-billed gulls is influenced by magnetic activity.

Recently Martin Lindauer and Herman Martin of the University of Frank-furt have demonstrated that honeybees give orientational responses to magnetic cues several thousand times weaker than the earth's field. Only a few years ago biologists were debating whether or not any organism could detect a magnetic field as weak as the earth's (approximate-ly half a gauss). The responses of honey-bees to magnetic cues now makes us wonder if one gamma (10^{-5} gauss) will not prove to be the lower limit. Indeed, a study that my colleagues and I have re-cently conducted suggests that the mag-netic-detection sensitivity of pigeons may rival that of honeybees. In four long series of tests over a period of three years we have found that fluctuations of less

than 100 gamma (and probably less than 40 gamma) in the earth's magnetic field, caused by solar flares and sunspots, appear to have a small but significant effect on the pigeons' choice of an initial bearing at the release site.

The question of how organisms detect magnetic stimuli is unanswered. We have very little idea what a magnetic sense organ should look like, or even where in the body we should expect to find it. Since magnetic flux can pass free-ly through living tissue, magnetic de-tectors might be anywhere inside the body. The search for these detectors has already begun in our laboratory and in others throughout the world. It promises to be a challenging undertaking.

Exciting as the discovery that mag-netism plays a part in avian navigation systems may be, we are in a sense back where we started. The weight of the evi-dence at present suggests that mag-netism simply provides a second com-pass, not the long-sought map. Hence we must continue our search. What other sources of information might the birds have?

One possibility that comes readily to mind in this age of long-range rocketry is that the birds might be capable of in-ertial guidance, that they might some-how detect and record all the angular ac-celerations of the outward journey to the release site, then double-integrate them to determine the direction home. Intrigu-ing as this possibility is, all the evidence is against it. Pigeons have been carried to release sites while riding on turn-tables or in rotating drums, yet this in-put of additional inertial "noise" has no effect; the birds orient homeward as ac-curately as control birds not so treated. Other pigeons that were carried to the release site while they were under deep anesthesia were able to determine the direction home with no difficulty. Pi-geons with a variety of surgical lesions of the semicircular canals—the principal detectors of acceleration in vertebrates—orient themselves accurately, whether they are tested under sunny conditions or overcast ones.

The hypothesis that pigeons may be able to use olfactory information in navi-gating has been advocated by Floriano Papi and his colleagues at the University of Pisa. The probability that this is the case seems low in view of the relatively poor development of the pigeon's olfac-tory system. Nonetheless Papi has some interesting experimental results, and it is too early to make a judgment on his pro-posal. We are currently conducting ex-periments to test his ideas.

By now the reader may well be won-dering why so little has been said about what might seem the most obvious pos-sible cue for homing pigeons: familiar landmarks. The reason is that there is abundant evidence that landmarks play a very small role in the homing process. In the course of tracking pigeons by air-plane Walcott and his colleague Martin Michener have repeatedly noted that when pigeons flying on an incorrect course encounter an area over which they have recently flown, they seldom give any indication of recognizing the familiar territory. Several other investi-gators, including members of our group, have found that pigeons clock-shifted six hours and released less than a mile from

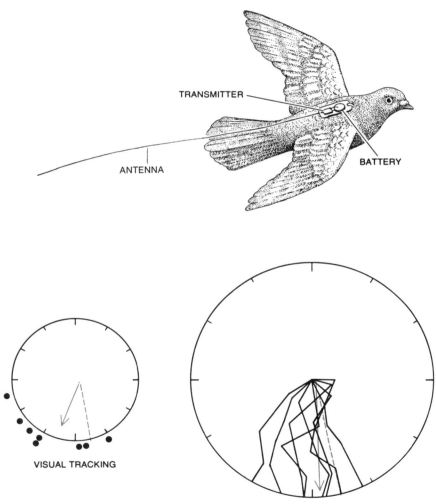

RADIO TRACKING OF PIGEONS is carried out from a receiver on the ground at the re-lease site or sometimes by a receiver on an aircraft. An FM transmitter and a battery are glued on the pigeon's back (top). The 19-inch antenna trails behind the bird as it flies. Data from radio tracking reveal that pigeons do not continue to fly in a straight line after they leave a release site but frequently alter their course. The vanishing bearings for eight pi-geons, as determined by observers with binoculars, and the bearings determined by simul-taneous radio tracking from the site are compared (bottom). The scale of the two circles is arbitrary. Visual tracking extends to one or two miles, depending on the flying height of the bird. Radio tracking extends to eight miles or more. Broken line indicates home direction.

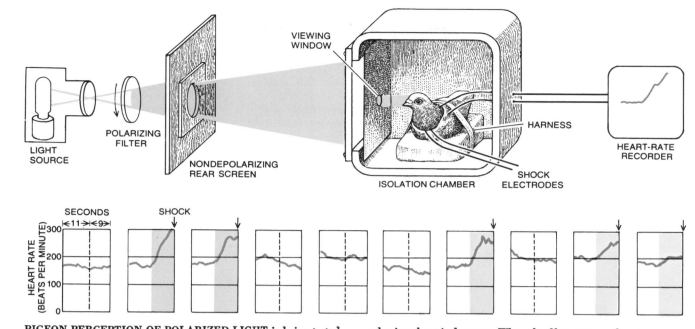

PIGEON PERCEPTION OF POLARIZED LIGHT is being tested in the author's laboratory by Melvin L. Kreithen. After electrodes for administering electric shock and for detecting the heart rate are attached, the pigeon is put in a harness and then is placed in a sealed soundproof chamber. Light is projected through a polarizing filter on a rotating mount and then through a nondepolarizing rear-projection screen. Part of the light enters the isolation chamber through a small window and falls on the pigeon's eye. The light comes on at random intervals. In some trials, which are also determined at random, the polarizing filter starts to rotate after 11 seconds; in others it does not. When the filter rotates, the pigeon receives a shock at the end of the light signal. When the filter does not rotate, no shock is given. After a number of trials the pigeon's heart rate begins to rise rapidly at the beginning of the rotation of the polarizing filter, indicating that the bird is able to sense the change in the plane of polarized light and is anticipating the shock that is to come. Recordings from a series of tests of a pigeon are shown (*bottom*). The colored block indicates the interval during which the polarizing filter rotates. In control runs during the corresponding interval (*to right of broken line*) no rotation occurs.

home, in territory over which they have flown daily during their exercise period, often vanish 90 degrees away from the home direction. Only a direct view of the loft building itself takes precedence over what their navigation system is telling them; nearby buildings or trees apparently do not serve as reference points under these conditions. In fact, even a view of the loft is not always effective, particularly at distances of a mile or more.

Perhaps most convincing of all are experiments conducted by Schmidt-Koenig and H. J. Schlichte of the University of Göttingen. They put frosted contact lenses over the eyes of pigeons, thus making it impossible for the birds to see any object that is more than a few meters away. Not only do these pigeons orient homeward when they are released as far as 80 miles away but also a surprising number of them actually get home. Schmidt-Koenig conducted some of his experiments at our Cornell lofts, and thus I had the opportunity of observing them at first hand. It was a remarkable experience. The birds arrived very high overhead and fluttered down to a landing in the fields around the loft.

Being unable to see the loft, they waited for us to pick them up and carry them the last few feet. These results suggest that the pigeon navigation system is often accurate enough to pinpoint the home location almost exactly without reliance on familiar landmarks; vision is necessary only for the final approach, frequently at a distance of less than 200 yards.

It will be apparent from all I have said that the task of uncovering the pigeon's navigation system is going to be a difficult one. The old idea that birds use a single method to determine the home direction has given way to the realization that there are probably multiple components in the system and that these components may be combined in a variety of ways, depending on such factors as weather conditions, the age of the bird and the bird's experience.

One approach that holds much promise for helping us tease apart the many elements in the system is the study of the ontogeny of navigational behavior. For example, we have found that bar magnets disrupt the initial orientation of very young pigeons released away from home for the first time in their life, even when the sun is visible. Moreover, normal first-

flight youngsters cannot orient under total overcast, even if they have previously been released for exercise in inclement weather. It seems, then, that inexperienced homing pigeons need both sun information and magnetic information. Various other manipulations that have little effect on experienced birds also disorient first-flight pigeons.

Perhaps with experience a pigeon learns to orient accurately with less information. Or perhaps experience is necessary to enable the pigeons to settle on a weighting scheme that allows them to decide what to do when they get conflicting information from different sources. Early results from some current experiments indicate that by training very young pigeons under conditions in which we severely restrict, or eliminate altogether, certain normally important environmental cues such as the sun, we may be able to induce the birds to settle on weighting schemes for evaluating directional cues that are quite different from normal. The availability of such birds would greatly facilitate the carrying out of experiments designed to clarify the roles of cues that are normally difficult to alter.

Another approach we are actively pursuing is an attempt to learn more about the sensory capabilities of pigeons. The more we learn, the more we become convinced that birds live in a sensory world very different from our own. For example, my student Melvin L. Kreithen has recently demonstrated that pigeons are remarkably sensitive to tiny changes in barometric pressure. Such a sensitivity might enable pigeons to get navigationally useful information from pressure patterns in the atmosphere. Kreithen and I have also recently obtained experimental evidence that pigeons can detect the plane of polarized light, which might

mean that pigeons, like honeybees, can continue using the sun as a compass on partially overcast days, when the sun's disk is hidden from sight but some blue sky remains visible.

It has long been known that the bearings chosen by pigeons at distant release sites, although roughly in the homeward direction, are almost never oriented directly toward home. Moreover, the mean bearings of repeated releases at any given site usually show a consistent deviation from home; there is, in effect, a relatively stable "release-site bias" that is characteristic of each location. At some

sites the bias is apparent only in the vanishing bearings obtained by visual tracking. The bias often becomes less marked when the final-contact bearings obtained by radio tracking are used, but at some sites the bias is still manifest when the birds move out of radio range (between six and 10 miles from the release site). In the hope that these biases might prove to be a key to local geophysical factors that could provide at least part of the map information for pigeons, we chose for intensive study several release sites where the biases were unusually large.

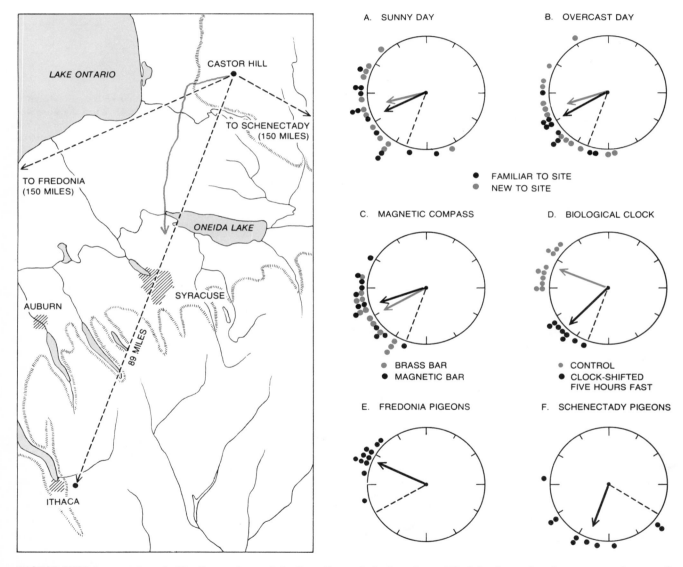

CASTOR HILL is approximately 89 miles northeast of the Cornell University pigeon lofts in Ithaca, N.Y. At Castor Hill the Cornell pigeons regularly choose an initial bearing that deviates clockwise from the true home direction. This occurs both on sunny days and on overcast days (A and B); thus the characteristic bias must not depend on the sun compass. The bias probably is not due primarily to the magnetic compass either, since under sunny conditions birds with bar magnets have about the same vanishing bearing as pigeons with brass bars (C). Pigeons whose internal

clocks have been shifted five hours fast choose a more homeward direction than normal pigeons, but the clock-shifted pigeons are less successful at getting home (D). Pigeons from another loft at Fredonia, N.Y., 150 miles west of Ithaca (E), and pigeons from Schenectady, N.Y., 150 miles east of Ithaca (F), choose bearings that also deviate clockwise from the true home bearing. It appears that the bias is a function of the site and not of the pigeons. The actual flight path of normal Cornell pigeons released at Castor Hill and tracked by an airplane is shown by the colored line on the map.

One such site is the Castor Hill Fire Tower, located 89 miles north northeast of our Cornell lofts. Here our pigeons regularly depart with a mean bearing that deviates roughly 60 degrees clockwise from the direction of home [*see illustration on opposite page*]. In a long series of experiments we have found that this clockwise bias is evident not only with experienced pigeons new to the site but also with pigeons that have been released at the site before. The same bias is found in very young pigeons on their first homing flight. It is found on both sunny and overcast days, so that it apparently has nothing to do with the sun compass, and it is found in pigeons wearing magnets, so that it probably has nothing to do with the magnetic compass either. It is even found when the pigeons are wearing frosted contact lenses; hence it must not depend on anything the pigeons see.

Wild bank swallows captured near Cornell and released at Castor Hill showed the same clockwise bias, indicating that the biasing factor, whatever it may be, affects other bird species in the same way. Pigeons borrowed from lofts 150 miles east and west of Cornell and released at Castor Hill show a similar clockwise departure bias relative to their home. Finally, pigeons clock-shifted five hours fast depart nearly straight toward home from Castor Hill but nonetheless have poorer homing success than control pigeons that depart with the usual 60-degree bias. In a joint experiment with Walcott, normal pigeons with radio transmitters attached to them were tracked by an airplane after their release from Castor Hill. We found that the birds turn onto a more homeward course when they are approximately 14 to 18 miles west of Castor Hill. It may be that the clock-shifted birds that have poor homing success make a corresponding turn when they are a similar distance from the release site and thus become directed away from home. We hope soon to learn if this is so.

We conclude, then, that the bias in the birds' initial bearings is not a biological error, that it is due not to some peculiarity of the birds but to a peculiarity of the location. The birds are probably reading the map cues correctly but the map itself is twisted clockwise at Castor Hill. Perhaps if we can learn what geophysical factors are responsible for this distortion of the map we will finally be on the way to understanding the ancient mystery of how pigeons home.

IV

EVOLUTION

IV EVOLUTION

INTRODUCTION

Evolution—the process by which new species arise—is difficult to study. Much of what we want to know happened long ago, and the kinds of controlled experiments laboratory scientists do cannot be applied. Some of the mechanisms of evolution can be studied in the laboratory, but its course must be learned primarily by examining the history of life on Earth. It is risky to draw inferences from living animals; every creature alive today has had an equal period of time in which to evolve. No contemporary animal or plant is an ancestor to any living thing. Much of our present knowledge of evolution has been gained by patient digging and searching for fossils, careful inference, a little guesswork, and a lot of luck. Unfortunately, very few creatures become fossilized when they die, and few fossils are ever uncovered by someone who is trained to study them.

Evolution works by the slow screening of chance genetic variations, which results in the selection of traits that enable an organism to survive longer and reproduce better than its less fortunate relatives. Genes that permit an organism to establish a separate ecological niche and reduce its need to compete with other creatures have great selective advantage.

Animals (and plants) rarely get an opportunity to rest on their genetic laurels. The environment is continually changing, and no terrestrial habitat is permanent. Plateaus are lifted up from the sea; mountains erode into plains. As habitats alter over the long span of geologic time, the organisms that live there are under pressure to change too. The process is one in which organisms tune in to the environment or, in the long run, drop out of the game.

Birds, like mammals, are believed to have evolved from reptiles (see Fig. 1). There is a variety of anatomical evidence to suggest their ancestor was a small dinosaur that walked on its hind legs. The most convincing evidence that birds are descended from a line of reptiles are four partial specimens of a small crow-sized animal unearthed in limestone beds in Bavaria (see Table 1). The creature, named *Archaeopteryx*, had a reptilian skeleton, including teeth and a bony tail, but it also had feathers and wings (see Fig. 2). Paleontologists would be hard put to imagine a better link between reptiles and birds.

REPTILES   BIRDS

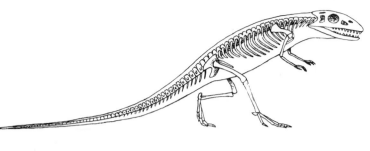
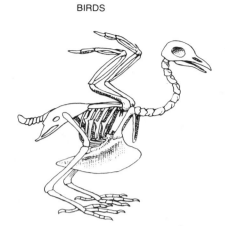

BONE

FORELIMB

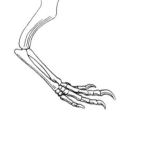

STERNUM

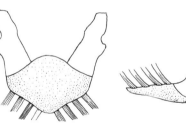
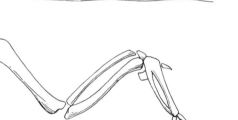

BOTTOM VIEW   SIDE VIEW

BOTTOM VIEW   SIDE VIEW

SKIN COVERING

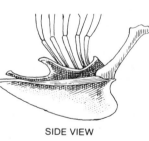

Figure 1. Evolution of birds from reptiles can be considered a process of adaptation by which birds solved the "problem" of flight. At the top of the illustration, the skeleton of a modern pigeon (right) is compared with that of an early reptile: a thecodont, a Triassic ancestor of dinosaurs and birds. Various reptile features were modified to become structures specialized for flight. Heavy, dense bone was restructured to become lighter but strong; the forelimb was lengthened (and its muscles and skin covering were changed) to become a wing; the reptilian sternum, or breastbone, was enlarged and deepened to anchor the wing muscles (even in *Archaeopteryx*, the Jurassic transition form between reptiles and birds whose sternum is pictured here, the sternum was small and shallow); scales developed into feathers. [From "Adaptation" by Richard C. Lewontin. Copyright © 1978 Scientific American, Inc. All rights reserved.]

TEETH PRESENT

THREE FREE, CLAWED
DIGITS IN WING

SKELETAL AXIS OF
TAIL LONG

Figure 2. Reconstruction of *Archaeopteryx*.

Archaeopteryx lived in the Upper Jurassic, 140 million years ago, when reptiles were the dominant form of animal and the large pterosaurs ruled the air. The immediate ancestors and descendants of *Archaeopteryx* are unknown; there is a 20-million-year gap in the fossil record after its appearrance. Nearly complete specimens of a few extinct aquatic birds, *Hesperornis* and *Ichthyornis*, have been discovered in sedimentary rocks of the Cretaceous Period. *Hesperornis* was a toothed, flightless, loonlike creature about 1.5 meters (5 feet) long (see Fig. 3). *Ichthyornis* was a small bird resembling a gull. Whether it also had teeth has not been determined.

A large number of the modern families of birds appeared 65 million years ago in the Tertiary Period. These include penguins, rheas, loons, cormorants, herons, ducks, vultures, hawks, grouse, cranes, and rails. In a sense, the more than 8,500 species of birds that are living today represent the top of an evolutionary iceberg of species that have become extinct. Paleontologist W. P. Brodkorb estimates that there have been approximately 154,000 species of birds. However, few of these hypothetical species have been unearthed. Approximately 1,700 species of birds have been identified from fossil remains. Of these, about 800 still exist. The Pleistocene Epoch, which began 2 million years ago, is believed to have hosted the greatest number of bird species that lived at any one time—an estimated 10,000 species.

The lack of described fossil birds is not due to a lack of material, argues Brodkorb, but to a lack of scientists willing to search for and study them. He notes that "Four authors are responsible for the description of one-third, seven authors for one-half, and fifteen authors for three-fourths of the known 900-odd paleospecies."

No one knows when the first bird flew. Some theorize that *Archaeopteryx* lived in trees and glided or flew from branch to branch. Baron Francis Nopsca, who was associated with the British Museum of Natural History, proposed in 1907 that *Archaeopteryx* and its immediate ancestors lived on the ground. This idea has recently been revived by Yale biologist John Ostrom (see, for example, his 1979 article in *American Scientist*). Ostrom argues that they used their feathered forelimbs to catch such prey as large insects, small lizards, and mammals and that their need for rapid movement gave a selective advantage to those that became airborne as they raced after their prey.

Whether feathers evolved before flight is another topic for debate. Flight may have evolved in a line of reptiles that had previously developed feathers as an insulation to help them to maintain a high body temperature. This hypothetical progenitor could have lived either in trees or on the ground; either lifestyle would give an advantage to animals with wings for forelimbs. Once airborne, even if the wings were used only for gliding, such animals would have found new ecological niches readily available, and the stage would have been set for the rapid evolution of the birds we see today.

TABLE 1.   THE FOSSIL HISTORY OF BIRDS.

Era	Period	Epoch	Events	Years since beginning of period or epoch
	Quaternary	Holocene	Modern birds. Passerine birds dominate.	11,000
		Pleistocene	All modern orders and families represented.	2×10^6
Cenozoic	Tertiary	Pliocene	Probable maximum number of bird species.	12×10^6
		Miocene	Majority of bird families represented.	26×10^6
		Oligocene	First appearance of grebes, shearwaters, storks, falcons, turkeys, and parrots.	37×10^6
		Eocene	Period of major bird evolution. Many modern groups, including penguins, rheas, loons, and pelicans.	53×10^6
		Paleocene	Rise of mammals.	62×10^6
Mesozoic	Cretaceous		Rise and extinction of toothed birds. First fossils of birds resembling cormorants, geese, and herons.	136×10^6
	Jurassic		Appearance of *Archaeopteryx*, flying reptiles. Dinosaurs rule.	190×10^6
	Triassic		First dinosaurs, egg-laying mammals.	225×10^6
Paleozoic			Age of invertebrates, fishes, and amphibians.	570×10^6

After various sources.

Figure 3. Reconstruction of *Hesperornis.*

Evolutionary change occurs most rapidly in small, reproductively isolated populations exposed to new habitats either through immigration or geologic change. Although mutations—the raw material of evolution—appear and disappear all the time in a population, the smaller the total population, the more likely it is for a favorable one to be transmitted to a relatively large number of progeny. For this reason, the Galapagos, the Hawaiian Islands, New Guinea, and other isolated islands are favorite spots for avian biologists to study evolution. The remarkable diversity of adaptation shown by the birds of the Galapagos was one of the clues that led Charles Darwin to formulate his theory of evolution. Even today, almost a century and a half later, the Galapagos continue to inspire scientists who visit them to study their animal and plant life. The first article in this section, by the late David Lack ("Darwin's Finches"), describes the 14 species of finches on the islands and the evidence that they are all the descendants of a common ancestor from the South American mainland. Lack emphasizes the importance of geographical isolation and the absence of competitors in the rapid evolution of these birds.

Another example of such an adaptive radiation of birds into different ecological niches is found in the Hawaiian honeycreepers, a family of song birds that live on the Hawaiian Islands. The remarkable diversity of beaks of these birds is shown in Figure 4. There are two large subfamilies: the Drepanidinae have curved bills for extracting nectar, and the Psittirostriinae have finchlike bills for cracking seeds. Some beaks are shaped like those of crossbills, useful for catching insects beneath leaf buds, and others are long and curved, adapted for probing crevices for insects. Biologists of the last century classified these

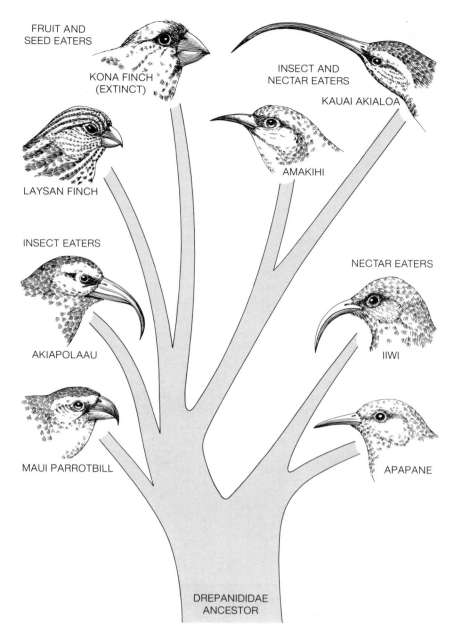

FRUIT AND
SEED EATERS

KONA FINCH
(EXTINCT)

INSECT AND
NECTAR EATERS

KAUAI AKIALOA

LAYSAN FINCH

AMAKIHI

INSECT EATERS

NECTAR EATERS

AKIAPOLAAU

IIWI

MAUI PARROTBILL

APAPANE

DREPANIDIDAE
ANCESTOR

Figure 4. Adaptive radiation of Hawaiian honeycreepers. The figure depicts approximate rather than exact relationships. The Akiapolaau removes bark to eat insects. The Maui Parrotbill specializes in beetle larvae. The Kona Finch is an extinct seed eater. The Laysan Finch eats seeds, fruits, and eggs of other birds. The Kauai akialoa is now very rare. The Amakihi probes for insects and drinks nectar. The Iiwi uses its long bill to reach deep into tubular flowers. The Apapane is the most common surviving species.

birds as 69 separate forms and placed them into four families and 18 genera. Today they are classified as one family and 22 species. Some species are intermediate to the two large subfamiles.

These birds are believed to be descended from a common ancestor that came from the North American mainland. Unfortunately, many of the species have become extinct as a result of diseases, destruction of habitat by human beings, and the introduction of dogs, cats, and other predators.

Geographic isolation is only one of several ways populations can become reproductively isolated, a necessity for the formation of new species. The possibility that behavioral cues can accomplish the same thing is the subject of the next selection ("Visual Isolation in Gulls"), by Neal Griffith Smith. The article is about how visual signals inhibit interbreeding between species of *Larus* gulls, which not only look alike but also live together.

Some hybridization does occur between species of *Larus* gulls. W. Hoffman, J. A. Wiens, and J. M. Scott of Oregon State University recently studied the extent to which the Glaucous-winged Gull and the Western Gull interbreed along a 180 kilometer (112 mile) stretch of coast in the state of Washington. Over half the birds in one breeding colony, on Destruction Island, were intermediate in eye coloration, iris color, shade of mantle, and wing-tip pattern compared to pure Glaucous-winged Gulls and Western Gulls. The population seemed in dynamic balance. On the one hand, most birds preferred to mate with partners similar in appearance to themselves, which tended to reduce the number of hybrids. On the other hand, the few matings between a hybrid and either pure species produced more eggs than matings between two birds of one of the pure species. A computer model suggested that an equilibrium between pure and hybrid forms could be maintained by annually adding less than two dozen of each species to the population of approximately 1,300 birds on the island. A lower immigration rate would favor the hybrids; a higher rate would favor the pure species. Perhaps the next step in the process of speciation studied on Destruction Island would be similar to that found by Smith, in which interbreeding was discouraged.

The populations we have been discussing consist of different species. There are other cases in which two distinct forms of the same species may coexist in a population, often without either exhibiting any obvious selective advantage. The mechanisms underlying this situation, termed polymorphism, and the significance of the phenomenon are matters of much discussion and study by evolutionists. Some may be stages in the continuing evolution of a new species, an earlier stage of the situations seen in the *Larus* gulls. Others may be due to a balance between the positive and negative effects of the genes involved in response to environmental factors. Even a small selective advantage is sufficient to permit a gene to establish and maintain itself in a population.

Figure 5. Percentage of bridled form of the Common Murre (Guillemot) at North Atlantic nesting sites. [After H. N. Southern, "Survey of Bridled Guillemots, 1959–1960," *Proceedings of the Zoological Society of London* 138:455–472, 1962.]

The second article, by H. N. Southern ("A Study in the Evolution of Birds"), concerns color phases of the Common Murre (called the Guillemot in Britain) and the 20-year study he undertook to understand their geographic distribution with the help of The British Trust for Ornithology, a society of amateur bird watchers. Breeding colonies of Guillemots in Britain have two kinds of birds within them, the common form, which has no eye ring, and the bridled form, which has a white eye ring. H. N. Southern began a study of the distribution and relative frequency of the bridled form of the Guillemot in the late 1930s. The results of the first and second censuses of the many breeding colonies are described in the article reprinted here. The first study established that the proportion of the form increased from southeast to northwest; the second study raised the question of whether the bridled form was rapidly decreasing, perhaps in response to a warming trend in the weather. A third census of the breeding colonies in 1959–1960 showed that the changes noted in the second census in 1948–1950 were fluctuations, and not part of a long-term trend. A summary of part of the results from all three studies, with data from breeding colonies from Spain to the Arctic Circle, is illustrated in Figure 5, which is adapted from the last report of the study. Averages of the values from the three censuses are included when available.

REFERENCES

Hoffman, W., J. A. Wiens, and J. M. Scott. "Hybridization Between Gulls (*Larus glaucescens* and *L. occidentalis*) in the Pacific Northwest." *The Auk* 95:442–458, 1978.

Ostrom, J. H. "Bird Flight: How Did It Begin?" *American Scientist* 67:46–56, 1979.

Southern, H. N. "Survey of Bridled Guillemots, 1959–1960." *Proceedings of the Zoological Society of London* 138:455–472, 1962.

9

Darwin's Finches

by David Lack
April 1953

These drab but famous little birds of the Galapagos Islands are a living case study in evolution. Isolated in the South Pacific, they have developed 14 species from a common ancestor

ON THE Galapagos Islands in the Pacific Charles Darwin in 1835 saw a group of small, drab, finch-like birds which were to change the course of human history, for they provided a powerful stimulus to his speculations on the origin of species—speculations that led to the theory of evolution by natural selection. In the study of evolution the animals of remote islands have played a role out of all proportion to their small numbers. Life on such an island approaches the conditions of an experiment in which we can see the results of thousands of years of evolutionary development without outside intervention. The Galapagos finches are an admirable case study.

These volcanic islands lie on the Equator in the Pacific Ocean some 600 miles west of South America and 3,000 miles east of Polynesia. It is now generally agreed that they were pushed up out of the sea by volcanoes more than one million years ago and have never been connected with the mainland. Whatever land animals they harbor must have come over the sea, and very few species have established themselves there: just two kinds of mammals, five reptiles, six songbirds and five other land birds.

Some of these animals are indistinguishable from the same species on the mainland; some are slightly different; a few, such as the giant land-tortoises and the mockingbirds, are very different. The latter presumably reached the Galapagos a long time ago. In addition, there are variations from island to island among the local species themselves, in-

dicating that the colonists diverged into variant forms after their arrival. Darwin's finches go further than this: not only do they vary from island to island but up to 10 different species of them can be found on a single island.

The birds themselves are less dramatic than their story. They are dull in color, unmusical in song and, with one exception, undistinguished in habits. This dullness is in no way mitigated by their dreary surroundings. Darwin in his diary succinctly described the islands: "The country was compared to what we might imagine the cultivated parts of the Infernal regions to be." This diary, it is interesting to note, makes no mention of the finches, and the birds received only a brief mention in the first edition of his book on the voyage of the *Beagle*. Specimens which Darwin brought home, however, were recognized by the English systematist and bird artist, John Gould, as an entirely new group of birds. By the time the book reached its second edition, the ferment had begun to work, and Darwin added that "one might really fancy that from an original paucity of birds in this archipelago, one species had been taken and modified for different ends." Thus obscurely, as an afterthought in a travel book, man received a first intimation that he might once have been an ape.

THERE ARE 13 species of Darwin's finches in the Galapagos, plus one on Cocos Island to the northwest. A self-contained group with no obvious relations elsewhere, these finches are usually

placed in a subfamily of birds named the *Geospizinae*. How did this remarkable group evolve? I am convinced, from my observations in the islands in 1938-39 and from subsequent studies of museum specimens, that the group evolved in much the same way as other birds. Consequently the relatively simple story of their evolution can throw valuable light on the way in which birds, and other animals, have evolved in general. Darwin's finches form a little world of their own, but a world which differs from the one we know only in being younger, so that here, as Darwin wrote, we are brought nearer than usual "to that great fact—that mystery of mysteries—the first appearance of new beings on this earth."

The 14 species of Darwin's finches fall into four main genera. First, there are the ground-finches, embracing six species, nearly all of which feed on seeds on the ground and live in the arid coastal regions. Secondly, there are the tree-finches, likewise including six species, nearly all of which feed on insects in trees and live in the moist forests. Thirdly, there is the warbler-like finch (only one species) which feeds on small insects in bushes in both arid and humid regions. Finally, there is the isolated Cocos Island species which lives on insects in a tropical forest.

Among the ground-finches, four species live together on most of the islands: three of them eat seeds and differ from each other mainly in the size of their beaks, adapted to different sizes of seeds; the fourth species feeds largely on prickly pear and has a much longer

THE 14 SPECIES of Darwin's finches are arranged at the left to suggest the evolutionary tree of their development. Grayish brown to black, all belong to the subfamily *Geospizinae*, divided broadly into ground finches (*Geospiza*), closest to the primitive form, and tree finches (mainly *Camarhynchus*), which evolved later. Of the tree species, 1 is a woodpecker-like finch (*C. pallidus*), 2 inhabits mangrove swamps (*C. heliobates*), 3, 4 and 5 are large, medium and small insect-

eating birds (*C. psittacula, pauper* and *parvulus*), 6 is a vegetarian (*C. crassirostris*), 7 is a single species of warbler-finch (*Certhidea*) and 8 an isolated species of Cocos Island finch (*Pinaroloxias*). The ground-finches, mainly seed-eaters, run thus: 9, 10 and 11 are large, medium and small in size (*G. magnirostris, fortis* and *fuliginosa*), 12 is sharp-beaked (*G. difficilis*), 13 and 14 are cactus eaters (*G. conirostris* and *scandens*). All of the species in the drawing are shown about half-size.

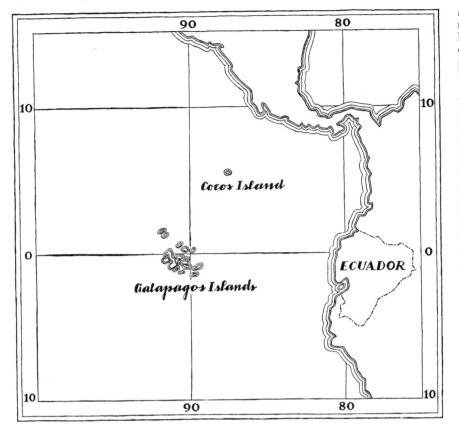

THE GALAPAGOS are shown some 600 miles west of Ecuador, above, and close up below. Cocos Island is not in the group, but it has developed one species of finch, presumed to have come originally from the mainland.

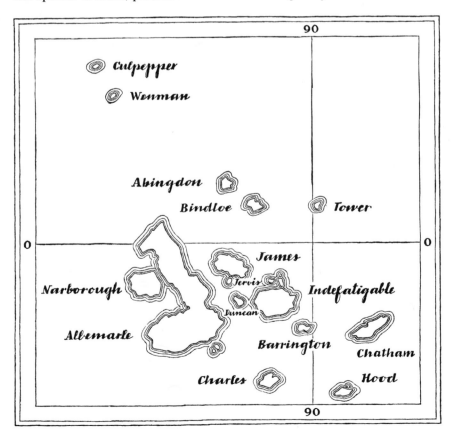

and more pointed beak. The two remaining species of ground-finches, one large and one small, live chiefly on the outlying islands, where some supplement their seed diet with cactus, their beaks being appropriately modified.

Of the tree-finches, one species is vegetarian, with a parrot-like beak seemingly fitted to its diet of buds and fruits. The next three species are closely alike, differing primarily in body size and in the size of their beaks, presumably scaled to the size of the insects they take. A fifth species eats insects in mangrove swamps. The sixth species of tree-finch is one of the most remarkable birds in the world. Like a woodpecker, it climbs tree trunks in search of insects, which it excavates from the bark with its chisel-shaped beak. While its beak approaches a woodpecker's in shape, it has not evolved the long tongue with which a woodpecker probes insects from crannies. Instead, this tree-finch solves the problem in another way: it carries about a cactus spine or small twig which it pokes into cracks, dropping the stick to seize any insect that emerges. This astonishing practice is one of the few recorded cases of the use of tools by any animal other than man or the apes.

The warbler-like finch is in its own way as remarkable as the Galapagos attempt at a woodpecker. It has no such wonderful habit, but in its appearance and character it has evolved much closer to a warbler than the other finch has to a woodpecker. Thus its beak is thin and pointed like that of a warbler; its feeding methods and actions are similar, and it even has the warbler-like habit of flicking its wings partly open as it hunts for food. For nearly a century it was classified as a warbler, but its internal anatomy, the color of its eggs, the shape of its nest and other characteristics clearly place it among the finches.

The close resemblance among Darwin's finches in plumage, calls, nests, eggs and display suggests that they have not yet had time to diverge far from one another. The only big difference is in their beaks, adapted to their different diets. It is reasonably certain that all the Galapagos finches evolved from one original colonizing form. What is unusual about them is the existence of several distinct species on the same island. In this we may have an indirect clue to how separate species establish themselves.

LET US consider first how new forms of an animal may originate from a common ancestor. When a member of the original species moves into a new environment, it is likely to evolve new features adapted to the new local conditions. Such geographical variations among animals are commonly found; in the Galapagos, for instance, the land birds other than finches vary from island to island, with only one form on each island. These forms are not distinct species but subspecies, or geographical races. Their differences, however, are hereditary and not trivial or accidental. There are several examples of such geographical variation among Darwin's finches. Three common species of the ground-finch, for instance, are found on most of the islands; they are large, medium and small, feeding on large, medium and small seeds respectively. Now on two southern islands the large species is missing, and here the medium species has a rather larger beak than elsewhere, presumably an adaptation to the large seeds available to it in the absence of the large species. Again, on another islet the small ground-finch is absent, and the medium species fills the gap by being rather smaller than elsewhere. On still other islets the medium species is missing and the small species is rather larger than elsewhere.

It seems clear that the beak differences among the subspecies of Darwin's finches are adaptive. Further, some of these differences are as great as those distinguishing true species.

What is likely to happen if a subspecies evolved in isolation on one island later spreads to an island occupied by another race of the same species? If the two populations have not been isolated for long and differ in only minor ways, they may interbreed freely and so merge with each other. But evidence from the study of insects suggests that if two populations have been isolated for a long time, so many hereditary differences will have accumulated that their genes will not combine well. Any hybrid offspring will not survive as well as the parent types. Hence natural selection will tend to intensify the gap between the two forms, and they will continue to evolve into two distinct species.

DARWIN'S finches provide circumstantial evidence for the origin of a new species by means of geographical isolation. Consider three different forms of the large insectivorous tree-finch. On the most southerly Galapagos island is a small dark form with a comparatively small beak. On another island to the northwest is a rather larger and less barred form. On the central islands is a yet larger and paler type with a larger, more parrot-like beak. Evidently these three forms had a common ancestor and evolved their differences in geographical isolation. The differences among them do not seem great enough to set them apart as separate species, and they would be classed as subspecies but for one curious circumstance: on the southernmost island the two extremes—the small dark form and the largest pale form—live side by side without merging.

Clearly these must be truly separate species. It seems likely that the large pale form spread from the central islands to the southern island in comparatively recent times, after both it and the small dark form had evolved into distinct species.

If differentiated forms are to persist alongside each other as separate species, two conditions must be met. First, they must avoid interbreeding. In birds this is usually taken care of by differences in appearance (generally in the color pattern) and in the song. It is no accident that bird-watchers find male birds so easy to recognize: correct identification is even more important for the female bird! Darwin's finches recognize each other chiefly by the beak. We have often seen a bird start to chase another from behind and quickly lose interest when a front view shows that the beak is that of a species other than its own.

The second requirement for the existence of two species together is that they must not compete for the same food. If they tend to eat similar food, the one that is better adapted to obtain that food will usually eliminate the other. In those cases where two closely related species live side by side, investigation shows that they have in fact evolved differences in diet. Thus the beak differences among

the various Galapagos finches are not just an insular curiosity but are adapted to differences in diet and are an essential factor in their persistence together. It used to be supposed that related species of birds overlapped considerably in their feeding habits. A walk through a wood in summer may suggest that many of the birds have similar habits. But having established the principle of food differentiation in Darwin's finches, I studied many other examples of closely related species and found that most, if not all, differ from one another in the places where they feed, in their feeding methods or in the size of the food items they can take. The appearance of overlap was due simply to inadequate knowledge.

NOW the key to differentiation is geographical isolation. Probably one form can establish itself alongside another only after the two have already evolved some differences in separate places. Evolutionists used to believe that new species evolved by becoming adapted to different habitats in the same area. But there is no positive evidence for that once popular theory, and it is now thought that geographical isolation is the only method by which new species originate, at least among birds. One of

THE WOODPECKER-FINCH is the most remarkable of Darwin's finches. It has evolved the beak but not the long tongue of a woodpecker, hence carries a twig or cactus spine to dislodge insects from bark crevices.

Darwin's species of finches provides an interesting illustration of this. The species on Cocos Island is so different from the rest that it must have been isolated there for a long time. Yet despite this long isolation, along with a great variety of foods and habitats and a scarcity of other bird competitors, the Cocos finch has remained a single species. This is because Cocos is an isolated island, and so does not provide the proper opportunities for differentiation. In the Galapagos, differentiation was possible because the original species could scatter and establish separate homes on the various islands of the archipelago. It is significant that the only other group of birds which has evolved in a similar way, the sicklebills of Hawaii, are likewise found in an archipelago.

Why is it that this type of evolution has been found only in the Galapagos and Hawaii? There are other archipelagoes in the world, and geographical isolation is also possible on the continents. The ancestor of Darwin's finches, for instance, must formerly have lived on the American mainland, but it has not there given rise to a group of species similar to those in the Galapagos. The answer is, probably, that on the mainland the available niches in the environment were already occupied by efficient species of other birds. Consider the woodpecker-like finch on the Galapagos, for example. It would be almost impossible for this type to evolve in a land which already possessed true woodpeckers, as the latter would compete with it and eliminate it. In a similar way the warbler-like finch would, at least in its intermediate stages, have been less efficient than a true warbler.

Darwin's finches may well have been the first land birds to arrive on the Galapagos. The islands would have provided an unusual number of diverse, and vacant, environmental niches in which the birds could settle and differentiate. The same may have been true of Hawaii. In my opinion, however, the type of evolution that has occurred in those two groups of islands is not unique. Similar developments could have taken place very long ago on the continents; thus our own finches, warblers and woodpeckers may have evolved from a common ancestor on the mainland. What is unique about the Galapagos and Hawaii is that the birds' evolution there occurred so recently that we can still see the evidence of the differentiations.

MUCH MORE is still to be learned from the finches. Unfortunately the wonderful opportunities they offer may not long remain available. Already one of the finches Darwin found in the Galapagos is extinct, and so are several other animals peculiar to the islands. With man have come hunters, rats, dogs and other predators. On some islands men and goats are destroying the native vegetation. This last is the most serious threat of all to Darwin's finches. Unless we take care, our descendants will lose a treasure which is irreplaceable.

Visual Isolation in Gulls

by Neal Griffith Smith
October 1967

*Some species of gulls live together and look alike,
yet they do not interbreed. How do the species remain
isolated? Experiments in the Artic indicate that they
do so by recognizing subtle visual signals*

Gulls look remarkably alike. That was the problem. Differences in appearance among the large gulls of the genus *Larus* can be subtle: a slight variation in size or a change in the color of the wing tips or of the eye and the small fleshy ring around the eye. Observing differences of this kind, an ornithologist discriminates among species of the genus. The problem arose from the fact that the gulls are equally discriminating. In some places *Larus* species that seem virtually indistinguishable nest side by side, yet they do not interbreed. How do gulls of one species avoid interbreeding with gulls of another?

The question of how species acquire and maintain their identity has received much attention in the century since the publication of Charles Darwin's *Origin of Species*. It is now well established that geographic isolation between populations is of prime importance in initiating the process by which species arise. Indeed, the gulls of the Northern Hemisphere have been cited as a classic example supporting this concept.

The common ancestor of the *Larus* gulls probably emerged in the Siberian region. As these gulls spread to the east and west, simple geographic distance began to inhibit the flow of genes between the most distant populations. By the time these populations had spread around the hemisphere and overlapped in western Europe, their respective genetic backgrounds were different enough so that hybrids between them were at some disadvantage; thus they did not interbreed. The advance and retreat of the ice during the Pleistocene epoch caused a further fracturing and recombination of these circumpolar gull populations. In some cases the differences evolved were not critical enough to confer a disadvantage on hybrids; thus the

rejoined populations interbred.

It seems clear that the mechanisms by which species discriminate among one another evolved gradually during the process of species formation. In the Canadian Arctic, and probably elsewhere in the north, the ice intruded between various gull populations at different times and for different lengths of time. Accordingly the isolating mechanisms were likely to be at different stages of development in different populations. By studying populations in such an area one can uncover what these mechanisms are.

It is one thing to identify differences in the appearance of two closely related species living side by side and infer that the differences function as a barrier to interbreeding. It is quite another to demonstrate that these features are actually utilized in the isolation of species. To explain how such features work is still another step. This article is primarily concerned with the last two problems. It also considers the evolutionary history of the *Larus* gulls, because the elucidation of a feature that is utilized in species isolation can suggest what the species were like in the past and how the isolation mechanisms evolved.

The four species of *Larus* gulls I have been studying comprise the Canadian portion of the complex of gull populations around the North Pole. The fact that the four species do not interbreed has been clearly established by other workers and myself. All four gulls have a white body and a gray back and wings. The largest in body size is the glaucous gull (*Larus hyperboreus*). The tips of its wings are white, the iris of its eye is yellow and the fleshy ring around the eye is an even brighter yellow. Colonies of glaucous gulls are found throughout the polar area; in the

eastern part of the Canadian Arctic they usually nest on cliffs. A more familiar species is the herring gull (*L. argentatus*), the only one of the four that breeds in the continental U.S. It is a medium-sized bird with wing tips that are partly black and partly white. Like the glaucous gull, the herring gull has a yellow iris; its eye-ring, however, is orange. In the Arctic this species usually nests on the ground in marshy areas. About the same size and coloration is Thayer's gull (*L. thayeri*), except that in this species the iris of the eye is dark brown and the eye-ring is a reddish purple. Thayer's gull nests almost exclusively on towering cliffs. The smallest of the four species (although not by very much) is Kumlien's gull (*L. glaucoides*), which also nests on cliffs. It is most like Thayer's gull: its eye-ring is reddish purple but the iris varies from clear yellow to dark brown. Its wing tips also vary in their amount of gray.

The common breeding grounds of these gulls are difficult to visit, and not much has been known about them. When I began my work, the evidence was that no one area was shared by all four species. In the course of trying to find such an area I spent three seasons (April to September) in the Canadian Arctic, during which I covered just under 2,000 miles by dogsled and canoe. During this time I studied three of the gulls (glaucous, Kumlien's and herring) I found nesting together on the south side of Baffin Island and a different trio (glaucous, Thayer's and herring) on nearby Southampton Island. Finally I discovered all four species nesting together on the east side of Baffin Island. It was never easy to find the ground-nesting herring gulls in association with the cliff-nesting species. Nesting on cliffs evolved as an adaptation against predators such as foxes; apparently competition with the other gulls for nesting sites has resulted in the herring gulls' occupying poorer sites. Nevertheless, where the surface allowed it and where the birds were safe from predators in a place such as a rocky islet, all the gulls would nest together.

There were a number of factors, for instance the habitat differences I have mentioned, that tend to reduce the possibility of mixed matings in the areas shared by different populations of gulls; here, however, I shall discuss only differences in external appearance among the species that function as major isolating mechanisms. In 1950 Finn Salomonsen, a Danish ornithologist, suggested that the color of the eye-ring might serve as a signal for differentiation between Kumlien's gull (reddish-

purple eye-ring) and the glaucous gull (yellow eye-ring). Although I tested the possible significance of all the differences in the gull's external appearance (with the exception of size), I concentrated on the color of the eye-ring.

In order to study the gulls closely it was necessary to catch them. At first I did so by stretching over a ledge a large fishnet under which food was placed. When the gulls were under the net, an Eskimo assistant and I rushed forward and dropped it, pinning the gulls to the ground. This was obviously an inefficient method, and later I used the drug tribromoethanol. Capsules of the drug were inserted into pieces of meat; after eating the meat the gulls quickly became anesthetized. In this way more than 1,800 gulls were trapped. After the gulls had been drugged they were immobilized with a surgical rubber band that pinned

their legs and wings to their bodies, and colored leg bands were put on them to make it possible to recognize individuals. Sex was determined by measuring bill, feet and wings; the males are usually larger. The determinations were confirmed by the subsequent behavior of the gulls.

One of my first thoughts had been that if markings and coloration play a role in the gulls' mating behavior, it should be possible to demonstrate it by changing these features artificially. This I now undertook to do. To change the color of the eye-ring I applied oil paint with a thin brush. The wing-tip pattern was changed with white or black ink after first wiping the feathers with alcohol so that the ink would penetrate. Judging from the behavior of the painted gulls neither of these procedures caused any physical irritation. On the

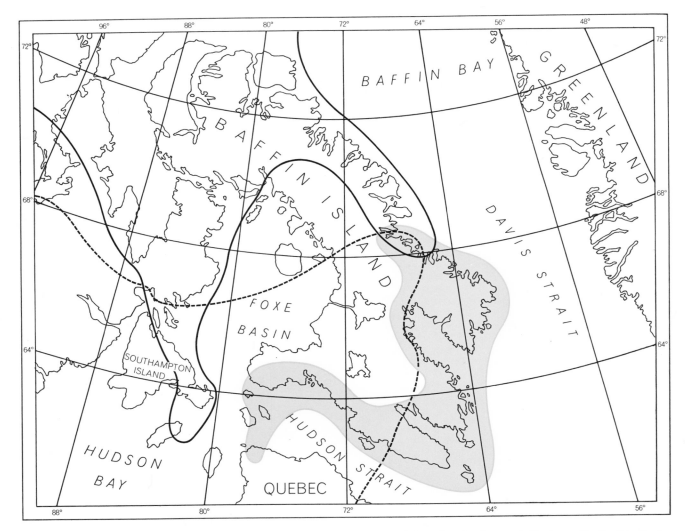

BREEDING RANGES of large *Larus* gulls lie in the eastern Canadian Arctic. Thayer's gulls (*black line*) and Kumlien's gulls (*colored area*) usually were found nesting in colonies on sea cliffs. The glaucous gull nests throughout this region; it was observed both on cliffs and on level ground. Herring gulls (*broken line*), a ground-nesting species, were found with the others only on rocky islands. Before discovering all four gulls on the east coast of Baffin Island, the author studied some species on Southampton Island.

other hand, when I attempted to change the color of a gull's back by spraying it with paint, the feathers stuck together and the gull tried repeatedly to remove the paint.

In my first season, after observing the behavior of individual pairs of glaucous, Kumlien's and herring gulls in a colony in southern Baffin Island, I captured a small group of the gulls. The eye-ring of each one was changed to the color of a different species. Over the yellow ring of the glaucous gull, for example, I painted a ring of reddish purple. All the female birds had copulated with males before the experiment but none had laid eggs. When the females returned to their nests, they were accepted by their mates. In the days that followed, however, the males would no longer mount, in spite of intense solicitation by the females. In all cases where the female's eye-ring color had been changed the pair did not remain together. Five of the males whose mates had been painted formed pairs with nonaltered females in adjacent territories. Copulation ensued, and after two weeks all the new pairs had eggs. The females I had painted left the colony.

In contrast to these findings, changing the eye-ring of a mated male gull appeared not to affect a pair's behavior. The females accepted their altered mates and the males responded to the soliciting behavior of the females. In the one case where both individuals of a mated pair were changed the results were exactly the same as they were when only the female was changed.

The results looked promising. Although the number of individuals involved was small (33 females and 30 males) and some important controls were lacking, I now had a working hypothesis, namely that in some way the eye-ring color of the females functioned as a stimulus for mounting by their mates and that this reaction was keyed to differences among the species.

The program for the next two seasons was to repeat the eye-ring experiments with the necessary controls and to explore the hypothesis in greater detail. Was it the fleshy eye-ring alone or the entire eye that functioned as a stimulus? Was the important factor color or was it contrast? In answering these questions the critical species would be Thayer's gull, with its dark eye-ring and dark iris. It was also of prime importance to test the function of eye-ring color and other physical features with unmated gulls. There was reason to be-

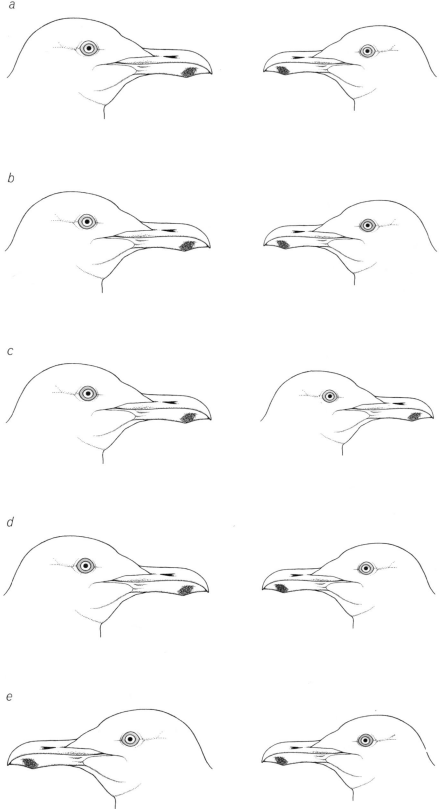

MATING BEHAVIOR OF GULLS changes when their appearance is artificially altered. Even when individuals of like species nest nearby, males and females of the same species normally mate (*a*). Such pairs still form even if an unmated female's eye-rings are painted to look like those of another species (*b*). Painted the same way, an unmated male fails to obtain a mate of his species (*c*). If the male is mated when his eye-rings are altered, his mate remains with him (*d*). When same change is made in the female, they usually separate (*e*).

lieve that the females choose the males, and it seemed unlikely that a mixed pair would form only to separate later because copulatory behavior was disrupted. There should also be an earlier isolating barrier.

In the experiments of these two seasons there were three major control groups: gulls that were drugged but not painted, gulls that were drugged and painted with their own color or pattern and gulls that were not captured but whose behavior was observed. My earlier findings with mated female gulls were confirmed in experiments that also shed light on the question of color v. contrast. A group of Kumlien's gulls was captured and their reddish-purple eye-ring was painted over either with a light color (yellow, orange or white) or a dark one (red or black). When the female gull had been painted with a light color, copulation usually stopped and the pair separated; in this regard an eye-ring painted white was the most effective. Dark colors had no significant effect. Exactly the reverse was true when the herring gull (orange eye-ring) and the glaucous (yellow) were painted in the same

way: dark colors inhibited copulation and light colors had no significant effect. Among the broken pairs were a number of female glaucous gulls whose yellow eye-ring had been changed to orange. This fitted the other results rather nicely, the orange eye-ring of the herring gull being darker than the yellow one of the glaucous gull.

When the same procedures were tried with Thayer's gull, however, there was no significant change in behavior. In this species it is not the eye-ring that stands out against the bird's white head, as it does in the other three species, but the entire orbital region—both the iris and the eye-ring are dark. This suggested that the orbital region as a whole functioned as a stimulus.

One could not paint the eye to change its color, but painting the reddish-purple eye-ring white reduces the contrast of the orbital region against the white head. After thus "erasing" the eye-ring I painted a larger one on the feathers around the eye. In making this "super-eye-ring" I used on various gulls the same assortment of colors as I had in the other experiments. One might think

HERRING GULL

EXTERNAL FEATURES vary among species. Each gull shown above differs from the

of the painted circle as the "eye-ring," the white feathers between it and the eye as the "iris" and the actual iris as the new "pupil." This may seem a bit far-fetched, and I do not mean to imply that this is what the gull sees, but the fact remains that in a significant number of cases where the female had been given a light-colored super-eye-ring copulation was inhibited and pairs separated. Apparently the stimulus to copulation was the contrast pattern of the ringed eye against the white head: dark color against white in Kumlien's and Thayer's gull and light color against white in the herring and glaucous gull.

In the course of these experiments I observed that a male occasionally mounted his altered mate but did not attempt copulation even when the female prodded his breast or rubbed her tail against his anal region. Earlier I had observed that copulation was invariably preceded by such tactile stimulation on the part of the females. I concluded that successful copulation probably involves both visual and tactile stimuli. (Auditory stimuli may also be involved, but this was not tested.) It appeared that the tactile stimuli were supplemental to other stimuli rather than independent of them; the eye-head contrast of the females played the major role.

Did the eye-head contrast play a role in the formation of pairs as well as in copulatory behavior? The eye-rings of a group of unmated female gulls were changed to determine if this made a significant difference in the species of the males with which they paired. The results showed no difference between this group and control groups. After a week or two, however, pairs in which the females had been given the "wrong" eye-head contrast separated; the males would not copulate. This of course further supported the role of eye-head

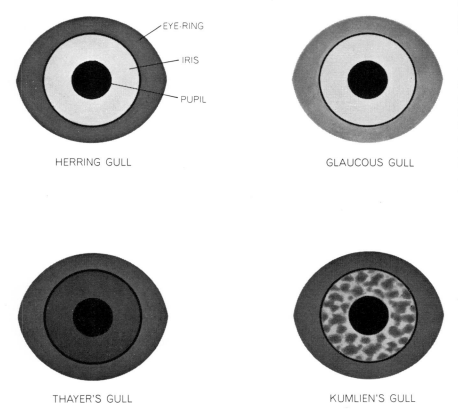

RINGED EYES of various colors, photographed in black and white, exhibit different color values. The orange eye-ring of the herring gull shows darker than the yellow ring of the glaucous gull. Darker still is the reddish-purple ring of Thayer's and Kumlien's gulls. In Thayer's gulls brown irises enforce the contrast of the orbital region against the white head; the iris of Kumlien's is lighter. Eye-head contrast acts as an interspecies barrier among gulls.

GLAUCOUS GULL

THAYER'S GULL

KUMLIEN'S GULL

others in size, in the coloration of the orbital region, back and wings and in the pattern of the wing tips. The author's experiments suggest that the wing-tip pattern serves to supplement the signal of eye-head contrast in preventing the formation of mixed pairs.

contrast.

When the same experiment was performed with unmated male gulls, the results were quite different. In one instance 91 percent of the male Thayer's gulls that had been changed by the super-eye-ring technique to the light-eyed condition failed to obtain mates of their own species. An experiment with glaucous and herring gulls also showed that if the eye-head contrast of unmated males was "wrong," they were significantly less successful in obtaining mates of the same species than the controls were.

The results suggested that in pair formation it is indeed the females that choose the males, and that they select males with an eye-head contrast like their own. In other words, the same feature works in two ways to isolate the species: in the males it serves the purpose of pair formation and in females the purpose of copulatory behavior. What role is played by other external differences? The color of the mantle (back and wings) of the *Larus* gulls varies from one species to another. Among the four species I studied the differences in mantle coloration were not pronounced; still it seemed worthwhile to attempt an evaluation of mantle color as a possible signal. As I have indicated, however, spraying paint on a gull's back has too great an effect on the gull's behavior to make for a sound experiment, and the role played by this feature remains obscure.

Tests of the wing-tip pattern displayed at rest suggest that this feature does function as a signal in species discrimination during pair formation. There was no significant change in behavior after alteration of the wing tips of female gulls, whether mated or unmated. On the other hand, alteration of the wing tips of unmated males indicated that the wing-tip pattern functions as a stimulus

to pair formation in combination with the eye-head contrast. This was shown by the fact that female gulls chose males with both "right" wing-tip pattern and eye-head contrast over males with only the "right" eye-head contrast. The wing-tip pattern alone is apparently not utilized in species discrimination during pair formation.

In several of the experiments male Thayer's gulls painted to appear light-eyed had been chosen by glaucous females. Since the females had the "wrong" eye-head contrast for the males, no copulation resulted and these mixed pairs did not remain together. After 59 Thayer's-glaucous pairs had formed I captured all but three of the glaucous females and altered them to the "right" contrast. Ten days later all 56 male Thayer's gulls had been observed to mount their altered mates, and about two weeks later 55 of the pairs had eggs. (One pair did not remain together.) Heavy ice on the rocks unfortunately forced me to abandon these colonies; I was never able to return to them. Before leaving I did collect several eggs, and they contained well-developed embryos. It may be that the mixed pairs produced hybrid offspring.

From the start of my experiments it had been clear that there was a strong correlation between the behavior that resulted from changing the eye-ring and the gonadal cycle of the gull. Two identical experiments, one performed 16 days before the first eggs were laid and the other 12 days later, yielded strikingly different results. I considered initially as a working hypothesis that the main component of the pair bond was the attachment of the individuals to each other, and that during and after the egg-laying period the main component of the bond became the attachment of the individuals to

the nest and the eggs. This hypothesis could account for certain pairs of gulls that had remained together even though the males had failed to respond to the solicitations of their altered mates. It could not, however, explain instances in which males continued to mount their mates after they had been painted and before egg-laying had begun. Moreover, the hypothesis offered no answer to the crucial question of what the physiological basis for the male's behavior is.

The solution to the problem was found in the relation between the internal physiological state of the male (indicated by the weight of the testes) and the number of times a pair had copulated. All but 12 of the 168 pairs of gulls that had remained together after the female had been given a different eye-ring had copulated six or more times before she had been painted. This number of copulations could be correlated with a certain weight of the testes attained in the male's gonadal cycle. I concluded that a gull whose testes had developed to the critical weight or beyond it would respond to a mate whether or not her eye-ring had been changed. The most telling evidence was that if the female's eye-ring was changed at a time before the critical weight was reached, the testes of her mate did not increase in weight—in fact, they diminished!

It is fairly well substantiated that gonadal development in many species is stimulated by changes in the daily cycle of daylight and darkness. On arriving in the Arctic in summer gulls are subjected to periods of daylight lasting almost 24 hours. This factor alone, however, could not cause the gulls' testes to develop beyond the level attained at the end of pair formation. Certain other stimuli must interact with light, and one of them—probably the most important one

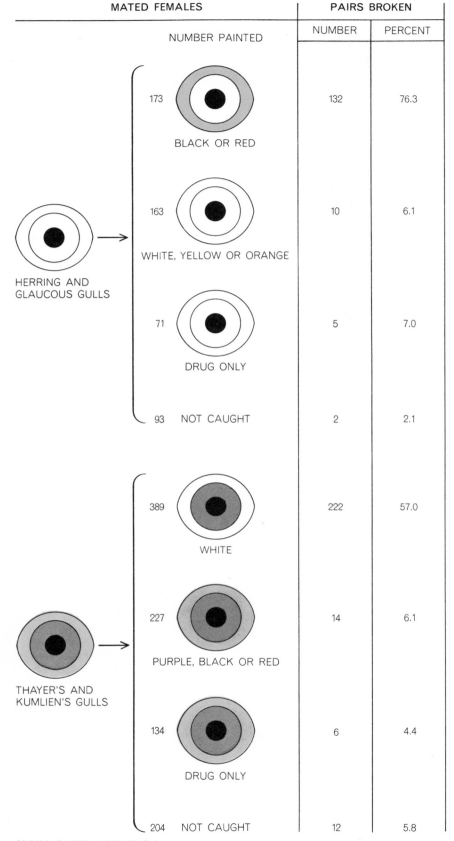

MATED FEMALES		PAIRS BROKEN	
	NUMBER PAINTED	NUMBER	PERCENT
HERRING AND GLAUCOUS GULLS	173 BLACK OR RED	132	76.3
	163 WHITE, YELLOW OR ORANGE	10	6.1
	71 DRUG ONLY	5	7.0
	93 NOT CAUGHT	2	2.1
THAYER'S AND KUMLIEN'S GULLS	389 WHITE	222	57.0
	227 PURPLE, BLACK OR RED	14	6.1
	134 DRUG ONLY	6	4.4
	204 NOT CAUGHT	12	5.8

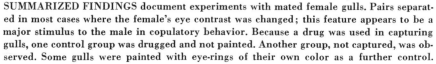

SUMMARIZED FINDINGS document experiments with mated female gulls. Pairs separated in most cases where the female's eye contrast was changed; this feature appears to be a major stimulus to the male in copulatory behavior. Because a drug was used in capturing gulls, one control group was drugged and not painted. Another group, not captured, was observed. Some gulls were painted with eye-rings of their own color as a further control.

—is the presence of a mate with the proper eye-head contrast.

Although I have no evidence for it, it seems likely on logical grounds that a similar mechanism functions in females during pair formation. Once a pair bond is formed and a series of hormonal events is activated, inhibition of the female's gonadal development does not occur, even when the original stimulus—the eye-head contrast of the male—is removed. In the female, as in the male, the interaction of stimuli and the hormonal background at different times in the season provides a species-isolating mechanism that appears to be wholly effective.

Thus far we have been considering the two questions raised at the beginning: What are the visual factors involved in species discrimination among the gulls, and how do these factors affect reproductive behavior? At this point I should like to take up the matter of how the mechanisms that isolate species have evolved. In this regard it is instructive to examine the natural variation in iris and wing-tip color that occurs in one species: Kumlien's gull.

The eye-ring color differs little among Kumlien's gulls and Thayer's gulls but the amount of dark pigment in their irises varies considerably. Kumlien's gull is by far the more variable, ranging from individuals with completely dark irises to those with completely clear eyes of yellow. I divided this variation into six classes, Class 1 being the darkest and Class 6 the clearest. On the south coast of Baffin Island, Kumlien's gulls live together with herring gulls and glaucous gulls. In this locale Kumlien's gulls with clear irises were almost entirely absent; they occupied classes from Class 1 to Class 4 or Class 5. On the east coast of Baffin Island, where Kumlien's gulls nested with Thayer's gulls and glaucous gulls, the situation was reversed. There almost all the Kumlien's gulls fell into the last three classes, being clear-eyed or nearly so.

This pattern can be explained in terms of the natural selection of the variations that will reduce the possibility of mixed mating. According to my experiments, the contrast of the eye-ring and iris against the white head is the chief factor in species discrimination among gulls. To avoid mixed pairings, then, selection favored dark-eyed individuals where Kumlien's gulls nested with the light-eyed herring gulls and light-eyed individuals where Kumlien's gulls nested with the dark-eyed Thayer's gulls. Apparently the dark eye-ring of Kumlien's gull has been adequate for species recognition between Kumlien's gull and the yellow-eye-ring glaucous gull. The orange eye-ring of the herring gull affords a darker contrast, however, and where herring gulls and Kumlien's gulls nest together the dark iris of the latter reinforces the eye-head contrast. It is interesting to note that in Greenland, Kumlien's gulls have light eyes; there herring gulls are not found and glaucous gulls are.

The amount of dark pigment in the iris of Kumlien's gull is highly correlated with the amount of pigment in the wing tips. Individual Kumlien's gulls with light irises, as found on the east coast of Baffin Island, have white wing tips; those with dark eyes, as found on the south coast of the island, have dark blotches on their wing tips. It has been suggested that this variation in wing-tip pattern is the result of hybridization between Thayer's gulls and Kumlien's gulls, but that is not the case. The two species are most unlike each other where they nest together; they are very much like each other where they do not live together but where each is associated with glaucous gulls and herring gulls. The explanation for the variation of the wing tip is simply that it reflects the correlation between the pigment in the iris and the wing tip and the results of selection for differences in iris color in different populations.

In the course of my earlier work I had come to the conclusion that female gulls chose males that in eye-head contrast and wing-tip pattern were most like themselves. This created a problem, because it implied that the female knows what it looks like. A series of observations and one experiment on the east coast of Baffin Island provided an escape from this dilemma and also showed how responsive to very slight evolutionary pressures the visual isolating mechanisms are. The experiment was one in which I had hoped to induce mixed matings between Kumlien's gulls and Thayer's gulls by painting the eye-rings of unmated male Kumlien's gulls black to increase the contrast. The males were chosen not by Thayer's gull females, however, but by females of their own species. I concluded that other features, perhaps the wing-tip pattern, were the critical ones in discrimination between the two species.

Then further investigation of Kumlien's gulls in this area where they overlapped with Thayer's gulls revealed a curious phenomenon. Although the ma-

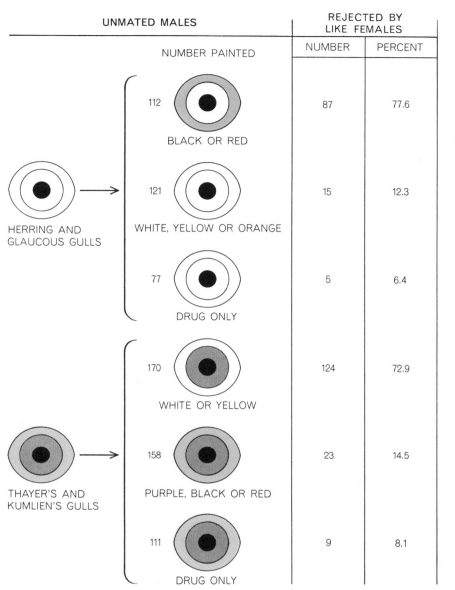

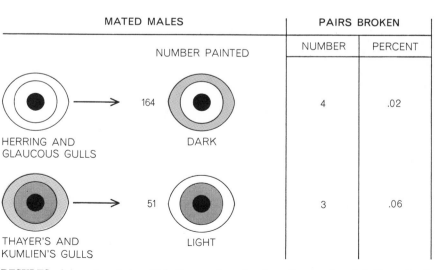

RESULTS of experiments in which the eye-ring of male gulls was altered indicate (*top*) that in pair formation the female chooses the male and that eye-head contrast is a factor in the choice. Changing the eye contrast of the male after a pair was formed (*bottom*) did not produce a change in mating behavior: nearly all the pairs of gulls remained together.

HEADS OF *LARUS* GULLS are almost identical except for the color of the eye and its encircling fleshy ring. At top on the opposite page are two Kumlien's gulls (*Larus glaucoides*), a species in which the iris varies from clear yellow to mottled brown. The eye-ring is reddish purple. Below appear two Thayer's gulls (*L. thayeri*). The eye-ring is the same as it is in Kumlien's gulls but the iris tends to be darker in this species. Next is a herring gull (*L. argentatus*), the only one that nests in the continental U.S. The glaucous gull (*L. hyperboreus*), shown last, has an eye-ring of yellow, which distinguishes it from the herring gull. Smallest gull is at top; largest at bottom. The painting was made by Guy Tudor.

jority of Kumlien's gulls in the area had clear yellow irises, there were many individuals (37 percent) with various amounts of iris pigmentation. If the gulls are viewed as two groups, one with iris pigmentation and one without it, a pattern emerges: in each group there is a striking preponderance of matings between individuals that look alike. Outside the overlap area mating is essentially random with respect to the presence or absence of iris pigmentation.

With this information in mind the results of the black-eye-ring experiment can be interpreted very differently. In this area dark-eyed males normally are chosen by dark-eyed females and clear-eyed males by clear-eyed females. Yet in the experiment even though 92 clear-eyed females were available for mating, they chose only four from the group of 41 clear-eyed males that had been painted to have a darker orbital region; 29 of these males were chosen by dark-eyed females. None of the 26 males with dark irises ringed in black were picked by light-eyed females. It can be seen that by increasing the eye-head contrast of unmated male Kumlien's gulls in this area, one can predict the iris coloration of the eventual mate.

Thus there was both observational and experimental evidence that the fe-male Kumlien's gulls of this area were discerning very slight differences in the eye-head contrast of prospective mates. This mating system probably evolved as a result of two primary pressures. The presence of small numbers of herring gulls in the overlap zone probably provided pressure to maintain the delicate balance between clear-eyed and dark-eyed Kumlien's gulls. Secondly, in order to avoid mixed pairings with Thayer's gulls, selection favored individual Kumlien's gulls that perceived slight eye-head contrast differences. The mating system among Kumlien's gulls, in which like mates with like, is a by-product of such selection. This view is supported by the fact that increasing the eye-head contrast of unmated males just outside the overlap zone had no detectable effect, whereas the same alterations within the zone produced major changes in the mating system.

At first, of course, it is difficult to imagine how female gulls manage to choose mates that look like themselves. Presumably they do not actually see themselves. (Mirrors are rare in the Arctic.) The answer may nonetheless be quite simple. It is known that many birds "imprint" on their parents soon after birth, and that they choose mates that look like their parents. Possibly gulls do the same. If eye color in gulls is inherited (as seems likely, although genetic information is lacking), then female gulls choose mates that look like themselves simply because they are looking for mates that look like their parents, and in most cases they themselves look like their parents. This hypothesis suggests that the Kumlien's gull mating system may simply represent an intensification of the normal process, that is, a female chooses a male most like her parents in eye-head contrast and wing tips.

To understand the evolution of these visual signals that function as reproductive isolating mechanisms one can examine the distribution of the large *Larus* gulls throughout the Northern Hemisphere. With the exception of the glaucous gull, all the other *Larus* gulls that overlap with the herring gull and are reproductively isolated from it have the contrast pattern of a dark eye against a white head. The populations that apparently hybridize with herring gulls have dark eye-rings but light irises. As I have indicated, dark eye-rings without dark irises are insufficient as isolating mechanisms against the orange-eye-ring herring gulls. The important point here is that the darkening of the eye region (principally the eye-ring) begins to develop in an isolated population. If the population becomes genetically so different from the one from which it was separated that on coming together again the two populations remain distinct, selection will favor a further increase in the darkening of the eye region, specifically a darkening of the iris. The end result is a sealing off of gene exchange.

A Study in the Evolution of Birds

11

by H. N. Southern
May 1957

*The head of the guillemot is either all black or bridled,
i.e., decorated with markings resembling spectacles. This
phenomenon, known as polymorphism, is a clue to the
operation of evolution*

On the seacoasts around the North Atlantic lives a bird of the auk family which is known in Europe as the common guillemot and in America as the murre. The bird has a white breast and black back: it looks not unlike a small penguin [*see photograph on this page*]. Generally the guillemot's head is all black, but there is a mutant form with white rings around its eyes, giving the appearance of spectacles. For well over a century the spectacled, or bridled, guillemot was a subject of controversy among naturalists. It was long classified as a separate species, but many maintained that it must be merely a variant of the common guillemot (*Uria aalge*), because the bridled and non-bridled forms were found living side by side in the same groups. It is now definitely established that the two forms are actually of the same species and represent only different color "phases" of the species.

The main topic of my article is a study of the guillemots, now in its second decade, which has cast significant light on the processes of adaptation and evolution. But first let us look into this matter of "phases," or the phenomenon called polymorphism. Among birds variations of form within a species are most commonly observed in the colors of the plumage, but they may apply to other traits. For instance, the crossbill, a bird whose upper beak crosses over the lower in scissor fashion, has two phases: in one variety the upper beak crosses to the right, in the other to the left. The bird lives mainly on the seeds of coniferous trees, and its curious beak is well adapted to prying apart the cones' tough scales to get at the seeds. I have watched crossbills dealing with the very hard cones of the Scots pine at the rate of one every two minutes, and since each cone

has 20 to 50 seeds to be extracted, this is no mean achievement. While working on a cone, "right-handed" birds always hold it in one particular direction, "left-handed" birds in the opposite way. The curious thing about this dimorphism is that in Europe right-handed crossbills

predominate, while in America the left-handed seem to be in the majority. It would be an interesting point to investigate further.

Color polymorphism among birds is very common. Most frequently the phase variations express themselves in darken-

SUBCOLONY OF GUILLEMOTS was photographed at the Bullers of Buchan, a turbulent inlet on the east coast of Scotland. The guillemot is a large bird; it stands about a foot high.

114

COLONIES OF GUILLEMOTS and kittiwakes nest on the ledges of a cliff on Noss Island, in the Shetlands north of Scotland.

Among the guillemots are both bridled and nonbridled forms. The proportion of bridled birds is larger than in colonies to the south.

BRIDLED PHASE OF THE GUILLEMOT is depicted at the bottom of this drawing; the nonbridled is at the top. Some naturalists believed bridled phase was a separate species.

ing, whitening or reddening of the normal plumage color. Many species of heron have both white and slate-blue forms—a situation which was highly confusing to early classifiers. Among the hawks, certain species (*e.g.*, the Australian gray goshawk and Eleanora's falcon) show strikingly different color phases. Some jaegers have both white-breasted and dark-breasted versions; buzzards vary over a wide range of phases from predominantly dark to predominantly light; many owls may have either gray or foxy-red plumage. There are also a number of cases of color polymorphism in the vast order of passerine birds (the small, perching birds). The Caribbean sugarbird, or banana quit, normally has a yellow and gray plumage, but on two islands in the Caribbean the sugarbird populations are almost entirely black. In Australia the Gouldian finch, a colorful little bird with a gay body plumage of amethyst, blue, green and yellow, usually has a black face but sometimes it is scarlet.

All this, of course, is of great interest to biologists. It is not surprising to find mutant forms within a species, but ordinarily mutants are very rare: the proportion of mutant genes maintained in a wild population of animals, it has been estimated, is only about one in 100,000 or one in a million. Mutations are usually detrimental. Many geneticists believe that populations are so sensitive to small selection pressures in the environment that there is virtually no such thing as a neutral gene: therefore any mutant gene must either completely replace its allele (opposite number) because it is advantageous, or be reduced to an extremely rare variant because it is disadvantageous.

How, then, can a mixed, polymorphic population persist, as it does in the color phases of birds? The English geneticists Ronald A. Fisher and Edmund B. Ford have proposed that this can be explained on the basis of the interplay of opposing factors, which maintain a balance between the contrasting phases. Ford cites the case of the butterflies whose coloring mimics that of distasteful species, so that they are unmolested by predators. Since the predators have to learn by experience, and since the mimics are not distasteful, it is obvious that they will not long survive if they come to predominate

over their inedible models. Therefore a mimetic form never outnumbers the distasteful species that it imitates. I have suggested that a somewhat similar mechanism controls the populations of the cuckoo. The cuckoo deposits its eggs in the nest of another bird (always one certain species) for hatching. If a particular "race" of cuckoos becomes too successful in getting its eggs hatched by the species it is parasitizing, the exploited host will decline in numbers and so too will the cuckoo.

Another factor supporting polymorphism is the phenomenon called heterosis, or "hybrid vigor." A mixture of genes often improves the viability of an animal species. The Australian finch I mentioned may be a case in point. In the wild, about one in three or four of these finches is red-headed. But bird breeders have found it very difficult to produce a pure line of red-headed finches, for many of the offspring suffer from fits. It is known that a single dominant gene is responsible for the red-headed phase of this finch. The breeding experiments certainly indicate that the heterozygote (individual with mixed genes) is far more viable than the homozygous red.

Now the most significant fact about the possession of a reservoir of mutant genes by a species is that it gives the species adaptability: it can respond readily to a change in its environment. Ford has illustrated this very convincingly with an instance of a color change in moths. The moths in question are species with camouflaging color schemes that hide them from predators in the wild. During the past 100 years many of these species, living in city areas where their former predators are absent, have become predominantly black—a change which is described as "industrial melanism." The black mutant used to be rare, but apparently it is more viable than the camouflaged type, and the absence of the old predators has allowed this advantage to be expressed.

The case of the Caribbean sugarbird also is suggestive. In most of the region the bird is yellow and gray. But on the island of Grenada the sugarbird population is largely black, with pockets of the normal type, and on Saint Vincent it is almost entirely black. It is tempting to conclude that we see there a species in various stages of adaptation to environmental conditions.

This kind of situation offers a beautiful opportunity to watch natural selection and evolution in action. The color phases of birds are sharply defined and easy to observe. They are controlled in a simple way by a single gene or group of genes. The bird population probably responds swiftly to variations in environmental conditions—from place to place and from year to year. This means that the processes of selection can be followed simply by counting the frequencies of the various color types at different places and at different times.

We selected the guillemots for such a study. During the early 1930s I often visited the sea cliffs of the British Isles where sea birds breed in vast numbers, and I came to realize that the bridled and nonbridled phases of the common guillemot were an ideal subject for investigation. The guillemot is a comparatively large bird—about a foot high—and is easily identified. The bridled form, with its white eye-ring and line running back from the eye toward the nape, can be picked out from a considerable distance with binoculars. Huge colonies of the bird nest on the open cliff ledges. And last but not least, the wild, rocky headlands and islands where they nest are most attractive places to visit.

So when, in 1937, Julian Huxley suggested that I should organize a large-scale inquiry into the bridled guillemot, I was easily persuaded. He proposed that I enlist the members of the British Trust for Ornithology, who are mainly amateurs, in a cooperative endeavor, and most of them were only too willing to take part. Their job was simply to visit the cliff colonies and count the numbers of bridled and nonbridled guillemots.

I think that many people enjoyed themselves doing these counts. At any rate, sufficient enthusiasm was displayed to cover during 1938 and 1939 practically all the known breeding colonies of any size in Great Britain and many in other countries as well. For my own part I took great pleasure in my round tour of the northernmost part of Scotland, extending to the Orkney Islands. I found guillemots on cliffs of sandstone which glowed red in the setting sun, on cliffs of pink granite, of black basalt and even of chalk. Some of the colonies of these birds have to be seen to be believed. Often several thousand birds nest within a space only 50 to 100 yards long on a cliff face some 200 to 300 feet high. A guillemot's "nesting" consists in laying a single egg on the bare rock. The birds are so close together that a continual rain of droppings falls from their ledges. A mile or so of cliff populated at this density adds up to a most startling sight. Even more startling is the noise that assaults one's ears. The birds "talk" constantly in a sort of muttering growl (*arrrrrr—arra-arra-arra*), and this roar from thousands of guillemot throats sounds very like a yard full of schoolchildren let out to play. I never hear the one without being irresistibly reminded of the other.

The results of that prewar survey were clear-cut. The frequency of the bridled character varied consistently with the latitude: at the southern end of the range, in Portugal, not a single spectacled guillemot was seen, but northward the proportion of bridled birds increased fairly regularly until it reached more than 50 per cent in Iceland. It was obvious that in some way the bridled trait, or something associated with it, conferred a considerable advantage in the northern part of the range, and that its absence was advantageous in the southern part. It also seemed probable that the selective advantages changed in a graded way in step with latitude.

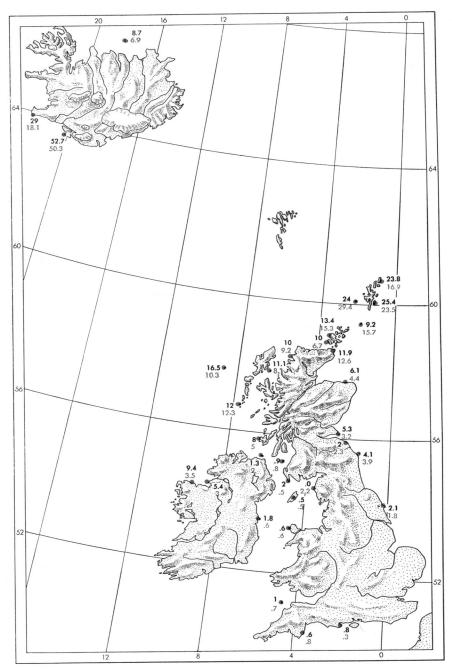

PERCENTAGE OF BRIDLED GUILLEMOTS in samples of guillemot colonies in the British Isles and Iceland is indicated by the numbers on this map. The black numbers give the percentage in 1938-39; the colored, the percentage in 1948-49. The percentage increases with latitude. In 10 years the proportion of bridled birds in most colonies decreased.

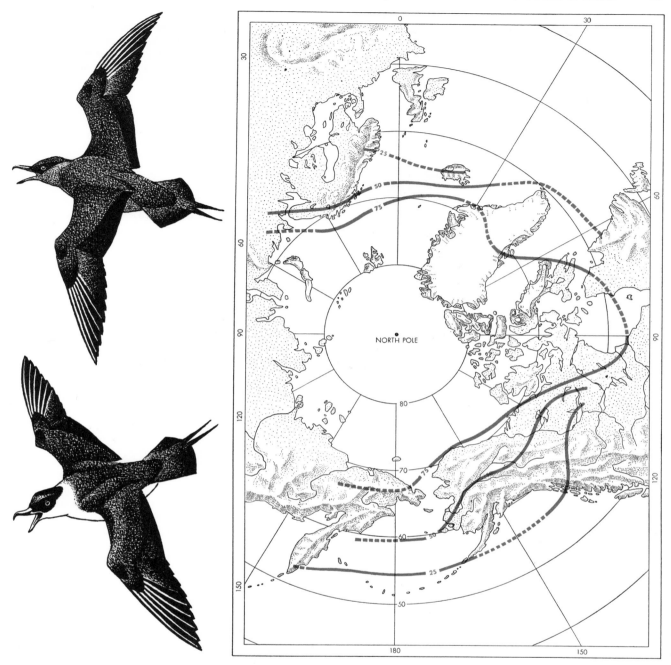

SKUA, like the guillemot a sea bird, has a dark phase (*upper left*) and a light phase (*lower left*). The percentage of the light phase, like that of the bridled guillemot, increases with latitude. The percentages are given by the contours in the map at right.

Two or three interesting details in this geographical gradient are worth mentioning. The percentage of bridled birds does not increase *quite* evenly with latitude. For instance, in the range up the west coast from the southernmost part of England to the Clyde River in Scotland the proportion of bridled birds rises only from .5 per cent to about 2 per cent, but in the next colonies northward, in the Hebrides, it jumps to about 8 per cent. This is in accord with an analysis of geographical patterns by Huxley, which predicts such jumps where there is a succession of relatively isolated breeding groups. A second point of interest is that in Iceland the bridled phase suddenly declines. In Iceland the common guillemot is gradually replaced by a different species, called Brünnich's guillemot, as one goes northward. Curiously, as the common guillemot declines so does the percentage of its bridled members, until finally it is down to 10 per cent on the island of Grimsey north of Iceland. Still another interesting point is that in northwestern Europe the gradient of increase in bridling does not run strictly from south to north but rather from southeast to northwest: at a given latitude the bridle percentage is higher to the west than to the east. This slanting arrangement coincides with the geographical influence of the Gulf Stream on climate in western Europe.

When we took stock of the results of that first survey, we felt we had collected the most complete and most extended picture of the geographical distribution of a genetic factor ever obtained. Now we faced the question: Was the situation a stable one or was an evolutionary change in progress? One possible interpretation was that the bridled gene was spreading south from a starting point near Iceland.

To settle the question we decided to repeat the survey 10 years later. When 1948 arrived, circumstances threatened to thwart our plan: private motoring was strictly rationed and it looked unlikely that we could reach the more remote nesting places. But by spreading the survey over three seasons and carrying out a large part of it by myself, I was

SHRIKES of the genus *Chlorophoneus* have four color phases in West Africa. At upper left in these semischematic drawings is the buff phase; at upper right, the scarlet; at lower left, the yellow; at lower right, the black. These birds have other colors.

able to get a fairly adequate cross section of counts.

The results were something of a surprise. In every area (except one) where we found any significant change in counts, the percentage of bridled guillemots *decreased*. In Iceland, for example, it dropped from 29 per cent to 18 per cent; on the island of Saint Kilda, from 17 to 10. Only in one small area did the proportion increase. The counts were not altogether conclusive, but they did establish fairly clearly that there was no general rise in the frequency of the bridled trait—in short, that the gene responsible for it was not spreading.

We are therefore left with two possible conclusions: either (1) the bridled and nonbridled phases of the guillemot are in long-term balance and the changes in counts on the second survey represent only random fluctuations around an average, or (2) the bridled phase is declining in frequency because of a general change in the environment. We know that a climatic change is in fact under way. There is plenty of evidence that during the past century the temperature difference between the Equator and the Poles has decreased: the ice caps have been retreating, and many species of birds and animals have been extending their ranges northward, especially in western Europe. If the bridled gene is better adapted to the colder climates, as its distribution suggests, then we should expect the warming change to reduce its over-all frequency. We are planning a third survey in 1958-59, and this should tell us more definitely whether such a decline is really occurring.

In the meantime I have been trying to learn more about the population dynamics of the guillemots, partly with a view to determining how rapidly any real change in the gene's frequency could take place. I have pursued these studies with help from the University of Aberdeen zoologists along a stretch of precipitous coastline in northeastern Scotland. We have surveyed certain colonies there each year for eight years and are beginning to get some answers.

On mainland cliffs the guillemots generally nest on inaccessible ledges, out of reach of foxes and other predators. But on a shaft of rock just off the coast, easily reached by boat, we found an accessible sub-colony of about 200 guillemots which we had no difficulty in catching and banding with colored rings. With a cautious approach we were able to slip a noose hanging from a long bamboo pole over the head of a bird and thus capture it for marking. Unhappily the

colored identifying bands faded after a couple of years, but they lasted long enough to give us most of the information we were seeking.

We learned, first, that guillemots move very little once they are established on a breeding site. The bird sticks to its own square foot of ledge, and the same individual turns up on the same ledge from one year to the next. No marked bird on the stack of rock off the coast moved over to the mainland quite close by. In short, the colonies are well isolated. Secondly, we found that the turnover of the population in a colony is slow. A guillemot, once it has survived to breeding age, has a long expectation of life. Young birds replace the older birds only slowly, for they suffer a heavy mortality during the early years before they have won a place on the ledge. The result is that any significant change in the ratio of bridled to nonbridled birds in a colony cannot take place very rapidly: over the eight years of our intensive study we found only random fluctuations in the ratio. This means that it will probably take several decades to see a real shift in the ratios.

Birds admittedly have many drawbacks as subjects for the study of evolution in progress. Their succession of generations is slow compared with that of invertebrates; many of them are difficult to acclimatize to captivity, where their inheritance might be studied conveniently. But, to look at the other side of the coin, birds are adaptable to a broad range of environmental differences, and so can give us a sweeping picture of geographical variation.

This kind of work also has another felicitous feature. A tremendous amount of amateur enthusiasm can be harnessed to it in a cooperative way. In the modern world the amateur naturalist no longer dominates the research scene as he did up to the last century. He no longer has abundant leisure, for one thing. But he still has unbounded zeal, and, in bits and pieces, can contribute what amounts in the aggregate to a great deal of time in field work. Amateur naturalists can, therefore, act as a tremendous extension of the eyes and ears of professional investigators—a function which they are usually only too glad to perform. The field of population genetics and of systematics in the broad sense is peculiarly susceptible to attack by the teamwork of professionals and amateurs. Supported by such a combination, the investigation of the patterns of life on our planet may become one of the most vigorous growing points in biology.

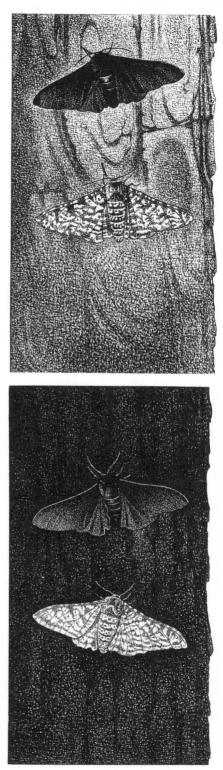

PEPPERED MOTH has two phases: normal and dark. In the upper drawing the two phases are shown on a relatively light tree trunk in the country; under these conditions the dark phase is the more visible to predators, and the light phase tends to survive. In the lower drawing the two phases are shown on a soot-darkened tree trunk in the city; in cities the dark mutant prevails because this form is fundamentally more viable in the absence of predators.

V

BEHAVIOR

BEHAVIOR

V

INTRODUCTION

Ornithologists are often asked if birds think and if they must be taught to fly, sing, eat, and mate. Under one guise or another, psychologists have been arguing for generations whether "nature" (e.g., heredity) or "nurture" (e.g., environment and experience) determine behavior—that is, the things an animal does to itself, others, and its environment. The truth seems to be somewhere between the two poles; birds have less spontaneous behavior than a mammal like man, but they have more than some behaviorists had previously suspected.

Each kind of activity (i.e., defense, feeding, courting and reproduction, sleep, body care) has both innate (hereditary) and modifiable (learned). components. Innate patterns of behavior are those we loosely call "instinctive"; they are inherited, often species-specific, stereotyped patterns of behavior elicited by simple stimuli known as releasers. Such signal-response combinations function without "thought" as we know it; the animal responds as if its behavior were a complicated reflex. Many of the complicated courting rituals of some birds probably proceed by a sequence of releasers, one partner evoking a response from the other as the reproductive behavior of the pair becomes synchronized. Even though the activities are complex, they are programmed, and not spontaneous. For example, as Carl Welty has pointed out in his textbook *The Life of Birds,* a goose will continue to roll an imaginary egg back to the nest with its lower mandible after the real one has been snatched away midway in the journey.

Learned behavior encompasses activities that are modified through experience. Few activities are wholly one or the other. Examples of innate behavior separate from any "learning" are the motions used by a bird to break out of its shell and the cessation of peeping of unhatched grouse in response to a warning call from their mother. An example of learning is the recently acquired ability of titmice and other birds in the British Isles to open and drink milk from bottles left at the door. Since 1921, over 11 species have developed the habit, learning how to remove paper, cardboard, and metal foil tops from the bottles.

In the previous section, the article "Visual Isolation in Gulls" discussed how markings on the heads of gulls help to keep the species apart at breeding time. Another function of such colored areas on the head or patterns in the mouth are as cues for the feeding of baby birds. The first article in this section ("How an Instinct is Learned"), by Jack P. Hailman, explores how these and other phases of feeding behavior of gulls are modified by experience after hatching.

The ritual nature of many of the visual cues used by birds—the fact that the responses are programmed—makes those birds vulnerable to exploitation by imposters. Mimicry is used by several bird groups, such as cuckoos and weaverbirds, to permit them to lay their eggs in the nests of others, where they are successfully hatched and raised by foster parents, often to the detriment of their own offspring. The article by Jürgen Nicolai ("Mimicry in Parasitic Birds") discusses a group of birds in Africa, the widowbirds or wydahs, related to weaverbirds. These birds have evolved remarkable specializations of feature and behavior in their mimicry of the finches whose nests they parasitize.

Another group of birds, the megapodes (the name refers to their large feet) of Australia and New Guinea, have developed perhaps an even more remarkable adaptation. They incubate their eggs in mounds and pits of rotting vegetation, replacing the heat from their bodies with that produced by bacterial decomposition of organic matter. H. J. Frith ("Incubator Birds") reports on their behavioral specializations and their ability to detect and adjust the temperatures of the incubators they construct.

The observation that newly hatched goslings would follow him rather than their mother if he was the first creature they saw after hatching led Konrad Lorenz to propose the existence of a psychological process in which an animal rapidly and permanently acquires an attachment to its parents. This "imprinting" has been considered a form of learning, and many studies of it have been done under controlled laboratory conditions. The third article in this section ("Imprinting in a Natural Laboratory"), by Eckhard H. Hess, describes how the author sets about studying the phenomenon under natural conditions.

A "territory" is any area that is defended by a bird against either sex of its own or another species. The concept has been one of the unifying ideas in ornithology since its development by English businessman and ornithologist H. Eliot Howard over 50 years ago. Defense of a territory by a bird may serve many ends: for example; it is an important part of the courtship behavior and pairing of many birds; it helps to regulate the population density of some species in an area, and it reduces losses of birds to predators.

Several kinds of territoriality are exhibited by birds (see Table 1). The most

TABLE 1.   KINDS OF TERRITORIES AND EXAMPLES OF BIRDS THAT ESTABLISH AND DEFEND THEM.

Mating, Nesting, and Feeding	Mating and Nesting	Mating only	Nesting only
thrushes	grebes	Prairie chicken	pelicans
sparrows	swans	grouse	penguins
warblers	finches	birds of Paradise	gulls
woodpeckers	Red-Winged	Hummingbirds	terns
meadowlarks	Blackbird		herons
cardinals	Yellow-Headed		doves
	Blackbird		cormorants
	Willet		

common is the defense of an area for feeding, courting, and nesting. In the majority of passerine birds, the males arrive at the breeding ground several weeks before the females. They then vie for possession of territories, singing loudly and scrimmaging with the males at the periphery of the land they have occupied. The area defended may be an acre for a bird the size of a sparrow or warbler. The territory may even be one the bird has held in the preceding season. The battles that occur are often rituals in which neither party is severely injured. However, the possibility of a more serious conflict is always present. When a stuffed bird is placed in the territory of an American Robin, the live bird continues to attack the dummy until it is torn apart. The behavior is stereotyped, elicited by color and shape, and not by the recognition by one bird of the presence of another living creature.

When the females arrive, each selects a male (or territory—the one goes with the other), and courtship, mating, nest building, and the rest of the activities involved in raising a family take place within the confines of the defended area. Much of the singing and dashing about of birds in the springtime is part of their territorial defense.

The territory defended by the male or the mated pair need not be used for every purpose associated with raising a family. Some birds, like the Red-winged Blackbird, feed communally, but jealously defend their mating and nesting sites. Colonial sea birds that nest on cliffs defend rather small areas. In crowded colonies, the nesting area may be defined by the distance that a sitting bird can reach out and jab with its bill. The nests of the Slender-billed Shearwater may be as close as nine per square meter; the nests of Brown Pelicans may be as close as two per square meter.

Polygamous birds, like the Prairie Chicken, defend only a mating site within a special display ground, or lek, where they call and posture for the benefit of the females. Most males never mate; only a favored few breed with the females that visit the mating ground. An elaborate system of courtship is described in the article by R. Haven Wiley ("The Lek Mating System of the Sage Grouse"), who has studied how the polygamous groups are established and maintained.

Strictly speaking, ecosystems themselves do not evolve. The plants and animals that compose them are the subjects of natural selection. Nevertheless, the interactions between life forms are important factors in the evolutionary process, and the outcome of these are communities—intricately related groups of plants and animals. The last article in this section ("Ecological Chemistry") by Lincoln Pierson Brower, considers the behavior of birds as part of an ecosystem. It deals with a subtle example of toxicity and mimicry in a food chain of plant, predator, and prey. Cardiac glycosides in milkweed are ingested by larva of the Monarch Butterfly, making them unpalatable to Blue Jays and conditioning the bird against eating them and other butterflies, such as the viceroy, that resemble the monarch.

REFERENCE

Welty, J. C. *The Life of Birds* (2nd ed.). Saunders, Philadelphia, 1975.

12

How an Instinct Is Learned

by Jack P. Hailman
December 1969

*A study of the feeding behavior of sea gull chicks
indicates that an instinct is not fully developed at
birth. Its normal development is strongly affected
by the chick's experience*

The term "instinct," as it is often applied to animal and human behavior, refers to a fairly complex, stereotyped pattern of activity that is common to the species and is inherited and unlearned. Yet braking an automobile and swinging a baseball bat are complex, stereotyped behavioral patterns that can be observed in many members of the human species, and these patterns certainly cannot be acquired without experience. Perhaps stereotyped behavior patterns of animals also require subtle forms of experience for development. In other words, perhaps instincts are at least partly learned.

In order to investigate this possibility, I chose a typical animal instinct for study: the feeding behavior of sea gull chicks. My colleagues and I have observed the animals in their natural environment and in the laboratory, where we have conducted a number of experiments designed to elucidate the development of the feeding behavior. Our conclusion is that this particular pattern of behavior requires a considerable amount of experience if it is to develop normally. Moreover, the study strongly suggests that other instincts involve a component of learning.

Sitting quietly in a blind near the nest of a common laughing gull, which breeds on coastal marsh islands in eastern North America, one can watch the feeding of the chicks. The parent lowers its head and points its beak downward in front of a week-old chick. If some time has passed since the last feeding, the chick will aim a complexly coordinated pecking motion at the bill of the parent, grasping the bill and stroking it downward. After repeated pecking the parent regurgitates partly digested food. The pecking motion of the chick is thus seen to be a form of begging for food. If one watches further, one sees the chick peck at the food, tearing pieces away and swallowing them. Pecking is therefore also a feeding action. When the chick and the one or two other chicks in the nest have had their fill, the parent picks up the remaining food and swallows it.

Further observation reveals several intricacies in the interaction of the parent and the chicks. If the parent fails to elicit pecking by merely pointing its bill downward in front of the chicks, it may swing its beak gently from side to side. Such a motion usually stimulates pecking. After the parent has regurgitated food onto the floor of the nest it waits for the chicks to feed. If they do not, the parent lowers its beak again and appears to point at the food. This action is likely to stimulate pecking. If it fails, the parent picks up the food in its mandibles and holds it in front of a chick. If this action elicits pecking, the parent drops the food again so that the chick can eat it readily.

We find in this apparently simple pecking behavior a number of questions concerning the possible role of experience in the development of begging. How does the chick come to stroke the parent's bill with its begging peck and to tear at the food with its feeding peck when the two movements are basically so similar? Why does the chick rotate its head sideways in the begging peck but not in the feeding peck? Does the chick require practice to perfect its aim and coordination? How does the chick come to peck when it is hungry and not peck when it is sated? Why does the chick not peck at the parent's red legs or other objects in its environment? How does the chick recognize food?

In order to answer these and many other questions our group studied chicks experimentally from the time of hatching through the first week of life. By that time the feeding behavior is well established. Moreover, by restricting the study to a short period after hatching we could be sure of controlling several of the elements of development in order to assess their contribution to the behavior. As is often the case, the study raised more questions than it answered, but it also provided a good deal of information.

Let us consider first the accuracy of the pecking aim. In order to investigate this matter we painted diagrammatic pictures of parent gulls on small cards [*see top illustration on page 127*]. The card in use was mounted on a pivoting rod that could be moved horizontally back and forth in front of a chick. We collected eggs in the field and hatched them in a dark incubator so that the chicks would not have received any visual stimuli before the test. Each chick was confronted with the two-dimensional model of the parent during the day of hatching and was allowed to make about a dozen pecks at the moving model. Each peck was marked on the card with a penciled dot.

Having made sure that the chick could be identified later, we put it in a nest in the field in exchange for a pipping egg (one that was almost ready to hatch). The chick thus began to experience normal rearing by its foster parents. On the first, third and fifth day after hatching we went to the nesting area and gathered up half of the chicks for further tests, and on the second, fourth and sixth day we tested the others. On each gathering day a chick was tested again on the model and then put back in the nest.

The tests showed that on the average only a third of the pecks by a newly hatched chick strike the model. On the first day after hatching more than half of the pecks are accurate, and by two days after hatching the accuracy reaches a steady level of more than 75 percent.

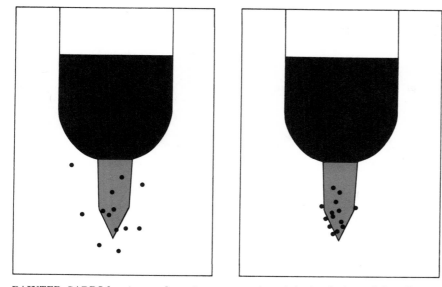

PAINTED CARDS bearing a schematic representation of the head of an adult gull were presented to chicks to test their pecking accuracy. Pecks are identified by dots. At left is the erratic record of a newborn chick, at right what the same chick did two days later.

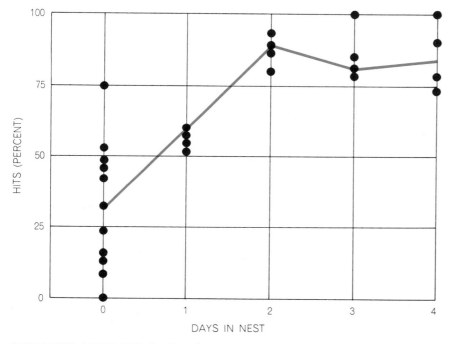

IMPROVING ACCURACY of pecking by an experimental group of chicks is charted. Each circle represents the record of one chick. After testing on cards at the time of hatching, the chicks were put into nests and fed by adult gulls. Half of the group was tested on the cards again on the first and third day and the other half on the second and fourth day. Fewer chicks are represented on those days than on the day of birth because it was not always possible to find each chick. The colored line shows the median accuracy for the chicks tested.

The record of a typical chick shows that the strokes become much more closely grouped and that in particular the horizontal error is greatly reduced.

How does this rapid increase in accuracy come about? In order to find out we designed a more extensive experiment involving the use as controls of two groups of chicks reared in the wild. Three experimental groups were reared in dark brooders so that they would not have any visually coordinated experience in pecking. One experimental group was force-fed in the brooder. A second group received no food for two days; the chicks lived on their ample reserves of yolk. The members of the third group did not hatch normally; instead the experimenter broke open the egg as soon as pipping started, took the chick out and placed it in an incubator. The reason for this procedure was to see if the movements of normal hatching had any effect on the accuracy of pecking.

On various days after hatching the chicks of all groups were photographed pecking at the stuffed head of an adult laughing gull. From the films we could ascertain the percentage of accurate pecks. Chicks of all five groups demonstrated an increasing accuracy with age, but only in the two control groups did the figure reach the normal level of more than 75 percent hits. The denial of the hatching experience had no effect on accuracy, but the denial of visual experience after hatching had a strong effect.

The most conservative interpretation of these results is that visual experience is necessary for the development of full accuracy in pecking but that a certain amount of improvement in accuracy is achieved without experience. Perhaps this amount results from improved steadiness of stance. Here again an element of experience may enter in, since the improvement in stance can most plausibly be attributed to the chick's practice in standing in the dark incubator.

How does the chick come to position itself at the correct distance to strike the bill or the model accurately? Our observations of newly hatched chicks suggest that a self-regulating form of behavior based on depth perception is at work. If an inexperienced chick is too close to the target at first, its pecking thrust against the bill or model is so strong that the chick is thrown backward as much as an inch. If the chick starts out too far from the target, the pecking thrust misses and the chick falls forward as much as two inches. Older chicks rarely make such gross errors, suggesting that the experience of overshots and undershots has helped the chick learn to adjust its distance.

It has often been implied that hunger is a learned motivation. Our experiments suggest that hunger has at least an unlearned basis from which to develop further. Several experiments showed that, as one might expect, if chicks were fed to satiation and tested with models at various times after feeding, the pecking rate increased with time since feeding. The same pattern appeared, however, with chicks we gave no opportunity to "learn" hunger. Chicks hatched and reared in dark incubators were force-fed to satiation when they were between 24 and 48 hours old and then were tested in light on models. At one hour after feeding they pecked at a mean rate of 6.2 pecks per two minutes and at two hours at 10.2 pecks, which is a statistically reliable difference.

a

b

c

d

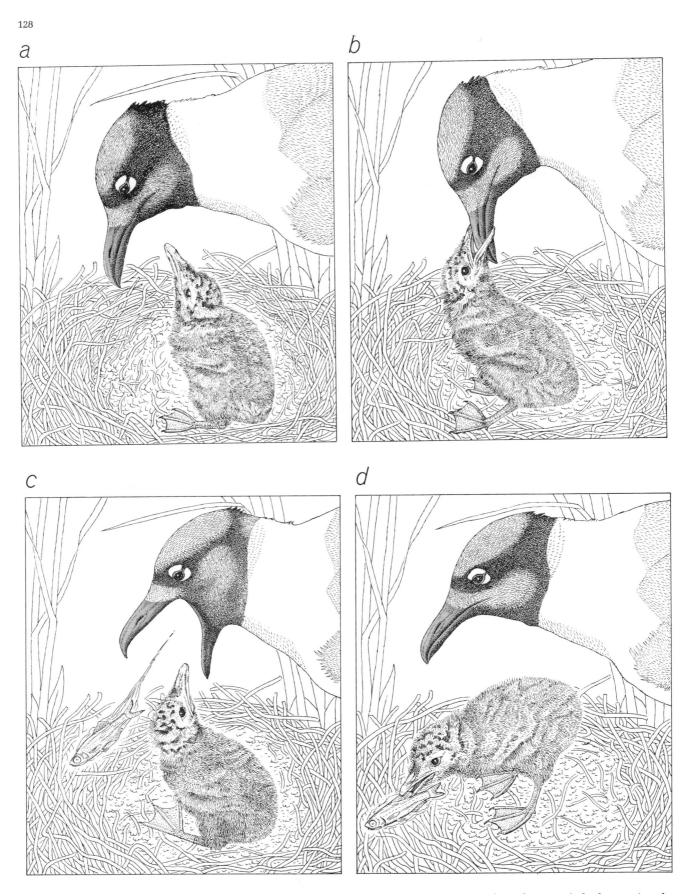

NORMAL FEEDING BEHAVIOR of a laughing gull chick in-cludes two separate but related types of pecking. A chick about three days old, which has largely perfected the feeding pattern, is portrayed. As the parent lowers its head (*a*) the chick aims a high-ly coordinated begging peck at the parent's beak, grasping the beak (*b*) and stroking it downward. Parent then regurgitates part-ly digested food onto the floor of the nest (*c*) and the chick begins to eat it (*d*) with a pecking action that is called the feeding peck.

By means of high-speed motion pictures we analyzed in detail the motor pattern of the begging peck. In a chick several days old the pattern, by then well developed, includes four major components: (1) the opening and subsequent closing of the bill; (2) the motion of the head up and forward toward the beak of the parent and then down and back toward the chick's body; (3) the rotation of the head to the side in anticipation of grasping the parent's vertical beak and then the return rotation to the vertical position, and (4) a slight push upward and forward with the legs [see illustration on page 128]. A frame-by-frame analysis of the motion pictures revealed considerable variation in the synchronization of components from peck to peck of individual chicks and from chick to chick. The variation decreases somewhat with age. Presumably the decrease reflects increasing coordination, although we have not investigated the phenomenon in detail.

Among the interesting points that emerged from the films was the observation that with chicks reared in the wild the anticipatory rotation of the head became more frequent with age. To see what effect visually guided pecking experience had on this change, we analyzed the films of the five groups of chicks used in the experiments on pecking accuracy. The results indicated that chicks reared without pecking experience seldom showed any development of the head-rotation component of pecking. A chick reared in the wild does not show the rotation on the day of hatching but then acquires it and improves it rapidly.

We do not know how experience brings about this development, but the films provide a suggestion. Sometimes when a naïve chick is striking forward with its mandibles spread apart and the parental bill or the model is not exactly vertical, the chick's upper mandible goes to one side of the target and the lower mandible goes to the other side. The thrust of the forward head movement then forcibly rotates the chick's head to the side. Perhaps this is how the rotary movement in anticipation of grasping the parental bill is learned.

One of the most interesting questions about pecking is how the chick recognizes its parent. Observations from a blind show that chicks do peck at objects other than the bill of a parent, including other parts of the parent's body, but that most of the pecks are aimed at the parental bill—increasingly so with age. These observations suggest that the newly hatched chick has only a vague mental picture of the parent and that the picture becomes sharper with age and experience. We investigated the question by making a number of models of heads and beaks [see illustration on next page]. By systematically eliminating or changing parts of the models we could discover the most effective stimulus for pecking. Usually a model was mounted on a rod that could be moved on a pivot in time to a metronome, so that the speed of movement would be known and could be controlled. In each experiment a chick was presented with five models, which were offered in a random order, and the number of pecks (usually per 30 seconds) was recorded.

The first problem was to find the most

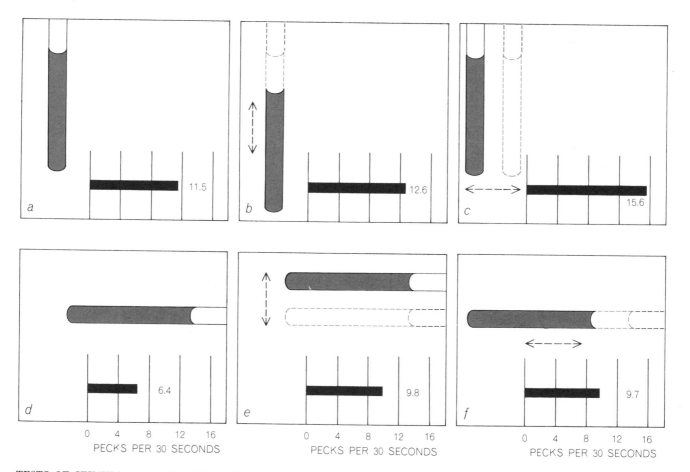

TESTS OF STIMULI were made with wooden dowels approximately the width of an adult gull's beak. The mean number of pecks in 30 seconds by a group of 25 chicks was recorded for (a) a vertical rod held stationary; (b) the same rod moved vertically; (c) the rod moved horizontally; (d) a stationary horizontal rod; (e) same rod moved vertically, and (f) the rod moved horizontally.

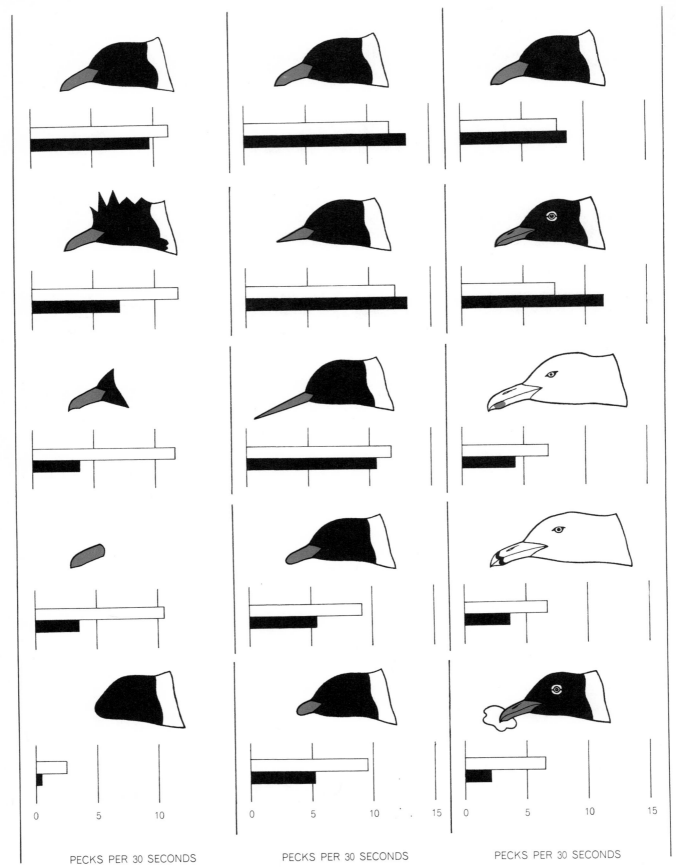

FEATURES OF HEAD that elicit the most pecks were tested with models presented in groups of five to newly hatched chicks (*white bars*) and older chicks (*black bars*). All the chicks were laughing gulls. The group of models in the column at right included models of the herring gull (*third from top*) and the ring-billed gull (*fourth from top*). A model holding food in its bill is also depicted.

effective stimulus for naïve chicks, which had been kept in dark incubators until being tested about 24 hours after hatching. In the first three experiments the naïve chicks responded equally to all five models presented except for the model lacking a bill. These experiments established that newly hatched chicks are responding primarily to features of the parent's bill rather than to features of the head or even to the presence of the head.

One of the first three experiments revealed an unexpected finding: laughing gull chicks do not discriminate between a model of their own parent and a model of an adult herring gull. The adults of these two species are strikingly different in appearance. The laughing gull has a black head with a red bill; the herring gull has a white head and a yellow bill with a red spot on the lower mandible. The laughing gull chicks responded to this red spot on the model.

If laughing gull chicks fail to distinguish their parent from the herring gull, what would herring gull chicks do? In order to answer this question and others we went to a large colony of herring gulls on an island of the Grand Manan archipelago in the Bay of Fundy and tested herring gull chicks with models of both species. The result was the same: newly hatched chicks failed to discriminate between the two species in their pecking. This result suggested that the chicks of both species were responding to simple features of form and movement provided by the red bill of the laughing gull or the red spot of the herring gull.

Even though the optimum stimulus for eliciting pecks is evidently a simple one, it apparently has features that enable the chick to distinguish it from other simple forms in its environment, such as the red leg of a parent or a blade of grass, because pecks are rarely aimed at such targets. We investigated the matter with simple dowel rods made of wood and painted red. A rod was presented to a chick both vertically and horizontally, and in each orientation it was held stationary, moved vertically and moved horizontally. Every vertical stimulus received higher peck rates than every horizontal one, but the most effective vertical rod was the one moved horizontally. This result accords well with the natural situation in which the parent's vertical bill is likely to be moved horizontally in front of the chick.

Further analysis of the results showed that the vertically moved vertical rod elicited no more pecks than the stationary vertical rod. In addition, both horizontal and vertical movement of the horizontal rod were equally effective and curiously were more effective than the stationary horizontal rod. The most cautious interpretation of these results is that two kinds of movement are instrumental in eliciting pecks from the newly hatched laughing gull chick. The first is horizontal movement, and the second is movement across the long axis of the rod. This interpretation explains why a vertical rod moved vertically is no more effective than a stationary vertical rod, since both stimuli lack both horizontal movement and movement across an axis. With a horizontal rod, however, vertical movement is across the long axis and therefore is as effective as horizontal movement (along the axis), and each kind of movement is better than no movement.

The next step was to try various speeds of movement of a vertical rod. We used five different speeds with three diameters of rod. The results showed that a width of about eight millimeters was preferred, independent of the rate at which the rod was moved, and that a speed of movement of 12 centimeters per second was chosen over higher and lower speeds regardless of the width. These results demonstrate well the exactness of the match that evolution has brought about between stimulus and responsiveness. The parent's beak measures 10.6 millimeters from front to back and 3.1 millimeters laterally; the mean width of beak seen by the chick is thus about eight millimeters. Furthermore, the horizontal soliciting movement of the parent's beak was calculated from high-speed motion pictures made at the nest and was found to average 14.5 centimeters per second.

A recent experiment has added another item to this picture of a chick's ideal stimulus. Vertical rods projecting from above the chick's eye level are much preferred to those that come from below. The preference is also shown for oblique objects. Such a choice would reduce the chick's responsiveness to the parent's legs, which of course project from the ground and join the parent's body at just about the chick's eye level.

We now understood, at least roughly, how the newly hatched chick discriminates between its parent's beak and other objects in its environment. The question we addressed next was whether or not this perception changes during the first few days of life. We presented the same three series of five simple cardboard models each to week-old chicks and found a large difference between those results and the results with newly hatched chicks. Older chicks were sensitive to small differences in shape and detail of the head and beak. Moreover, the older chicks discriminated readily between their laughing gull parent and the model of the herring gull. To see if older herring gull chicks also came to prefer their own parent, we marked individual chicks and tested them on about the fourth day of life and about the seventh. The longer they had been in the nest, the greater their response to the model of their own parent and the less to the model of the laughing gull.

Was this change in perception due to conditioning experience with the parent that feeds the chick? To find out we worked with herring gull chicks that had been reared in an incubator. We divided them into three groups. If a chick was in the first group, it was fed a small amount of food when it delivered several pecks to a model of a laughing gull; if it was in the second group, it was fed for pecking at a model of its own species. The third group, which served as a control, was fed without first pecking at any model. At the end of two days of training each group was responding more, in discrimination tests without a reward of food, to the model on which it had been trained. Although the experiment is preliminary, it suggests that conditioning with a reward of food could account for the changes seen in wild chicks.

In sum, our findings indicate that the newly hatched chick responds best to a very simple stimulus situation. Although the experimenter can construct a model that is even more effective than the parent, the characteristics of the parent match the chick's ideal more closely than any other object in the environment. As a chick is fed by its parents, however, it develops a much more specific mental picture of the parent. Chicks a week old peck only at models that closely resemble the parent.

Our results did not appear consistent with certain earlier findings of the ethologists Nikolaas Tinbergen and A. C. Perdeck, who studied the herring gull. They found that if the red spot on the beak of the parent gull was moved to the forehead of a model, the model received few pecks. Since all the stimulus elements were thought to be the same in the two models, merely arranged differently, this classic experiment has been interpreted as showing the highly configural nature of the newly hatched herring gull's perception of the parent.

We thought the question of whether or not all the stimulus elements are in

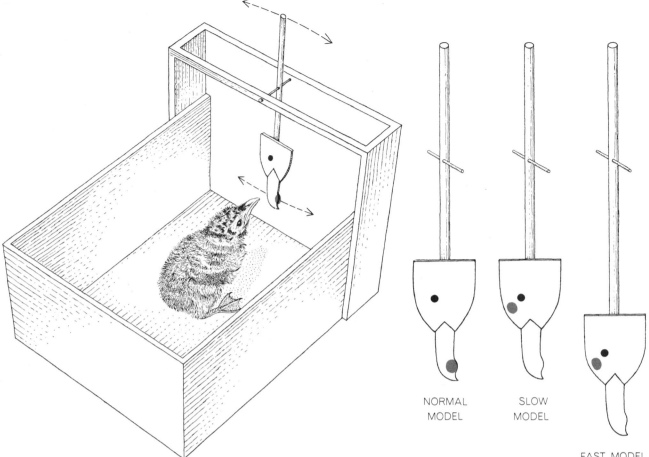

LABORATORY APPARATUS was designed to test the effect of three models of the herring gull on the pecking rate of chicks. The normal model had the gull's red spot in its natural position on the beak. The "slow" model had the spot on the forehead; the spot moved more slowly than the one on the "fast" model when it was swung back and forth because it was closer to the pivot point.

NORMAL MODEL

SLOW MODEL

FAST MODEL

fact the same needed investigation. The Tinbergen-Perdeck models were hand-held, so that when the model was moved in a pendulum-like manner with the hand as the pivot point, the spot on the forehead moved more slowly than the spot on the beak and through a shorter arc. Moreover, a chick had to stretch higher to peck at the forehead spot.

For these reasons we repeated the Tinbergen-Perdeck experiment, adding a third model. It was a forehead-spot model mounted on a rod in such a way that the forehead spot was the same distance from the pivot point as the bill spot was in the other model [*see illustration above*]. In addition our apparatus had a floor of adjustable height so that the chick's eye could always be positioned level with the red spot, whether the spot was on the bill or on the forehead. We called our third model the "fast" forehead-spot model, because the spot on it moved faster than the one on the "slow" Tinbergen-Perdeck model. If our hypothesis about movement were correct, the new, fast forehead-spot model should

be as effective as the bill-spot model.

The results were unequivocal. Newly hatched chicks responded as readily to the fast forehead-spot model as to the conventional model with the spot on the bill. Now we tested the same chicks after they had had three days in the nest and then seven days. This test showed that, as we had now come to expect, the bill-spot model improved steadily in relation to both the old and the new version of the forehead-spot model.

The classical interpretation of the Tinbergen-Perdeck experiment was that it demonstrated the existence of an innate releasing mechanism, which was conceived to be an unlearned perceptual mechanism that is activated by highly configural stimuli. Our experiment shows the gull chick's perception to be activated by a less configural simple shape when it is unlearned and by a highly configural shape when it is learned. The experiment suggests the need for reinvestigation of other results thought to be examples of innate releasing mechanisms.

The results also suggest the need for reinterpretation of another widely held concept in the behavioral sciences: classical conditioning. In the familiar example represented by the experiments of Ivan Pavlov an animal is presented with a new conditioning stimulus before it receives or just as it receives the usual stimulus that elicits the response of interest. After a number of these paired presentations the animal comes to respond to the conditioned stimulus alone. Pavlov's classic experiment involved ringing a bell before a dog was exposed to the smell of food; in time the dog would salivate merely in response to the bell.

Psychologists have long wondered how useful this cross-modal conditioning is to animals in their ordinary activities. Why should such a learning capability be evolved when it seems to be so little used under normal conditions? Our results suggest an answer worthy of further testing. As the chick develops its perceptual preference it is responding to simple features of the parent (the unconditioned stimuli) but is being presented simultaneously with all the complexities of the parental head (the conditioned stimulus). As a result of feeding, the chick comes to demand the more subtle features of the stimulus before it will peck.

This developmental process, which I have termed "perceptual sharpening," can be distinguished from the classical conditioning of laboratory experiments by the fact that the conditioned and unconditioned stimuli are physically identical. Perhaps the capability for classical conditioning has evolved primarily as a mechanism for perceptual sharpening, and the traditional experiments involving classical conditioning are in fact dealing with what is essentially an artifact of perceptual sharpening. At this stage my argument is no more than a hypothesis.

Although we have studied many more aspects of pecking that cannot be related briefly here, one should be mentioned: the recognition of food. Do newly hatched chicks recognize food when they encounter it? To find out, we placed food in dishes in the four corners of a small box and watched incubator-reared herring gull chicks find their first meal. The number of seconds taken to find food was inversely related to the pecking rate. This is the result to be expected if chicks are finding the food solely by trial and error.

If the chicks are allowed to feed until satiated and are then removed from the box until they are hungry again, they find food in the box much more quickly. The time required reaches a minimum by the third trial. This change cannot be attributed to an increase in the pecking rate, since the pecking rates in the second and subsequent trials are only slightly higher than in the first trial. The experiment shows that chicks can learn rapidly to identify food, or at least its location.

If the newly hatched chick does not initially recognize food, must it rely on trial-and-error searching to get its first bite and thereby initiate the rapid learning? Observation and experiment show that several mechanisms exist to help accelerate the first discovery of food. Recall that if a chick does not peck at food, the parent picks the food up in its beak. Quite often, in first feedings I have seen from a blind, the chick continues to peck at the parent's beak after the parent has regurgitated food onto the floor of the nest. Eventually the parent picks the food up and the chick strikes it during a peck at the bill. The observation suggests that the poor pecking accuracy of newly hatched chicks may be adaptive, ensuring that the chick at least occasionally misses the parent's bill and strikes the food instead.

Another mechanism to assist the rapid learning of what food is involves the siblings in the nest. A chick will often peck at the white bill tip of another chick. In an ordinary clutch of three eggs the chicks hatch at intervals of about 12 hours, so that the older chicks have already been fed by the time a younger one appears. If a younger chick pecks at the bill of an older one while the older one is pecking at food, which it now recognizes, the younger chick's peck will probably also strike the food. Observation from a blind has shown that the first bite of food does come about in this way at times.

We tested the recognition of food with three groups of incubator-reared herring gull chicks. In one control group each chick was put alone into the small box with food; each chick in the two experimental groups had a companion. In one group the companion was equally naïve about food, and in the other group the companion had eaten earlier in the box. The results showed that the solitary chicks took the longest time to find food. The chicks with equally naïve companions took the next-longest time, and the

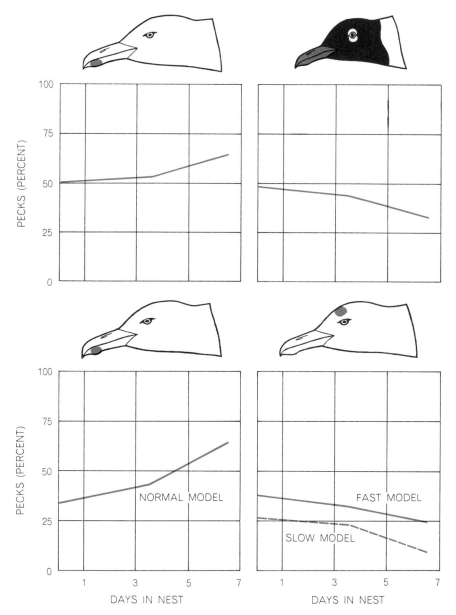

RECORD OF RESPONSES by herring gull chicks to various models shows changes as the chicks grow older. The model at top left is of a herring gull's head; the one at top right is of a laughing gull's. At bottom are two models of the herring gull; the one at left has the red spot in its normal place, and in the one at right it is on the forehead of the model.

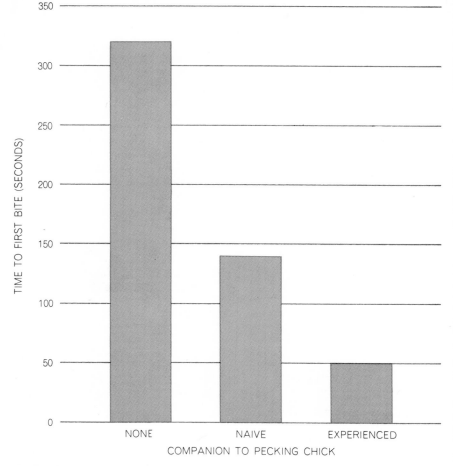

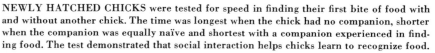

COMPANION TO PECKING CHICK

NEWLY HATCHED CHICKS were tested for speed in finding their first bite of food with and without another chick. The time was longest when the chick had no companion, shorter when the companion was equally naïve and shortest with a companion experienced in finding food. The test demonstrated that social interaction helps chicks learn to recognize food.

chicks with experienced companions took the least time [*see illustration above*].

These differences cannot be accounted for merely on the basis of increased exploratory trial-and-error pecking by the newly hatched chicks with companions, because the companion's bill actually diverted pecks from exploration. The naïve companion did cause the newly hatched chick to move about more in the box and

therefore to find food more quickly than the solitary chicks did. The experienced companion must have had a further effect, inasmuch as each naïve chick in this group first discovered food when it was pecking at the bill of its companion while the companion was pecking at food.

We can now summarize the developmental picture yielded by our investigation. The newly hatched gull chick begins life with a clumsily coordinated, poorly aimed peck motivated by hunger and elicited by simple stimulus properties of shape and movement provided only by a parent or sibling. The chick cannot recognize food, but by aiming at the bills of its relatives and missing it strikes food and rapidly learns to recognize it. As a result of the reward embodied in the food, the chick comes to learn the visual characteristics of the parent. Through practice in pecking its aim and depth perception improve steadily. The chick also learns to rotate its head when begging from the parent, and thus its begging peck and feeding peck become differentiated.

The picture strongly suggests that the normal development of other instincts entails a component of learning. It is necessary only that the learning process be highly alike in all members of the species for a stereotyped, species-common behavioral pattern to emerge. The example of the gulls also shows clearly that behavior cannot meaningfully be separated into unlearned and learned components, nor can a certain percentage of the behavior be attributed to learning. Behavioral development is a mosaic created by continuing interaction of the developing organism and its environment.

Mimicry in Parasitic Birds

13

by Jürgen Nicolai
October 1974

Various species of birds lay their eggs in the nest of another bird, which then incubates the eggs and feeds the young. The widow birds of Africa achieve this result by some remarkable feats of mimicry

The number of eggs a female animal produces is inversely proportional to the probability that the egg will give rise to a female that produces more eggs. All invertebrate animals and most lower vertebrates need to broadcast eggs by the hundreds and thousands in order to ensure the existence of subsequent generations. The number of eggs laid by a bird, although much smaller, also reflects the probability of reproductive success. Consider the greatest of ocean birds, the wandering albatross. It occupies breeding grounds on isolated islands of the Southern Hemisphere where it is completely undisturbed, and the female albatross lays a single egg every other year. In contrast, most species of European tits and both species of goldcrests respond to the stresses of severe winters and numerous predators by laying two yearly clutches of eggs, each numbering between eight and 12.

Any bird that is subject to severe environmental stress or predation pressure is at a reproductive disadvantage. It must incubate its eggs with the heat of its own body, and so the eggs must be kept all in one place, usually in a nest. A predator therefore needs to search out only a single target. One group of birds, the turkeylike megapods of Australasia and the Pacific, has surmounted this handicap by an ingenious stratagem. Instead of building nests they pile up mounds of plant material where they bury their eggs to be incubated by the warmth of plant decay [see "Incubator Birds," by H. J. Frith, beginning on page 142]. Still other bird species have discovered another solution to the problem. They deposit their eggs, one at a time, in the nest of another species; the eggs are then incubated and the hatchlings raised by the host.

Birds that practice this kind of parasitic parenthood are found around the world. Among them are various members of the cosmopolitan family of cuckoos, some species of American cowbirds, a black-headed duck (*Heteronetta atricapilla*) in South America, all species of honey guides and certain weaverbirds in Africa. I have investigated the behavior of this last group, observing in particular the several species of a subfamily, the Viduinae, within the family of weaverbirds. The birds in this subfamily are commonly called widow birds. My work has been conducted both in the field and in our laboratory at the Max Planck Institute for Behavioral Physiology in Seewiesen.

Although a parasitic bird has overcome the disadvantage of putting all its eggs in one nest, the very nature of its solution to the problem introduces certain other difficulties. For one thing, if parasitic parenthood is to be successful, the parasite's reproductive cycle must be synchronized with the cycle of the host species. For another, it would be fatal if the host rejected either the parasite's egg or the hatchling that emerged from it. With respect to the egg a strategy of mimicry has evolved. For example, parasitic cuckoos lay eggs with markings that closely resemble those of the host's eggs. Widow-bird eggs are unmarked, as are their host's; they differ from the eggs of the host species only slightly in size and shape.

With respect to the acceptance of the hatchling the parasite strategies that have evolved are various. Several species of cowbirds punch tiny holes in the host's eggs before depositing their own, thus ensuring that no host egg ever hatches. An African honey-guide hatchling emerges from its egg armed with formidable hooks at the tip of its beak; its host's offspring are all soon fatally wounded, leaving the parasite to consume all the food the host provides. Some cuckoo nestlings simply nudge their foster siblings out of the nest during the first few days of life; others mature so much more rapidly than their nestmates that the foster siblings' development is inhibited and they die prematurely.

In the long run, of course, strategies that result in the death of the host's young are unproductive. The parasitic parent needs to use the nests of several host pairs each year and a dwindling host population means fewer nests. The widow birds have evolved a strategy that circumvents this problem; like the egg strategy, it is imitative. Each widowbird nestling is indistinguishable from its host's nestlings in size, in color and markings, in gesture and in call. Thus the intruders can grow up among their alien nestmates with no risk of being rejected by their foster parents. Such a strategy ensures that the numbers of the host population do not diminish.

It seems surprising that the widow birds should have evolved this particular strategy. Their chosen hosts—various species of finches, the entire family Estrildidae—are noted for having mouths that are colored and marked in a complex and conspicuous manner [see *illustration on page 136*]. No two of the 125 species of estrildid finches have identical mouth markings. The color of the palate may be whitish, red, yellow or bluish. The palate markings may form a three-spot pattern or a five-spot pattern or may be only a fine horseshoe-shaped line; the spots themselves may be black or violet. Moreover, the fledglings' gape papillae vary in shape and color. They may be ivory white, cornflower

136

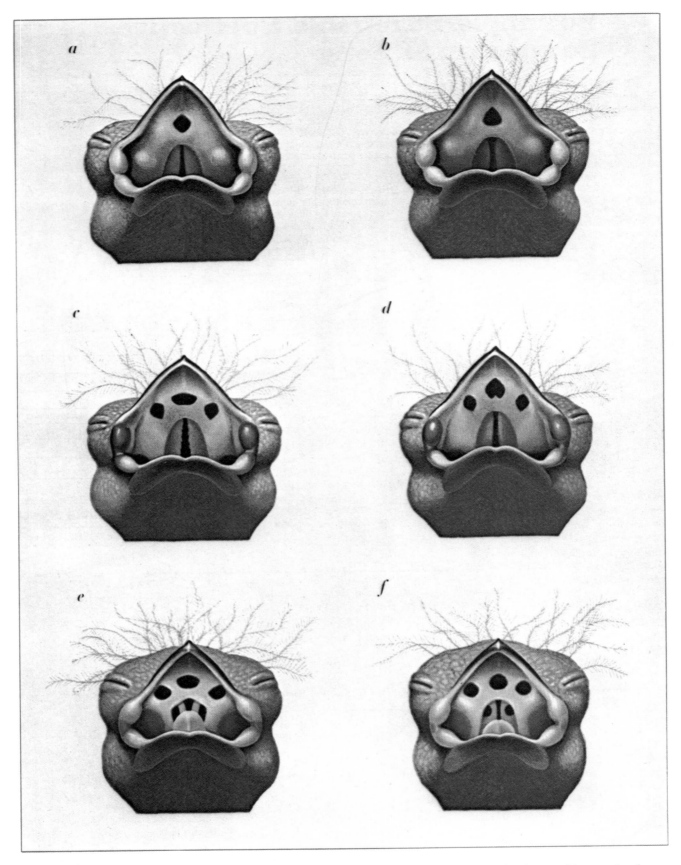

MOUTH MARKINGS of host nestlings, which stimulate the host parents' feeding response, are mimicked in detail by all the parasitic species of African widow birds. Shown here are the markings of a host-species nestling, the melba finch (*a*), and its parasitic sib-ling, the paradise widow bird (*b*), of a second host species, the purple grenadier (*c*), and its parasite, the straw-tailed widow bird (*d*), and of a third host-parasite pair, Jameson's fire finch (*e*) and the purple combassou (*f*). Many other mimicries of the type are known.

blue, yellow or faintly violet, and they may appear as simple thickenings or resemble small pearl-shaped warts.

In parallel with these elaborate mouth markings there has evolved among the estrildid finches a precise, genetically based "knowledge" of species-specific patterns and stimulus-receiving mechanisms that are correspondingly selective. By the simple experimental method of placing nestlings of one finch species in the nest of other species my colleagues and I have demonstrated that the parent birds will feed only the nestlings that display the appropriate species-specific markings. Even minor deviations in pattern are noted by the parent birds, and the deviants are ruthlessly weeded out by starvation.

A parasite nestling constantly interacts with its foster parents from the time of its emergence until it leaves the nest. The host birds are thus an essential part of the parasite's environment. The host sets a series of examples that instructs the parasite with respect to such matters as environmental standards and feeding habits. One instance of this process of parallel adaptation is the synchronization of the parasite's and the host's reproductive cycle.

Most species of estrildid finches breed during the rainy season. The finches' gonads begin to swell when, after months of drought, a series of showers brings the vegetation to renewed life. The timing is appropriate because the increase in the food supply that comes with the rainy season makes it easier to feed nestlings. Several finch species begin their breeding activities when the rains start; others do not begin until the middle of the rainy season or toward the end of it. A few species, such as the yellow-winged pytilia and the aurora finch of West Africa, delay their breeding until the dry season, a time when they find feeding conditions appropriate.

In each of these instances the parasitic widow birds synchronize their reproductive cycle with that of their host. One element in the cycle is that when courtship begins, the male widow bird displays a splendid and conspicuous plumage. The molt into breeding plumage occupies a period of four to six weeks. This means that the maturation of the widow bird's gonads, which initiates the molt, actually occurs sometime before the host's gonads mature.

To cite some examples, the paradise widow bird and the straw-tailed widow bird have hosts that breed during the rainy season. That requires the male

PARASITIC ADULTS, the female (*a*) and male (*b*) paradise widow bird, do not in any way mimic the appearance of the foster parents of their young, the female (*c*) and male (*d*) melba finch. The male paradise widow bird is seen in its bright breeding plumage.

widow birds to develop their breeding plumage before the end of the dry season. Similarly, two species of widow bird, the Togo paradise widow bird and the Kongo paradise widow bird, have hosts that breed during the dry season. The male parasites' molt must therefore take place toward the end of the rainy season. Under these circumstances it is clear that the onset of the parasites' reproductive activity cannot simply be triggered by the onset of the hosts'; it is evidently set in motion by some kind of seasonal rhythm. The specific rhythms remain unidentified but one is justified in assuming that, because the rainy and dry seasons follow each other with great regularity in most of Africa, the gonads of rainy-season breeders begin to be stimulated after the passage of a certain length of dry-season time, and vice versa.

Now, in any fine-tuned system of parasitic adaptation one of the greatest potentials for disruption is accidental hybridization between species of parasites that are closely related and coexist in the same area. As far as the widow birds are concerned, any hybrid offspring would display intermediate mouth markings rather than markings that match those of their foster siblings. That in turn means they would be refused food by the host species of both parents. This hazard, with its long-term potential for the extinction of all widow birds, has been avoided by the evolution of a kind of behavior that is unknown among other parasitic birds. In brief, when the male widow bird sings, it includes in its song certain unique finch-species phrases it has learned from its foster parents.

Widow birds are polygamous. At the start of the breeding season a male stakes out a large territory that it defends against potential rivals. Throughout the breeding season the male perches on certain selected trees and bushes in the territory and sings its unique melody. If one compares the songs of various widow-bird species, either by listening or by analyzing sound spectrograms, it soon becomes apparent that the songs of all species have a few phrases in common. For example, they all include harsh chattering sounds; the motif is evidently related to the vocalizations produced by the widow birds' closest relatives, the bishop birds of the subfamily Euplectinae. Since these chatterings appear to represent an ancient genetic heritage, we call them widow-bird phrases.

The major portion of any male widow bird's song consists of quite different vocalizations. Its motifs vary from one

YOUNG PARASITES, unlike adult parasites, closely resemble their host siblings in appearance. Profiles at left show a paradise widow-bird nestling (a) and a melba-finch nestling (b) 13 days after hatching; profiles at right show a straw-tailed widow-bird nestling (c) and a purple-grenadier nestling (d) 15 days old. The young are independent after five weeks.

species to another, and each species-specific repertory perfectly imitates the motifs characteristic of the widow bird's finch host. We therefore call such motifs host phrases. They include the finch's long-distance call, its contact call, its distress and anger calls, its greeting phrases and, of course, its routine song. The parasite's mimicry of this repertory is so exact that it sounds like the finch's to the human ear and looks like it in a spectrogram [see illustration on page 139]. Furthermore, the host finch itself cannot distinguish between the widow bird's imitation and the song of its own species.

Let us examine in detail the song of one widow-bird species. The straw-tailed widow bird of East Africa (Tetraenura fischeri) ranges over the scrub savanna of that region from southern Tanzania northward into Ethiopia and Somalia. The male's breeding plumage is black and yellow and its four conspicuously elongated central tail feathers look like yellowish blades of dry grass. During the breeding season the male perches high in small trees or thornbushes and twitters its song unceasingly from early morning until sunset. The first motif in its repertory is usually the contact call of its finch host, the purple grenadier,

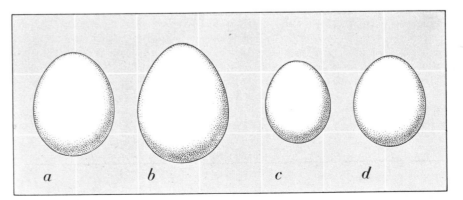

MIMICRY IN THE NEST extends to the size and shape of the egg laid by the parasite. At left is the egg of the melba finch (a) and of the paradise widow bird (b); the parasite's egg is only slightly larger and more rounded than the host's. At right is the egg of another host, the red-billed fire finch (c), and the egg of its parasite, the black-winged combassou (d). As centimeter grid shows, the host and parasite eggs are virtually identical in size and shape.

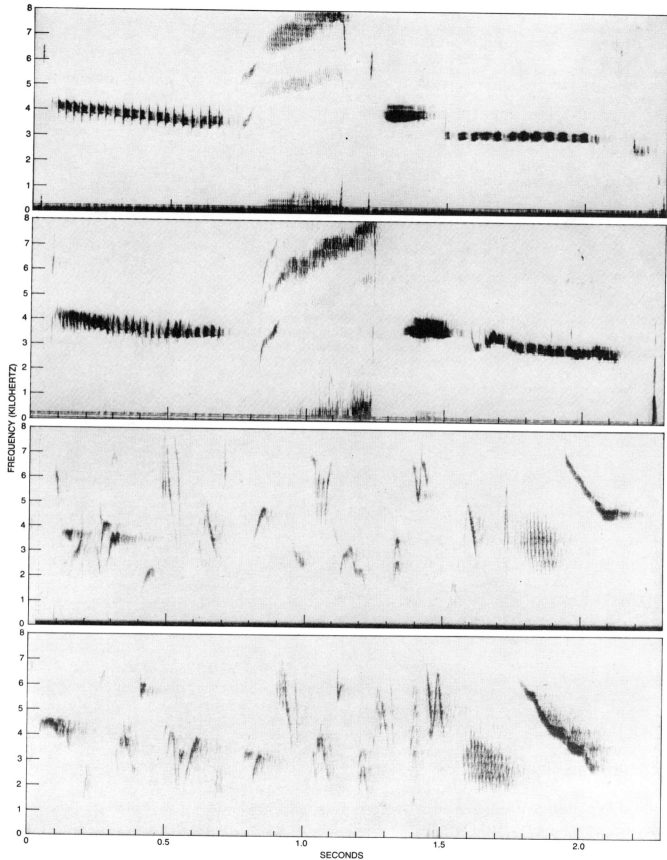

SONG MIMICRY, a meticulous imitation of the host male's call, learned by the parasite male while a juvenile, is demonstrated by these paired sonograms. The top sonogram shows the final seconds of a Damara melba finch's song; the sonogram directly below it is mimicry of this part of the finch's song by a male paradise widow bird. The third sonogram shows a two-second segment of the song of the violet-eared waxbill; the fourth is mimicry of this segment of the song by the waxbill's parasite, the shaft-tailed widow bird.

140

BREEDING PLUMAGE of parasitic widow birds develops during a four-to-six-week period. Seen here are a male straw-tailed widow bird (*a*) and its host, a purple grenadier (*b*), and below them a male purple combassou (*c*) and its host, a Jameson's fire finch (*d*). The parasite's breeding cycle must synchronize with its host's to ensure synchronous egg-laying; in order to grow breeding plumage, however, a parasite must enter its breeding cycle first.

Uraeginthus ianthinogaster; this is a long trill. The mimicked phrase is repeated several times, increasing and decreasing in loudness. It is followed by other elements of the host's repertory. They include the brief "call" phrase used by the male to attract the female, the male's clacking song, a chase call, whispering nest calls and the shrill begging calls that fledglings use; in all, the mimic's repertory includes a total of eight finch motifs. Each mimicked vocalization is separated from the next by an interval, and each lasts the same length of time as the host's. The finch potpourri is interspersed with three different widow-bird phrases that, like the mimicked host melodies, occur in unpredictable sequences. The eight finch motifs give the male straw-tailed widow bird effective command of the entire vocabulary of the purple grenadier.

The same pattern of host-melody mimicry is apparent in almost all other species of widow birds. The shaft-tailed widow bird of South Africa (*Tetraenura regia*) mimics the repertory of its host, the violet-eared waxbill (*Uraeginthus granatinus*). Each of the five species of the paradise widow-bird genus (*Steganura*) copies the host melody of the particular species of the finch genus (*Pytilia*) it parasitizes. The same is true of the seven species in the genus of short-tailed black combassous (*Hypochera*) that mimic all seven species of the genus of fire finches (*Lagonosticta*). Indeed, in only two instances has it been impossible to demonstrate the presence of host phrases in a widow bird's song; these cases are the two species of the genus *Vidua,* the blue widow bird of East Africa and the pin-tailed widow bird, which is found in the sub-Saharan regions of the continent.

By determining which are the host phrases in a male widow bird's song, it is even possible to predict the identity of the host when it is not known. Such predictions have been made more than once in our laboratory after careful analysis of the songs of captive widow-bird males, and I was later able to prove their accuracy. In the field in East Africa we found the appropriate young parasites among the nestlings of exactly those species of estrildid finches that had been identified as probable hosts.

The use of host melodies in widow-bird singing serves a vital purpose: it is a barrier to hybridization. How this isolating mechanism is acquired is best shown by a review of the widow-bird life cycle. The young nestlings' first weeks of life, as they share the nest of their host siblings, are ones of constant contact with their foster parents. The parasites become independent at the age of five weeks, but even after that they continue to live for some time among their host siblings. It is only later that they form a flock with other juveniles of their own species.

During these weeks of dependence and association the young widow birds are imprinted to the host species; this imprinting is a decisive factor in their later reproductive behavior. When, at the age of seven to eight weeks, the widow-bird juveniles first engage in premature sexual behavior as all songbirds do, there arises in the parasites a quite narrow and specific interest in the activities of the host species. Whereas other songbirds not only play at building nests during this phase but also feed and court one another, the attention of the juvenile widow bird is concentrated on two aspects of its hosts' adult behavior. The focus of interest depends on the sex of the widow bird.

As the female widow bird approaches sexual maturity her interest is concentrated on the hosts' reproductive cycle. The parasite checks frequently on the progress of the host pair's nest-building. The female also synchronizes her own ovulation with that of the host female; this ensures that her own egg is ready at about the time the host female produces her second or third egg. As a consequence the young parasite will hatch at about the same time that its host siblings do and will be their equal in the competition for food.

The male widow bird's concentration is differently oriented. During the most impressionable phase of its youth its interest is focused on the vocalizations of the male foster parent. The parasite evidently disregards the songs of any other species of bird; as a result, when it reaches maturity, it is able to reproduce its host's sound patterns exactly. Although the female parasite does not sing, she becomes similarly song-imprinted, and a memory of the host's repertory remains with her for life. The imprinting becomes evident when ovulation takes place and the female's sexual drive is aroused. Once the female widow bird is in search of a mate, she "knows" that the only appropriate male partner is one who can recite the same calls and notes she heard from her foster father while she was still a nestling. Only when the courting male corresponds to this prototype will the female widow bird allow mating.

Superficially it might seem that the male's signal is merely a kind of lure, for example "I grew up among the same host species that you did!" In my view the signal contains a message with a much deeper biological meaning; it might be paraphrased as "I have inherited the same adaptive characteristics that you have and so our offspring will have the same chances of survival."

It is clear that the adult widow birds' general adaptation to their hosts' song repertory, breeding rhythms and feeding habits, along with their nestlings' perfect mimicry of foster-sibling markings, movements and calls, can only have been the result of an extended evolutionary process. As we have come to know the identity of more and more host species of estrildid finches some of the mechanisms of the process responsible for these unusual adaptations have become apparent. It seems that in effect the potential for the evolution of a new species of widow bird has arisen in the past only when a new species of host finch has evolved.

Consider the relations between hosts and parasites from a taxonomic viewpoint. Two species of the widow-bird genus *Tetraenura* are known: the straw-tailed widow birds and the shaft-tailed. The estrildid finches parasitized by these two related widow-bird species are also two species of the same genus, *Uraeginthus*. In turn five species of paradise widow birds are the parasites of five species of another finch genus, and the seven species of combassous are linked to seven species of fire finch. Even though the specific hosts of the two widow birds of the genus *Vidua* remain unknown, we are certain that they are one or another of the species in the finch genus *Estrilda*.

Such species-to-species relations can be understood only if one assumes that a long time ago the widow birds began to arise from a single viduine prototype species that had started to parasitize a single species of estrildid finches. When this ancient estrildid species began to evolve into several species, the widow birds were forced to follow suit, because only by doing so could they evolve mouth markings sufficiently like those of the evolving new species of potential hosts. Of course, each widow-bird population that failed to achieve such an adaptive process was destined to become extinct, since its mismarked offspring would starve to death in the nests of hostile hosts. In this way the evolution of the adaptively successful widow-bird species both parallels and reflects the evolution of their chosen hosts among the numerous species of estrildid finches.

14 Incubator Birds

by H. J. Frith
August 1959

These extraordinary fowl hatch their eggs not by sitting on them but by putting them in a hot place. Some species even rake together dead leaves, the decay of which heats the eggs

On the mainland of Australia and the islands to the north lives a family of rather dull-looking black or brown birds about the size of domestic fowl. Called Megapodiidae, after their big feet, they rarely fly, have raucous calls and are seldom seen by man. These birds are of interest because they do not brood their eggs with the heat of their bodies as other birds do but hatch out their young in incubators. Depending upon their habitat, the various megapode species have developed different ways of finding and generating heat short of sitting on the eggs themselves. They bury their eggs in sunwarmed sand, in volcanoes or in compost heaps where fermentation supplies the heat. One Australian species, the mallee fowl, constructs huge mounds of soil and vegetable matter, enlisting both the heat of the sun and of fermentation, and manages to keep the temperature within a degree or so of 92 degrees Fahrenheit throughout the incubation period despite the vagaries of an often hostile climate. The chicks never see their parents. They hatch deep beneath the soil, dig their way upward to the surface and run away into the bush, fully feathered and able to fend for themselves from the start.

The first Europeans to hear of the incubator birds were survivors of Magellan's ill-fated 1519-1522 expedition around the world. One of them, Gemelli Careri, described in his memoirs a bird about the size of a small fowl that laid eggs bigger than itself and buried them in the ground to hatch from the heat of the sun and sand. The people of Europe at that time accepted mermaids and devils as normal inhabitants of the earth, but found the idea of birds building their own incubators too fantastic to believe. Careri's tale was rejected as just another sailor's yarn.

When early settlers in Australia discovered large mounds in the inland scrub, they marveled that aboriginal mothers should build such big sand

MALE MALLEE FOWL WATCHES FEMALE as she prepares to lay half-pound egg in hole he has dug in incubator mound. Egg will roll down to where female here has her head. Of this male the author says: "His co-operation has immensely assisted our studies."

castles to amuse their children. Later settlers in the north of the continent found really enormous mounds. They deduced that these monuments were the tombs of dead warriors. The natives, however, denied building mounds for either children or the dead. They stoutly claimed the mounds were birds' nests. But who could believe such a fantastic story from uncultured savages? The settlers continued to doubt the bushmen until 1840, when the pioneer naturalist John Gilbert took the obvious step of digging into the mounds. Sure enough, he found birds' eggs. The aborigines chuckled.

When I first heard of these mound builders, I wondered why other birds had not adopted this habit. Why should they not deposit their eggs in an incubator and lead a life of leisure instead of exposing themselves to the cares and dangers of the common method of incubation? Now, after a decade of studying the mallee fowl, I no longer wonder. The construction and maintenance of its incubator mound call for great skill and stamina and ceaseless heavy work for most of the year. Normal incubation must be easier in every way.

The megapodes that live on small islands in Celebes and the Moluccas have adopted somewhat less arduous methods. There the climate is warm and the temperature varies little during the day or over the course of a year. The shaded soil of the jungle, where these birds live, remains somewhat too cool. But the sand on the beaches becomes uniformly warm to a relatively great depth. The birds simply go to an exposed beach, dig a small pit deep enough to find the right temperature, and lay their eggs in it. In some places old lava-flows across the beaches have weathered to black sand. Here the birds unerringly choose the black sand for egg pits; presumably the better heat-absorbing properties of black sand make it slightly warmer. The jungle fowl, however, must face one difficulty. The beach is often as much as 20 miles away. Since they lay an egg every few days for several weeks, returning to the forest in between, their life during breeding season must be a constant promenade. A few of the birds do find warm spots in the forest soil at the edges of warm springs, and lay their eggs there.

The most widely distributed of all megapodes is the jungle fowl Megapodius. It is found from the Nicobars in the west to Fiji in the east, and from the Philippines to the central Australian coast, living on small coral atolls, larger

DIGGING MALE MALLEE FOWL works at dawn in spring. He opens his egg-incubator mound to let out heat of fermenting matter and keep the eggs at 92 degrees Fahrenheit.

IN MIDSUMMER the bird adds more soil to his already high mound to increase its insulation from hot sun. Fermenting leaves under the buried eggs now give off much less heat.

BY AUTUMN the male must work at midday to scoop out the mound and allow the sun's heat to penetrate to the eggs. He rebuilds the mound with sand warmed by the noon sun.

islands and on the continent itself. As might be expected, it is the most adaptable of the megapodes and varies its incubation method to suit each location.

On small islands this species lives in the jungle near the beach and lays its eggs in pits dug in the beach, side by side with the turtles that heave themselves from the sea for the same purpose. On islands where there is volcanic activity, Megapodius digs egg pits in places where steam issues from the ground and, on some islands, even in the volcanic ash of active craters. On larger islands and in Australia, the fowl lives in fairly dense forests and jungles at long distances from the exposed beaches and with no volcanic heat at hand. Here Megapodius adapts the heat of rotting vegetable matter to do the work of incubation.

The hard-working birds build mounds of soil and leaf material that may reach 50 feet in diameter and 15 to 20 feet in height. In open scrub near the seashore, where the sun shines brightly, they incorporate less organic material in their incubators. Such mounds represent perhaps no more than a first improvement on the simple egg-pit, elevating the pits for drainage and for safety from the tide. In dense jungle, however, where little sun reaches the ground, the mound will be almost entirely vegetable, and much heat is generated by fermentation. Between these two extremes are many mounds of intermediate composition. I find it remarkable that a bird is able to estimate the amount of organic matter it must add to a heap of soil so that the heat generated by fermentation is just enough to bridge the gap between the soil temperature and the temperature necessary for incubation. It almost suggests that these birds understand some chemistry.

Another group of megapodes, the brush turkeys, live in the dense, steamy rain forests of Australia and New Guinea, where the sun seldom penetrates. These birds find no difficulty in generating heat by fermentation, and depend on it entirely. The brush turkeys' mounds are heaps of rotting leaves 12 to 15 feet in diameter, scratched up from the forest floor with practically no soil. The mound is built in spring and, when it is wet with the summer rains, ferments so vigorously that, as we shall see, the birds are obliged to take active steps to control the heat.

The jungle fowl on their sunny beaches near the Equator, and the brush turkeys with masses of organic matter at hand, have no great difficulty finding sufficient heat for purposes of incubation. With the mallee fowl it is quite different.

This bird inhabits inland Australia, a region of semideserts and arid scrub with an annual rainfall of as little as eight inches. The hard, dry leaves do not rot where they fall. Instead, they are eaten by termites or they wither and blow away, and there is practically no leaf litter on the ground. Even if leaves are heaped up, they do not ferment but remain dry and are eventually burned by a brush fire or swept away by the wind. Clearly a bird wanting to generate heat by fermentation here has formidable obstacles to overcome.

Nor is solar heat dependable in this landscape. The air temperature ranges from 112 degrees F. to as low as 17 degrees. The days are blazing hot and the nights may be freezing cold. The temperature of the soil near the surface fluctuates madly, and the temperature deeper in the soil is only 60 degrees.

The ingenious mallee fowl is equal to the problem. It is the male bird that takes charge, building the incubator mound, tending it constantly and seldom going more than 200 yards away. He induces the leaf litter to ferment by burying it in the ground during the winter, when it is moist. The work begins in May (the Australian "November"), when he digs a hole 15 feet in diameter and three to four feet deep. Through the winter he rakes in the leaf litter from 30 to 40 yards around, piling it in the hole. Then, in August, he covers the heap with soil up to two feet thick. The organic matter is usually moist from the few winter showers and, sealed off from the dry air and sun, soon begins to ferment, raising the temperature in the mound. If it has been a dry winter and the leaves do not ferment, the birds abandon the mound and do not breed in that year.

The female is an egg-producing machine. She lays the first egg in mid-September and the last egg in late February or early March. She weighs only 3.5 pounds, but she justifies Careri's report of her by laying a half-pound egg and valiantly laying one every four to eight days for a total of as many as 35 in a season. Since an egg needs seven weeks to hatch, many of the chicks have already hatched and taken off long before the last eggs are laid—true assembly-line production.

During the whole time that eggs are in the mound the male carefully regulates the temperature. Many birds aim at exactly 92 degrees F., though others permit fluctuation between 90 and 95 degrees. When the last egg hatches, the mound is dug out and prepared for a new charge of organic matter.

To use natural heat and to regulate it so closely, the birds must have a highly developed sense of temperature. In 1952 I set out to learn how the mallee fowl goes about it.

I found that the mound temperature will rise to 115 degrees F. in the spring if the male is kept away from it. The heat then quickly leaves as the fermentation burns itself out. I built mounds without organic matter and found that the temperature rises very slowly when heat comes only from the sun, and never reaches 92 degrees. When the internal temperature in a normal undisturbed mound rises to 92 degrees, the male goes to work and keeps it from going higher. Later in the season he must reverse his strategy and work to maintain the temperature in the mound above the declining temperature of the soil. He does so by balancing the heat from his two sources: fermentation and sun. The temperature of the eggs seldom fluctuates more than one degree during the whole season.

The male actually varies his activity from day to day according to the weather, but in general he follows three successive routines as conditions change during the breeding season. In the spring he must reduce the amount of fermentation heat reaching the eggs. He visits the mound before dawn each day and digs rapidly until he nears the egg chamber. After allowing just enough heat to escape he refills the hole with cool sand.

Later in the summer the sun gets very hot, and much heat moves by conduction from the surface of the mound to the egg chamber. Some heat still moves

SEVEN MEGAPODE SPECIES are depicted on the opposite page. They are: (1) *Alectura lathami* of eastern Australia; (2) *Megapodius freycinet*, spread throughout the South Pacific area; (3) *Aepypodius arfakianus*, which lives in New Guinea areas above 3,000 feet; (4) *Leipoa ocellata*, the mallee fowl of southern Australia; (5) *Tallegallus jobiensis* of New Guinea; (6) *Eulipoa wallacei* of the Moluccas, and (7) *Megacephalon maleo* of the Celebes Islands.

up also from the organic matter, though fermentation is slowing by this time. The eggs thus tend to overheat, and the bird must do something to reduce the temperature. There is little he can do to slow the fermentation rate, but he does lower the rate of solar conduction. Daily he adds more soil to the mound. As the mound grows higher and higher, the eggs for a while are more thoroughly insulated from the sun. After

a time, apparently, the bird can build the mound no higher, and a wave of heat begins to go down toward the eggs again. Now the male bird visits the mound each week or so in the early morning, removes all the soil and scatters it in the cool morning air. When it is cool, he collects it and restores it to the mound. This is strenuous work, but effective in destroying the heat wave in the incubator. The temperature in

the egg chamber remains steady at 92 degrees.

When autumn comes, the bird is faced with the opposite problem: falling temperature in the mound. The mound no longer generates fermentation heat, and the daily input of solar heat is declining. The bird now changes his activities to meet the challenge. Whereas he had scratched and scattered the sand to cool it in the early morning, often before

MEGAPODE HABITATS cover much of the South Pacific area, as shown on this map. *Megapodius freycinet*, the most widespread

of all, varies its incubator-building habits with location. *Leipoa ocellata*, the mallee fowl of southern Australia, is the hardest work-

dawn, he now comes to the mound each day at about 10 a.m., when the sun is shining on it. He digs almost all the soil away and spreads it out so that the mound resembles a large saucer, with the eggs only a few inches below the surface. This thin layer of soil, exposed to the midday sun, absorbs some heat, but not enough to maintain the temperature throughout the night. The saucer must be refilled with heated sand.

ing, because it lives in arid country where it is very difficult to get leaves to ferment.

Throughout the hottest part of the day the bird scratches over the sand he has removed from the mound, exposing all of it to the sun. As each layer gets hot, he returns it to the mound. He times the work so that the incubator is restored with layers of heated sand by 4 p.m., when the sun is getting low.

We thought it possible that all this temperature-control work could be merely part of a fixed behavior pattern evolved by natural selection to suit the seasons. But the birds, while changing their work with the season, make day-to-day adjustments. On an exceptionally hot spring day they do not open a mound; instead they pile more sand on top, presumably to insulate the eggs from the sun. Similarly, during a series of dull days in autumn, the birds build a mound up higher to conserve the interior heat, rather than scooping it out to spread the sand at midday. Our observations suggested that the birds know what is happening inside the mound and vary their activity deliberately. We decided to see whether the birds could detect unusual temperatures in the mound and cope with them.

In one case we sabotaged an actively fermenting mound by removing all the organic material. The internal temperature quickly fell from 92 to 60 degrees. The male bird had been visiting the mound daily to release heat. On his next visit he detected the fall in temperature. Although it was October, he immediately began his autumn type of digging and opened the mound in the heat of the day to warm it. He did this every day, but the spring sun was not strong enough. He only managed to get the mound to 80 degrees by midsummer. In December this male was slaving away warming his mound, while all the others were busy cooling theirs. Obviously he was aware that something was afoot.

In another series of experiments we installed heating elements in a mound so that we could control its temperature. By switching the heat on or off we were able to keep the male on the jump, making him change from working to warm the mound to striving to cool it. He always detected our trickery and was so efficient that our thermostats and our 240-volt generator could barely cope with his efforts. He almost won the struggle to keep the eggs at 92 degrees.

We have no doubt that the broad pattern of activity—the time of day a bird comes to the mound, whether he opens it on a given day, and so on—is determined by the weather. But our ob-

servations and experiments show that the work actually done on the mound in the course of a particular day is determined by its internal temperature. This implies that the birds can actually measure temperature. How else could they detect the variations we had caused inside the mound with our heating elements?

When a bird is working, he frequently pauses and buries his bill in the mound, withdrawing it filled with sand, which then trickles out. The work that follows is clearly influenced by the results of this probing. We have little doubt that this is the temperature-measuring action and that the bird's "thermometer" is inside the bill; it may be either the tongue or soft palate.

The temperature-taking is particularly significant during egg-laying. The male mallee fowl opens the mound, a job that takes an hour or more. The female then comes out of the scrub and probes the place in the egg chamber that he has exposed. If she is not satisfied, she goes off and sits under a bush, and the male must refill the hole and dig another one. This may happen three or four times before she is satisfied that her egg will be placed in a suitably warm spot.

The brush turkeys measure the temperature in the same manner, but their temperature-control work is neither so prolonged nor so precise. The male brush turkey is also in charge of the mound, and he savagely drives off the female except when she wishes to lay eggs. After the mound is built, in August, the male daily turns over the fermenting material while clouds of steam rise from it. He thus keeps it well aerated until the first burst of fierce heat from the rapid fermentation has passed. Then he allows the female to lay, and for the rest of the season watches over the mound. When fermentation lags he scratches small amounts of fresh material onto the mound, and when it gets too hot he digs out the center to cool it.

The jungle fowl's task is even simpler. Those that lay in warm sand simply choose a spot with exactly the right temperature. Those that build fermentation mounds do not attempt to control them, as the mallee fowl does, apart from judging the initial composition. They do, however, select the spot for the eggs. As the season advances they scrape additional material onto the mounds, starting new cycles of fermentation in successive layers. It seems probable that for each egg the jungle fowl choose the layer that is in the appropriate state of fermentation. They probe their mounds with their bills, just as the other megapodes do, no doubt to help decide where to place each egg.

All of this egg-laying, egg-burying, mound-building and temperature-control work is directed, of course, to only one end: the production of offspring. But the birds' preoccupation with eggs keeps them so busy that they have no time for their chicks. As a result young megapodes are probably more precocious than the nestlings of any other bird.

The mallee chick hatches three feet beneath the soil; we have watched them do so behind glass. The egg bursts and the chick immediately begins his struggle, moving slowly and spasmodically upward. The journey can take 15 to 20 hours. At last its head comes through; it breathes fresh air and takes stock of the situation. The outlook must be grim. Alone and defenseless, the infant is exposed to any predator that happens along; there is little food and no water.

The chick at last works free of the mound, tumbles down the side, and struggles to the nearest bush for shelter. Here it rests for a couple of hours and then moves purposefully off into the world. It is already able to run swiftly and soon can fly up to a limb to roost in safety. Throughout its early life it remains solitary and flees from anything that moves, including other mallee fowl.

The egg that yields a mallee fowl that grows up in turn to tend its own mound in the bush is one of a small minority.

The incubator system is not particularly efficient, discounting the unremitting toil it involves for the bird. Many eggs fail to hatch because of mishaps to the mound, the commonest one being thunderstorms that catch the mound open and drench its interior. Foxes and other predators dig out and eat large numbers of the oversized eggs. The chicks that do hatch often suffocate before they escape. All in all, the megapodes are no more successful in breeding than other ground-nesting birds.

How, then, did they come to possess the mound-building habit? Some observers believe it is a survival from birds' reptilian ancestors. As the prehistoric reptiles began to develop wings and feathers, so the story goes, one group retained the habit of burying its eggs, as do turtles, crocodiles and many reptiles of today. Having watched the labors of the male mallee fowl and the less spectacular but equally precise work of the brush turkeys, however, I refuse to believe that it is a primitive characteristic. Every observation suggests that the incubation process is very highly developed and specialized.

It is more likely that the ancestors of the present-day megapodes were ground-nesting birds that developed the habit of covering their eggs with sand or leaves when leaving the nest, as a protection against predators. Several present-day birds, in fact, do this. Natural selection favored these individuals, perhaps because the covering tended to prevent severe fluctuations in the egg temperature and even, by accidental

fermentation, provided some extra heat. The use of fermentation heat could have increased as the birds extended their range from the sunny beaches into the dense, shady forests.

To explain the temperature-control work of the mallee fowl we need only consider Australia's climatic history. Originally the interior of the continent was well watered and supported rain forests. It is probable that the ancestors of the mallee fowl ranged the forests building large leafy mounds like those of the present-day brush turkeys. In the Pleistocene epoch an arid cycle began, and deserts and scrub gradually replaced the forests. The birds then adopted the habit of covering the mound with sand to conserve its moisture and absorb the heat of the sun.

While the course of evolution that selected the mound-building habit may have helped the megapodes to survive, it certainly did not give them an easy way of life. It is strange to see a mallee fowl panting heavily, out in a clearing under the blazing desert sun, grimly digging in a huge pile of sand. When everything else in the bush is still and resting, the mallee fowl works. One early observer wrote: "Its actions are suggestive of melancholy, for it has none of the liveliness that characterizes almost all other birds, but stalks along in a solemn manner as if the dreary nature of its surroundings and its solitary life weighed heavily on its spirits."

Although I have a deep personal interest in these birds, I must admit that is a fair comment. They do seem to have little to live for.

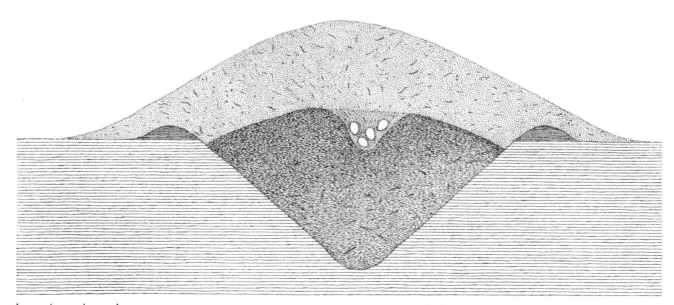

FEET 1   2   3   MALLEE FOWL MOUND cross section shows pit in which bird places rotting organic matter, with egg chamber on it. Heaped over eggs and compost is sandy soil. Lumps at side of pit are old soil from hole.

15

"Imprinting" in a Natural Laboratory

by Eckhard H. Hess
August 1972

*A synthesis of laboratory and field techniques has
led to some interesting discoveries about imprinting,
the process by which newly hatched birds rapidly
form a permanent bond to the parent*

In a marsh on the Eastern Shore of Maryland, a few hundred feet from my laboratory building, a female wild mallard sits on a dozen infertile eggs. She has been incubating the eggs for almost four weeks. Periodically she hears the faint peeping sounds that are emitted by hatching mallard eggs, and she clucks softly in response. Since these eggs are infertile, however, they are not about to hatch and they do not emit peeping sounds. The sounds come from a small loudspeaker hidden in the nest under the eggs. The loudspeaker is connected to a microphone next to some hatching mallard eggs inside an incubator in my laboratory. The female mallard can hear any sounds coming from the laboratory eggs, and a microphone beside her relays the sounds she makes to a loudspeaker next to those eggs.

The reason for complicating the life of an expectant duck in such a way is to further our understanding of the phenomenon known as imprinting. It was through the work of the Austrian zoologist Konrad Z. Lorenz that imprinting became widely known. In the 1930's Lorenz observed that newly hatched goslings would follow him rather than their mother if the goslings saw him before they saw her. Since naturally reared geese show a strong attachment for their parent, Lorenz concluded that some animals have the capacity to learn rapidly and permanently at a very early age, and in particular to learn the characteristics of the parent. He called this process of acquiring an attachment to the parent *Prägung*, which in German means "stamping" or "coinage" but in English has been rendered as "imprinting." Lorenz regarded the phenomenon as being different from the usual kind of learning because of its rapidity and apparent permanence. In fact, he was hesitant at first to regard imprinting as a form of learn-

ing at all. Some child psychologists and some psychiatrists nevertheless perceived a similarity between the evidence of imprinting in animals and the early behavior of the human infant, and it is not surprising that interest in imprinting spread quickly.

From about the beginning of the 1950's many investigators have intensively studied imprinting in the laboratory. Unlike Lorenz, the majority of them have regarded imprinting as a form

of learning and have used methods much the same as those followed in the study of associative learning processes. In every case efforts were made to manipulate or stringently control the imprinting process. Usually the subjects are incubator-hatched birds that are reared in the laboratory. The birds are typically kept isolated until the time of the laboratory imprinting experience to prevent interaction of early social experience and the imprinting experience. Various objects

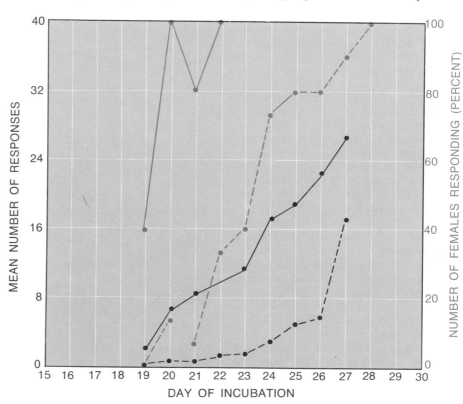

VOCAL RESPONSES to hatching-duckling sounds of 15 female wild mallards (*broken curves*) and five human-imprinted mallards (*solid curves*), which were later released to the wild, followed the same pattern, although the human-imprinted mallards began responding sooner and more frequently. A tape recording of the sounds of a hatching duckling was played daily throughout the incubation period to each female mallard while she was on her nest. Responses began on the 19th day of incubation and rose steadily until hatching.

have been used as artificial parents: duck decoys, stuffed hens, dolls, milk bottles, toilet floats, boxes, balls, flashing lights and rotating disks. Several investigators have constructed an automatic imprinting apparatus into which the newly hatched bird can be put. In this kind of work the investigator does not observe the young bird directly; all the bird's movements with respect to the imprinting object are recorded automatically.

Much of my own research during the past two decades has not differed substantially from this approach. The birds I have used for laboratory imprinting studies have all been incubated, hatched and reared without the normal social and environmental conditions and have then been tested in an artificial situation. It is therefore possible that the behavior observed under such conditions is not relevant to what actually happens in nature.

It is perhaps not surprising that studies of "unnatural" imprinting have produced conflicting results. Lorenz' original statements on the permanence of natural imprinting have been disputed. In many instances laboratory imprinting experiences do not produce permanent and exclusive attachment to the object selected as an artificial parent. For example, a duckling can spend a considerable amount of time following the object to which it is to be imprinted, and immediately after the experience it will follow a completely different object.

In one experiment in our laboratory we attempted to imprint ducklings to ourselves, as Lorenz did. For 20 continuous hours newly hatched ducklings were exposed to us. Before long they followed us whenever we moved about. Then they were given to a female mallard that had hatched a clutch of ducklings several hours before. After only an hour and a half of exposure to the female mallard and other ducklings the human-imprinted ducklings followed the female on the first exodus from the nest. Weeks later the behavior of the human-imprinted ducks was no different from the behavior of the ducks that had been hatched in the nest. Clearly laboratory imprinting is reversible.

We also took wild ducklings from their natural mother 16 hours after hatching and tried to imprint them to humans. On the first day we spent many hours with the ducklings, and during the next two months we made lengthy attempts every day to overcome the ducklings' fear of us. We finally gave up. From the beginning to the end the ducks

remained wild and afraid. They were released, and when they had matured, they were observed to be as wary of humans as normal wild ducks are. This result suggests that natural imprinting, unlike artificial laboratory imprinting, is permanent and irreversible. I have had to conclude that the usual laboratory imprinting has only a limited resemblance to natural imprinting.

It seems obvious that if the effects of natural imprinting are to be understood, the phenomenon must be studied as it operates in nature. The value of such studies was stressed as long ago as 1914 by the pioneer American psychologist John B. Watson. He emphasized that field observations must always be made to test whether or not conclusions drawn from laboratory studies conform to what actually happens in nature. The disparity between laboratory results and what happens in nature often arises from the failure of the investigator to really look at the animal's behavior. For years I have cautioned my students against shutting their experimental animals in "black boxes" with automatic recording devices and never directly observing how the animals behave.

This does not mean that objective laboratory methods for studying the behavior of animals must be abandoned. With laboratory investigations large strides have been made in the development of instruments for the recording of behavior. In the study of imprinting it is not necessary to revert to imprecise naturalistic observations in the field. We can now go far beyond the limitations of traditional field studies. It is possible to set up modern laboratory equipment in actual field conditions and in ways that do not disturb or interact with the behavior being studied, in other words, to achieve a synthesis of laboratory and field techniques.

The first step in the field-laboratory method is to observe and record the undisturbed natural behavior of the animal in the situation being studied. In our work on imprinting we photographed the behavior of the female mallard during incubation and hatching. We photographed the behavior of the ducklings during and after hatching. We recorded

CLUCKS emitted by a female wild mallard in the fourth week of incubating eggs are shown in the sound spectrogram (*upper illustration*). Each cluck lasts for about 150 milliseconds

all sounds from the nest before and after hatching. Other factors, such as air temperature and nest temperature, were also recorded.

A detailed inventory of the actual events in natural imprinting is essential for providing a reference point in the assessment of experimental manipulations of the imprinting process. That is, the undisturbed natural imprinting events form the control situation for assessing the effects of the experimental manipulations. This is quite different from the "controlled" laboratory setting, in which the ducklings are reared in isolation and then tested in unnatural conditions. The controlled laboratory study not only introduces new variables (environmental and social deprivation) into the imprinting situation but also it can prevent the investigator from observing factors that are relevant in wild conditions.

My Maryland research station is well suited for the study of natural imprinting in ducks. The station, near a national game refuge, has 250 acres of marsh and forest on a peninsula on which there are many wild and semiwild mallards. Through the sharp eyes of my technical assistant Elihu Abbott, a native of the Eastern Shore, I have learned to see much I might otherwise have missed. Initially we looked at and listened to the undisturbed parent-offspring interaction of female mallards that hatched their own eggs both in nests on the ground and in specially constructed nest boxes. From our records we noticed that the incubation time required for different clutches of eggs decreased progressively between March and June. Both the average air temperature and the number of daylight hours increase during those months; both are correlated with the incubation time of mallard eggs. It is likely, however, that temperature rather than photoperiod directly influences the duration of incubation. In one experiment mallard eggs from an incubator were slowly cooled for two hours a day in a room with a temperature of seven degrees Celsius, and another set of eggs was cooled in a room at 27 degrees C. These temperatures respectively correspond to the mean noon temperatures at the research station in March and in June. The eggs that were placed in the cooler room took longer to hatch, indicating that temperature affects the incubation time directly. Factors such as humidity and barometric pressure may also play a role.

We noticed that all the eggs in a wild nest usually hatch between three and eight hours of one another. As a result all the ducklings in the same clutch are approximately the same age in terms of the number of hours since hatching. Yet when mallard eggs are placed in a mechanical incubator, they will hatch over a two- or three-day period even when precautions are taken to ensure that all the eggs begin developing simultaneously. The synchronous hatching observed in nature obviously has some survival value. At the time of the exodus from the nest, which usually takes place between 16 and 32 hours after hatching, all the ducklings would be of a similar age and thus would have equal motor capabilities and similar social experiences.

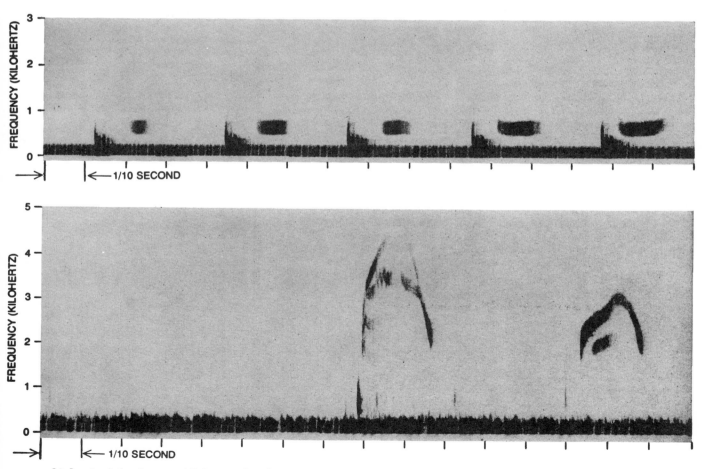

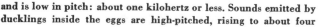

and is low in pitch: about one kilohertz or less. Sounds emitted by ducklings inside the eggs are high-pitched, rising to about four kilohertz (*lower illustration*). Records of natural, undisturbed imprinting events in the nest provide a control for later experiments.

Over the years our laboratory studies and actual observations of how a female mallard interacts with her offspring have pointed to the conclusion that imprinting is related to the age after hatching rather than the age from the beginning of incubation. Many other workers, however, have accepted the claim that age from the beginning of incubation determines the critical period for maximum effectiveness of imprinting. They base their belief on the findings of Gilbert Gottlieb of the Dorothea Dix Hospital in Raleigh, N.C., who in a 1961 paper described experiments that apparently showed that maximum imprinting in ducklings occurs in the period between 27 and 27½ days after the beginning of incubation. To make sure that all the eggs he was working with started incubation at the same time he first chilled the eggs so that any partially developed embryos would be killed. Yet the 27th day after the beginning of incubation can hardly be the period of maximum imprinting for wild ducklings that hatch in March under natural conditions, because such ducklings take on the average 28 days to hatch. Moreover, if the age of a duckling is measured from the beginning of incubation, it is hard to explain why eggs laid at different times in a hot month in the same nest will hatch within six to eight hours of one another under natural conditions.

Periodic cooling of the eggs seems to affect the synchronization of hatching. The mallard eggs from an incubator that were placed in a room at seven degrees C. hatched over a period of a day and a half, whereas eggs placed in the room at 27 degrees hatched over a period of two

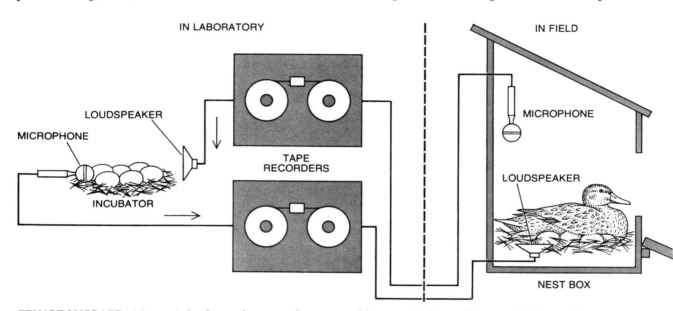

FEMALE MALLARD sitting on infertile eggs hears sounds transmitted from mallard eggs in a laboratory incubator. Any sounds she makes are transmitted to a loudspeaker beside the eggs in the laboratory. Such a combination of field and laboratory techniques permits recording of events without disturbing the nesting mallard and provides the hatching eggs with nearly natural conditions.

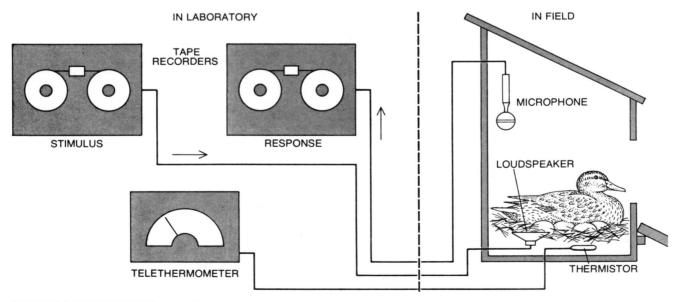

REMOTE MANIPULATION of prehatching sounds is accomplished by placing a sensitive microphone and a loudspeaker in the nest of a female wild mallard who is sitting on her own eggs. Prerecorded hatching-duckling sounds are played at specified times through the loudspeaker and the female mallard's responses to this stimulus are recorded. A thermistor probe transmits the temperature in the nest to a telethermometer and chart recorder. The thermistor records provide data about when females are on nest.

and a half days (which is about normal for artificially incubated eggs). Cooling cannot, however, play a major role. In June the temperature in the outdoor nest boxes averages close to the normal brooding temperature while the female mallard is absent. Therefore an egg laid on June 1 has a head start in incubation over those laid a week later. Yet we have observed that all the eggs in clutches laid in June hatch in a period lasting between six and eight hours.

We found another clue to how the synchronization of hatching may be achieved in the vocalization pattern of the brooding female mallard. As many others have noted, the female mallard vocalizes regularly as she sits on her eggs during the latter part of the incubation period. It seemed possible that she was vocalizing to the eggs, perhaps in response to sounds from the eggs themselves. Other workers had observed that ducklings make sounds before they hatch, and the prehatching behavior of ducklings in response to maternal calls has been extensively reported by Gottlieb.

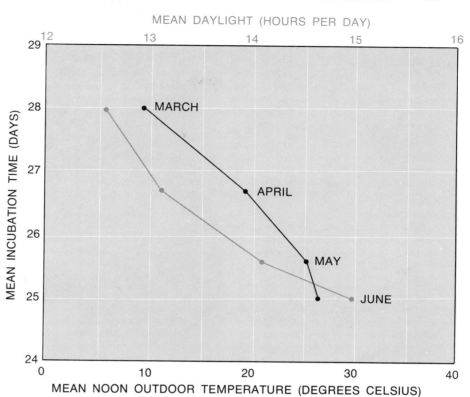

INCUBATION TIME of mallard eggs hatched naturally in a feral setting at Lake Cove, Md., decreased steadily from March to June. The incubation period correlated with both the outdoor temperature (*black curve*) and the daily photoperiod (*colored curve*).

We placed a highly sensitive microphone next to some mallard eggs that were nearly ready to hatch. We found that the ducklings indeed make sounds while they are still inside the egg. We made a one-minute tape recording of the sounds emitted by a duckling that had pipped its shell and was going to hatch within the next few hours. Then we made a seven-minute recording that would enable us to play the duckling sounds three times for one minute interspersed with one-minute silences. We played the recording once each to 37 female mallards at various stages of

NEST EXODUS takes place about 16 to 32 hours after hatching. The female mallard begins to make about 40 to 65 calls per minute and continues while the ducklings leave the nest to follow her. The ducklings are capable of walking and swimming from hatching.

incubation. There were no positive responses from the female mallards during the first and second week of incubation. In fact, during the first days of incubation some female mallards responded with threat behavior: a fluffing of the feathers and a panting sound. In the third week some females responded to the recorded duckling sounds with a few clucks. In the fourth week maternal clucks were frequent and were observed in all ducks tested.

We found the same general pattern of response whether the female mallards were tested once or, as in a subsequent experiment, tested daily during incubation. Mallards sitting on infertile eggs responded just as much to the recorded duckling sounds as mallards sitting on fertile eggs did. Apparently after sitting on a clutch of eggs for two or three weeks a female mallard becomes ready to respond to the sounds of a hatching duckling. There is some evidence that the parental behavior of the female mallard is primed by certain neuroendocrine mechanisms. We have begun a study of the neuroendocrine changes that might accompany imprinting and filial behavior in mallards.

To what extent do unhatched ducklings respond to the vocalization of the female mallard? In order to find out we played a recording of a female mallard's vocalizations to ducklings in eggs that had just been pipped and were scheduled to hatch within the next 24 hours. As before, the sounds were interspersed with periods of silence. We then recorded all the sounds made by the ducklings during the recorded female mallard vocalizations and also during the silent periods on the tape. Twenty-four hours before the scheduled hatching the ducklings emitted 34 percent of their sounds during the silent periods, which suggests that at this stage they initiate most of the auditory interaction. As hatching time approaches the ducklings emit fewer and fewer sounds during the silent periods. The total number of sounds they make, however, increases steadily. At the time of hatching only 9 percent of the sounds they make are emitted during the silent periods. One hour after hatching, in response to the same type of recording, the ducklings gave 37 percent of their vocalizations during the silent periods, a level similar to the level at 24 hours before hatching.

During the hatching period, which lasts about an hour, the female mallard generally vocalizes at the rate of from zero to four calls per one-minute interval. Occasionally there is an interval in which she emits as many as 10 calls. When the duckling actually hatches, the female mallard's vocalization increases dramatically to between 45 and 68 calls per minute for one or two minutes.

Thus the sounds made by the female mallard and by her offspring are complementary. The female mallard vocalizes most when a duckling has just hatched. A hatching duckling emits its cries primarily when the female is vocalizing.

After all the ducklings have hatched the female mallard tends to be relatively quiet for long intervals, giving between zero and four calls per minute. This continues for 16 to 32 hours until it is time for the exodus from the nest. As the exodus begins the female mallard quickly builds up to a crescendo of between 40 and 65 calls per minute; on rare occasions we have observed between 70 and 95 calls per minute. The duration of the high-calling-rate period depends on how quickly the ducklings leave the nest to follow her. There is now a change in the sounds made by the female mallard. Up to this point she has been making clucking sounds. By the time the exodus from the nest takes place some of her sounds are more like quacks.

The auditory interaction of the female mallard and the duckling can begin well before the hatching period. As I have indicated, the female mallard responds to unhatched-duckling sounds during the third and fourth week of incubation. Normally ducklings penetrate a membrane to reach an air space inside the eggshell two days before hatching. We have not found any female mallard that vocalized to her clutch before the duckling in the egg reached the air space. We have found that as soon as the duckling penetrates the air space the female begins to cluck at a rate of between zero and four times per minute. Typically she continues to vocalize at this rate until the ducklings begin to pip their eggs (which is about 24 hours after they have entered the air space). As the eggs are being pipped the female clucks at the rate of between 10 and 15 times per minute. When the pipping is completed, she

SOUND SPECTROGRAM of the calls of newly hatched ducklings in the nest and the mother's responses is shown at right. The high-pitched peeps of the ducklings are in the

DISTRESS CALLS of ducklings in the nest evoke a quacklike response from the female mallard. The cessation of the distress calls and the onset of normal duckling peeping sounds

drops back to between zero and four calls per minute. In the next 24 hours there is a great deal of auditory interaction between the female and her unhatched offspring; this intense interaction may facilitate the rapid formation of the filial bond after hatching, although it is quite possible that synchrony of hatching is the main effect. Already we have found that a combination of cooling the eggs daily, placing them together so that they touch one another and transmitting parent-young vocal responses through the microphone-loudspeaker hookup between the female's nest and the laboratory incubator causes the eggs in the incubator to hatch as synchronously as eggs in nature do. In fact, the two times we did this we found that all the eggs in the clutches hatched within four hours of one another. It has been shown in many studies of imprinting, including laboratory studies, that auditory stimuli have an important effect on the development of filial attachment. Auditory stimulation, before and after hatching, together with tactile

stimulation in the nest after hatching results in ducklings that are thoroughly imprinted to the female mallard that is present.

Furthermore, it appears that auditory interaction before hatching may play an important role in promoting the synchronization of hatching. As our experiments showed, not only does the female mallard respond to sounds from her eggs but also the ducklings respond to her clucks. Perhaps the daily cooling of the eggs when the female mallard leaves the nest to feed serves to broadly synchronize embryonic and behavioral development, whereas the auditory interaction of the mother with the ducklings and of one duckling with another serves to provide finer synchronization. Margaret Vince of the University of Cambridge has shown that the synchronization of hatching in quail is promoted by the mutual auditory interaction of the young birds in the eggs.

Listening to the female mallards vocalize to their eggs or to their newly hatched offspring, we were struck by the

fact that we could tell which mallard was vocalizing, even when we could not see her. Some female mallards regularly emit single clucks at one-second intervals, some cluck in triple or quadruple clusters and others cluck in clusters of different lengths. The individual differences in the vocalization styles of female mallards may enable young ducklings to identify their mother. We can also speculate that the characteristics of a female mallard's voice are learned by her female offspring, which may then adopt a similar style when they are hatching eggs of their own.

The female mallards not only differ from one another in vocalization styles but also emit different calls in different situations. We have recorded variations in pitch and duration from the same mallard in various nesting situations. It seems likely that such variations in the female mallard call are an important factor in the imprinting process.

Studies of imprinting in the laboratory have shown that the more effort a duckling has to expend in following the im-

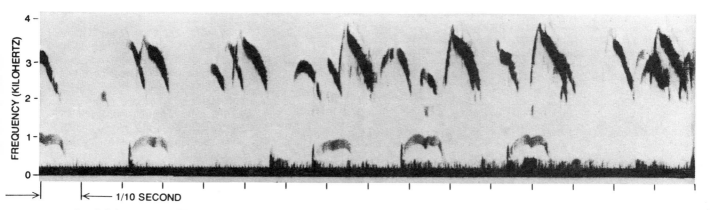

two-to-four-kilohertz range. They normally have the shape of an inverted *V*. The female mallard's clucks are about one kilohertz and last about 130 milliseconds. After the eggs hatch the vocalization of the female changes both in quantity and in quality of sound.

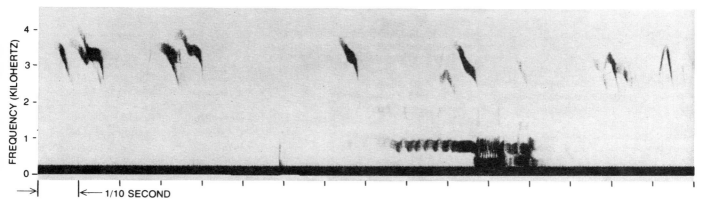

is almost immediate, as can be seen in this sound spectrogram. The female mallard's quacklike call is about one kilohertz in pitch and has a duration of approximately 450 milliseconds. The call is emitted about once every two seconds in response to distress cries.

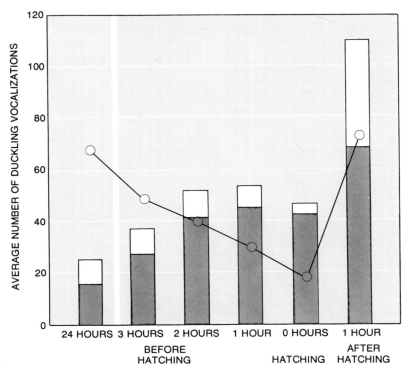

NUMBER OF SOUNDS from ducklings before and after hatching are shown. The ducklings heard a recording consisting of five one-minute segments of a female mallard's clucking sounds interspersed with five one-minute segments of silence. The recording was played to six mallard eggs and the number of vocal responses by the ducklings to the clucking segments (*gray bars*) and to the silent segments (*white bars*) were counted. Twenty-four hours before hatching 34 percent of the duckling sounds were made during the silent interval, indicating the ducklings initiated a substantial portion of the early auditory interaction. As hatching time approached the ducklings initiated fewer and fewer of the sounds and at hatching vocalized most in response to the clucks of the female mallard.

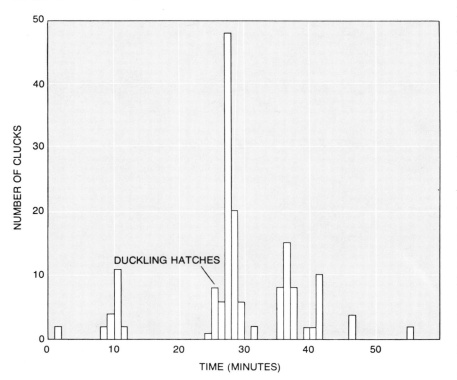

CLUCKING RATE of a wild, ground-nesting female mallard rose dramatically for about two minutes while a duckling hatched and then slowly declined to the prehatching rate. Each bar depicts the number of clucks emitted by the female during a one-minute period.

printing object, the more strongly it prefers that object in later testing. At first it would seem that this is not the case in natural imprinting; young ducklings raised by their mother have little difficulty following her during the exodus from the nest. Closer observation of many nests over several seasons showed, however, that ducklings make a considerable effort to be near their parent. They may suffer for such efforts, since they can be accidentally stepped on, squeezed or scratched by the female adult. The combination of effort and punishment may actually strengthen imprinting. Work in my laboratory showed that chicks given an electric shock while they were following the imprinting object later showed stronger attachment to the object than unshocked chicks did. It is reasonable to expect similar results with ducklings.

Slobodan Petrovich of the University of Maryland (Baltimore County) and I have begun a study to determine the relative contributions of prehatching and posthatching auditory experience on imprinting and filial attachment. The auditory stimuli consist of either natural mallard maternal clucks or a human voice saying "Come, come, come." Our results indicate that prehatching stimulation by natural maternal clucks may to a degree facilitate the later recognition of the characteristic call of the mallard. Ducklings lacking any experience with a maternal call imprint as well to a duck decoy that utters "Come, come, come" as to a decoy that emits normal mallard clucks. Ducklings that had been exposed to a maternal call before hatching imprinted better to decoys that emitted the mallard clucks. We found, however, that the immediate posthatching experiences, in this case with a female mallard on the nest, can highly determine the degree of filial attachment and make imprinting to a human sound virtually impossible.

It is important to recognize that almost all laboratory imprinting experiments, including my own, have been deprivation experiments. The justification for such experiments has been the ostensible need for controlling the variables of the phenomenon, but the deprivation may have interfered with the normal behavioral development of the young ducklings. Whatever imprinting experiences the experimenter allows therefore do not produce the maximum effect.

Although our findings are far from complete, we have already determined enough to demonstrate the great value of studying imprinting under natural conditions. The natural laboratory can be profitably used to study questions about imprinting that have been raised but not answered by traditional laboratory experiments. We must move away from the in vitro, or test-tube, approach to the study of behavior and move toward the in vivo method that allows interaction with normal environmental factors. Some of the questions are: What is the optimal age for imprinting? How long must the imprinting experience last for it to have the maximum effect? Which has the greater effect on behavior: first experience or the most recent experience? Whatever kind of behavior is being studied, the most fruitful approach may well be to study the behavior in its natural context.

16

The Lek Mating System
of the Sage Grouse

by R. Haven Wiley, Jr.
May 1978

In a lek system a large percentage of the females mate with a small percentage of the males. How the system operates among the sage grouse of the Rockies is examined in detail

Of all the bizarre rituals in animal courtship few are more impressive than the lek mating system of the sage grouse. On the high sagebrush plateaus of the Rocky Mountain region both sexes congregate during the breeding season at communal display grounds, or leks (originally a Scandinavian word meaning play). There the males display repeatedly. Although 50 or 60 male sage grouse may gather at a lek, most of the visiting females copulate only with the same one or two males, and most of the males find no mates at all.

The lek mating system, characterized by a transitory association of both sexes at a regular location and extremely unequal copulatory success among the males, has evolved among distantly related species of birds, including certain grouse, birds of paradise, sandpipers, weaver finches and the manakins and cotingas of Central and South America. It is also found among insects, fishes and mammals. Because the system is such a clear case of unequal matings by males it has long fascinated zoologists. I felt that an example as extreme as that of the sage grouse might clarify some general principles of animal mating systems. For this reason I recently undertook a three-year study of sage grouse mating.

In winter, when the sagebrush plateaus are swept by snow and high winds, the sage grouse depend almost entirely on one evergreen plant, the big sagebrush, for both shelter and food. These grouse are among the largest birds of their family and show a marked sexual dimorphism: adult males average 2.5 kilograms in weight and adult females only 1.2 kilograms. Beginning in the first warm days of February the males congregate at leks scattered on the sagebrush plains. Throughout March and April and on into May each male returns morning after morning to his particular lek and to a particular position within the lek. Female grouse visit the lek for a much briefer period, usually some 20 days in April.

Activity on a lek begins at first light, an hour or so before sunrise, and continues for three or four hours. During this period the males spend much of their time repeating what early observers of sage grouse dubbed "the strut." The male inflates his elastic esophageal sac by heaving the sac upward and then letting it fall. By doing so twice he expands the sac until it contains some four liters of air. Then, contracting the superficial muscles of his chest, he compresses the inflated sac and suddenly releases the compressed air. The result is a resonant popping sound, much like the sound of a cork being pulled from a bottle. Each cycle of inflation and release takes a little more than three seconds; between struts the male usually stands in a conspicuous attitude, his white neck feathers ruffled and his tail feathers cocked vertically. Elaborate displays are characteristic of lek-mating animals, but sage grouse reach an extreme of grotesque behavior.

When the female grouse visit the lek in April, they arrive in large numbers around sunrise and tend to congregate in a dense pack at the center. The one or two males near the center strut back and forth through the congregation of females and copulate with them at intervals. Each female usually copulates only once and then leaves to make her nest, sometimes as much as four kilometers away from the lek. The female lays six to eight eggs, incubates them for 26 days on the average and rears the young birds without any further association with a male.

Of the 50 or 60 males that attend a lek during the breeding season the large majority never copulate at all and only a few copulate repeatedly. In the course of a season a successful male mounts from 20 to 60 females; I once recorded 34 successful copulations by the same male in a single morning. Overall at least 90 percent of the copulations at any particular lek are participated in by no more than 10 percent of the males present.

Earlier naturalists who were interested in Charles Darwin's theory of sexual selection were particularly intrigued by the lek mating system. For example, when Edmund Selous described the leks of the black grouse in England in 1909, he emphasized the competition among the males and the selection of the most vigorous males by the visiting females. Indeed, for decades before data on polygynous behavior in other animals became available lek-forming birds provided the prime examples for the theory of sexual selection. Today, with detailed studies, we are in a better position to understand the social interactions that generate the unequal distribution of matings on leks. My own studies show that sage grouse exhibit many features of behavior that are present in other lek-forming animals, although in a less exaggerated form.

One characteristic of leks is their traditional location. The sage grouse return year after year to virtually the same spot. For example, in 1949 Robert Patterson of the Wyoming Game and Fish Commission located all the sage grouse leks in 650 hectares (some 1,600 acres) of sagebrush in the western part of the state. He repeated his survey in 1950 and 1951. He found no new leks but observed that every lek recurred in the same location each year. The record for documented adherence to one location belongs to the Muddy Springs lek near Laramie, Wyo., first studied by John Scott of the University of Wyoming in 1940 and 1941. The location of the Muddy Springs lek had not changed when I worked in the area 28 years later.

Not only the lek itself but also the mating center, a small inner area about 10 meters in diameter where most of the copulations occur, is found in the same

MATING CENTER at a sage grouse communal display ground, or lek, in Wyoming is crowded with female grouse. A male grouse, much larger than the females, here appears to be even larger than usual be-cause it has inflated its esophageal sac with air in the course of a court-ship display known as a strut. The skin over the sac protrudes promi-nently and the male's head is hidden in a ruff of white neck feathers.

UPRIGHT FAN of tail feathers is part of the male sage grouse's dis-play posture. Raising the tail feathers brings the shorter, brown feath-ers under them into view; their white tips form a distinctive pattern that differs from male to male, as is evident in these photographs. Memorizing the different patterns enabled the author to identify in-dividual males in sight of his blind and to follow their movements.

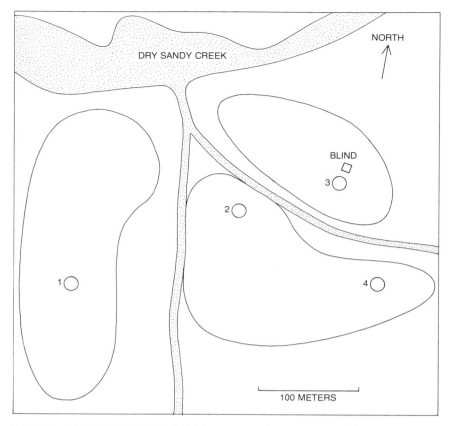

LARGE LEK IN WYOMING included three zones where males occupied territories; those zones contained a total of four mating centers, each center some 50 square meters in extent. Most of the females congregated at these centers. Every morning in season more than 250 males gathered at the lek. The author's blind was set up next to one of the four mating centers (*upper right*). Intermittent tributary streams feed Dry Sandy Creek; hence the name of the lek.

place year after year. Scott, Patterson and I have all observed this consistency of location, although in small leks or leks disturbed by human activities the location of the mating centers seems to be less consistent.

Sage grouse leks vary in the number of males in attendance. At some small leks only a few males congregate; some large ones have more than 400 males, although such a large number is unusual. In any event when more than 50 or 60 males congregate, the lek always has more than a single mating center. Thus in a really large lek one can expect to find one mating center for about every 50 males. This means that a large lek is in effect an aggregate of smaller ones, so that the basic unit of sage grouse social organization is a lek covering about two hectares (five acres) that is visited in season by as many as 50 or 60 male grouse and has a single mating center some 50 square meters in extent.

Even a biologist shivering in his blind at dawn, alone on the vast Wyoming plains, finds a big lek an imposing spectacle. Each arriving male grouse settles in its territory within the lek morning after morning to strut and to defend its boundaries against intrusion by other males. If one male should strut near the boundary of another male's terri-

tory, the challenged male will often respond by shifting its own strutting closer to the threatened boundary. Periodically neighboring males will interrupt their strutting for an outright boundary encounter. The encounters can begin suddenly, with one male rushing at another that has come too close to the line. The two males end up almost side by side, each facing past the other; they jockey back and forth a few steps at a time.

Occasionally tension mounts and actual fighting breaks out. Holding positions roughly side by side, the two males beat each other vigorously with their wings. Normally neither male is clearly defeated. As with territorial encounters in other animal species, the contestants soon back away into their respective domains. Injuries must occur occasionally, but I never saw a male hurt in one of these encounters.

Accurate observation of this kind of behavior requires an ability to identify every male grouse individually. Rather than risk upsetting the birds by capturing them for artificial marking, I learned to identify individuals by the unique pattern formed by the feathers under their cocked tail; the short feathers under the tail are chocolate brown with white tips, and no two patterns are

exactly alike. In each year of my study I soon came to recognize every male within sight of my blind.

I was also able to plot the location of each boundary encounter within a radius of 30 to 50 meters from the blind by making a detailed map of the terrain; the map included every bunch of sagebrush and clump of grass in view. The plotting was further assisted by laying out small flags in a grid near the blind. I also used a 16-millimeter motion-picture camera to monitor the activities of the males. By filming at the time-lapse rate of one frame every four seconds I could generally record the behavior of as many as five males over a two-hour period beginning at sunrise. When I plotted the locations of boundary encounters on the map, it turned out that the lines of demarcation between adjacent males' territories were precise: many boundaries were defined to within a meter or less. Territories near the mating center were smaller than territories toward the outer edge of the lek: no more than 30 square meters compared with 100.

My observations established that each male sage grouse reigns supreme within its own territory. Most important, within its own territory each male can copulate without being challenged by a neighboring male. It is only when a male mounts a female close to a territorial boundary that the neighboring male dashes forward and precipitates a confrontation that interrupts the copulation. Any male grouse, regardless of its success or lack of success in mating with the females, is subject to a neighboring male's attack if it attempts copulation too near a territorial boundary.

To occupy a territory within or near the mating center of a lek is to enjoy a great advantage in copulation; a male so situated will copulate repeatedly, whereas its immediate neighbors copulate only rarely. In spite of this discrepancy the less successful neighbor will not intrude on the more successful male to interrupt copulation, and the more successful one will not intrude on the less successful one, unless either attempts copulation too near the territorial boundary. Clearly a male sage grouse becomes successful in mating not because of any ability to interrupt other males' attempts at copulation but because it has obtained a territory that coincides with a mating center.

Naturalists in the past were uncertain whether the male grouse at leks evinced territorial behavior, in which neighbors meet as equals at mutual boundaries, or a dominance hierarchy, in which dominant males exclude subordinate ones from an opportunity to mate. Actually the social interactions of male sage grouse are a blend of these two classic patterns of behavior. Neighboring males meet at boundaries more or less as equals. They only occasionally intrude into each other's territories, even when one mates frequently and the other does not. Yet males are attracted to the mating center within a lek. As a result each male tends to strut most of the time near its territorial boundary closest to the mating center. At the same time it guards against intrusions from neighbors whose territories lie farther from the mating center than its own. I found that each male attacks those neighbors farther from the mating center more often than the neighbors attack the more central male. In effect the males practice "polarized territoriality": they are ranked in a dominance hierarchy in accordance with the distance of their territories from the mating center.

What behavioral responses of the female grouse establish the mating center? One hypothesis, proposed by the first naturalists to study leks, is that male grouse differ from one another and that the females, following some criterion of form or behavior, choose to mate with the most attractive male on the lek and thereby transform its territory into a mating center. The hypothesis seems plausible at first; the casual observer at a lek soon sees that the males adjacent to the breeding center strut more often than males farther removed, spend more time in the strutting posture and also have more frequent boundary encounters with neighboring males. Conceivably any one or all of these actions might attract females. One must be cautious, however, about accepting such an explanation. The possibility cannot be excluded that the greater activity of the males near the center is the result of the females' congregating there rather than the cause. If males are more active when they are near females, then regardless of how the females select a place to congregate the males at the selected site would exhibit the greatest activity.

To test these alternative explanations I recorded the activities of male grouse located either centrally or peripherally on the lek under conditions of equivalent proximity to the females. Time-lapse photography helped me to document the males' behavior in three different circumstances: when females were inside the territorial boundary of the male being observed, when females were inside the territory of an immediately neighboring male and when no females were in either the observed male's territory or the territory of any of its immediate neighbors.

In the first instance I found that the males strutted frequently, often at an apparently maximum rate (in excess of six struts per minute). They strutted less often when the females were present only in a neighbor's territory, and they scarcely strutted at all when no females were in adjacent territories. Thus there were no consistent behavioral differences between successful and unsuccess-

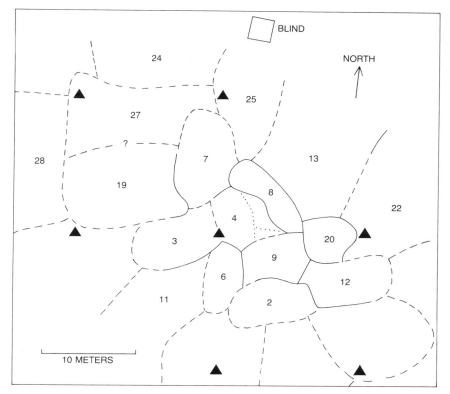

MALE TERRITORIES surrounding one mating center at the Dry Sandy lek were occupied by 20 grouse at the time of the author's observations. Each bird was assigned an identifying number; the four numbers in colored circles identify yearling males in their first season on a lek. The two numbers in colored squares identify the most sexually active males; the four numbers in colored triangles identify males that also copulated but less frequently. Black triangles locate grid-corner flags, aids to territory mapping; boundaries with broken lines are known less accurately than those with solid lines. Colored rectangle outlines lek area shown enlarged in the illustration below. Only the six males so identified and none of the 14 other identified birds nor the many males with territories farther from the mating center succeeded in mating.

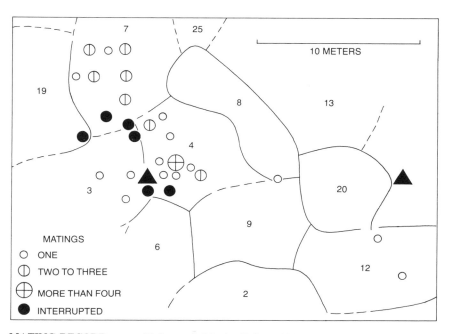

MATING RECORD over a 20-day period in April shows high activity on the part of males No. 7 and No. 4, lower activity on the part of males No. 3, No. 9 and No. 12 and no activity at all on the part of male No. 8. Six mating efforts were interrupted, all of them when the male concerned attempted copulation at a point too near the boundary of a neighboring territory.

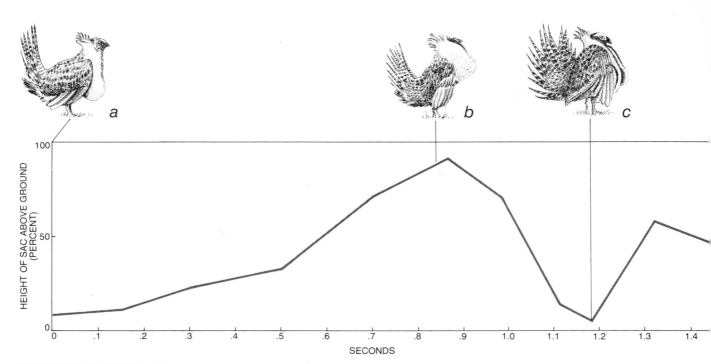

STRUTTING SEQUENCE of the male sage grouse during a single three-second strut is illustrated at the top. The graph at the bottom shows variations in the height of the male's esophageal sac expressed as a percent of the maximum; a near-maximum is seen in illustra-

ful males under conditions of equivalent proximity to females.

Jon Hartzler of the University of Montana has also attempted to discover individual differences between successful and unsuccessful male sage grouse at varying distances from females. For his criterion he used the absolute distance between the male and the female rather than the female's presence in the male's territory or absence from it. He found that successful males are slightly more active than unsuccessful ones at the same distance from the female. The difference in our respective findings might be due to our different criteria regarding a male's proximity to females. At the moment it is not clear whether behavioral differences of individual males affect the females' choice of a place to mate. The fact remains that the more frequent strutting activity of male grouse adjacent to the lek mating center is primarily the effect of the females'

MATING-CENTER ACTION during a 25-minute period in mid-April at the Ford's Creek lek in Montana can be followed in the eight frames from a time-lapse film reproduced here. The mating-center area coincided with the territory of one male grouse; a caret above each of the frames locates the male. Some seven females and four males can be seen in the first frame; the females are congregated inside the mating center (middle), and male A (caret) has just moved toward one edge of its territory to confront one of three neighboring males. The encounter lasted for less than four seconds; in the next frame male A has returned to the assembly of females. In the third frame, some five minutes later, male A has moved to the opposite side of the territory, where a female solicits copulation. In the fourth frame, less

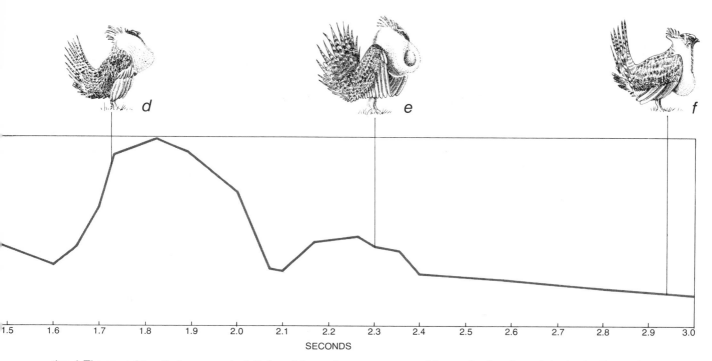

tion d. The upward toss that accompanies inflation of the sac is seen in b and d; the contraction that produces a popping sound is seen in e, some 2.3 seconds after the male begins its display. All male sage grouse strut in the same manner with only minor individual variations.

congregating there and not the cause.

In actuality a female grouse might choose a mating place in ways other than by discriminating between differences in the behavior of males. For example, the males' territories are smaller near the mating center than they are at the periphery of the lek, so that the con- gregation of males is densest near the center. The females might recognize this difference in density and choose to mate in the areas that have the denser concentration of displaying males. The density information, although not specific enough to locate the mating center exactly, would identify its general location.

Another possible cue is even more ambiguous. A mating center is usually located at a point within the lek where the growth of sagebrush is sparse. There are usually several such comparatively bare spots within the lek, yet only one will be the site of a mating center.

A highly specific cue for the location

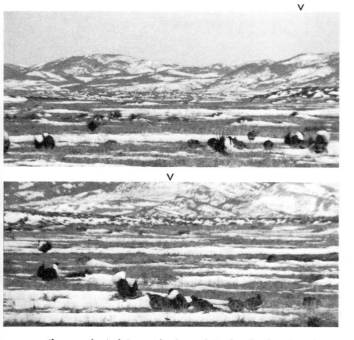

than a minute later, male A copulates for the first time (*zoom lens close-up*). Some three minutes later (*fifth frame*) male A and a second female copulate; neighboring males continue to display. Less than two minutes later (*sixth frame*) the neighboring males are dispersed to the far reaches of their territories and only one of the three (*right rear*) is in camera range. Male A struts alone amid the female assembly. Some four minutes later (*seventh frame*) male A copulates for the third time. The bird copulated five more times in the next eight minutes, thereby inseminating all but one of the nine females that had gathered at the mating center in the morning. By the ninth minute (*eighth frame*) male A has moved to the right to confront the male that occupies this adjacent territory. The gathering of females is dispersing.

of the mating center is the presence of a tight pack of females. This information, however, would be available only to those females that arrived at the lek later in the morning than the rest.

My own observations show that females arriving at a lek tend to follow one another and to stop as a group even when they are still some distance from the mating center. This attention of the females to one another's behavior might enable the females that were breeding for the first time to follow more experienced ones to the mating center, but only if the experienced ones had already learned the location of the center earlier in the breeding season or remembered the location from a previous year. A characteristic of one-year-old females noted by Robert Eng of Montana State University and Paul Dalke of the University of Idaho and their colleagues provides a mechanism whereby experienced females might cue novices. Eng and Dalke found that novice females arrive at the lek later and lay their eggs later in the breeding season than second-season and older females do. In other words, mature guidance is available to the novices.

So far it is uncertain which combination of cues guides the female sage grouse in selecting a place to mate. Two facts—that females follow one another on the lek and that they gather in a dense cluster at the mating center—suggest, however, that interactions between the females themselves, and not merely the females' response to the males' displays, control most if not all of the females' breeding behavior.

The key question here is clearly not "How do females choose a particular male to mate with?" but "How do males acquire territories at a mating center?" The recurrence of a mating center in the same location within a lek year after year cannot reflect an enduring preference of the female grouse population for individual male grouse. This becomes obvious when one considers that mortality in the male grouse population runs at a rate of about 50 percent per year. To learn how some males reach the mating center one must focus on the social dynamics that regulate territorial accession.

On the leks that I observed the process of accession can be described as centripetally oriented filling of vacancies. Whenever a male grouse disappeared overnight, the vacancy it left was occupied by one or more neighboring birds whose territory was farther from the mating center. I never saw a male fill a vacancy that was farther from the center than its own territory.

The vacancy-filling process was gradual. Often on the first day none of the missing male's neighbors made any major intrusion on the vacant territory. Over the next day or two, however, a peripheral neighbor would extend its strutting activities farther and farther until the vacancy had been transformed into its new territory. The inward movement of course left the newcomer's former territory vacant and would initiate an inward shift by the next most peripheral neighbor.

The process is not always precisely predictable, even though no males move in an outward direction and none leapfrog over an intervening territory. For example, two neighbors equidistant from the center sometimes divide a more central vacancy between them, but on other occasions one bird lays claim to the whole of the more central vacancy and the other ignores the newly created vacancy and remains in its old territory. Regardless of such details, within any one mating season the male grouse tend to move gradually closer to the mating center simply by filling vacancies.

That male grouse continue their progress toward the mating center year after year seems likely for several reasons. For one thing, in many species of lek-forming grouse the males maintain at least perfunctory contact with their leks throughout the year. On warm days in the fall and winter they visit their leks briefly in the morning. They do not usually strut much on these off-season occasions, but the visits could enable individual males to maintain contact with their lek neighbors on a year-round and even a year-to-year basis. In this connection, banding studies have demonstrated that once a male grouse has established a territory on one lek the bird rarely moves to another lek in subsequent breeding seasons.

Observations of lek activity in late winter, just before the male grouse begin to congregate in earnest, reveal an absence of vigorous competition for central positions. Only a few of the males established on the lek will show up on any one morning, and the birds are relatively inactive. Thus it seems reasonable to suppose the filling of vacancies due to winter mortality is a gradual process, beginning with the return of the surviving males to their approximate former positions. It is certainly the case among sharp-tailed grouse, as Henry Kermott of the University of Minnesota has documented in detail. He found that the process of gradual movement toward the mating center begins in the male's first breeding season and continues from year to year.

First-year sage grouse males, easily recognizable because their tail feathers are less sharply pointed than those of older males, arrive at the lek much later in the breeding season than the older males. The young males probably visit a number of leks before settling at one of them. Most of the first-year males have yet to establish their own territories on a lek by the time the female grouse arrive. By the middle of April, when copulation is in progress, the young males take up positions on the periphery of the lek. In due course they begin normal territorial behavior, coming regularly each morning to reoccupy their chosen domain. Here the luck of the draw can play a part in the young males' future success. Leks are seldom exactly symmetrical. As a result some of the first-year males will find fewer occupied territories between them and the mating center than others will. At the same time the advantage of a superior initial position can be nullified if the random death of older birds does not vacate intervening territories.

The evidence hence suggests a consistent hypothesis for male sexual success

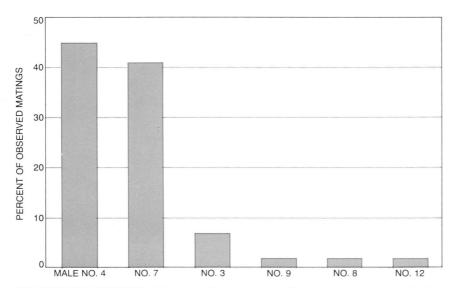

SEASON-LONG RECORD of the six mating males at the Dry Sandy lek shows that the two most active birds were responsible for 86 percent of the 42 copulations observed at the center.

51 OBSERVATION PERIODS

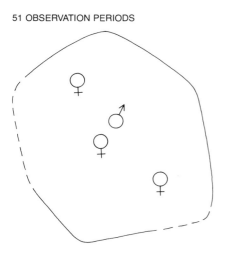

36 OBSERVATION PERIODS

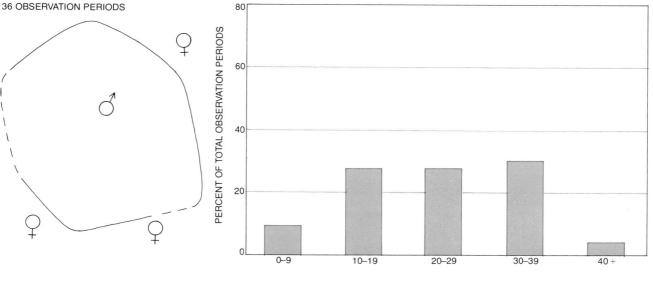

66 OBSERVATION PERIODS

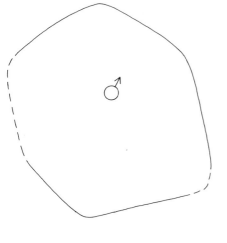

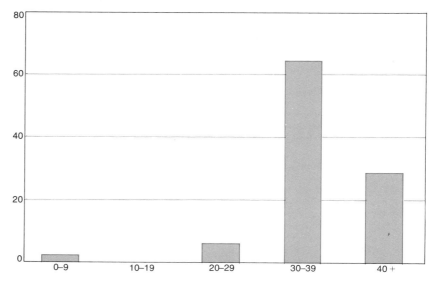

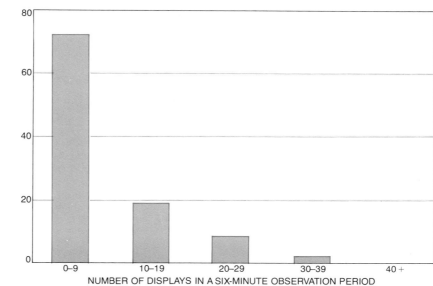

FREQUENCY OF DISPLAYS by male sage grouse is directly related to the nearness of females. A total of 51 observations proved that males usually displayed more than 30 times during a six-minute interval when females were inside a male's territory (*top*). When the females were outside a male's territory but inside a neighboring territory (*center*), the frequency was lower, although males still strutted between 10 and 39 times every six minutes. When no females were adjacent (*bottom*), most male displays fell to fewer than 10 in six minutes.

along the following lines. In its first year the male grouse establishes a territory at the edge of a lek. In successive years the bird tends to return both to the same lek and to the same general location within the lek. The bird's location shifts centripetally both within a season and from year to year, and its progression toward the mating center—and mating success—remains probabilistic throughout. Although there is undoubtedly a good deal of variation in the ages of males that reach the mating center, the first-year males will virtually never mate and the second-year males are less likely to achieve mating success than older males. Thus there is a regular ontogenetic trajectory, or developmental progression, by which a male achieves full reproductive success. In the simplest terms, the key to success is age before beauty.

What has been said so far applies to males. Is there any such ontogenetic trajectory for the female grouse? Evidently not. Almost all the females mate each season; they begin to reproduce in their first year and lay about the same number of eggs annually as long as they survive. The young male grouse, on the other hand, not only rarely reproduce but also are less developed than older males in terms of morphology and physiology. Their plumage is not as developed as the older males', and even at the height of the breeding season their testes are smaller.

I have termed this difference in the life cycles of male and female sage grouse sexual "bimaturism," a condition analogous to sexual dimorphism. Bimaturism is characteristic not only of the sage grouse and other lek-displaying birds but also of most if not all animals with polygynous mating systems. Even human society is not exempt: where polygynous marriage is practiced the difference in age between the male (older) and the female (younger) at first marriage is substantial.

So far I have attempted to analyze the behavioral mechanisms that regulate the structure of the sage grouse lek system. How might such a social system have evolved? One feature of the system—the congregation of displaying males—could have evolved, at least among grouse, in a straightforward way. Clustering at mating time would have adaptive value for grouse in open habitats by virtue of protecting the displaying males from predators' surprise attacks in the dim light at dawn. Polygynous grouse that live in forests do not form leks; the individual males occupy large territories and perform their displays at widely dispersed locations. In open country, however, the males of all polygynous grouse species display in aggregations. The presence of so many watchmen, so to speak, affords each male some protection from predators

such as eagles and coyotes. Indeed, I have witnessed several close escapes from attacking eagles that seemed to know the location of the lek. The predators, flying close to the ground, used low ridges for cover, and often they approached unobserved within 100 meters of the lek before their final dash.

What is more difficult to explain is the evolution of a social structure that features such an extremely unequal distribution of copulations by males; sage grouse practice the most extreme polygyny known among birds. Most biologists now agree that the evolution of social behavior, like the evolution of any other trait, is best explained in terms of the optimization of the individual's "Darwinian fitness," that is, the optimization of the rate at which the genes of the individual are conveyed to its descendants. An explanation of the evolution of a mating system must explain the advantages of the system with respect to the Darwinian fitness of both males and females.

As to male fitness in polygynous societies, the delay before males achieve successful reproduction complicates matters. The rate at which an individual's genes propagate to its descendants depends not only on the individual's fecundity but also on the age at which the individual and its descendants begin to breed. In simple terms, a delay in reproduction increases the generation time and thus lowers the rate at which descendants multiply. A male that delays reproduction in effect tends to sacrifice the advantages of high fecundity once breeding begins.

To see how this works, consider an imaginary bird society. Its males and females have identical survival rates but the males begin to reproduce at a later age than the females. More males than females in each cohort will die before they reach breeding age; as a result fewer males than females will breed in any one season. Such a society necessarily engages in polygyny.

Imagine further that the size of the population is constant, so that over a lifetime each bird leaves on the average one descendant of the same sex, and also that once the males begin to breed they all share the available females equally. In such a simple society polygyny offers neither advantages nor disadvantages to the male. The longer the males defer breeding, the more fecund they are when they begin to breed. The two effects exactly compensate for each other. Yet for the delayed-breeding characteristic of lek-mating males to have evolved at all the individual male grouse must realize some advantage in terms of the propagation of their descendants.

Two oversimplified and inadequate theories of male advantages in lek mating systems have long had currency. They may be called respectively the "sex appeal" theory and the "trial by ordeal"

theory. The first theory proposes that successful males in polygynous societies possess a higher evolutionary fitness than unsuccessful males because they have higher fecundity. The second theory proposes that the successful males have a higher fitness because they have survived longer. As we have seen, however, the high fecundity of successful male grouse does not necessarily mean that such males have higher evolutionary fitness, and neither does a greater life span. Fitness consists, rather, in the optimum distribution of the individual male grouse's time and energy to the promotion of its survival and the exercise of its fecundity over the entire span of its life.

One hypothetical advantage for males in polygynous societies seems at least plausible. If males that breed less are more likely to survive, such an increase in survival, if it is sufficient, could increase the evolutionary fitness of the males that defer reproduction to later ages. Whether or not a hypothesis along these lines can help to explain sage grouse polygyny is not yet clear. Verification in the field would not be easy; it would require comparisons of the longevity and fecundity of males that start breeding at different ages.

When earlier naturalists speculated on fitness, they often equated the behavioral competition between individuals with evolutionary competition. My findings on sage grouse show that this equation cannot be accepted in every case. Competition of the first kind has to do with which individual wins fights, whereas competition of the second kind has to do with which individual's genes pass on to descendants. After observing a lek it would be tempting to conclude that the successful males are simply the winners in a competition with the unsuccessful males. In a behavioral sense they are: the males at the mating center exclude intruders from their territory by means of threat and overt aggression. That, however, is not necessarily evolutionary competition. If indeed males increase their evolutionary fitness by deferring full reproductive activity, then the fact that an older male successfully excludes a younger male from the opportunity to copulate might have nothing to do with differences in Darwinian fitness. Quite possibly both grouse are acting in accordance with an evolutionary strategy that enhances the fitness of both.

Does the polygynous mating system offer any advantages to the female grouse? One consequence of such mating is reduced or nonexistent parental care by males. Of the 16 grouse species, 12 are polygynous, and only one of the four monogamous species practices dual parental care. Single parenthood would certainly be disadvantageous for the monogamous and polygynous species alike if grouse nestlings required, as many newly hatched birds do, a prolonged period of feeding until they mature to a state of independence. As it happens, however, all 16 species of grouse, like domestic chickens, give rise to precocial young that are able to follow their mother and feed themselves soon after hatching. Hence a potential disadvantage of polygynous mating has been largely nullified. Nevertheless, three species of grouse have single parental care but practice monogamy. Evi-

dently the evolution of a social pattern of single parenthood, and for that matter the evolution of the precocial young that makes single parenthood possible, although necessary prerequisites to the evolution of polygyny, are scarcely sufficient causal factors.

On balance the adaptive advantage gained by the female grouse depends on the advantages of the male's strategy. Each female's genes are transmitted equally to its male and female descendants: consequently the best strategies for

each sex are not in conflict. By breeding with males that practice the optimal male strategy the females increase their own evolutionary fitness: the rate at which their genes propagate to descendants. Hence from generation to generation both the male and the female sage grouse have evolved a mating relationship in accordance with a delicate balance between the disadvantages of single parental care and the advantages of sexual bimaturism.

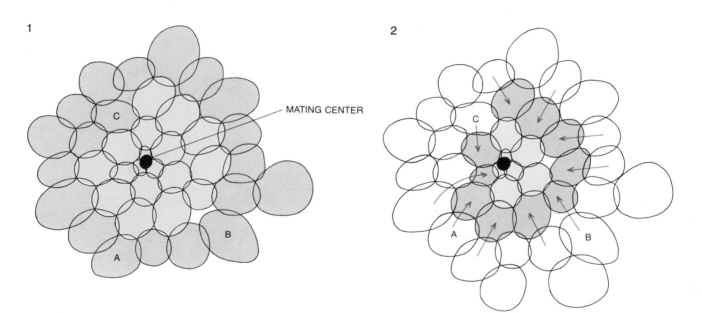

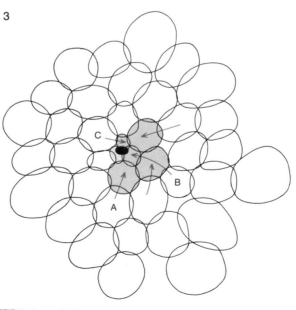

PROGRESSION TO MATING CENTER is shown in idealized form here. At start (1) 20 young males have established territories (gray) on the periphery of a lek during their first mating season; the more central positions are occupied by older males. By chance the territory of male C is closer to the mating center (black) than the territories of males A and B are. By the next spring (2) about half of the preceding year's yearlings have died, as have half of the older males. Males A, **B and C and others of their cohort (gray) are now closer to the mating center; the better starting position of male C has brought it closest. The following year (3) only five of the cohort still survive. The territories of males B and C now overlap the mating center, and the territory of male A is adjacent to it; the ontogenetic trajectories of males B and C mean that they will sire many of the young produced during the season. Male A, if it survives, will probably reach center the next year.**

Ecological Chemistry

17

Lincoln Pierson Brower
February 1969

*Certain insects feed on plants that make substances
that are poisonous to vertebrates. Hence the insects
are unpalatable to bird predators. These relations
have surprising results*

Many plants synthesize chemical compounds that apparently serve no purpose in the plant's metabolism. Some of these compounds are quite complex, and even if they were simple it would be puzzling that the plant should make them; the synthesis calls for a considerable expenditure of energy. Why, then, does the plant manufacture these substances? One reasonable explanation is that they promote the survival of the plant either by repressing the growth of competing plants and parasitic microorganisms or by repelling insects or other animals that would otherwise feed on it.

There is reason to believe this is only part of the story of the secondary substances made by plants. My colleagues and I (at Amherst College, the University of Oxford and the University of Basel) find evidence that such substances can play a much subtler role in a community of interacting plants and animals. For example, certain plants manufacture compounds that are poisonous to vertebrates, but certain insects are able to feed on the plants. An insect that feeds on such a plant ingests the poison and is therefore unpalatable to vertebrate predators. Moreover, an insect that does not feed on the plant can mimic the appearance of the insect that does, and is thus avoided by predators even though it is palatable. In the light of such relationships one begins to perceive that the study of secondary substances can be characterized as ecological chemistry.

A striking instance of the effectiveness of the secondary substances in repelling animals is provided in Costa Rica by the milkweed *Asclepias curassavica.* In the province of Guanacaste large herds of cattle completely avoid the plant even though it grows abundantly in the grass. The cattle do so with good

reason: this plant and others belonging to the large family Asclepiadaceae often cause sickness in livestock and occasionally death.

The poisons in the asclepiads have attracted much attention among pharmacologists and organic chemists because the substances are chemically similar to the drug digitalis; they share with it the remarkable property of having a highly specific effect on the vertebrate heart. These drugs, called cardiac glycosides or cardenolides, cause a weak and rapidly fluttering heart to beat more strongly and more slowly. Like most other drugs, cardiac glycosides produce side effects. One of profound importance is the activation of the nerve center in the brain that controls vomiting. Pharmacologists working with cats and pigeons have found that the dosage necessary to cause emesis is just about half the amount required to cause death. Hence an animal that eats a food containing cardiac glycosides will, provided that it is capable of vomiting, rid itself of the poisons before a lethal amount can be absorbed. In other words, although the animal suffers a very unpleasant gastronomic experience, vomiting protects it from being killed by the poisonous food.

In contrast to the animals that are made ill by eating milkweeds containing cardiac glycosides are the animals that eat the plants with no apparent adverse effects. For example, milkweeds are the exclusive food of the larvae of an entire group of tropical insects: the Danainae, which includes the familiar monarch and

queen butterflies. Naturalists have observed for more than a century that insect-eating vertebrates, particularly birds, avoid these butterflies. A widely accepted hypothesis has been that the predators avoid the butterflies because the larvae have assimilated the poisonous substances from the milkweeds. The implications of this hypothesis are most interesting: the Danaine butterflies not only must have developed the ability to feed on the poisonous milkweeds but also apparently are able to use the poisonous substances against their predators.

We undertook to test this hypothesis with a threefold approach. First, our group at Amherst reared a large number of monarchs on *Asclepias curassavica,* and John Parsons of Oxford subjected them to a series of pharmacological tests. Assaying extracts of the butterflies, he found that they contained cardiac glycosides similar to digitalis in their effects. Second, with new facilities at Amherst we were able to rear some two pounds of monarchs (1,540 butterflies) on *A. curassavica,* and Tadeus Reichstein of the University of Basel chemically analyzed both the butterflies and the plants. His results showed that the plant and the butterfly contain at least three cardiac glycosides that are identical. They are calactin, calotropin and calotoxin [*see bottom illustration on page 175*].

In the course of rearing the butterflies and plants for chemical analysis we had begun our third line of attack. By selec-

REACTION OF BLUE JAY to palatable and unpalatable monarch butterflies appears in the photographs on the following page. At top the jay attacks a palatable butterfly *(1),* eats it *(2),* and later eats another monarch *(3).* When the same jay is presented *(4)* with a monarch that is unpalatable because it fed on poisonous milkweed at the larval stage, the bird eats only part of it *(5)* and then reacts *(6).* Soon it vomits *(7),* and after drinking water it vomits again *(8).* It soon recovers *(9)* but rejects subsequent monarchs on sight.

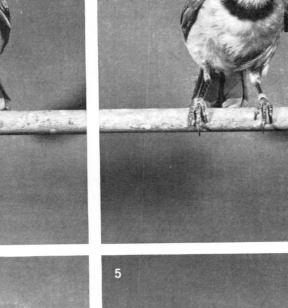

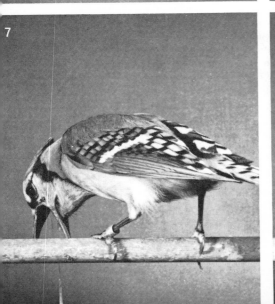

tive breeding we obtained a strain of monarch butterflies that could develop on cabbage, a plant known to lack cardiac glycosides. Our assumption was that cabbage-reared monarchs would prove acceptable to our test birds, which were blue jays captured locally. At first all our blue jays were extremely reluctant to attack the monarchs. We found, however, that if we deprived the jays of food for several hours, they would become hungry enough to attack and eat the butterflies. Once the jays had been induced to try the monarchs they would accept them readily whenever we offered them and would devour them with no signs of sickness.

Having broken down the initial reluctance of the blue jays, we then offered them monarchs reared on *A. curassavica*. Most of the birds promptly ate at least one butterfly. Within 12 minutes, on the average, every bird became violently ill, vomiting the ingested material and continuing to vomit as many as nine times over a half-hour period. All the birds recovered fully within about half an hour.

In preparation for our feeding experiments we had also cultivated several other milkweed plants in our greenhouse. Much to our surprise, one species from the tropical Western Hemisphere, *Gonolobus rostratus,* produced monarch adults that were as acceptable to birds as the cabbage-reared butterflies were. As the reader can readily imagine, we were delighted when Reichstein analyzed our *Gonolobus* plants and found that they completely lack cardiac glycosides. These findings showed clearly that the palatability of the monarch butterfly is directly related to the kind of plant eaten by the larvae: if the plant contains cardiac glycosides, the adult butterflies also contain them, and if the plant lacks the poisons, the butterflies also lack them.

The next question we asked was: Is there a spectrum of palatability in monarch butterflies that is dependent on the particular plants the larvae eat? To investigate the matter we first determined which species of milkweed produce emetic butterflies. Our technique was to induce the birds to eat the nonemetic butterflies reared on *Gonolobus* and then to offer them butterflies reared on a variety of other milkweeds. So far we have found that three species of *Asclepias* common in eastern North America produce palatable butterflies, whereas two milkweeds from the southeastern U.S. produce emetic ones. In addition we have discovered that monarchs

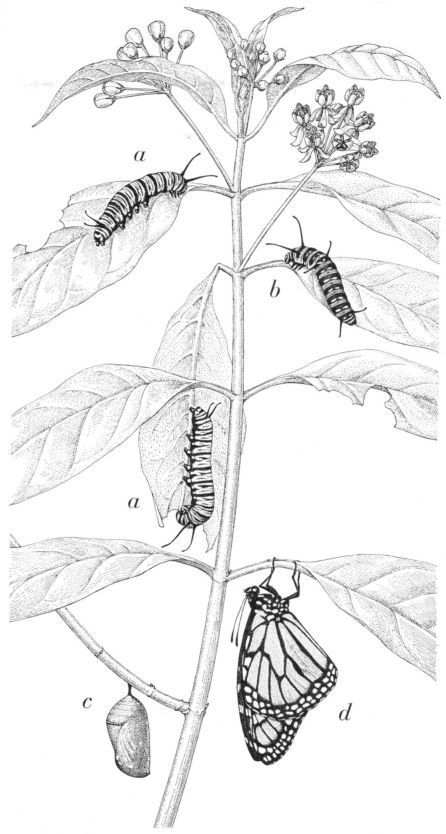

ECOLOGICAL SETTING of the plant-butterfly-bird relationship includes the milkweed *Asclepias curassavica* and the larval stage of such butterflies as the monarch (*a*) and the queen (*b*). The plant produces substances called cardiac glycosides, which have a strong effect on the vertebrate heart. Larvae assimilate the substances, which are retained by adults, so that an adult monarch (*d*) is unpalatable to birds. At *c* is a monarch butterfly chrysalis.

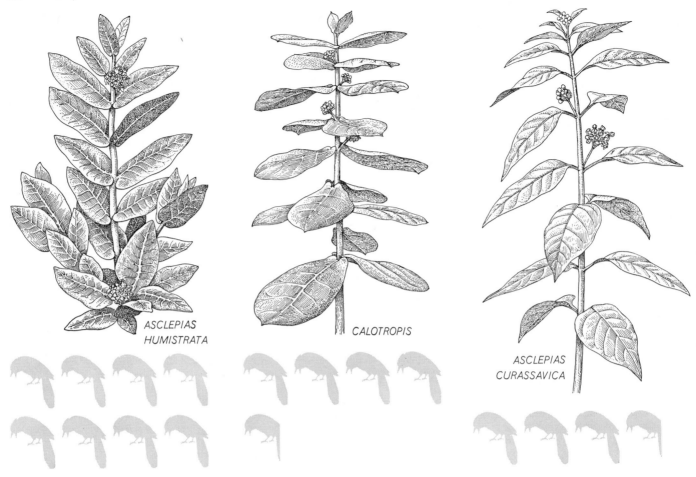

RELATIVE TOXICITY of several milkweeds and of monarch butterflies raised on them is expressed in terms of blue jay emetic units. The units represent the number of blue jays that will be made ill by the poisons in one monarch butterfly raised on a given

reared on two African milkweeds belonging to the genera *Calotropis* and *Gomphocarpus* are emetic.

Having established this emetic series, William N. Ryerson (who is now at Yale University) and I developed a new method for comparing the degree of toxicity of the monarchs reared on the various plants. The technique consists in drying adult butterflies and grinding them to a fine powder, which we load into gelatin capsules that are force-fed to the birds. In this way we could determine the precise dosage of butterfly needed to cause emesis. Then, on the basis of the average weight of both monarch butterflies and blue jays, we calculated the number of blue jay emetic units per monarch butterfly [*see top illustration on this page*]. The experiments showed that a monarch that has eaten *Asclepias humistrata* contains enough poison to make approximately eight blue jays vomit; a butterfly reared on *Calotropis procera* contains 4.8 blue jay emetic units; one that has eaten *A. curassavica*, 3.8 units, and one that has eaten *Gomphocarpus*, .8 unit. In other words, there is a palatability spectrum, and the most unpalatable butterfly is at least 10 times as emetic as the most palatable one. Since the genus *Asclepias* consists of 108 known species in North America alone, and there are

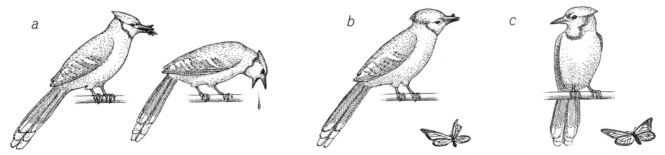

GOURMAND-GOURMET HYPOTHESIS put forward by the author holds that a bird can reject a poisonous insect at three physiological levels. To a naïve bird (*a*) flavor conveys no particular information, so that the bird will eat any food it finds and is a gourmand. When a bird is made ill by an insect, it associates the flavor of the insect with the illness and thereafter can reject a similar insect by tasting it (*b*), so that the bird becomes something of a gourmet. At that level, however, the bird must still take the time to catch the insect. Hence birds usually learn to reject such insects on sight (*c*), which is the most efficient level of rejection.

GOMPHOCARPUS

GONOLOBUS

plant. For example, a single butterfly raised on milkweed *Asclepias humistrata* contains enough cardiac glycosides to cause emesis in eight blue jays (*left*). *Gonolobus* is nonemetic.

several other genera of milkweed on the continent, it seems likely that the spectrum of palatability is very wide indeed.

Moreover, we have here an ecologically important criterion for measuring the palatability of food to wild animals. Clearly a butterfly is unsuitable food if it causes emesis, but if it carries less than an emetic dosage, it could serve as an emergency ration during periods of food shortage, provided that the birds ate successive individuals at a sufficiently slow rate. Measuring palatability by the criterion of emesis not only is more objective than many of the vague concepts of palatability that are so often discussed in the technical literature of biology but also provides insight into the kinds of problems that confront wild animals in their quest for food.

I have mentioned that most of the blue jays we trained to eat the nonemetic butterflies subsequently ate without hesitation the first highly emetic one we gave them. After recovering from their bout of vomiting the birds usually rejected all subsequent monarchs on sight

alone. By again depriving the jays of food, however, we were able to induce them to attack another nonemetic monarch. Now instead of swallowing the butterfly rapidly a bird would peck it apart, manipulate the mangled pieces in its bill and often regurgitate pieces several times before finally swallowing them.

This behavior has led us to propose a new way of looking at the biological significance of taste; we call it "the gourmand-gourmet hypothesis." According to this hypothesis items of food in the natural environment have a variety of flavors that in themselves convey no relevant information to a vertebrate animal eating the food for the first time. Hence the naïve animal will initially accept a wide range of food. If the animal eats the food and then vomits, however, it will associate the taste signals present in the food as it is expelled through the mouth with the noxious experience of the entire emesis syndrome. In other words, just as an animal can learn to associate an unpleasant experience with the color pattern of a food item and subsequently to reject the food on sight, so

can it probably associate the taste of the food with the noxious effects. Initially a gourmand, the animal becomes by conditioning a gourmet, and for the rest of its life the taste signals in its food convey relevant information. Once conditioned in this way the animal will exercise judgment in assessing the taste of potential food items.

A plant-eating animal or a prey-catching one will always be confronted with a wide potential of food items in its natural environment. In terms of our blue jay–monarch butterfly system it is important to realize that the bird has three levels at which it can reject a poisonous butterfly. The most basic level is the automatic gastronomic rejection brought on by the emetic effect of the cardiac glycoside. Clearly this is the least efficient form of rejection, since the bird not only is made sick but also loses any food that was in its crop before it ate the poisonous insect. Once the bird has suffered this noxious primary experience and has learned to avoid food with the particular flavor, it can reject the same type of butterfly merely by tasting it. This is the second level of rejection. It too is rather inefficient, because if it is to operate, the bird must first catch the butterfly. The most efficient level of rejection is provided by the capacity to associate the visual characteristics of the food with its unpalatability, since the bird then need neither get sick nor even waste time catching the insect in order to determine its flavor.

The fact that many naturally occurring plant poisons, including alkaloids and cardiac glycosides, are bitter is highly relevant. The poison itself could very well be tasteless, provided that it was always associated with a flavor that could serve as a cue for conditioning predators. These considerations raise the possibility that certain plants and prey animals have flavors usually associated with particular poisons but actually lack the poisons. They would thus be exhibiting a form of mimicry.

Mimicry in insects usually refers, of course, to the imitation by one species of the distinctive coloration of another species. One can see how natural selection favored the evolution of distinctive coloring in unpalatable species, because the coloration operates as a cue that reminds the predator of its earlier unpleasant experience. The warning coloration is of advantage to both prey and predator: the prey is less frequently attacked, and the predator can hunt more efficiently because it does not need to waste time catching unpalatable insects.

LIMENITIS ARTHEMIS   *LIMENITIS ARCHIPPUS*   *DANAUS PLEXIPPUS*

BATESIAN MIMICRY, named for the 19th-century English naturalist Henry W. Bates, arises when a palatable insect comes to look like an unpalatable one, thereby sharing the unpalatable one's capacity to repel predators. An example is the North American butterfly *Limenitis.* From its original form (*left*) it has evolved a form (*center*) that mimics the monarch butterfly *Danaus* (*right*).

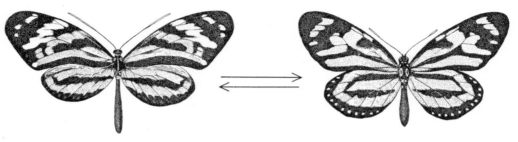

HIRSUTIS MEGARA   *LYCOREA CERES*

MÜLLERIAN MIMICRY, named for the 19th-century German zoologist Fritz Müller, appears when two species of unpalatable insects come to look alike. An example from Trinidad is the resemblance between butterflies *Hirsutis megara* from the family Ithomiidae (*left*) and *Lycorea ceres* from the family Danaidae (*right*). Similarity enables each species to gain protection from the other.

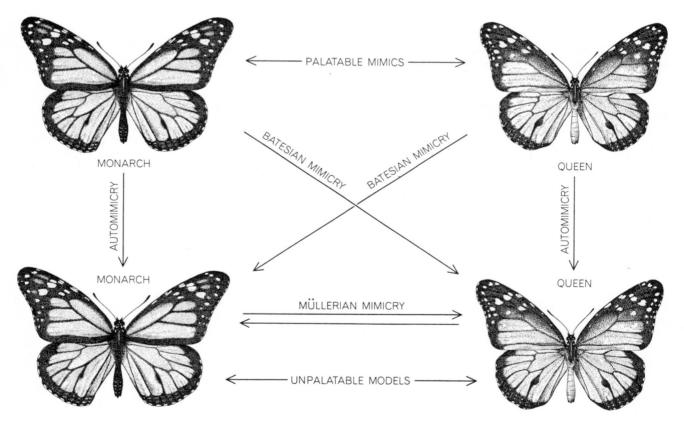

MULTIPLE MIMICRY found in Trinidad between monarch and queen butterflies is charted. Palatable monarchs resemble unpalatable queens in Batesian mimicry, as is the case with palatable queens resembling unpalatable monarchs. Unpalatable monarchs and queens resemble each other in Müllerian mimicry. Automimicry describes recent discovery that not all monarchs and queens are unpalatable. The term refers to the fact that palatable butterflies gain protection from unpalatable ones of the same species.

Once unpalatable insects with a warning coloration evolved, the opportunity arose for natural selection to favor modifications in palatable species so that they came to look like unpalatable ones. This phenomenon, which is called Batesian mimicry after the 19th-century English naturalist Henry W. Bates, is widespread and involves many different groups of insects and other prey organisms. The mimic takes advantage of the fact that the predator has learned to avoid the model: the unpalatable prey with a warning coloration. Clearly the mimic must not become too common with respect to the model or the system would tend to break down because the predators would so frequently encounter palatable mimics.

Another form of mimicry is called Müllerian after Fritz Müller, a German zoologist of the late 19th century. It entails resemblances among unpalatable insects. Tropical regions abound with groups of unpalatable insects that have come to look alike because natural selection has favored the evolution of a few common warning colorations. This type of mimicry benefits predators by reducing the number of color patterns that need to be remembered. The prey benefit because the numbers of individuals that are killed in each group of Müllerian mimics are reduced: once predators learn to avoid one species on sight they will tend to reject them all.

If, as our experiments suggest, certain plants and prey insects have the flavors usually associated with particular poisons but do not contain the poisons, they would be flavor mimics and would gain the usual advantages of Batesian mimicry. Other foods could contain different poisons but have similar flavors. They would gain the mutualistic advantage of

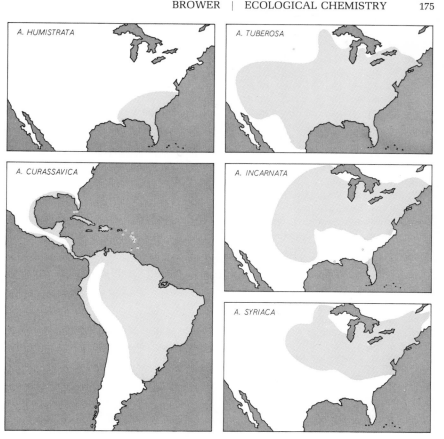

APPROXIMATE DISTRIBUTION of five species of milkweed of the genus *Asclepias* is indicated. The two species at left produce cardiac glycosides, so that butterflies feeding on the plants are unpalatable to birds. The three species at right lack the cardiac glycosides.

Müllerian mimicry.

The fact that monarch butterflies exhibit a spectrum of palatability from completely acceptable to totally unacceptable has led us to propose an extension of mimicry theory to include what we call automimicry. In our view butterflies that feed on poisonous plants can serve as unpalatable models and protect the individuals of their own species that have not fed on such plants. Since both butterflies are of the same species, the palatable individuals can be called automimics of the unpalatable ones. The advantage gained by an automimic is somewhat greater than the protection secured by a Batesian mimic; whereas the Batesian mimic has evolved a close re-

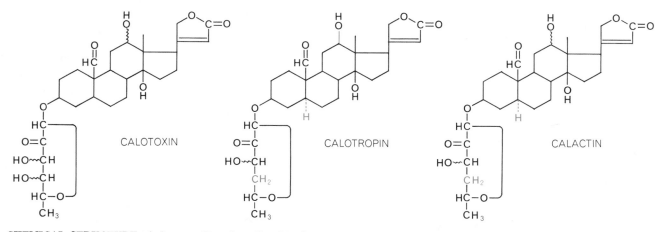

CHEMICAL STRUCTURE of three cardiac glycosides found in both the milkweed *A. curassavica* and the monarch butterflies that feed on the plant is indicated. Assays of the plants and butterflies were made by Tadeus Reichstein of the University of Basel. It was he also who hypothesized the structures of calotropin and calactin on the basis of the known structure of calotoxin (*left*).

semblance to its model, the automimic is a perfect mimic because it is a member of the same species.

We have calculated that if birds continued eating monarchs until they encountered an emetic one, and they then stopped eating monarchs, the protection afforded a butterfly population in which only half of the individuals are unpalatable would be nearly as great as if the entire population were unpalatable. Let us assume, for example, that a bird can eat up to 16 butterflies but stops eating them as soon as it eats an unpalatable one. Under these circumstances a butterfly population with 50 percent unpalatable members would suffer only 7 percent more predation than a population with 100 percent unpalatable members. Indeed, at the same level of predation a population that was only 25 percent unpalatable would still gain an immunity of 75 percent. As the level of potential predation increases, the advantage of automimicry tends to stabilize [*see illustration on this page*].

It might seem ecologically strange for prey that can become unpalatable simply by eating poisonous plants to feed on nonpoisonous ones. Yet we have found thus far that only two out of eight species of North American milkweeds produce emetic butterflies. The two are *Asclepias curassavica* and *A. humistrata.* We were surprised to find that three very common eastern species—*A. syriaca, A. tuberosa* and *A. incarnata*—produce palatable butterflies. These species are widely fed on by monarch larvae. Evidently this is the key to understanding the selective advantage of automimicry: If the majority of milkweeds in a given area are nonpoisonous, the monarchs will be forced to lay eggs on those plants and will deposit eggs on poisonous milkweeds only when they can find them. Automimicry enables the species to more than double its numbers without losing much of its protection from predation.

Our studies have established that wild populations of monarchs do include both palatable and unpalatable individuals. Last fall we collected a number of wild monarchs in western Massachusetts during their southward migration and subsequently dried and force-fed one butterfly each to 50 blue jays. Twelve of the butterflies (24 percent) caused emesis; the other ones proved to be palatable automimics. This finding agrees well with the minimum proportion of unpalatable individuals needed to confer a substantial automimetic advantage as shown in the illustration at the right. It will be interesting to press further with the investigation to discover what milk-weeds in the Northeast do produce emetic butterflies.

On the Caribbean island of Trinidad monarch butterflies live together with another species of the Danainae, the queen butterfly. In this part of their range both butterflies look very much alike in size and color pattern, and it has been assumed that they both are unpalatable species enjoying the mutualistic protection of Müllerian mimicry. In this area, as in North America, several species of asclepiad plants are available as food. The monarch lays its eggs almost exclusively on the common and poisonous *A. curassavica* but occasionally feeds on other asclepiads lacking cardiac glycosides. As one would expect, the majority (65 percent) of the monarchs from this area are emetic.

On the other hand, the queens are rarely found on *A. curassavica,* and only 15 percent of the adults captured are emetic. In the laboratory, however, the queens lay their eggs on the plant and freely feed on it. It seems likely that in this area of Trinidad the monarch somehow partly displaces the queen to the nonpoisonous milkweeds, which is why relatively few queens become emetic.

Yet the queens in Trinidad have evolved a great similarity to the monarchs in color pattern, which is not the case over most of the range where the two species live together. Hence the queens that are palatable gain the advantage of Batesian mimicry of the predominantly unpalatable monarch population, and the unpalatable queens share a Müllerian advantage with the unpalatable monarchs. At the same time the palatable monarchs are protected by the unpalatable monarchs and the palatable queens are protected by the unpalatable queens, so that automimicry is also involved. Thus in Trinidad the mimetic relations of the two species are complex and simultaneously involve Batesian mimicry, Müllerian mimicry and automimicry [*see bottom illustration on page 174*].

The discovery that certain insects can assimilate plant poisons they in turn employ as a defense against their predators provides a remarkable example of what George Gaylord Simpson has called the opportunistic aspect of evolution. Clearly ecological chemistry and its implications provide a fertile field for extending our understanding of the interrelations of ecology, sensory physiology and animal behavior.

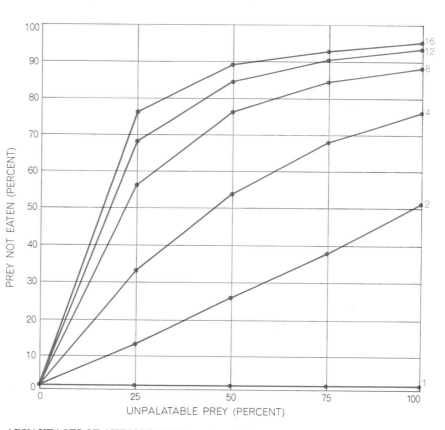

ADVANTAGES OF AUTOMIMICRY are charted for six levels of predation. Colored numbers refer to the maximum number of prey eaten by a single predator in a given time. A butterfly population in which only 25 to 50 percent of the individuals are unpalatable from having fed on poisonous plants is almost as well protected as if all individuals were emetic.

VI

PHYSIOLOGY AND SONG

VI PHYSIOLOGY AND SONG

INTRODUCTION

T he body plan of birds has been greatly influenced by their ancestry, method of reproduction, size, and dual modes of locomotion. Many of the features we think of as birdlike are actually those of their reptilian ancestors. These include specialized organs for hatching (egg teeth and hatching muscles), a special organ in the eye (pecten), scales, and hollow bones. Indeed, since T. H. Huxley, generations of comparative anatomy students have been taught to think of birds as "glorified reptiles."

FEATURES THAT BIRDS AND REPTILES HAVE IN COMMON

Large-yolked eggs	Single ear bone
Nucleated red blood cells	Special rib processes
Egg-tooth and hatching muscle	Supporting bones in eye
Vestigial claws on wings	Airsacs
of some birds	Few skin glands
Pecten in eyes	Ball-and-socket
Scales	attachment of skull to
Hollow bones	the neck

The fact that most birds both fly and walk drastically affects the arrangement of their bodies (see Fig. 1). The large sternum and the flight muscles attached to it help balance the bird in flight, and the fused synsacrum and the muscles of the legs balance the bird when it is standing. Birds stand on their toes, like dogs and horses. The long tarsometatarsal bone makes the ankle joint of a bird functionally like the knee joint of a human. The joint comparable to our knee is tucked up close to the body of a bird.

The anatomy and physiology of birds is much influenced by the large, hard-shelled egg they lay. The four-pound Kiwi lays a one-pound egg, one-fourth its body weight! Even though most birds lay eggs relatively smaller than that of the Kiwi, the pelvic region is enlarged, and usually only the left ovary and oviduct are functional. (Some hawks have both left and right ovaries.)

The testicles and ovaries vary greatly in size during the breeding cycle. Because birds have specific breeding seasons, they are spared from carrying large, partially formed eggs around inside their bodies. The stages in the production and structure of the avian egg are discussed in the article by T. G. Taylor ("How an Eggshell is Made"). It tells how a hen mobilizes up to 10 percent of her bone calcium in one day to supply material for the egg shell and describes the special bone structures in which calcium for eggs is stored.

The avian egg is a remarkable system; it provides all the nutrients needed for the growth and development of the embryo, except oxygen. The way that gases are supplied to the embryo through the egg is the subject of the article

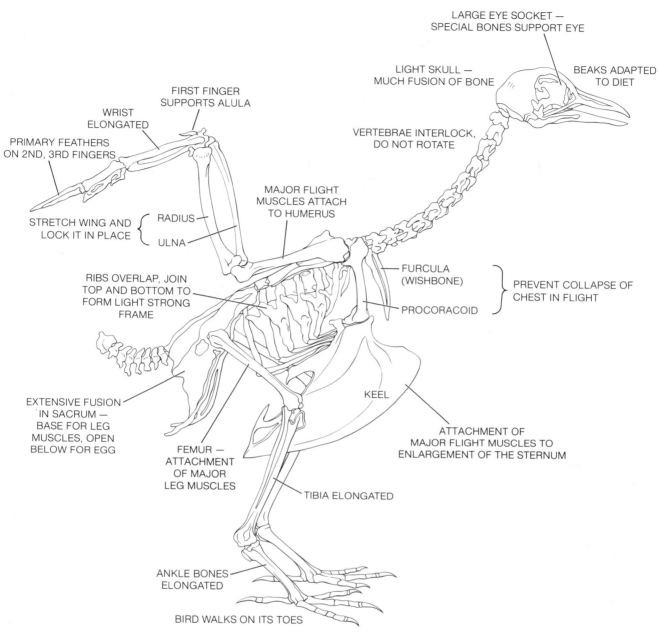

LARGE EYE SOCKET —
SPECIAL BONES SUPPORT EYE

LIGHT SKULL —
MUCH FUSION OF BONE

BEAKS ADAPTED
TO DIET

FIRST FINGER
SUPPORTS ALULA

WRIST
ELONGATED

VERTEBRAE INTERLOCK,
DO NOT ROTATE

PRIMARY FEATHERS
ON 2ND, 3RD FINGERS

MAJOR FLIGHT
MUSCLES ATTACH
TO HUMERUS

STRETCH WING AND
LOCK IT IN PLACE

RADIUS

ULNA

FURCULA
(WISHBONE)

PREVENT COLLAPSE OF
CHEST IN FLIGHT

RIBS OVERLAP, JOIN
TOP AND BOTTOM TO
FORM LIGHT STRONG
FRAME

PROCORACOID

EXTENSIVE FUSION
IN SACRUM —
BASE FOR LEG
MUSCLES, OPEN
BELOW FOR EGG

KEEL

ATTACHMENT OF
MAJOR FLIGHT MUSCLES TO
ENLARGEMENT OF THE STERNUM

FEMUR —
ATTACHMENT
OF MAJOR
LEG MUSCLES

TIBIA ELONGATED

ANKLE BONES
ELONGATED

BIRD WALKS ON ITS TOES

Figure 1. Special features of the skeleton of birds.

by Hermann Rahn, Amos Ar, and Charles V. Paganelli ("How Bird Eggs Breathe"). Their studies reveal the precise arrangement of the egg shell pores and membranes that regulate the rate of air movement into the egg. If the movement is too rapid, the egg will lose too much water and the embryo will dry out; if it is too slow, the embryo will suffocate. From the molecular structure of its pores and membranes to its overall shape, the anatomy of the bird egg has been selected over millions of years to conform to the physics of gas flow and the energy requirements of the growing embryo.

The small size of many birds has much to do with their high rates of metabolism. Small animals have high surface-to-volume ratios and tend to radiate away much of the heat they produce. They must eat often in order to maintain a high body temperature, as discussed earlier in "The Energetics of Bird Flight," by Vance A. Tucker.

The muscles of birds are positioned and designed for both flying and walking. Flight muscles and leg muscles form two separate compact masses that determine the center of gravity of the body of the bird. Flight muscles make

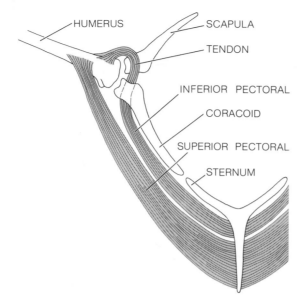

Figure 2. Positions of muscles that lift (inferior pectoral) and lower (superior pectoral) the wing. [After J. C. Welty, *The Life of Birds*, Saunders, Philadelphia, 1975.]

up much of the muscle mass of a flying bird; they are usually about one-fifth the body mass of flying birds and one-third the body mass of a snipe or a hummingbird.

Many specialties are built into the design of the muscles of birds. Some have even been shifted from the back to the front of the body to lower the center of gravity. In the usual body plan of a vertebrate, the forelimb is lifted by muscles of the back and pulled down by those of the chest. In birds, the muscle that lifts the wing, the inferior pectoral, lies in front of the bird, beneath the major breast muscle, the superior pectoral. A tendon-and-pulley system enables the muscle to lift the wing from "below" (see Fig. 2).

The leg tendons of passerine (perching) birds are modified to save the bird energy when on its perch. Tendons connect muscles in the upper leg to the toes and pass behind the ankle joint and through cartilage sheaths. When the bird lands on a branch, its own weight closes its toes, enabling it to perch passively, without having to expend energy by contracting its muscles. In addition, tiny projections on the tendons act like ratchets, gripping ribs on the tendon sheaths to prevent the tendons from slipping (see Fig. 3). Another locking system is found in the wings of birds. Bony processes lock the bones together when the wings are extended, providing a rigid framework for the muscle to pull against (see Fig. 4).

Have you ever wondered if there were any physiological significance to the color of the muscles of a bird? The red leg and the white breast muscles of chickens and pheasants differ in their structure and function. There are at

TABLE 1   PROPERTIES OF RED AND WHITE MUSCLES.

Property	Red	White
Fiber Size	Small	Large
Capillaries	Many	Few
Myoglobin	High	Low
Mitochondria	Many	Few
Glycolysis	Low	High
Oxidize Fat	High	Low
Oxidize Sugar	Low	High
Contraction	Slow	Fast

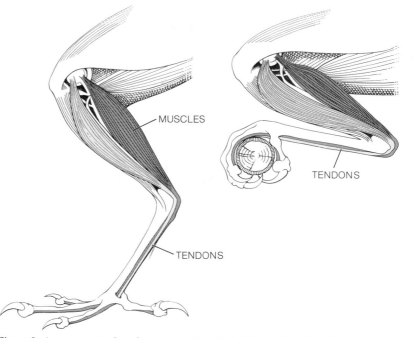

MUSCLES

TENDONS

TENDONS

Figure 3. Arrangement of tendons in perching birds. The tendons that join the muscles of the upper leg to the toes extend behind the ankle; when the bird lowers itself on a branch, the tendons are pulled and the toes automatically close.

least two kinds of muscle fibers in birds and mammals. The properties of the two kinds are listed in Table 1. "Slow-red" fibers are small and rich in myoglobin, which helps give them a dark red color. They have many mitochondria and are surrounded by many capillaries. Such fibers contract relatively slowly and are adapted to sustained exercise. They burn sugar and fat to carbon dioxide and water. "Fast-white" fibers are larger, with less myoglobin and fewer capillaries and mitochondria. They are adapted to fast contractions over short periods of time and burn sugar instead of fat. Some "red" fibers may be fast-contracting too.

Birds with predominately "white" fibered flight muscles, such as pheasants, leap into the air when flushed, but tire soon, and cannot fly long distances. Birds with "red" flight muscles are capable of more sustained activity. Ducks can fly all day at 80 kilometers (50 miles) per hour during their migration.

Both birds and mammals have evolved effective lungs with large air capacities, but they differ in design. Mammals have spongy lungs that expand and contract, moving air and exchanging oxygen for carbon dioxide in blind sacs (the alveoli). Avian lungs (see Fig. 5) are small, inelastic, and connected to a series of air sacs in the body cavities that extend, in some birds, into the large hollow bones. Air flows through all but the smallest tubes, exchanging gases with the blood regardless of whether air is being inhaled or exhaled. If the flow of air stops, the bird suffocates. This is one reason why it is important not to hold a small bird too tightly! Air sacs were once thought to cool the inner parts of the body, particularily the testes, but the actual temperature in the air sacs is high; the flow of air removes heat from the body but doesn't reduce the temperature of the organs.

The gizzard is a special organ of the bird's stomach that functions to break up food mechanically. It has hard walls, is heavily muscled, and contains grit—small stones that the bird has swallowed. Hundreds of years ago, Italian biologist Lazzaro Spallanzani (1729–1799) showed that turkeys can break up steel needles in their gizzard. Owls and other carniverous birds regurgitate unmacerated, undigested materials such as bones, hair, and feathers in pellets known as castings. Gizzards are almost absent in fruit-eating birds, but are large in birds that eat mollusks and vegetation. The gizzard of a goose may contain 30 grams of grit. Whether grit is needed for proper digestion is unclear. Some whalers once thought that penguins used grit as ballast.

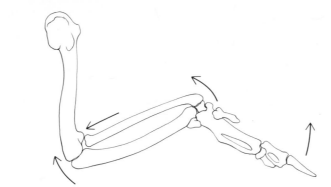

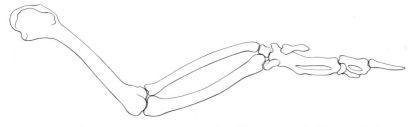

Figure 4. Wing-bone geometry. Extending the elbow automatically extends the wrist. [After Sir James Gray, *Animal Locomotion*, W. W. Norton, New York, 1968.]

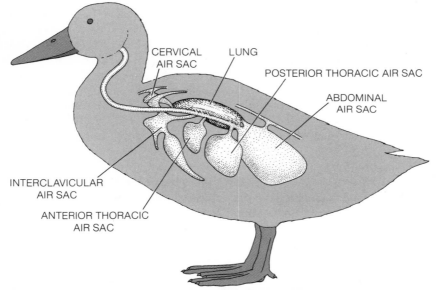

Figure 5. Lungs and air sacs of birds. [From "How Birds Breathe" by Knut Schmidt-Nielsen. Copyright © 1971 by Scientific American, Inc. All rights reserved.]

The avian intestine is short compared to that of mammals. It is broad, short, and thin-walled in meat- and fruit-eating birds, longer and more developed in seed eaters. One difference between the digestive systems of birds and mammals is that birds have caeca, blind tubes that grow out of the posterior end of the small intestine. They are longest in seed eaters, much reduced in hummingbirds and swifts, and absent in parrots. They may provide sites for the production of vitamins, such as vitamin K, through bacterial fermentation, and they may be important in the breakdown of cellulose.

The cloaca is the common opening of the digestive tract, the ureters, and the reproductive system. Birds defecate often; food rapidly moves through the gut. The time of passage may be only 20 minutes in a Starling and as little as 2 hours in a bird the size of a chicken. A magpie may digest a mouse in no more than 3 hours.

Excreta of birds are a combination of wastes from the digestive tract and urine from the kidneys. The paired kidneys filter chemicals from the blood, resorb water, and maintain the composition of the blood stream. The excretory system of birds is designed to save water and minimize weight. Their nitrogenous wastes are disposed of with little loss of water. The kidneys resorb most of the fluid brought to them by the bloodstream and excrete mostly insoluble uric acid in the form of a pasty material instead of soluble urea as in mammals. In addition, birds have no bladder, which makes them more compact and lighter—an obvious advantage to animals that fly.

The excretions of birds have recently taken on new importance to wildlife biologists and breeders of birds. Extremely sensitive radioactive immunological assays have been developed in some laboratories, such as that of Arthur Risser at the San Diego Zoo, to test for the presence of sex hormones in the droppings of birds. Because males and females of many species of birds look alike, it is difficult for breeders of birds to know whether the birds they are trying to mate are of the same or different sexes and whether they are in a condition to breed. An interesting and related project is that of D. M. Fry, an avian biologist at the University of California at Davis, who is applying the radioimmune-assay technique to study the reproductive state of the small population of California Condors that hover on the brink of oblivion in the Sespe Mountains north of Los Angeles. Once their sex and physiological state are known, wildlife biologists may be better able to help prevent their extinction.

Many birds live near or on salt water and have no access to fresh drinking water. Sea water is so concentrated that drinking it will unbalance the tissue fluids of most mammals, including humans. Marine birds like albatrosses, cormorants, penguins, ducks, and pelicans have special glands on the outside of the skull above the eyes that secrete excess salt into the nostrils, enabling the birds to dispose of the salt in the sea water that they drink. The first article in this section, by Knut Schmidt-Nielsen ("Salt Glands"), describes the discovery and investigation of these organs. Research done since that article was become more specialized in the salt glands. Specifically, the mechanism uses action of a mechanism that operates in various cells of the body but which has become more specialized in the salt glands. Specifically, the mechanism is the same sodium pump that bails sodium out of muscle and nerve cells, as well as acetylcholine, the compound released from nerves that signals muscles to contract.

Birds have a preen gland at the base of the tail. The gland secretes an oil that birds rub over their feathers with their beaks. It is believed to be important in waterproofing and waxing the feathers. Birds have no sweat glands. The skin is loose and thin. Like other animals, birds reduce their body temperature in hot weather by evaporative cooling. Even though they lack sweat glands, water is evaporated from their bodies through the skin; they also lose water by panting and moving their wings.

Birds, particularily raptors, are noted for their keen vision. Eyelids and nictating membranes protect the eyeballs of birds. Birds have both rods (for night vision) and cones (to perceive color in daylight). The cones are concentrated in regions of high visual acuity known as foveae. Eagles and other raptors have two foveae, one for monocular side vision and the other for binocular forward vision (as shown in Fig. 6). Humans and other mammals have a single fovea in the back of the eye. The cone cells of certain diurnal birds contain highly colored droplets of oil, which may be red, orange, yellow, or green. The exact function of these droplets is unknown; whether they serve as internal sunglasses to heighten vision is a matter for speculation.

The bony rings that encircle the eyes of birds help to maintain their shape. They elongate the eyes of owls, lending a telescopic effect and keeping all parts of the retina in focus. The pecten (Fig. 6) is a fleshy structure that projects into the eyeball of birds and reptiles from the head of the optic nerve. Its shape and position are characteristic of the species in birds. It is highly vascularized and may have a nutritive function.

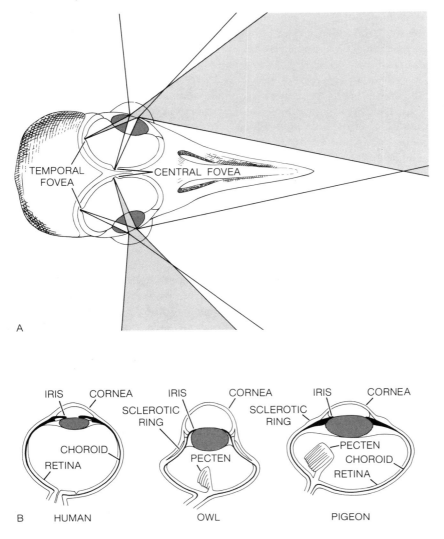

Figure 6. Eyes of Birds. *A.* Diagram of the double fovea of a raptor. *B.* Comparison of eyes of human, owl, and pigeon.

The brain of birds is constructed differently from that of a mammal. The cerebral cortex is smooth instead of being highly furrowed as in mammals, and the cerebellum is much enlarged. The article by Laurence Jay Stettner and Kenneth A. Matyniak ("The Brain of Birds") discusses the design of the brain of birds. They present evidence that having a brain designed differently from our own does not necessarily mean that birds are incapable of what we would recognize as intelligent behavior.

Birds are the most lyrical of animals. They probably were singing their songs before our ancestors ever thought of using rocks to beat out rhythms instead of beating on each other. Although songbirds often seem to be singing for the sheer joy of it, the vocalizations of birds are not merely self-expressions. Their primary purpose is communication; they constitute a kind of language. Birds have two general kinds of vocalizations: calls and songs. Calls are short phrases, usually never more than four to five notes. (Scientists have distinguished ten different calls of the chicken, each with its own significance; thirteen calls have been reported for the Smooth-Billed Ani, consisting of "shouts, chucks, chuckles, whines, quacks, whews.") Songs are usually a series of notes, produced in a sequence and forming a recognizable pattern. In general, calls communicate alarm, rally flocks, and intimidate enemies and competitors.

Songs are often part of the reproductive cycle; they are used in establishing territories, attracting members of the opposite sex, synchronizing sex behavior, and strengthening the pair bond.

Behaviorist W. H. Thorpe found that the Chaffinch, a European songbird, has two kinds of calls, one directional and the other nondirectional. When they see a hawk or an owl perched in a tree, they give a soft, low-pitched "chink-chink-chink" call. This attracts other small birds, and, together, they "mob" the predator. If the hawk is flying, the Chaffinch takes cover in the brush and gives a high-pitched "seeet" call, causing other Chaffinches to take cover and peer upward. The low frequency and short duration of the "chink" call make it easy for a listener to locate the caller. On the other hand, the high frequency and slurred beginnings and ends of the "seeet" call tend to obscure the position of the caller. Many birds use similar warning sounds. Listen for them next time you go for a walk in the forest or fields.

There are both instinctive and learned components of bird song. Bullfinches whose cochlea were removed to deafen them sang as well as normal birds for over a year, and deafened Blackbirds faithfully reproduced pitch and rhythm for several years. However, birds raised in isolation do not sing the way birds do in the wild. Isolated Chaffinches produce extremely simple songs. In the wild, Chaffinches learn part of their song during the first year of life. Populations of White-crowned Sparrows living within a few miles of one another but separated by geographic barriers have slightly different songs (one might almost say dialects). For example, White-crowned Sparrows in the hills of Berkeley and Oakland, California, sound noticeably different from those in Marin County, just across San Francisco Bay.

The article by W. H. Thorpe ("Duet-Singing Birds") reports on the extraordinary ability of forest birds to engage in mutual song, whereby one starts a song and the other completes it with remarkable precision.

There seems to be more than one opinion about how birds sing. Many ornithologists think of the vocal machinery of a bird as if it were a woodwind instrument: Air moving from the lungs vibrates the membranes in the syrinx (the "voice box" of birds), and the windpipe (trachea) acts as an organ pipe. The longer and wider it is, the deeper are the tones; the shorter and narrower it is, the higher are the tones. The voice of a hen rises when its trachea is experimentally shortened. The last article in this section ("How Birds Sing") is by Crawford Greenewalt, an avid student and researcher of birds and former president and chairman of the board of E. I. duPont de Nemours & Company, who challenges the woodwind theory on the basis of analyses of bird songs done at the Bell Telephone Laboratories. Regardless of how they do it, birds are indeed Nature's pre-eminent musicians.

18 Salt Glands

Knut Schmidt-Nielsen
January 1959

*A special organ which eliminates salt with great
efficiency enables marine birds to meet their fluid needs
by drinking sea water. Similar organs have been found
in marine reptiles*

As the writers of stories about castaways are apt to point out, a man who drinks sea water will only intensify his thirst. He must excrete the salt contained in the water through his kidneys, and this process requires additional water which is taken from the fluids of his body. The dehydration is aggravated by the fact that sea water, in addition to common salt or sodium chloride, also contains magnesium sulfate, which causes diarrhea. Most air-breathing vertebrates are similarly unable to tolerate the drinking of sea water, but some are not so restricted. Many birds, mammals and reptiles whose ancestors dwelt on land now live on or in the sea, often hundreds of miles from any source of fresh water. Some, like the sea turtles, seals and albatrosses, return to the land only to reproduce. Whales, sea cows and some sea snakes, which bear living young in the water, have given up the land entirely.

Yet all these animals, like man, must limit the concentration of salt in their blood and body fluids to about 1 per cent—less than a third of the salt concentration in sea water. If they drink sea water, they must somehow get rid of the excess salt. Our castaway can do so only at the price of dehydrating his tissues. Since his kidneys can at best se-

PETREL EJECTS DROPLETS of solution produced by its salt gland through a pair of tubes atop its beak, as shown in this high-speed photograph. The salt-gland secretions of most birds drip from the tip of the beak. The petrel, however, remains in the air almost continuously and has apparently evolved this "water pistol" mechanism as a means of eliminating the fluid while in flight.

crete a 2-per-cent salt solution, he must eliminate up to a quart and a half of urine for every quart of sea water he drinks, with his body fluids making up the difference. If other animals drink sea water, how do they escape dehydration? If they do not drink sea water, where do they obtain the water which their bodies require?

The elimination of salt by sea birds and marine reptiles poses these questions in particularly troublesome form. Their kidneys are far less efficient than our own: a gull would have to produce more than two quarts of urine to dispose of the salt in a quart of sea water. Yet many observers have seen marine birds drinking from the ocean. Physiologists have held that the appearance of drinking is no proof that the birds actually swallow water, and that the low efficiency of their kidneys proves that they do not. Our experiments during the past two years have shown that while the physiologists are right about the kidneys, the observations of drinking are also correct. Marine birds do drink sea water. Their main salt-eliminating organ is not the kidney, however, but a special gland in the head which disposes of salt more rapidly than any kidney does. Our studies indicate that all marine birds and probably all marine reptiles possess this gland.

The obvious way to find out whether birds can tolerate sea water is to make them drink it. If gulls in captivity are given only sea water, they will drink it without ill effects. To measure the exact amount of sea water ingested we administered it through a stomach tube, and found that the birds could tolerate large quantities. Their output of urine increased sharply but accounted for only a small part of the salt they had ingested. Most of the salt showed up in a clear, colorless fluid which dripped from the tip of the beak. In seeking the source of this fluid our attention was drawn to the so-called nasal glands, paired structures of hitherto unknown function found in the heads of all birds. Anatomists described these organs more than a century ago, and noted that they are much larger in sea birds than in land birds. The difference in size suggested that the glands must perform some special function in marine species. Some investigators proposed that the organs produce a secretion akin to tears which serves to rinse sea water from the birds' sensitive nasal membranes.

We were able to collect samples of the secretion from the gland by inserting a thin tube into its duct. The fluid turned

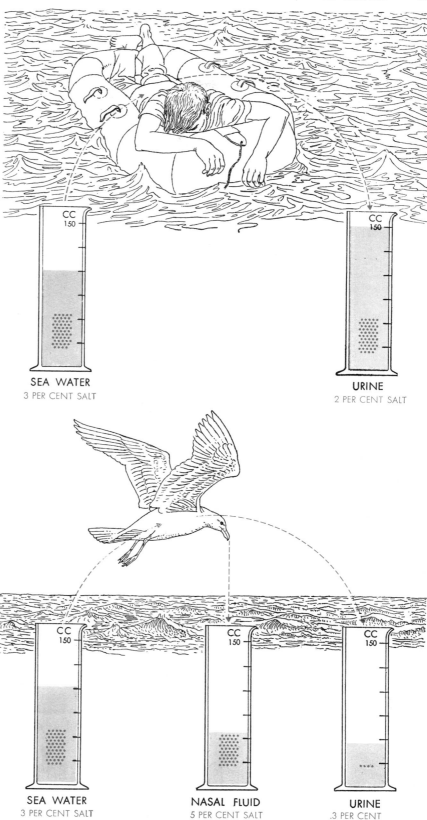

SALT EXCRETION IN MEN AND BIRDS is compared in these drawings. Castaway at top cannot drink sea water because in eliminating the salt it contains (*colored dots*) he will lose more water than he has drunk. His kidney secretions have a salt content lower than that of sea water. Gull (*below*) can drink sea water even though its kidneys are far less efficient than a man's. It eliminates salt mainly through its salt, or "nasal," glands. These organs, more efficient than any kidney, secrete a fluid which is nearly twice as salty as sea water.

out to be an almost pure 5-per-cent solution of sodium chloride—many times saltier than tears and nearly twice as salty as sea water. The gland, it was plain, had nothing to do with rinsing the nasal membranes but a great deal to do with eliminating salt. By sampling the output of other glands in the bird's head, we established that the nasal gland was the only one that produces this concentrated solution.

The nasal glands can handle relatively enormous quantities of salt. In one experiment we gave a gull 134 cubic centimeters of sea water—equal to about a tenth of the gull's body weight. In man this would correspond to about two gallons. No man could tolerate this much sea water; he would sicken after drinking a small fraction of it. The gull, however, seemed unaffected; within three hours it had excreted nearly all the salt. Its salt glands had produced only about two thirds as much fluid as its kidneys, but had excreted more than 90 per cent of the salt.

The fluid produced by the salt gland is about five times as salty as the bird's blood and other body fluids. How does the organ manage to produce so concentrated a solution? Microscopic examination of the gland reveals that it consists of many parallel cylindrical lobes, each composed of several thousand branching tubules radiating from a central duct like bristles from a bottle brush. These tubules, about a thousandth of an inch in diameter, secrete the salty fluid.

A network of capillaries carries the blood parallel to the flow of salt solution in the tubules, but in the opposite direction [see illustration on opposite page]. This arrangement brings into play the principle of counter-current flow, which seems to amplify the transfer of salt from the blood in the capillaries to the fluid in the tubules. A similar arrangement in the kidneys of mammals appears to account for their efficiency in the concentration of urine [see "'The Wonderful Net," by P. F. Scholander, SCIENTIFIC AMERICAN, April, 1957]. No such provision for counter-current flow is found in the kidneys of reptiles, and it is only slightly developed in birds.

Counter-current flow, however, does not of itself account for the gland's capacity to concentrate salt. The secret of this process lies in the structure of the tubules and the cells that compose them.

The microscopic structure of a salt-gland tubule resembles a stack of pies with a small hole in the middle. Each "pie" consists of five to seven individual cells arranged like wedges. The hole, or lumen, funnels the secretion into the central duct. When we inject dye into the lumen, colored fluid seeps out into a system of irregular crevices in the walls of the tubule. More detailed examination with the electron microscope reveals a similar, interlocking system of deep folds which extend inward from the outer surface of the tubule. This structure may be important in that it greatly multiplies the surface area of the cell. It is worth noting that cells with similar, though shallower, folds are found in the tubules of the mammalian kidney.

Evidently some physiological mechanism in the cell "pumps" sodium and chloride ions against the osmotic gradient, from the dilute salt solution of the blood to the more concentrated solution in the lumen. Nerve cells similarly "pump" out the sodium which they absorb when stimulated [see "The Nerve Impulse and the Squid," by Richard D. Keynes; SCIENTIFIC AMERICAN Offprint 58]. Of course the mechanisms in the two processes may be quite different. In the tubule cells the transport of sodium and chloride ions seems to involve the mitochondria, the intracellular particles in which carbohydrates are oxidized to produce energy.

The similarities between the salt gland and the mammalian kidney should not obscure their important differences. For one thing, the salt gland is essentially a much simpler organ. The composition of its secretions, which apart from a trace of potassium contain only sodium chloride and water, indicates that its sole function is to eliminate salt. In contrast, the kidney performs a variety of regulatory and eliminative tasks and produces a fluid of complex and variable composition, depending on the animal's physiological needs at a particular time.

The salt gland's distinctive structure, elegantly specialized to a single end, enables it to perform an almost unbelievable amount of osmotic work in a short time. In one minute it can produce up to half its own weight of concentrated salt solution. The human kidney can produce at most about a twentieth of its weight in urine per minute, and its normal output is much less.

Another major difference between the two glands is that the salt gland functions only intermittently, in response to the need to eliminate salt. The kidney, on the other hand, secretes continuously, though at a varying rate. The salt gland's activity depends on the concentration of salt in the blood. The injection of salt solutions into a bird's bloodstream causes

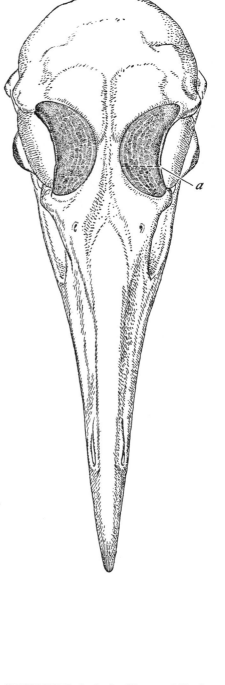

STRUCTURE of salt gland is essentially the same in all sea birds. In the gull the glands lie above the bird's eyes, as shown at left. Cross section of a gland (a) shows that it consists of many lobes (b). Each of these

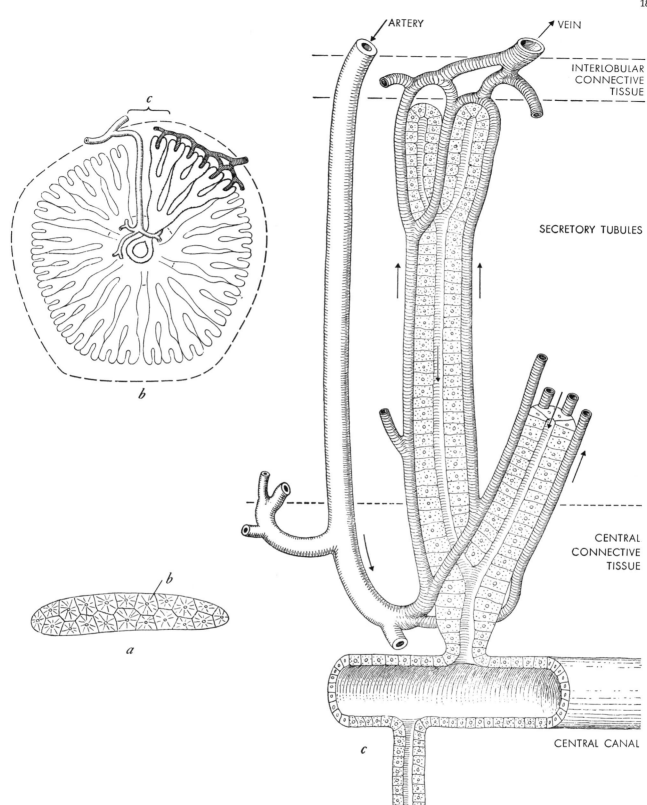

ARTERY

VEIN

INTERLOBULAR
CONNECTIVE
TISSUE

SECRETORY TUBULES

CENTRAL
CONNECTIVE
TISSUE

CENTRAL CANAL

lobes contains several thousand branching tubules which radiate
from a central duct like the hairs of a bottle brush. Enlargement
of a single tubule (c) reveals that it is surrounded by capillaries
in which blood flows counter to the flow of salt secretion in the
tubule. This counter-current flow, which also occurs in the kidneys
of mammals, facilitates the transfer of salt from the blood to the
tubule. The tubule wall, only one cell thick, consists of rings of
five to seven wedge-shaped cells. These rings, stacked one on top of
another, encircle a small hole, or lumen, through which the salty
secretion flows from the tubule into the central canal of the lobe.

the gland to secrete, indicating that some center, probably in the brain, responds to the salt concentration. The gland responds to impulses in a branch of the facial nerve, for electric stimulation of this nerve causes the gland to secrete.

While the structure and function of the salt gland is essentially the same in all sea birds, its location varies. In the gull and many other birds the glands are located on top of the head above the eye sockets [*see illustrations on this page*]; in the cormorant and the gannet they lie between the eye and the nasal cavity. The duct of the gland in either case opens into the nasal cavity. The salty fluid flows out through the nostrils of most species and drips from the tip of the beak, but there are some interesting variations on this general scheme. The pelican, for example, has a pair of grooves in its long upper beak which lead the fluid down to the tip; the solution would otherwise trickle into the pouch of the lower beak and be reingested. In the cormorant and the gannet the nostrils are nonfunctional and covered with skin; the fluid makes its exit through the internal nostrils in the roof of the mouth and flows to the tip of the beak.

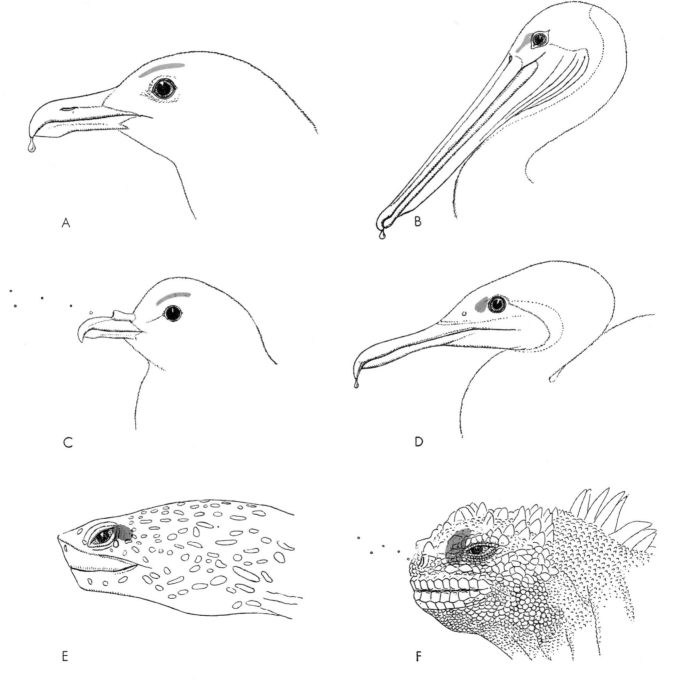

LOCATION OF SALT GLAND (*color*) varies in different species of marine birds and reptiles. In the gull (*A*) the gland's secretions emerge from the nostril and drip from the beak; in the cormorant (*D*) the fluid flows along the roof of the mouth. The pelican (*B*) has grooves along its upper beak which keep the fluid from dripping into its pouch; the petrel (*C*) ejects the fluid through tubular nostrils. In the turtle (*E*) the gland opens at the back corner of the eye; in the marine iguana (*F*) it opens into the nasal cavity.

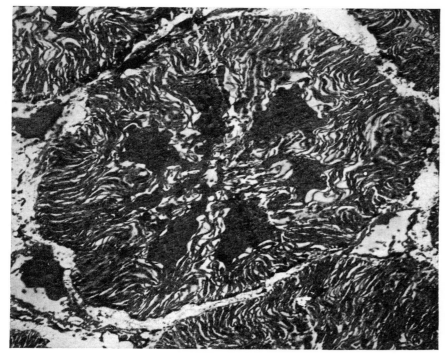

CROSS SECTION OF SALT-GLAND TUBULE is shown magnified about 5,700 diameters in this electron micrograph made by William L. Doyle of the University of Chicago. To emphasize the cell-structure the specimen was kept in a solution which shrank and distorted the cells and their nuclei. Most of the material of the cells lies in folded, leaflike layers; cells with a somewhat similar structure are found in the kidney tubules of mammals.

The petrel displays an especially interesting mechanism for getting rid of the fluid. Its nostrils are extended in two short tubes along the top of its beak. When its salt glands are working, the bird shoots droplets of the fluid outward through the tubes [*see illustration on page 186*]. This curious design may reflect a special adaptation to the petrel's mode of life. Though the bird remains at sea for months at a time, it rarely settles down on the water to rest. Presumably the airstream from its almost continuous flight would hamper the elimination of fluid from the bird's nostrils, were it not for the water-pistol function of the tubes.

Our studies so far have demonstrated the existence of the salt gland in the herring gull, black-backed gull, common tern, black skimmer, guillemot, Louisiana heron, little blue heron, double-crested cormorant, brown pelican, gannet, petrel, albatross, eider duck and Humboldt penguin. These species, from a wide variety of geographical locations, represent all the major orders of marine birds. There is little doubt that this remarkable organ makes it possible for all sea birds to eliminate salt and live without fresh water.

The discovery of the salt gland in sea birds prompted us to look for a similar organ in other air-breathing sea animals.

In *Alice's Adventures in Wonderland* the Mock Turtle weeps perpetual tears because he is not a real turtle; real turtles, at least the marine species, also weep after a fashion. A. F. Carr, Jr., a distinguished specialist in marine turtles, gives us a vivid account of a Pacific Ridley turtle that came ashore to lay its eggs. The animal "began secreting copious tears shortly after she left the water, and these continued to flow after the nest was dug. By the time she had begun to lay, her eyes were closed and plastered over with tear-soaked sand and the effect was doleful in the extreme." Thus Carr makes it clear that the turtle's tears do not serve to wash its eyes free of sand, an explanation that otherwise might seem reasonable. The suggestion that the turtle weeps from the pangs of egg-laying is even wider of the mark.

With the loggerhead turtle as our subject, we have found that the sea turtle's tears come from a large gland behind its eyeball. The tears have much the same composition as that of the salt-gland secretions of the sea bird. Thus it would seem more than likely that the turtle's "weeping" serves to eliminate salt. The salt gland of the turtle has a structure similar to that of the gland in sea birds, with tubules radiating from a central duct, and it seems that this structure is essential for the elaboration of a fluid with a high salt concentration. The similarity is the more striking because the location of the gland in the turtle indicates that it has a different evolutionary origin. Still a third independent line of evolution may be represented by the salt gland in the Galápagos marine iguana, the only true marine lizard.

Anatomical studies of the other marine reptiles—the sea snakes and the marine crocodiles—have established that their heads contain large glands whose function may be similar to that of the salt gland. When we succeed in obtaining living specimens of these creatures, we expect to determine whether their glands have the same function.

Investigations of marine mammals thus far indicate that these animals handle the elimination of salt from their systems in a more conventional manner. The seal and some whales apparently satisfy their need for water with the fluids of the fish on which they feed. The elimination of such salt as these fluids contain requires kidneys of no more than human efficiency. But other whales, and walruses, whose diet of squid, plankton or shellfish is no less salty than sea water, must surely eliminate large quantities of excess salt even if they do not drink from the ocean itself. Our knowledge of their physiology suggests that their kidneys, which are more powerful than ours, can eliminate all the salts in their food. Some mammalian kidneys do function at this high level. The kangaroo rat, whose desert habitat compels it to conserve water to the utmost, can produce urine twice as salty as the ocean, and thrives in the laboratory on a diet of sea water and dried soybeans [see "The Desert Rat," by Knut and Bodil Schmidt-Nielsen; SCIENTIFIC AMERICAN Offprint 1050].

We should like to study salt excretion in whales, but these animals are obviously not easy to work with. We have undertaken, however, some pilot studies on seals. When we injected them with salt solutions that stimulate the salt glands of birds and reptiles, they merely increased their output of urine. Methacholine, a drug which also stimulates the salt gland, gave equally negative results. Whatever the seal's need to eliminate salt, its kidneys are evidently adequate to the task. We must therefore assume that the salt gland has evolved only in the birds and reptiles, animals whose kidneys cannot produce concentrated salt solutions.

19 The Brain of Birds

by Laurence Jay Stettner and Kenneth A. Matyniak
June 1968

*Since birds have a smaller cerebral cortex than
mammals, are they less intelligent than mammals?
Recent work suggests that they may simply use other
parts of the brain to effect intelligent behavior*

In the lexicon of insult few terms are as disparaging as "bird brain." The derivation of the term is obvious. In comparison with the brains of even the most primitive mammals the avian brain seems a pathetic object. The brain of a bird is not only tiny in size but also notably backward in development of the cerebral cortex, the principal organ of intelligence in the higher animals. Yet investigations of the intelligence of animals have shown that the physical aspect of the bird brain is deceiving. Birds have demonstrated in test after test that they are capable of highly intelligent behavior, sometimes surpassing the abilities of mammals with greatly superior cortical development. These findings indicate that studies of the avian brain could be a revealing guide to the sources and evolution of intelligent behavior.

That birds possess certain remarkable sensibilities has of course been noted ever since bird-watching began. Their uncanny powers of navigation in long migrations, their intricate nest-building and their devoted parental behavior have impressed all students of these animals. Still, these activities could be attributed to inborn, stereotyped patterns of behavior rather than to intelligence. They have generally been regarded as "instinctive" in nature, not involving the flexibility and ability to learn that are the earmarks of intellectual activity. The modern studies of the learning abilities of birds by B. F. Skinner of Harvard University and by other investigators, however, cast a completely new light on avian intelligence. Skinner, who used the pigeon as one of his principal subjects in his experimental studies of learning,

found that pigeons were quite flexible in adjusting their behavior to a variety of learning tasks. By now a considerable body of evidence on the learning capacities of birds has been accumulated by a number of investigators, including our group at Wayne State University. Let us review the findings.

It is not easy to devise an experiment that affords a clear test of animal intelligence, and it is still more difficult to design one that will serve for comparative testing of various animals. The Bryn Mawr College psychologist M. E. Bitterman succeeded in working out a relatively simple type of problem that tests an animal's mental flexibility or, in other words, its ability to solve a problem by repeatedly changing or modifying its behavior to meet new conditions [see "The Evolution of Intelligence," by M. E. Bitterman; SCIENTIFIC AMERICAN, January, 1965]. The test is called "multiple reversal." After the animal has learned to choose between two symbols (say a circle rather than a square) in order to obtain a food reward, the "correct" symbol is reversed (from the circle to the square), so that the animal must now switch to choosing the symbol that was previously unrewarded. The experimenter repeats the reversal many times, and the animal's learning is measured by how soon it "catches on" that after the selection of one symbol is no longer rewarded it must switch to the other to gain the reward again. Bitterman found that fishes did not show any improvement in learning such a problem; after each reversal they made about the same number of fruitless selections of the old rewarded symbol before they switched to the new one. Rats, on the other hand, improved as the reversal program proceeded; they made fewer and fewer fruitless trials and eventually learned to switch to

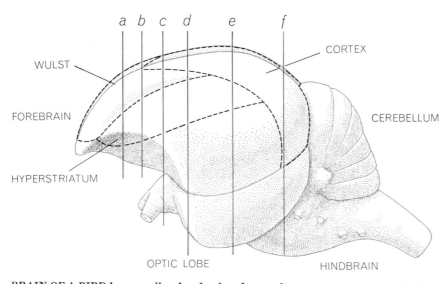

BRAIN OF A BIRD has a small and undeveloped cortex but an extensive striatum that lies above the brain's large optic lobe. The brain illustrated is that of a quail, the bird used in the authors' experiments. Broken lines surround the cortex and two parts of the striatum, the *"Wulst"* and the hyperstriatum. Vertical lines identify the areas seen in transverse section in the illustration on the opposite page, in which the cortex and striatum are contrasted.

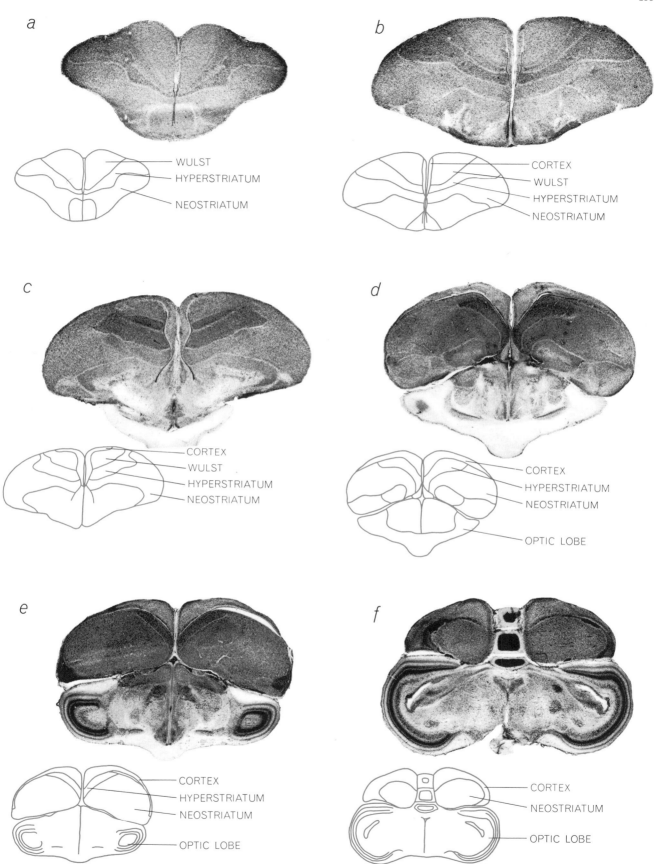

a

WULST
HYPERSTRIATUM
NEOSTRIATUM

b

CORTEX
WULST
HYPERSTRIATUM
NEOSTRIATUM

c

CORTEX
WULST
HYPERSTRIATUM
NEOSTRIATUM

d

CORTEX
HYPERSTRIATUM
NEOSTRIATUM

OPTIC LOBE

e

CORTEX
HYPERSTRIATUM
NEOSTRIATUM

OPTIC LOBE

f

CORTEX
NEOSTRIATUM

OPTIC LOBE

TRANSVERSE SECTIONS of a quail's forebrain appear in these six micrographs. The outline drawing below each micrograph shows the salient anatomical features. The smallness and shallowness of the cortex, in contrast to the extensive area occupied by various components of the striatum, is evident in sections *b*, *c* and *d*. The cortex becomes enlarged only toward the rear of the forebrain.

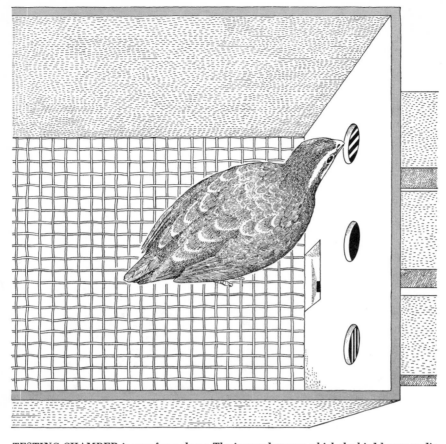

TESTING CHAMBER is seen from above. The images between which the bird learns to discriminate are projected on translucent "pecking plates" that can be reached through the holes in the chamber wall. When the bird pecks the right image, it is rewarded with food.

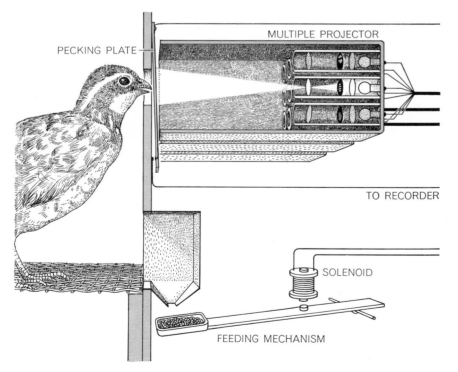

CUTAWAY VIEW of testing apparatus shows one of three multiple projectors and part of the circuitry connecting the pecking plate with the solenoid-actuated food lift. The bird's correct and incorrect responses to the various projected stimuli are recorded automatically.

the new symbol after only one or two unsuccessful trials at the old.

How do birds do in this test? Bitterman noted that pigeons showed the same "more intelligent" pattern that rats did. And the pigeon is by no means the most proficient learner among the birds. Experiments in our laboratory and by Robert Gossette of Hofstra University have demonstrated that crows, ravens, magpies, myna birds and parrots surpass the pigeon's performance in reversal learning. On the whole, birds do at least as well as many mammals on this measure of learning capacity.

Let us go on to a somewhat more exacting measure: a sophisticated test designed to measure the learning ability of primates rather than of lower mammals such as the rat. In this test, designed by Harry F. Harlow of the University of Wisconsin, the animal must learn a general approach for successful solution of various problems that involve the same principle but are presented in different physical forms. The animal is required to "learn how to learn" the answer; in technical terminology, the subject must form a learning "set." For instance, the animal may be confronted with a bowl and a shoe and receive a food reward if it touches the bowl rather than the shoe. The objects are then shifted about in further trials, and the animal must learn to choose the bowl every time, regardless of its position. After learning this lesson the animal is presented with a series of pairs of objects that entail the same type of recognition. There are a number of forms of the test; the irrelevant variable may be some factor other than the positions of the objects. Harlow has found that in the first presentation it may take a rhesus monkey, for example, some 50 to 60 trials to learn to touch the correct object regardless of position, but in later presentations the animal eventually is able to identify the rewarded object in only one or two trials. Harlow and other investigators have demonstrated that this type of test provides a measure of differences in intelligence among the various primates. Those with a more highly developed cerebral cortex show a greater capacity for forming learning sets. Thus New World cebid monkeys do better than the more primitive marmosets, rhesus monkeys do better than New World monkeys and chimpanzees in turn do better than rhesus monkeys. Learning set has been regarded as a supertest suitable only for primates; the performance of lower mammals on this test is consistently very poor.

How, then, do birds fare on learning

a   *b*   *c*

REWARD   REWARD   REWARD

REVERSAL LEARNING occurs in two steps. At first the animal learns that one visual pattern, in this example horizontal stripes, is rewarded regardless of where it may appear ("*a*" and "*b*"). Next the previously unrewarded pattern is made rewarding (*c*) and the number of wrong responses before discovery of the reversal is noted. As tests continue, the higher animals learn to reverse more quickly.

set? So far only two representatives—the pigeon and the chicken—have been tested, and both did better than any non-primate mammal had done; in fact, the chickens even outperformed the marmoset!

A still more complex learning task for animals is the "oddity" problem: selection of the odd member among three stimuli, two of which are alike. The complexity is introduced by changing the display or the odd stimulus from one trial to the next. For example, in Trial 1 the presentation may be circle, circle, square in a horizontal row; in Trial 2, square, circle, circle; in Trial 3, square, square, circle, so that the odd member is no longer a square but a circle. The animal cannot attach its response to a particular shape or position; it must take the total situation into account and respond to a relationship. Can birds master such a problem? The answer is yes. Monkeys, cats *and* pigeons have shown the ability to learn to pick out the odd member of a given trio of objects.

The oddity problem can be carried a step further. Is the animal capable of forming a learning set from such an experience, that is, can it generalize the oddity principle by applying it to various stimuli? Having learned to pick the odd figure out of circles and squares, will it also be able to do so when it is presented with, say, two rectangles and a triangle or two shoes and a bowl? To the human mind such a transfer of learning seems so elementary that one might suppose it should not be at all difficult for any animal that is capable of solving the initial oddity problem. It turns out that such is not the case. Even monkeys have some difficulty with the problem; they learn to generalize the oddity prin-

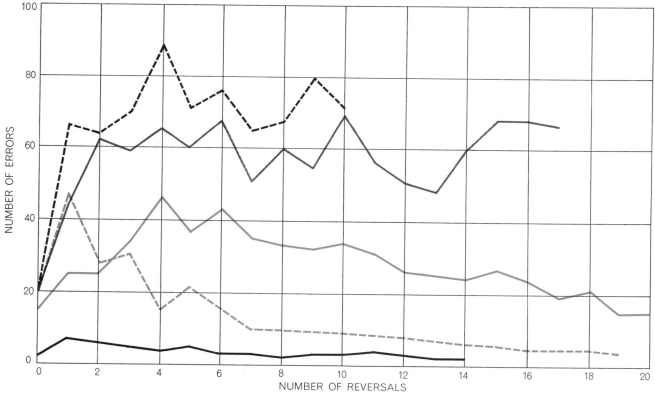

MULTIPLE-REVERSAL SCORES made by animals representing three vertebrate classes are compared. The lowest class tested, fishes, showed no improvement in learning. The same proved true of rats, members of the highest class tested, when they had suffered brain damage. Normal rats quickly mastered the problem. Pigeons did so almost as quickly as rats, and myna birds outdid pigeons. Data, except those for myna birds, are from studies by M. E. Bitterman of Bryn Mawr College. Robert Gossette of Hofstra University ran the myna tests.

ciple only after they have undergone the experience of solving many different oddity problems in succession. On the other hand, cats, as J. M. Warren of Pennsylvania State University has found, do not form the oddity learning set even after mastering 30 individual oddity problems. What the cat cannot accom-

plish, however, the canary can. Nicholas Pastore of Queens College of the City University of New York presented canaries with an array of nine three-dimensional objects, eight of which were identical. After the birds had learned that selection of the odd object brought a food reward, on later trials with new sets

of objects they picked out the odd object in each set at the very first exposure.

Consider next another intellectual capacity: the ability to count or, more precisely, to respond to the property of number. Even primates have considerable difficulty with this task. Herbert Woodrow of the University of Illinois

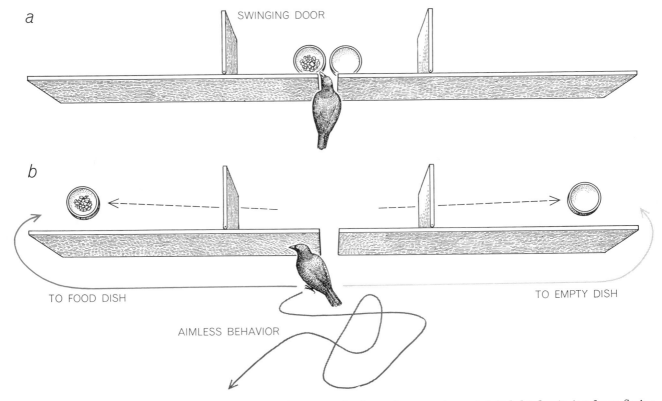

ANIMAL DILEMMA was devised by L. V. Krushinsky of Moscow State University. An animal feeds from one of two bowls by reaching through a narrow slot in the center of a wide screen (*a*). The bowls are then moved out of sight behind swinging doors. Seeing the bowl with food in motion, the animal may pursue it or not (*b*). Movement in the correct direction allows the feeding to resume.

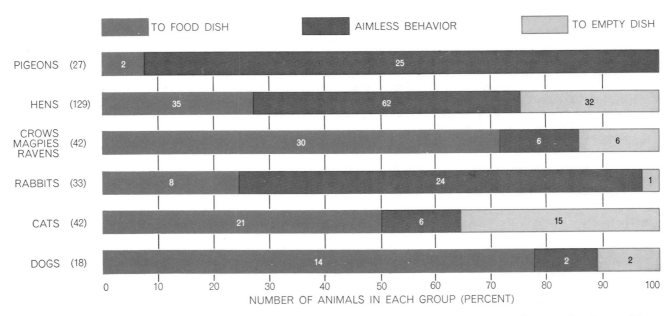

PERFORMANCE of birds and mammals in solving the Krushinsky problem is compared in this graph. Dogs made the best scores, but crows and their relatives were nearly as good as dogs and better than cats or rabbits. Hens outscored rabbits; pigeons did worst.

found, for example, that it took 21,000 trials to teach a monkey to distinguish reliably between the sounding of two tones and the sounding of three. For lower mammals such a task is of course a great deal more formidable. Frank Wesley of Portland State College attempted to teach rats to discriminate a single tone from two tones, but after 3,000 trials had produced no observable progress he gave up.

Birds, on the other hand, consistently master counting problems a great deal more complex than these. For example, the German ethologist Otto Koehler and his co-workers trained pigeons to discriminate four "objects" (or stimuli) from five, and they found in various experiments that ravens and parakeets could learn to "count" up to seven. In one form of these tests a raven was shown a key card with a certain number of spots on it and then was presented with an array of containers, each with a different number of spots on the lid; if the raven chose the lid displaying the same number of spots as the key card did, it was rewarded with a worm. The raven learned to find the matching number up to as many as seven spots, regardless of variation in the sizes, shapes or arrangements of the spots. This ability to respond to number per se, without reference to other properties of the stimulus, seems to be very unusual indeed among animals. For instance, the German zoologist Bernhard Rensch found that an elephant (which presumably ranks high in intelligence among mammals), after learning to discriminate a card with three circles on it from one with four circles, failed completely when the symbols were switched from circles to squares, and it took the animal 440 trials to learn this "new" problem [see "The Intelligence of Elephants," by B. Rensch; SCIENTIFIC AMERICAN, February, 1957]. In contrast, the Wayne State University psychologist Leland Swenson showed that a raven, confronted with a similar switch, solved it readily; the bird, having learned to discriminate one circle from two, scored better than 90 percent in trials in which the symbol was changed from the circle to a square, a triangle or an irregular form.

L. V. Krushinsky of the U.S.S.R., in an ingenious series of experiments at Moscow State University, has uncovered still another facet of avian intelligence. He places two bowls behind a slit in the center of a large screen; one bowl contains food and the animal eats from it. Then both bowls are suddenly moved out of sight, one to the left and one to the right. The problem in this case is

one not of learning but of making a modest extrapolation from the visual information available to the animal; if the animal goes around the screen on the side toward which the food bowl has disappeared, it regains the food. Krushinsky has tested dogs, cats, rabbits, pigeons, hens, crows, magpies and ravens on this problem. Rabbits, hens and pigeons do poorly; they tend to move around haphazardly after the food disappears, and most of them do not go behind the screen. Cats go around the screen, but they are as likely to go to the wrong side as to the correct one; it takes many repetitions of the experiment for the cat to catch on and move to the correct side each time. Only dogs, crows and crow relatives solve the problem immediately. A majority of them go promptly and directly to the correct side of the screen the first time they are presented with the case of the disappearing bowls.

Here, then, is another demonstration of a bird's capacity for intelligent behavior. Moreover, the test differentiates among the birds, showing that crows and their relatives are superior to the hen and the pigeon (whose performance is the poorest). The fact that these birds best the cat and match the performance of the dog indicates a surprisingly high level of mental power for a bird brain.

The general tenor of all the results reviewed above is unmistakable. It is true that the total volume of evidence so far is not large, and many more comparative studies will have to be made in order to arrive at an accurate and detailed evaluation of the intellectual capacities of birds. Nevertheless, the consistency of the evidence already established cannot be ignored. It points to the conclusion that birds are capable of intelligent achievements equaling or even exceeding those of many mammals. Even if future studies should reestablish mammalian superiority, it cannot be denied that birds show some mental capabilities that have long been thought to belong solely to animals with a well-developed cerebral cortex.

Krushinsky has recently written: "The last decades have markedly changed the previously widespread idea that the behavior of birds is less plastic than the behavior of mammals." It cannot be said that the new view is shared by scientists generally. Many of them are still reluctant to accept the full implications of the experimental evidence, primarily because the avian cerebral cortex is so obviously primitive. It has therefore become essential to take a closer look at the avian brain to see if it has developed

some other structure that may account for the birds' apparent intellectual abilities.

There is little question that among mammals the degree of intelligence depends on the size and complexity of the cerebral cortex. The organ shows a clear picture of evolutionary development going up the mammalian order. In the rat the cortex is smooth (without folds or convolutions) and is comparatively undeveloped in the frontal area; in the dog the cortex has a larger surface, some convolutions and greater frontal development; in the monkey it is still further expanded and more convoluted, and in man the cortex has become so extensive and complex that it is plainly distinguishable from that of all other animals. Within any single species (including man) the intelligence of normal individuals cannot be correlated with differences in their cortical development (at least not on the basis of present knowledge), but where there are major differences in cortical development from one species of mammal to another one finds a clear correlation with the degree of intelligence.

In both mammals and birds the cerebrum, or forebrain, contains two major types of structure: the cortex and a lower portion called the striatum. The two structures were inherited from the reptiles. They developed very differently, however, in the mammals and the birds. In the mammals the cortex became dominant, overgrowing and covering the striatum until, in man, the nerve cells of the striatum are deeply buried and intermingled with cortical fibers that have invaded the forebrain interior. In the birds, on the other hand, the main development has taken place in the striatum, while the cortex has become a thin layer of tissue covering only the top and side surfaces of the forebrain. The striatum in birds is a totally integrated, highly organized mass of nerve nuclei and fiber tracts and makes up most of the bulk of the cerebral hemispheres. In particular, the uppermost part of the striatum, called the hyperstriatum, is a well-developed structure that is not present at all in mammals.

A number of years ago the Harvard Medical School neurologist Stanley Cobb, a pioneer in comparative investigations of the brains of birds, suggested that the cortex played little or no part in the mental processes of birds; in fact, he noted that in their case the anatomy indicated a negative correlation between cortical development and intelligence. He deduced that the principal function of the cortex in birds was in relation to

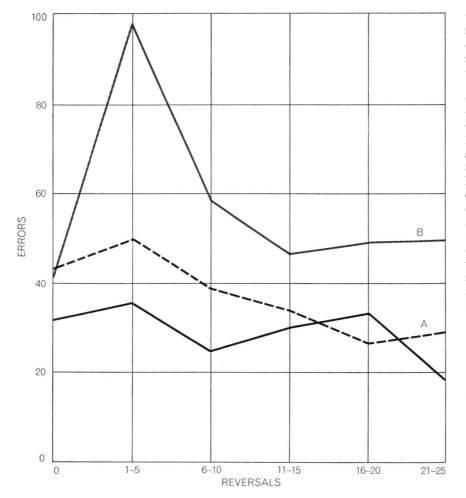

BRAIN DAMAGE resulting from surgical removal of the cortex and of both *Wulst* and cortex produces alterations in the capability of quail to improve reversal learning scores. Solid black line shows improved performance of normal birds over 25 trials. Other lines show performance of birds that were deprived of cortex (*A*) and of both brain tissues (*B*).

the sense of smell, and that as the more advanced avian species came to depend less on this sense the cortex shrank in size and importance. From his many anatomical studies of the brains of birds Cobb concluded that the avian "organ of intelligence" was not the cortex but the hyperstriatum.

Cobb did this on the grounds that examination of the brains of various birds had shown that species considered to be more intelligent have a more highly developed hyperstriatum; for example, in the crow, the parrot and the canary this organ is more prominent than in the chicken, the quail and the pigeon. More precise anatomical evidence supporting the notion that "hyperstriatum is to birds what cortex is to mammals" has recently come from the detailed work on avian brain structure done by Harvey Karten at the Massachusetts Institute of Technology. Karten has described an area of the hyperstriatum that receives the same type of neural connec-

tions in the avian brain as the vision area in the cortex of a mammal's brain.

Various items of evidence involving behavior tend to support these anatomical findings. It has long been known that complete removal of the cortical tissue from a bird's brain does not noticeably impair the animal's motor or sensory abilities, whereas a mammal deprived of its cortex becomes at the least severely handicapped in these respects. Recently H. P. Ziegler of the City University of New York showed that pigeons with extensive damage to their cortex could still perform normally in tests of visual discrimination such as learning to peck at a cross rather than a circle. On the other hand, he found that damage to the hyperstriatum greatly impaired birds' performance in such a test. Krushinsky found in his experiments that the performance of birds on the "around the screen" problem was perfectly correlated with the size of the hyperstriatum; the larger this structure (in proportion to

the total size of the cerebrum), the more readily the bird solved the problem. In contrast, the size of a bird's cortex was not at all correlated with ability to solve the problem.

The next inviting step is to explore the hyperstriatum of birds, with a view to finding out what specific structures within that organ are involved in given levels of learning ability. We have begun such experiments in our laboratory. Since Bitterman's multiple-reversal test had proved to be an effective means of differentiating among different species of animals with respect to their learning ability, and these differences in performance presumably reflected some critical difference in their neurological makeup, we selected the multiple-reversal test for our first experiments. As the initial structure for study we chose a bump on the top of the hyperstriatum called the *Wulst*. (It was so named by German investigators.)

Using bobwhite quail as our subjects, we removed the *Wulst* surgically and proceeded to examine the birds' capabilities. They recovered from the operation very quickly and appeared perfectly normal in their movements, eating and drinking behavior, reactions to people and so on. We first submitted the birds to tests involving only a simple form of learning. They learned to peck at a lighted window for food and to choose between vertical and horizontal stripes. Their behavior in these trials was so normal that we came to the conclusion they would certainly pass the multiple-reversal learning test. On the very first reversal problem, however, the birds showed in dramatic fashion that the operation had indeed seriously impaired some aspect of their intellectual functioning. Every bird that had had its *Wulst* removed displayed tremendous difficulty in learning to reverse its choice; this was true even of two birds that before the operation had been trained to a high level of proficiency in reversal. Evidently the *Wulst* not only contained neurological machinery involved in the reversal learning process but also was involved in the function of memory.

Clearly the birds' difficulties with the reversal test were not due to any impairment of their basic motor, sensory or motivational functions. The brain-damaged birds did not differ from normal ones in their movements, their pecking speed and persistence, their pecking accuracy, their responses to food or their ability to learn to make a simple choice between two different visual stimuli. In fact, in the reversal test they continued to peck consistently at the stimulus that had previously represented a food reward, which convincingly demonstrates that they were able to see the differences between the stimuli.

There are indications that some parts of the avian cortex, as well as the *Wulst*, may be involved in reversal learning. In our original experiments we removed much of the overlying cortical tissue along with the *Wulst*. Later, in order to pin down what tissues were actually involved, we tested birds with only the *Wulst* removed and others with only cortical tissue removed. All the birds that lacked only the *Wulst* showed deficiencies in reversal learning, confirming that it is an important structure in avian learning capacity. Removal of parts of the cortex, on the other hand, left this ability unimpaired in most cases. In some instances, however, cortical excision did impair the ability, although

not as much as excision of the *Wulst* did. We are now investigating the possibility that some part or parts of the cortex are functionally involved with the *Wulst* in the higher learning processes.

The discovery of the intellectual capabilities of the avian hyperstriatum has given us a fascinating new avenue for the investigation of brain processes. As a "thinking machine" that is now found to possess many of the capacities of the mammalian cortex, the hyperstriatum is much more accessible to study than the cortex, and its basic operations should be simpler to unravel. Indeed, the hyperstriatum may turn out to be a kind of Rosetta stone for brain researchers. Investigators of the neurology of higher mental processes have been struggling for many years to decipher the message written in the almost impene-

trable code of the extraordinarily complex mammalian cerebral cortex. In the hyperstriatum we now have another message that says almost the same thing but in a simpler code. By analyzing the simpler code and comparing the two codes, which obviously are related to each other, it should be possible to speed up progress toward understanding the basis of intelligence.

It was the lowly fruit fly that provided the key that opened the door to the modern study of heredity and the eventual decipherment of the genetic code, and the giant axon of the squid similarly has made large contributions to our understanding of the transmission of messages by the nervous system. Perhaps the much maligned bird brain will eventually make a key contribution to the understanding of how the brain works to produce intelligent behavior.

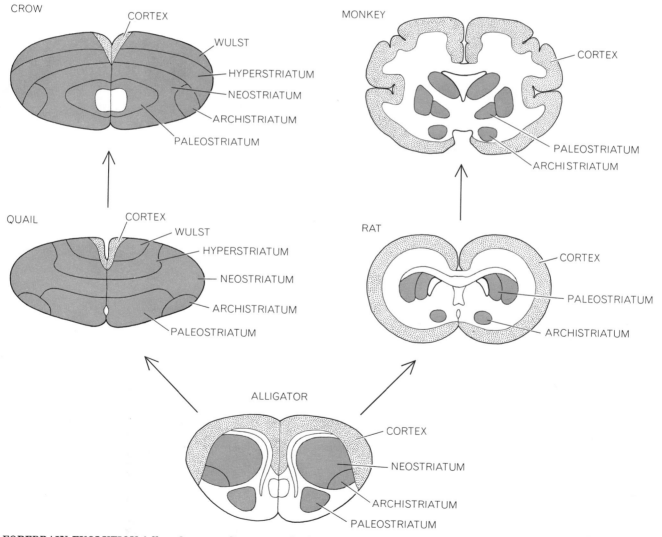

FOREBRAIN EVOLUTION followed separate lines among birds and mammals. Both groups stem from reptilian ancestors, represented here by an alligator's brain seen in transverse section. In it striatal tissue is more abundant than cortical tissue. The trend cli-maxes in the great enlargement of the hyperstriatum among the birds noted for highly intelligent behavior, such as crows. Among mammals the evolutionary trend progressed in the opposite direction, fostering development of a larger and more complex cortex.

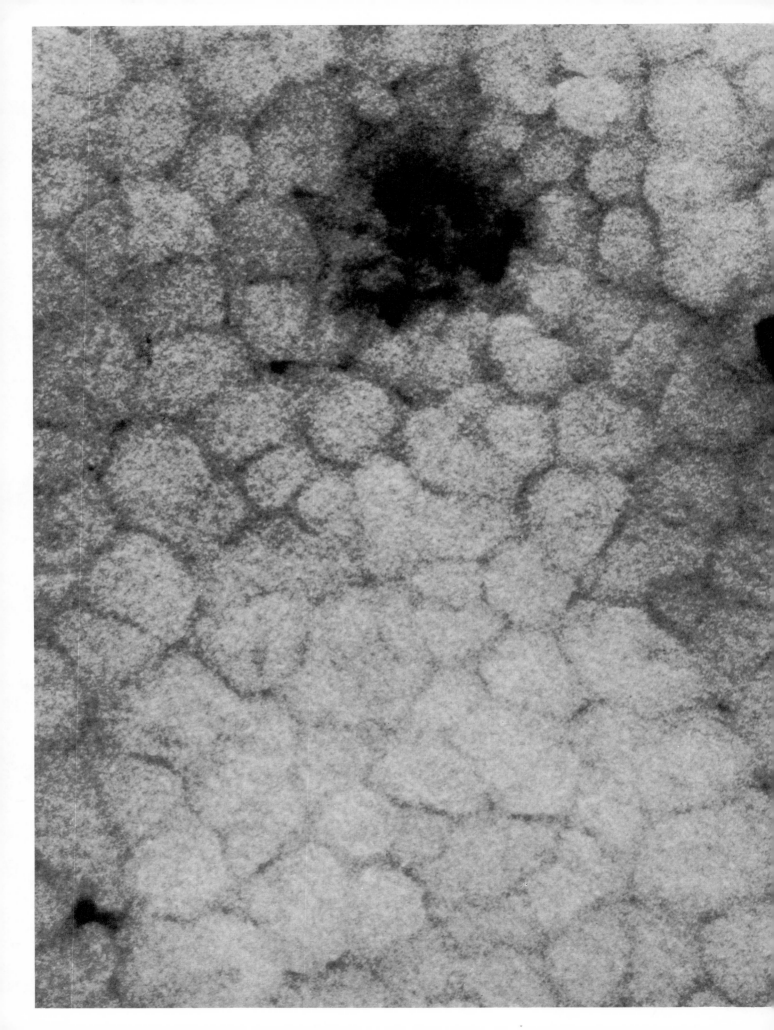

How An Eggshell Is Made

20

T. G. Taylor
March 1970

*Eggshell is largely crystalline calcium carbonate. The
calcium comes partly from the hen's bones, and when
necessary the hen can mobilize 10 percent of her bone
for this purpose in a day*

To a housewife an egg is an article of food, and its shell serves to protect it from physical damage and to prevent the entry of dirt and microorganisms. To the hen an egg is a potential chick, and the shell serves not only as a protective covering but also as a source of calcium for the embryo and as a membrane through which the embryo respires. The eggshell performs its various functions with high efficiency, which is remarkable considering the number of eggs (five to seven a week) that the hen turns out. What is even more remarkable is the process whereby the hen obtains the substantial supply of calcium needed for the formation of the eggshells. The element comes in large part from her bones. Indeed, in extreme cases the hen can mobilize for this purpose as much as 10 percent of her total bone substance in less than a day! The physiology of this unusual process rewards close examination.

In its immature state the egg is one of many oöcytes, or unripened ova, in the ovary of the hen. Each oöcyte is encased in a membrane one cell thick; the entire structure is termed a follicle. At any one time follicles of various sizes, containing yolks at different stages of development, can be found in the ovary. Normally follicles ripen singly at a rate of one a day in hens that are laying regularly. There are occasional pauses. On

the other hand, two follicles sometimes ovulate at the same time, giving rise to a double-yolk egg.

Ovulation takes place within six or eight hours after the release of a high level of a hormone produced by the pituitary gland. The release of the hormone is related to the time of onset of darkness, and it normally occurs between midnight and about 8:00 A.M. It follows that the hen always ovulates in daylight. Moreover, since it takes about 24 hours after ovulation to complete the formation of the egg, the egg is also laid during the daylight hours.

Once the yolk is released from the ovary all the remaining stages of egg formation take place in the oviduct, which consists of several distinct regions: the infundibulum, the magnum, the isthmus, the shell gland (uterus) and the vagina [*see illustration on page 203*]. The oviduct, like the ovary, is on the left side of the hen's body; a vestigial ovary and a vestigial oviduct are sometimes found on the right side in a mature bird, but they normally degenerate completely during the development of the embryo. One can only speculate on the evolutionary reason for the disappearance of the right ovary and oviduct. A reasonable guess is that two ovaries were disadvantageous because of the problem of providing enough calcium for the shells of two eggs at once. Birds have enough of a job supplying calcium for one egg a day. Certain species of wild birds have retained two functional ovaries and oviducts. It is not known how ovulation is controlled in these species, but apparently wild birds do not lay two eggs in one day.

After the ovum is released from the follicle it is engulfed by the funnel-like infundibulum of the oviduct. It is

here that the egg is fertilized in hens that have been mated. As the yolk passes along the oviduct, layers of albumen are laid down in the magnum. The proteins of the albumen, which constitute the egg white, are synthesized in the magnum from amino acids removed from the blood. The synthesis is continuous, and in the periods between the passage of yolks down the oviduct albumen is stored in the tissue of the magnum. The addition of the layers of albumen to the yolk takes about four hours.

The next stage in the formation of the egg is the laying down of two shell membranes, an inner one and an outer one, around the albumen. The membranes are formed in the thin, tubular isthmus. When the membranes are first laid down, they cover the albumen tightly, but they soon stretch. By the time the egg enters the shell gland they fit quite loosely.

The egg passes the next five hours in the process known as "plumping." This entails the entry of water and salts through the membranes until the egg is swollen. The plumping period appears to be an essential preliminary to the main process of shell calcification, which occupies the next 15 to 16 hours.

The shell is composed of calcite, which is one of the crystalline forms of calcium carbonate. A sparse matrix of protein runs through the crystals of the shell. The final stage in the formation of the egg is the deposition of a cuticle on the fully calcified shell; this is accomplished just before the egg is laid.

Let us now look at the structure of the eggshell in rather more detail. From the accompanying illustration [*bottom of page 205*] it will be seen that the shell is attached to the outer membrane by hemispherical structures known as mam-

CHICKEN'S EGGSHELL consists mainly of columns of calcite, a crystalline form of calcium carbonate. They appear on the opposite page in an X-ray micrograph made through the thickness of a shell by A. R. Terepka of the University of Rochester; enlargement is 370 diameters. Large dark spot at top center is a "glassy" region of less opaque mineral; to its right is a pore.

millary knobs. Histochemical studies have shown that the cores of the knobs consist of a protein-mucopolysaccharide complex rich in acid groups, and that anchoring fibers run from the outer membrane into the knobs.

The cores of the mammillary knobs are laid down as the membrane-covered egg passes through the part of the oviduct called the isthmo-uterine junction; it is between the isthmus and the shell gland. It seems probable that the knobs are calcified soon after they are formed, before the egg enters the shell gland, and that they subsequently act as nuclei for the growth of the calcite crystals comprising the shell. Modern ideas on the mechanism of biological calcification—whether in bones, teeth, eggshells or any of the other places where calcium is deposited in animal bodies—emphasize the importance of crystal growth. Earlier theories seeking to explain the mechanism laid much stress on the role of precipitation of calcium salts from supersaturated solutions, but in the light of more recent evidence this concept no longer seems valid.

The mechanism whereby the mammillary knobs are calcified is not well understood. It is thought to involve the binding of calcium ions to the organic cores of the knobs by means of the sulfonic acid groups on the acid-mucopolysaccharide-protein material of which the cores are composed. It is suggested that the spatial arrangement of the bound calcium ions is the same as it is in the lattice of the calcite crystal, so that these oriented calcium ions act as seeds or nuclei for the growth of calcite crystals forming the shell. Some years ago my colleagues and I found that the isthmus contains extremely high concentrations of both calcium and citric acid, the former reaching a maximum of about 90 milligrams per 100 grams of fresh tissue and the latter about 360 milligrams. We concluded that the high level of calcium in this region may be of significance in the calcification of the mammillary knobs.

The main part of the shell was once known as the spongy layer but has more recently come to be called the palisade layer. It is composed of columns of tightly packed calcite crystals; the columns extend from the mammillary knobs to the cuticle. Occasional pores run up between the crystals from spaces formed where groups of knobs come together. The pores reach the surface in small depressions that are just visible to the unaided eye on the outside of the shell. It is through these pores that the embryo takes in oxygen and gives out carbon dioxide during the incubation of the egg.

The raw materials for the formation of the calcite crystals, namely the ions of calcium and carbonate, come from the blood plasma. The shell gland is provided with an extremely rich supply of blood. Careful measurements have shown that the level of plasma calcium falls as the blood passes through the gland when the calcification of a shell is in progress but does not fall when there is no egg in the gland.

Changes in the level of calcium in the blood of female birds during the breeding season have engaged the attention of many workers since 1926, when Oscar Riddle and Warren H. Reinhart of the Carnegie Institution of Washington discovered that breeding hen doves and pigeons had blood calcium levels more than twice as high as those found in cocks or nonbreeding hens. Adult males, nonbreeding females and immature birds of both sexes have plasma calcium levels of about 10 milligrams per 100 milliliters, whereas the level in females during the reproductive period is usually between 20 and 30 milligrams per 100 milliliters. For many years it was assumed that the high level of plasma calcium found in laying females was related to the trait of producing eggs with calcified shells, but it is generally recognized now that it is related to the production of large, yolky eggs. The extra calcium in the blood of laying birds (as compared with nonlaying ones) is almost entirely bound to protein. In contrast, the level of ionic calcium, which is the form of calcium mainly used in the formation of the eggshell, is about the same in laying and nonlaying hens.

The particular protein concerned in the binding of the increased plasma calcium is the phosphorus-containing protein phosvitin. It is the characteristic protein of the egg yolk. Phosvitin has a great affinity for calcium: the greater the amount of this phosphoprotein in the blood, the higher the level of plasma calcium. Phosvitin is synthesized in the liver under the influence of estrogen and is carried in the blood (in combination with lipid material) to the follicles developing in the ovary. Similar proteins are found in the blood of all animals that lay yolky eggs, including fishes, amphibians and reptiles, and yet neither fishes nor amphibians lay eggs with calcified shells, and among the reptiles only the Chelonia (turtles and tortoises) and the Crocodilia do so.

In the passage of blood through the shell gland there is a fall in both the protein-bound calcium (also termed nondiffusible calcium because the molecules of the protein to which it is bound are too large to diffuse through a semipermeable membrane) and in the diffusible calcium, the latter being mainly in the form of calcium ions. The two forms of calcium appear to be in equilibrium with each other. It seems likely that calcium

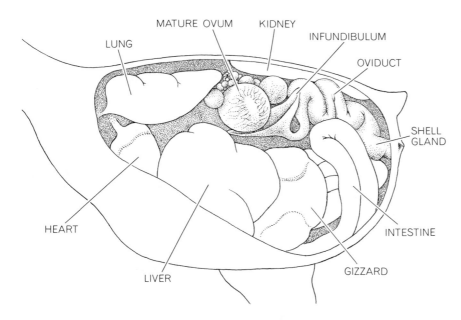

REPRODUCTIVE TRACT of the chicken is indicated in relation to the other organs in the body cavity. The single ovary and oviduct are on the hen's left side; an undeveloped ovary and an oviduct are sometimes found on the right side, having degenerated in the embryo.

in the form of ions is taken up from the plasma by the shell gland and that the level of ionic calcium is partly restored by the dissociation of a portion of the protein-bound calcium.

So much for the calcium ions. The origin of the carbonate ions is much harder to explain. At the slightly alkaline level of normal blood (pH 7.4) their concentration is extremely low, and it is the bicarbonate ion that predominates.

Theories to explain the formation of carbonate ions center on the enzyme carbonic anhydrase, which is present in high concentration in the cells lining the shell gland. One theory assumes that two bicarbonate ions are in equilibrium with a molecule of carbonic acid and a carbonate ion, with the equilibrium strongly in favor of the bicarbonate ions. The hypothesis is that the carbonic acid is continuously being dehydrated to carbon dioxide gas under the influence of the carbonic anhydrase, and that carbonate ions continuously diffuse or are pumped across the cell membranes into the shell gland, where they join calcium ions to form the calcite lattice of the growing crystals in the eggshell. An alternative theory, proposed by Kenneth Simkiss of Queen Mary College in London, is that the carbonate arises directly in the shell gland by the hydration of metabolic carbon dioxide under the influence of carbonic anhydrase.

The main evidence in support of the intimate involvement of carbonic anhydrase in eggshell formation is that certain sulfonamide drugs, which are powerful inhibitors of the enzyme, inhibit the calcification of shells. By feeding laying hens graded amounts of sulfanilamide, for example, it is possible to bring about a progressive thinning of the shells. Eventually, at the highest levels of treatment, completely shell-less eggs are laid.

On the average the shell of a chicken's egg weighs about five grams. Some 40 percent of the weight, or two grams, is calcium. Most of the calcium is laid down in the final 16 hours of the calcification process, which means that it is deposited at a mean rate of 125 milligrams per hour.

The total amount of calcium circulating in the blood of an average hen at any one time is about 25 milligrams. Hence an amount of calcium equal to the weight of calcium present in the circulation is removed from the blood every 12 minutes during the main period of shell calcification. Where does this calcium come from? The immediate source is the

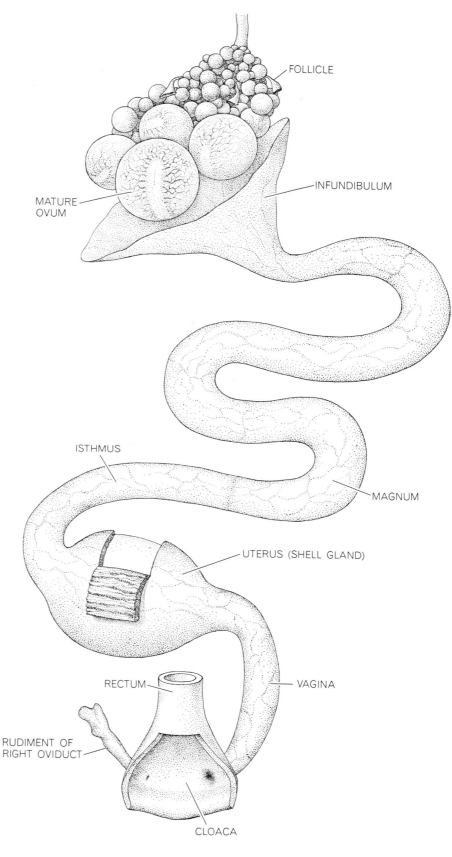

OVARY AND OVIDUCT of the chicken are involved in the formation of the egg. The shell is formed in the uterus, which is also called the shell gland. The principal steps in the formation of a chicken's egg are shown in the illustration at the top of the next two pages.

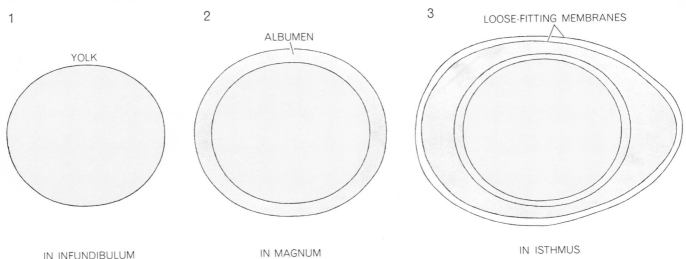

DEVELOPMENT OF EGG begins with the ovulation of a fully developed yolk from the ovary. It enters the infundibulum and begins moving along the oviduct. Layers of albumen are laid down in the magnum; the process takes about four hours. Two membranes

blood, but the ultimate source is the food. It has been demonstrated, however, that during the period of shell formation the hen is unable to absorb calcium from the intestines rapidly enough to meet the full requirement of the shell gland, no matter how much calcium is supplied in the food. When the rate of absorption from the gut falls short of the rate at which calcium is removed from the blood by the shell gland, the deficit is made good by the liberation of calcium from the skeleton.

This process has been demonstrated convincingly by the use of a radioactive isotope of calcium, calcium 45. Cyril Tyler of the University of Reading fed the isotope to laying hens daily and employed autoradiography to detect the amount of radioactive calcium deposited in the eggshells. (Beta particles given off by the calcium 45 of dietary origin blackened the X-ray film that was in contact with sections of shell, and the distribution of the isotope was thus visualized.) After the hens had been fed the radioactive calcium for a week the skeleton became intensely labeled, so that it was no longer possible to distinguish food calcium from bone calcium deposited in the shell. Accordingly the labeled calcium was withdrawn from the food, so that any calcium 45 deposited in the shells from then on must have come from the skeleton. Radioactive calcium appeared in abundance in the shells.

The mobilization of skeletal calcium for the formation of eggshell increases as the dietary supply of calcium decreases. When food completely devoid of calcium is fed, all the shell calcium comes from the bones. If a hen is fed a low-calcium diet, she will mobilize something like two grams of skeletal calcium in 15 to 16 hours. That is 8 to 10 percent of the total amount of calcium in her bones. Clearly hens cannot continue depleting their skeleton at this rate for long. When the food is continuously low in calcium, the shells become progressively thinner.

The hen's ability to mobilize 10 percent of her total bone substance in less than a day is quite fantastic but not unique: all birds that have been studied are able to call on their skeletal reserves of calcium for eggshell formation, and the rate of withdrawal is impressively high. This ability is associated with a system of secondary bone in the marrow cavities of most of the animal's bones. The secondary bone, which is called medullary bone, appears to have developed in birds during the course of evolution in direct relation to the laying of eggs with thick, calcified shells.

Strange to say, considering the fact that people had been killing birds for food for thousands of years and examining bones scientifically for at least a century, this unusual bone was not reported until 1916, when J. S. Foote of Creighton Medical College observed it in leg bones of the yellowhammer and the white pelican. The phenomenon was then forgotten until Preston Kyes and Truman S. Potter of the University of Chicago discovered it in the pigeon in 1934.

Medullary bone is quite similar in structure to the cancellous, or spongy, bone commonly found in the epiphyses (the growing ends) of bones. It occurs in the form of trabeculae, or fine spicules, which grow out into the marrow cavity from the inner surface of the structural bone. In males and nonbreeding females the marrow cavities of most bones are filled with red marrow tissue, which is involved in the production of blood cells. The spicules of medullary bone ramify through the marrow without interfering with the blood supply.

Medullary bone is found only in female birds during the reproductive period, which in the domestic fowl lasts many months. (In wild birds it lasts only a few weeks.) Medullary bone is never found in male birds under normal conditions, but it can be induced in males by injections of female sex hormones (estrogens). In hen birds medullary bone is produced under the combined influence of both estrogens and male sex hormones (androgens). It is thought that the developing ovary produces both kinds of hormone.

The formation and breakdown of medullary bone have been studied more closely in the pigeon than in any other bird. Pigeons lay only two eggs in a clutch; the second egg is laid two days after the first one. A pigeon normally lays the first egg about seven days after mating. The medullary bone is formed during this prelaying period. By the time the first egg is due to be provided with its shell, the marrow cavities of many bones of the skeleton are almost filled with bone spicules, which have grown steadily since the follicles developing in the ovary first started to secrete sex hormones.

About four hours after the egg enters the shell gland marked changes begin in

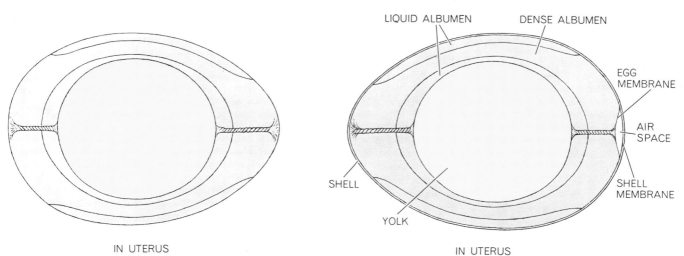

LIQUID ALBUMEN   DENSE ALBUMEN

EGG MEMBRANE

AIR SPACE

SHELL

SHELL MEMBRANE

YOLK

IN UTERUS   IN UTERUS

are added in the isthmus. At first they fit tightly, but by the time the egg enters the shell gland they have stretched so that the egg can undergo a five-hour process called plumping. The formation of the shell occupies the 15 to 16 hours needed to complete the egg.

the medullary bone. Within a few hours its cellular population has been transferred from one dominated by osteoblasts, or bone-forming cells, to one dominated by osteoclasts, or bone-destroying cells. The phase of bone destruction continues throughout the period of shell calcification. The calcium released from the bone mineral is deposited on the shell as calcium carbonate, and the phosphate liberated simultaneously is excreted in the urine.

The breakdown of the medullary bone persists for a few hours after the egg is laid. Then, quite suddenly, another phase of intense bone formation begins. This phase lasts until the calcification of the shell of the second egg starts; at that time another phase of bone destruction begins. No more bone is formed in this cycle. Resorption of the medullary bone continues after the second egg of the clutch is laid until, a week or so later, all traces of the special bone structure have disappeared and the marrow cavity regains its original appearance.

What mechanism might account for the rapid change from bone formation to bone destruction and vice versa?

One suggestion is that variations in the level of estrogen control the cyclic changes in the medullary bone. There can be little doubt that the high level of estrogen plus androgen in the blood plasma is primarily responsible for the induction of medullary bone during the prelaying period; the drop in the level of estrogen or androgen or both after the second egg of the clutch is laid might well give rise to the bone destruction. It is difficult to see, however, how the fine degree of control necessary to induce bone destruction when calcification of the first eggshell is due to start, and to

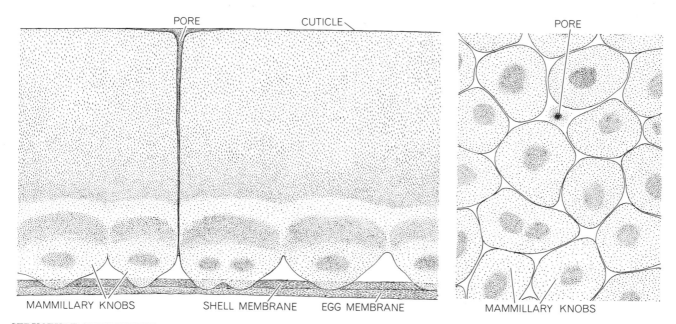

PORE   CUTICLE   PORE

MAMMILLARY KNOBS   SHELL MEMBRANE   EGG MEMBRANE   MAMMILLARY KNOBS

STRUCTURE OF EGGSHELL is portrayed in cross section (*left*) and in a tangential section (*right*) made through the layer containing the hemispherical mammillary knobs. The knobs, which attach the shell to the outer membrane of the egg by fibers, have an organic core; the rest of the structure is made of oriented ions of calcium that apparently act as seeds for the shell's calcite crystals.

reverse the process soon after it is completed, can be exercised by changes in the secretion of sex hormones, presumably from the single follicle present in the ovary and possibly from the recently ruptured follicle.

The control mechanism that my colleagues and I consider more likely is one mediated by the parathyroid gland. The role of this gland is to regulate the level of calcium ions in the blood. A drop in the level of plasma calcium causes the release of parathyroid hormone from the gland, and the hormone brings about a resorption of bone tissue through the agency of the bone cells (osteoclasts and enlarged osteocytes). Both organic matrix and bone mineral are removed together, and the calcium and phosphate are released into the blood. The level of plasma calcium is thus restored; the phosphate is excreted.

Bone resorption under the influence of parathyroid hormone is largely due to an increase in the number and activity of osteoclasts. The histological picture

observed in the medullary bone of pigeons at the height of eggshell calcification bears a strong resemblance to the resorption of bone in rats and dogs following the administration of parathyroid hormone. Leonard F. Bélanger of the University of Ottawa and I have recently shown that the histological changes in the medullary bone of hens treated with parathyroid hormone were very similar to those occurring naturally during eggshell formation.

It has been shown that the level of diffusible calcium in the blood drops during eggshell calcification in the hen; the stimulus for the release of parathyroid hormone is therefore present. The hypothesis that the parathyroid hormone is responsible for the induction of bone resorption associated with shell formation is also consistent with the time lag between the end of the calcification of the eggshell of the first egg in the pigeon's clutch and the resumption of medullary bone formation.

When hens are fed a diet deficient

in calcium, they normally stop laying in 10 to 14 days, having laid some six to eight eggs. During this period they may deplete their skeleton of calcium to the extent of almost 40 percent. It is interesting to inquire why they should stop laying instead of continuing to lay but producing eggs without shells. Failure to lay is a result of failure to ovulate; once ovulation takes place and the ovum enters the oviduct, an egg will be laid, with or without a hard shell.

The question therefore becomes: Why do hens cease to ovulate when calcium is withheld from their diet? The most probable answer seemed to us to be that the release of gonadotrophic hormones from the anterior pituitary gland is reduced under these conditions. To test this hypothesis we placed six pullets, which had been laying for about a month, on a diet containing only .2 percent calcium—less than a tenth of the amount normally supplied in laying rations.

After five days on the deficient diet, when each hen had laid three or four eggs, we administered daily injections of an extract of avian pituitary glands to three of the experimental birds. During the next five days each of these hens laid an egg a day, whereas two of the untreated hens laid one egg each during the five days and the third untreated hen laid three eggs. We concluded that the failure to produce eggs on a diet deficient in calcium is indeed due to a reduction in the secretion of pituitary gonadotrophic hormones.

The mechanism of pituitary inhibition under these conditions has not been established. It is possible that the severe depression of the level of plasma calcium inhibits the part of the brain known as the hypothalamus, which is known to be sensitive to a number of chemical influences. The secretion of gonadotrophins in mammals is brought about by hormone-like factors released by the hypothalamus, but it is not known if the same mechanism operates in birds.

Plainly the laying of eggs with highly calcified shells has profound repercussions on the physiology of the bird. The success of birds in the struggle for existence indicates that they have been able to meet the challenge imposed on them by the evolution of shell making. Many facets of the intricate relations between eggshell formation, the skeletal mobilization of calcium, the ovary and the parathyroid and anterior pituitary glands await elucidation, but the general picture is now clear.

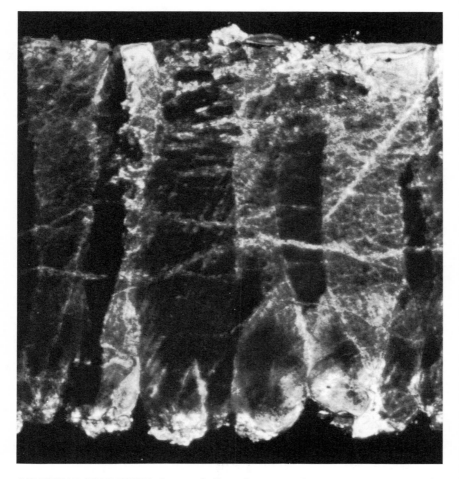

COLUMNAR STRUCTURE of an eggshell stands out in a photomicrograph also made by Terepka, using polarized light. The shell is seen in cross section at an enlargement of 325 diameters. The lumpy structures at bottom are the mammillary knobs of the eggshell.

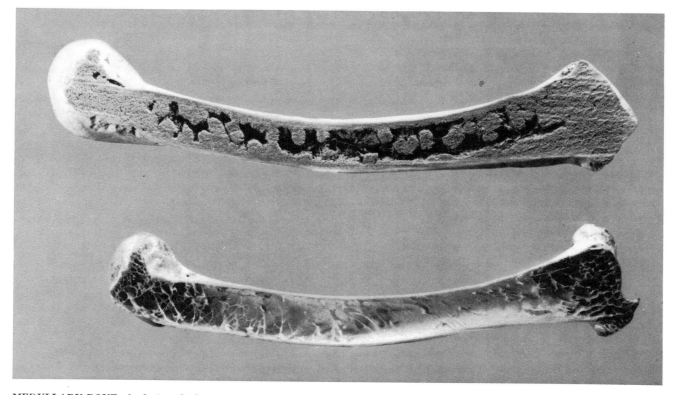

MEDULLARY BONE of a laying chicken contains the reserve of calcium that the hen draws on in forming the eggshell. Medullary bone in the femur of a laying chicken is shown at top; the struc- ture consists of trabeculae, or fine spicules, of bone that grow into the marrow cavity from the inside of the structural bone. The femur of a nonlaying bird (*bottom*) shows no medullary bone.

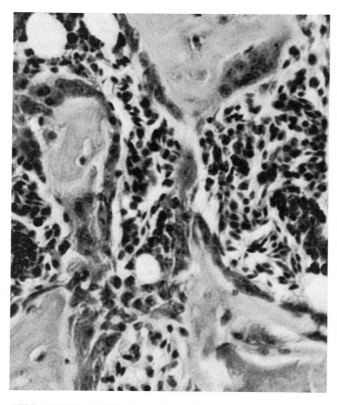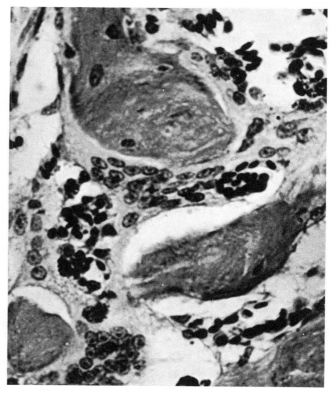

CELL POPULATION of medullary bone differs according to whether the bone is being built up or broken down. The bone is dominated by osteoblast cells (*left*) when the hen is accumulating a reserve of calcium and by osteoclast cells (*right*) when she is draw- ing on the reserve. The cells are the small, dark objects; the larger, gray objects are trabeculae. The bone is femur of a chicken; enlarge- ment is 600 diameters. These micrographs were made by Werner J. Mueller and A. Zambonin of Pennsylvania State University.

21

How Bird Eggs Breathe

by Hermann Rahn, Amos Ar, and Charles V. Paganelli
February 1979

*Bird embryos take up oxygen and discharge carbon
dioxide by simple diffusion through microscopic pores
in the eggshell. The process is regulated largely by pore
geometry, which varies among bird species*

The bird egg is a self-contained life-support system for the developing bird embryo. All the nutrients, minerals, energy sources and water utilized by the embryo during its incubation are already present in the freshly laid egg, so that the egg requires only warming by the parents and periodic turning to prevent the adhesion of the embryo to the shell membranes. Still, the egg lacks one crucial requirement: oxygen, which drives the metabolic machinery of the embryonic cells so that they can execute the complex maneuvers of development. How does the egg breathe, taking up oxygen from the surrounding atmosphere and discharging carbon dioxide, the waste product of respiration?

Gas exchange is usually associated with the periodic inhalation of a fluid medium (air or water), which carries oxygen to the capillaries of the lungs or the gills and removes carbon dioxide from the respiratory organ with each exhalation. The lungs or the gills are driven by muscles whose rate of pumping is determined by metabolic demand and controlled by the nervous system. Yet the eggs of birds and other organisms (such as insects, spiders, amphibians and reptiles) show no respiratory movements, and there are no air currents within the egg that could transport oxygen to the capillaries of the growing embryo. Instead the egg "breathes" by diffusion through thousands of microscopic pores in the shell.

The existence of these pores was first demonstrated in 1863 by John Davy, a member of the Royal Society from Edinburgh, without the aid of a microscope. He placed an egg in a jar of water and evacuated the air above the surface of the water with a vacuum pump. He noted that small bubbles of gas formed on the surface of the egg, and he deduced that there are minute openings in the shell.

Gas moves through the pores by the passive process of diffusion: the tendency for a high concentration of a molecule to run downhill to an area of lower concentration. Diffusion takes place because of the kinetic energy of gas molecules and does not require the direct expenditure of metabolic energy by the embryo; the lower concentration of oxygen inside the egg brings new oxygen molecules in through the pores from the outside, where the concentration is higher. Conversely, the concentration of carbon dioxide inside the egg causes those molecules to diffuse toward the outside, where there are essentially none. These diffusion processes are governed by the available pore area of the shell, the length of the pores and the concentration differences of the gases diffusing across the shell.

The water content of the air within the egg is greater than that of the air outside it, and so the pores will also allow water molecules (which are smaller than oxygen molecules) to diffuse out. Animals have evolved many specialized adaptations for conserving water, but bird eggs seem designed to lose it at a controlled rate. Most of the energy needed for embryonic development is taken from the fat stores of the yolk, and for every gram of fat burned an almost equal mass of metabolic water is generated. Therefore the relative water content of the egg will increase during incubation unless water is lost. If the relative water content at hatching is to equal that of the freshly laid egg, about 15 percent of the initial mass of the egg must be lost as water. As breeders of domestic fowl well know, this amount of water loss is essential for successful hatching.

Over the 21 days of its incubation a typical chicken egg weighing 60 grams will take up about six liters of oxygen and give off 4.5 liters of carbon dioxide and 11 liters of water vapor. Because of the water loss the egg will weigh only 51 grams after 21 days of incubation, and the newly hatched chick will weigh about 39 grams (subtracting the weight of the shell and the respiratory membranes). Investigations in our laboratories and in others have been aimed at elucidating the diffusive mechanisms responsible for this transfer of gases.

The three layers of the egg's integument—the shell and the two underlying membranes—should be familiar to anyone who has ever peeled a boiled egg. All three layers are laid down in less than 24 hours as the naked egg cell passes down the oviduct of the hen into the shell gland or uterus [see "How an Eggshell Is Made," by T. G. Taylor beginning on page 200]. The eggshell itself has an outermost layer called the cuticle (it is missing in some species), which is a very thin sheet of organic material, often cracked to expose the surface of the eggshell proper. The shell consists of secreted calcium carbonate, which forms columnar calcite crystals incorporating a small amount of organic material. Imperfect packing of the calcite crystals leaves spaces between them that traverse the thickness of the shell, giving rise to the microscopic pores.

The outer and inner shell membranes consist of a meshwork of organic fibers. The fibers of the outer shell membrane are attached to the inside of the eggshell through the mammillary cones, the centers of crystallization of the eggshell during its formation. The two membranes differ in diameter of fiber, coarseness of weave and total thickness. The inner side of the inner membrane is lined with a thin "film" that appears to be continuous rather than simply an extension of the fibers. Soon after the egg is laid the spaces between the fibers in the two membranes are filled with gas.

The pores in the eggshell are the only path of gaseous communication between the outside environment and the embryonic membranes. They are cylindrical in shape and their openings are sometimes covered with secreted organic or inorganic particulate material. Careful etching of the shell with acid followed by staining makes the pores visible to the unaided eye: the typical chicken egg has about 10,000 distributed over its surface. The dimensions and numbers of the pores are established in the shell gland before the egg is laid; thereafter they remain unchanged. As we shall see, the shape, size and number of the pores in the eggshell vary among bird species, and it is the aggregate geometry of the pores that determines the diffusing capacity of the eggshell.

Since the bird embryo cannot directly control its gas exchange, the permeability or conductance of the shell and membranes to gases must be delicately adjusted to meet the embryo's metabolic needs. If the gas conductance is too high, the oxygen requirement of the embryo will be amply met but too much water will be lost, resulting in dehydration. If the gas conductance is too low, the embryo will either suffocate for lack of oxygen, be poisoned by its own carbon dioxide or drown in its own metabolic water. A happy medium must be struck that provides optimal gas pressures in the embryo and ensures a finite loss of water from the egg.

Water is lost from the egg at a con-stant rate, but the uptake of oxygen increases considerably over the course of incubation. In the chicken the first 18 days of incubation are designated the prenatal period. On days five and six the chorioallantois (the respiratory organ of the embryo, analogous to the placenta of mammals) extends out from the embryo, making contact with the continuous film lining the inner membrane and establishing a network of capillaries. By day nine the chorioallantois has invested about half of the inner surface of the

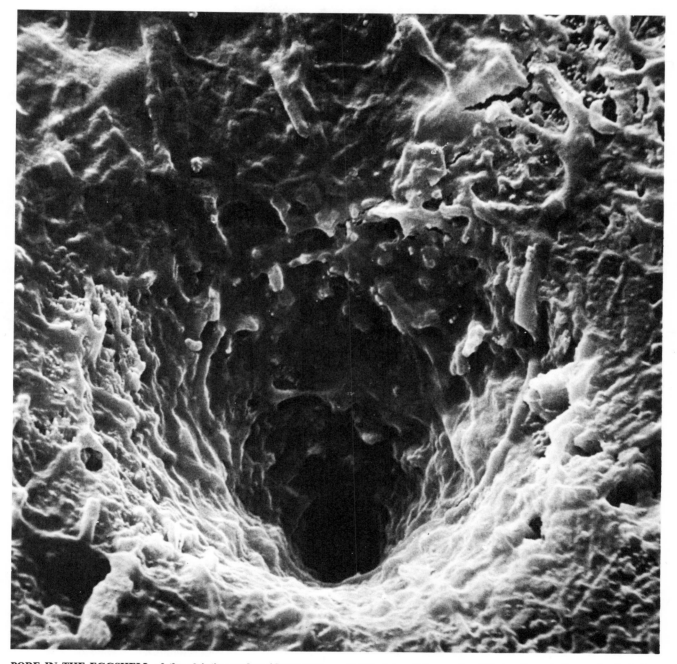

PORE IN THE EGGSHELL of the plaintive cuckoo (*Cacomantis merulinus*) of Java is magnified 3,800 diameters in this scanning electron micrograph. The conical pore opening narrows into a cylindrical tube a few micrometers in diameter that passes entirely through the eggshell. Atmospheric oxygen enters the egg and metabolic carbon dioxide leaves it by passive diffusion through thousands of similar pores distributed over the egg surface. This view of the pore opening is unusually clear; in most eggs the pores are concealed by secreted organic or inorganic material. Micrograph was made by J. H. Becking of Institute for Atomic Sciences in Agriculture in the Netherlands.

shell, and by about day 12 it has completely covered the inner surface. (The inner and outer shell membranes lie between the chorioallantois and the eggshell proper.)

During the prenatal period oxygen and carbon dioxide are exchanged across the chorioallantois and water vapor is continually lost. Since the shell is rigid, gas enters to replace the lost water and forms an air cell at the blunt end of the egg. The air cell increases steadily in size until it occupies about 15 percent of the internal volume of the egg at the end of incubation. The gas within the air cell is continuous with the gas found between the fibers of the outer and inner membranes. This continuity can be demonstrated by injecting pressurized air into the air cell underwater, causing air bubbles to escape from pores all over the surface of the egg. The gas tensions in the air cell are nearly identical with those in the air spaces of the shell membranes, so that the air cell provides a convenient site for sampling the gases within the egg.

The oxygen consumption of the embryo increases slowly during the first week and a half of incubation. Between days 10 and 14 it rises steeply to reach a plateau of 600 milliliters of oxygen per day prior to hatching. This value is the maximal amount of oxygen that can be obtained by passive diffusion through the fixed pores of the shell. Six hundred milliliters of oxygen per day may not seem very impressive to the reader (who will consume that amount in two minutes), but the molecular traffic through the 10,000 pores in the eggshell is remarkably intense. Every second a net of about 20 trillion (20×10^{12}) oxygen molecules flows into the egg through each pore and 14 trillion molecules of carbon dioxide and 12 trillion molecules of water vapor flow out.

Nevertheless, the rigors of hatching require more oxygen than simple diffusion can provide. Where does the additional oxygen come from? Nature has provided a simple solution to this problem: on about day 19 the chick penetrates the air cell at the blunt end of the egg with its beak, a process called internal pipping. The chick then begins to breathe from the air cell, ventilating its previously unused lungs. Internal pipping is a crucial event: it allows the chick's lungs and their air sacs to be inflated so that oxygen is transported to the lungs by convection, or bulk flow.

The period of active breathing from the air cell within the confines of the intact egg is called the paranatal period, because the chorioallantois is still functional. During this period oxygen is therefore delivered by both diffusion and convection.

About six hours after the chick has penetrated the air cell it pips the shell, that is, it makes a small hole with the egg tooth on its upper beak and breathes atmospheric air for the first time. By now lung function is well enough established to allow the significant increase in oxygen consumption required for the final effort of hatching. At the same time chorioallantoic function begins to wane, although it persists to the end, when the respiratory membranes are left clinging to the inside of the shell as the chick emerges and the postnatal period begins. The smooth transition from passive gas transport to active gas transport is accomplished in from 24 to 36 hours.

It is now known that the flow of oxygen from the atmosphere to the blood

DEMONSTRATION OF PORES in the eggshell without the need for a microscope can be achieved by injecting pressurized air into the air cell at the blunt end of a chicken egg. Bubbles emerge from the entire surface of the egg, indicating that it contains thousands of minute openings. This experiment is similar to one first performed by John Davy of Edinburgh in 1863. Photograph was made by Dennis R. Atkinson of State University of New York at Buffalo.

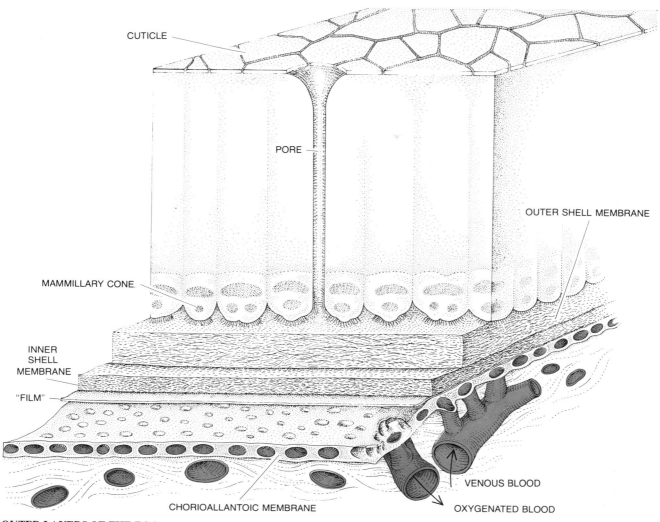

CUTICLE

PORE

OUTER SHELL MEMBRANE

MAMMILLARY CONE

INNER
SHELL
MEMBRANE

"FILM"

VENOUS BLOOD

OXYGENATED BLOOD

CHORIOALLANTOIC MEMBRANE

OUTER LAYERS OF THE EGG participating in gas exchange are shown in this cross section covering a depth of about .4 millimeter. The outermost layer is the cuticle, a thin organic sheet. Under it is the shell proper, made up of columns of calcite crystals and traversed by pores. The pores terminate in the loose, fibrous outer membrane; the outer and inner membranes differ in fiber diameter, coarseness of weave and total thickness. The very thin inner surface of the inner membrane, termed the "film," is most probably a continuous sheet. Attached to the film is the chorioallantois (the respiratory organ of the embryo), which is analogous to the placenta of mammals. Venous blood (*blue*) pumped by the embryonic heart flows to the chorioallantoic membrane, where it is replenished with oxygen that has diffused through the pores. Oxygenated blood (*red*) then travels to embryonic tissue. Simultaneously carbon dioxide diffuses out of venous blood.

capillaries of the chorioallantois is regulated by a series of barriers to diffusion: the shell and the inner and outer shell membranes. Respiratory physiologists express the permeability of a membrane to gas in terms of its conductance: the reciprocal of its resistance to diffusion. The partial pressures of the respiratory gases are commonly expressed in torr, or millimeters of mercury, one torr being equal to 1/760 of standard atmospheric pressure (the combined partial pressures of all the gases in the atmosphere at sea level, including nitrogen, oxygen and carbon dioxide).

There is a drop of some 100 torr between the partial pressure of oxygen in the atmosphere (154 torr) and that in the newly oxygenated blood of the chorioallantois (58 torr). Nevertheless, an oxygen pressure of 58 torr in the blood is nearly sufficient to saturate the blood with oxygen, which is carried to all the tissues of the embryo. The venous blood returning from the embryo has an oxygen pressure of 22 torr. It passes through the chorioallantois, where it is replenished with newly diffused oxygen to a pressure of 58 torr. Conversely, the partial pressure of carbon dioxide drops from 47 torr in the venous blood to 38 torr in the oxygenated blood.

Measuring the gas conductance between the inner membrane and the chorioallantois proved to be extremely difficult because the gas partial pressures in the air cell and in the oxygenated blood must be measured simultaneously. This experimental problem was solved by Hiroshi Tazawa of Yamagata University, with whom two of us worked last year in the laboratory of Johannes Pii-

per at the Max Planck Institute for Experimental Medicine in Göttingen.

To measure the partial pressures of oxygen and carbon dioxide in the egg, Tazawa glued to the shell over the air cell a hypodermic syringe that was partly filled with air, so that the air in the syringe was in direct contact with the gas in the air cell. Over a period of a few hours the partial pressures of oxygen and carbon dioxide in the syringe and the air cell came into equilibrium. By analyzing the gas partial pressures in the syringe it was therefore possible to determine those in the air cell. To measure the gas pressures in the oxygenated blood Tazawa made a small hole in the eggshell and implanted an ultrathin catheter, or plastic tube, in the chorioallantoic blood vessel that carries oxy-

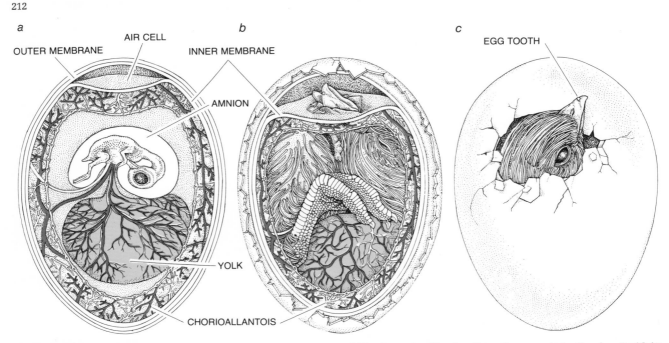

a OUTER MEMBRANE · AIR CELL · *b* INNER MEMBRANE · AMNION · *c* EGG TOOTH · YOLK · CHORIOALLANTOIS

SHIFT TO ACTIVE BREATHING during the 21-day incubation period of the chicken embryo takes place in two steps. The prenatal period (*a*) is the first 18 days of development. Beginning at day five the chorioallantois protrudes from the embryo and covers the inner shell membrane with a net of capillaries that supply the embryo with oxygen and remove carbon dioxide. Water vapor also diffuses continually from the egg; the liquid water that is lost is replaced by gas to form an air cell at the blunt end of the egg. The paranatal period

(*b*) begins on day 19, when the embryo penetrates the air cell with its beak, a process called internal pipping. The embryo then begins to breathe from the air cell, inflating its lungs and air sacs for the first time, although the chorioallantois still continues to function. About six hours later the chick breaks through the eggshell with the egg tooth at the tip of its upper beak (*c*) and starts to breathe atmospheric air. At this time chorioallantoic function begins to wane. Illustration is based on one by Hans-Rainer Duncker of the University of Giessen.

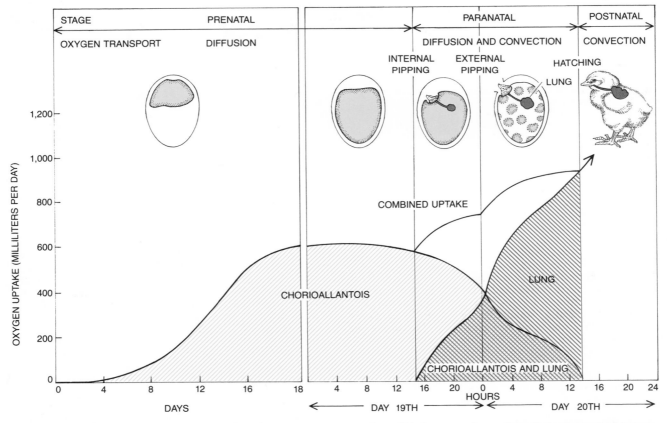

STAGE — PRENATAL — PARANATAL — POSTNATAL

OXYGEN TRANSPORT — DIFFUSION — DIFFUSION AND CONVECTION — CONVECTION

INTERNAL PIPPING — EXTERNAL PIPPING — HATCHING — LUNG

COMBINED UPTAKE

CHORIOALLANTOIS

LUNG

CHORIOALLANTOIS AND LUNG

OXYGEN UPTAKE (MILLILITERS PER DAY)

1,200 — 1,000 — 800 — 600 — 400 — 200 — 0

DAYS: 0 4 8 12 16 18

DAY 19TH: 4 8 12 16 20 0 4 8 12

HOURS

DAY 20TH: 16 20 24

OXYGEN CONSUMPTION of the chicken embryo increases considerably over the course of incubation. The increase is gradual for the first week and a half, but between days 10 and 14 oxygen consumption rises sharply. On days 19 and 20 there is a gradual switchover from diffusive gas exchange through the chorioallantois to active breathing through the lungs. By the time the chick emerges from the egg its lungs are already working efficiently. This graph is based on work done by A. H. J. Visschedijk of the University of Utrecht.

genated blood to the embryo. The air in the syringe and a sample of the oxygenated blood were removed simultaneously and analyzed for their oxygen and carbon dioxide levels.

With this approach Tazawa found that the partial pressure of oxygen in the air cell is about 50 torr higher than that in the oxygenated blood, whereas the carbon dioxide pressure is 2.5 torr higher in the oxygenated blood than it is in the air cell. The fact that there is a 50-torr difference in oxygen pressure between the air-cell gas and the blood calls for explanation. It is unlikely that the air-filled spaces normally present between the fibers of the inner shell membrane are responsible. The difference may be caused partly by the resistance to diffusion of the thin continuous film between the inner shell membrane and the chorioallantoic epithelium. Another possibility is that some venous blood (with its low oxygen pressure of 22 torr) bypasses the capillaries where gas exchange takes place and mixes with fully oxygenated blood, thereby lowering its oxygen pressure to 58 torr. Of course, both phenomena may operate.

In summary, as one traces the partial pressure of oxygen from the atmosphere to the oxygenated blood leaving the chorioallantois of the chick, one finds only two areas where large differences in oxygen pressure exist: the shell proper and the inner shell membrane. The shell alone, however, is responsible for almost the entire partial-pressure difference for both carbon dioxide and water vapor.

Given the task of designing an efficient gas-exchange system, the respiratory physiologist would logically try to maximize oxygen conductance. In the egg, however, such purely respiratory considerations must be balanced against other factors important for the survival of the embryo. These factors include the need for an eggshell thick enough to provide mechanical protection for the embryo, to prevent harmful bacteria from invading the egg, to conserve essential fluids and to maintain the proper carbon dioxide pressure for a normal acid-base balance.

Having learned some of the principles that govern gas exchange in the chicken egg, we became curious about some of the other 8,500 species of bird eggs, which cover a broad range of shapes and sizes. The smallest egg known, laid by one of the 150 species of hummingbirds, weighs a quarter of a gram; it takes 240 of these eggs to equal the weight of a single 60-gram chicken egg. At the other end of the range is the egg of *Aepyornis,* the recently extinct elephant bird of Madagascar, which had an average weight of nine kilograms, equivalent to 150 chicken eggs. The *Aepyornis* eggshell alone weighed two kilograms, more than the fresh weight of an

entire ostrich egg, which at 1.5 kilograms is the largest egg laid by an existing bird.

How do the shape and dimension of the pores differ in small and large eggs? Cyril Tyler and K. Simkiss of the University of Reading answered this question by impregnating eggshells with plastic and then dissolving away the

shells, thereby obtaining microscopic casts of the pores. These casts have demonstrated that the pores are widely variable in shape, even within a single species. We also became interested in other aspects of respiration in the eggs of different species. For example, how does the gas conductance of the shell vary with egg size? Is there a relation between

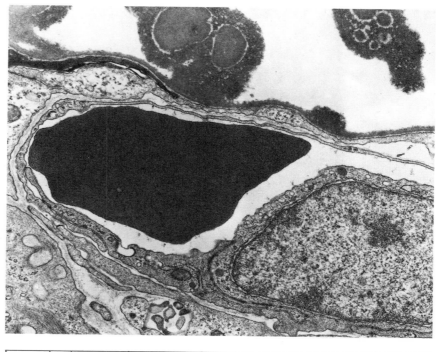

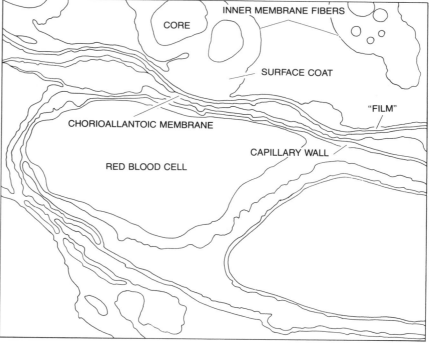

INTERFACE separating the inner shell membrane and the chorioallantois appears in this electron micrograph. At the top some of the fibers of the inner shell membrane are shown in section, coated with a fluffy material. The continuous line below the fibers is the thin film lining the inner membrane, to which the outer membrane of the chorioallantois is attached. The dark, irregular object in the center is a red blood cell shown in oblique section. Micrograph, the magnification of which is 18,400 diameters, was made by Ewald Weibel of University of Bern.

214

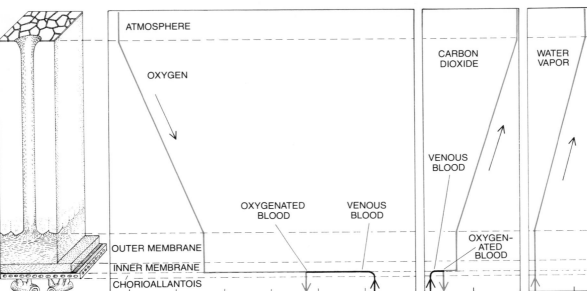

PROFILE OF GAS PRESSURES across the shell and the respiratory membranes is depicted for an 18-day-old chicken egg immediately prior to internal pipping. The various layers provide a series of barriers to diffusion that differ considerably in their conductance. A large change of gas pressures across a layer means that it has a low conductance; a small change means that the layer has a high conductance. The graphs indicate that both pore and film have a low conductance for oxygen; only the pore has a low conductance for carbon dioxide.

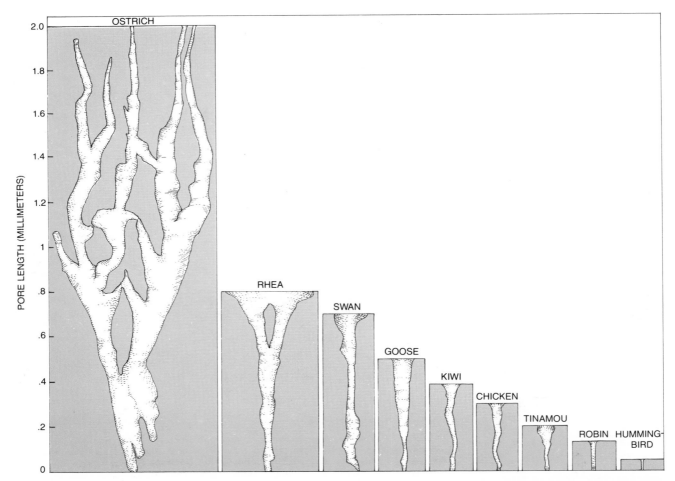

SHAPE OF SHELL PORES changes with increasing egg size. The length of the pores ranges from two millimeters in the ostrich egg to .04 millimeter in the hummingbird egg. Illustration is based on pore casts made by Cyril Tyler and K. Simkiss at University of Reading.

egg size and the oxygen concentration in the air cell at the end of incubation? How does oxygen consumption vary as a function of egg size? And finally, how is water loss related to egg size and the length of incubation?

Knowing that gas exchange across the eggshell proceeds entirely by diffusion, we first sought to develop a method to measure the gas conductance of intact eggs that was simple enough to use in field laboratories. The solution to this problem was provided by the laws of diffusion published in 1855 by Adolph Fick, who was professor of physiology at Zurich and later at Würzburg. Fick had the perceptiveness to realize that the mathematical description of heat flow in solids developed 30 years earlier by Jean-Baptiste Fourier could equally well apply to molecules diffusing through solids, liquids or gases.

The movement of gas by diffusion through a permeable barrier depends on the random motion of the gas molecules and the difference between the concentration of the diffusing species on one side of the barrier and the concentration on the other side. Since collisions among gas molecules are more frequent in a concentrated gas than in a dilute one, the molecules will tend to move from the side of higher concentration to the side of lower concentration.

A simplified version of Fick's law of diffusion states that the quantity of a given gas diffusing in a unit of time through the pores of an eggshell will be directly proportional to the area of the pores available for diffusion and to the difference between the concentration of the diffusing gas at one end of the pore and the concentration at the other end. On the other hand, the rate of diffusion will be inversely proportional to the length of the diffusion path (in this case the length of the pores through the eggshell). In other words, the gas conductance of the eggshell depends on the ratio of pore area to pore length. Doubling the area available for diffusion of a gas or doubling the concentration difference of that gas across the shell will double the rate of passage, whereas doubling the pore length will halve the rate of passage, all other factors remaining equal. Thus if one could measure the flux of a gas and divide it by the concentration difference of that gas across the pores, one would be able to calculate the conductance of the shell for that gas.

After trying several methods for measuring shell conductance we finally hit on a very simple one. If eggs are kept in a desiccator at a constant temperature and are removed only briefly once a day for weighing, they lose weight at a rate that remains constant over many days. This weight loss results entirely from the diffusion of water vapor through the pores of the shell into the dry atmo-

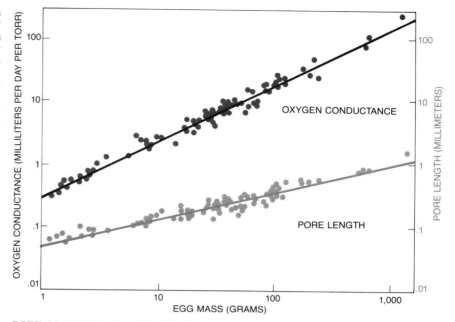

PORE LENGTH AND OXYGEN CONDUCTANCE increase at different rates with increasing egg mass, as is shown in this graph encompassing data from the eggs of some 90 species from different parts of the world. For every tenfold increase in mass the oxygen conductance of the eggshell increases 6.5 times but the pore length increases only 2.7 times. Pore length probably increases slower because the eggshell must be thin enough for the embryo to hatch.

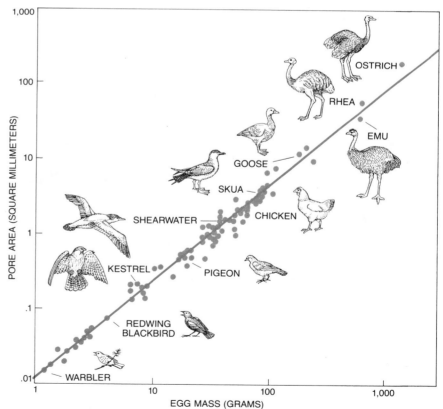

TOTAL PORE AREA, the sum of all the pores available for diffusion, increases almost 18 times with every tenfold increase in egg mass. For example, the fraction of total shell area occupied by pores jumps from .02 percent in the chicken egg to .2 percent in the ostrich egg. Rapid rise in pore area with increasing egg mass accounts for the fact that oxygen conductance (ratio of total pore area to pore length) increases 6.5 times for every tenfold increase in egg mass.

sphere of the desiccator. Dividing the daily weight loss by the water-vapor pressure between the inside of the egg and the environment yields the water-vapor conductance of the shell. Since the diffusion path through the shell for oxygen and carbon dioxide is the same as that for water, the water-vapor conductance can be converted into the oxygen conductance. Determining the oxygen conductance in this way is relatively easy: the only necessary tools are a desiccator, an accurate balance and a thermometer.

Adding calipers to this armamentarium enables one to measure the thickness of the shell, which is equivalent to the length of the pores. Knowing the conductance and the pore length, one can calculate from Fick's law the total functional pore area: the sum of all the individual pores available for the diffusion of gases. (In the chicken egg the 10,000 pores have an aggregate cross-sectional area of two square millimeters.)

Over the past seven years we and others have determined the conductance of hundreds of freshly collected eggs in various parts of the world. The eggs, ranging in mass from one gram to 1,500 grams, were obtained from 90 species and 15 orders of birds. We have consistently found that the gas conductance of eggs increases with the size of the egg. This trend was expected, because the oxygen demand of the embryo prior to internal pipping is greater in large eggs than it is in small ones. The rate of increase is not, however, directly proportional to the mass of the egg: with every tenfold increase in mass there is only a 6.5-fold increase in oxygen conductance.

A second interesting observation is that with every tenfold increase in egg mass the length of the pores increases only 2.7 times. This trend can perhaps be explained in terms of a balance of adaptive factors operating in the course of evolution. The thickness of the shell (which determines the length of the pores) is established to withstand the gravitational stresses of the contents of the egg and the weight of the incubating parent, but the thickness is also limited by the requirement that the embryo be able to break through it during hatching. This last presumably explains why eggshells increase in thickness in less than direct proportion to the size of the egg.

What are the structural consequences of a gas conductance that increases 6.5-fold and a pore length that increases 2.7-fold with each tenfold increase in egg mass? Fick's law states that the total functional pore area is directly proportional to the product of the gas conductance and the pore length. The pore area will therefore increase about 18-fold (6.5 × 2.7) for each tenfold increase in egg mass. For example, a 600-gram rhea egg, with a shell about three times thicker than that of a 60-gram chicken egg, will have a total pore area that is about 18 times larger.

We can now appreciate that the structural elements of the shell (pore area and pore length) determine its gas conductance, a functional property that can be related to the embryo's metabolic requirements and the oxygen-pressure difference across the eggshell. Here again Fick's law gives us the quantitative relation among these variables: the oxygen-pressure difference across the shell is equal to the oxygen consumption of the egg divided by the oxygen conductance of the shell.

Let us take as an example a hypothetical egg whose oxygen conductance is 10 milliliters per day per torr (that is, 10 milliliters of oxygen diffuse across the shell each day for each torr of oxygen-pressure difference). If the egg consumes 500 milliliters of oxygen per day, the oxygen-pressure difference across the shell must be 50 torr. Since the partial pressure of oxygen in the atmosphere is about 150 torr, the partial pressure of oxygen in the air cell of the egg (to which the blood of the embryo is exposed) will be 100 torr, or about 14 percent.

In order to explore the relation between shell conductance and the metabolism of the embryo, we compared the oxygen consumption of the egg just before internal pipping with the oxygen

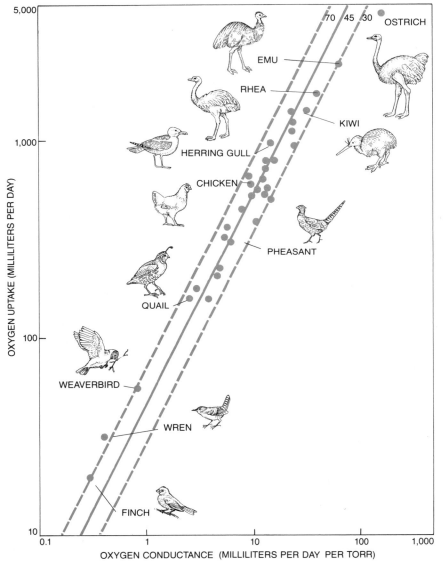

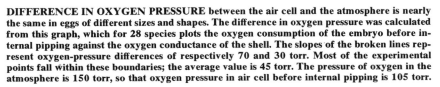

DIFFERENCE IN OXYGEN PRESSURE between the air cell and the atmosphere is nearly the same in eggs of different sizes and shapes. The difference in oxygen pressure was calculated from this graph, which for 28 species plots the oxygen consumption of the embryo before internal pipping against the oxygen conductance of the shell. The slopes of the broken lines represent oxygen-pressure differences of respectively 70 and 30 torr. Most of the experimental points fall within these boundaries; the average value is 45 torr. The pressure of oxygen in the atmosphere is 150 torr, so that oxygen pressure in air cell before internal pipping is 105 torr.

conductance of the eggshell in 28 species [*see illustration on opposite page*]. The list of known values for the oxygen consumption of the eggs of many species, large and small, was greatly expanded by the work of three investigators at the University of California at Los Angeles, Donald F. Hoyt, David Vleck and Carol Vleck. Knowing the oxygen consumption of the eggs and the conductance of the eggshells, we could then utilize Fick's law to calculate the oxygen pressure in the air cell. We found that the value was approximately the same for all 28 species: about 105 torr of oxygen, or 15 percent. This value was verified by directly sampling the air cell in 13 species. In addition the measured value of carbon dioxide in the air cell averaged 35 torr, or about 5 percent.

These values of oxygen and carbon dioxide in the air cell just prior to internal pipping are nearly identical with those found in the lungs of adult birds. Therefore the oxygen conductance of the eggshell appears to be matched to the egg's uptake of oxygen to "anticipate" the oxygen demand of the embryo prior to internal pipping and to provide in the air cell the oxygen and carbon dioxide pressures characteristic of the adult bird. A. H. J. Visschedijk of the University of Utrecht has suggested that these gas pressures initiate the final act of hatching and prepare the embryo for its postnatal existence.

It is remarkable that the gas conductance of the eggshell is calibrated to the mass of the embryo to yield nearly the same final concentrations of oxygen and carbon dioxide in eggs of different sizes. The general plan for shell porosity and function is even more impressive if one considers that the incubation period of bird eggs may vary from 11 days in some of the smaller species to 70 or more for the eggs of the tube-nosed birds, such as the wandering albatross.

So far we have not considered in detail the loss of water from the egg, which proceeds at a constant rate throughout incubation. Water loss in any given egg is independent of metabolic rate and yet appears to be necessary for successful hatching. The reason for this is not fully understood but may concern the state of hydration of the embryo.

Rudolf Drent of the University of Groningen was the first to point out that the daily rate of water loss during natural incubation is related to egg mass. Surveying data in the biological literature, he demonstrated that in 45 species of birds the daily rate of water loss increases 5.6 times for every tenfold increase in egg mass. We subsequently noted that an even more precise relation between water loss and egg mass could be derived if we calculated the total amount of water lost during the incubation period and plotted this value against the initial mass of the egg. Our

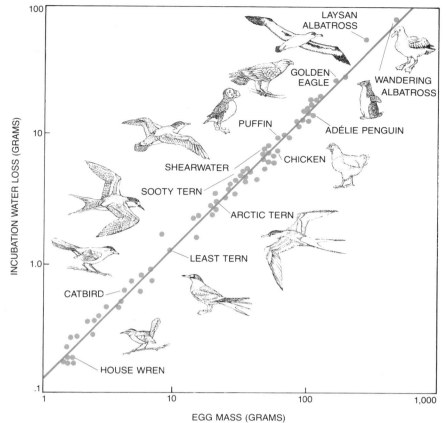

LOSS OF WATER during incubation is independent of the metabolic rate of the embryo, yet it appears to be essential for successful hatching. Here the total amount of water lost during incubation has been plotted against the initial mass of the egg. The graph includes data obtained from 65 species of eggs ranging in size from one gram to 500 grams, with incubation times ranging from 11 to 70 days. There is a remarkably consistent trend: regardless of egg mass or incubation time, the typical egg will lose 15 percent of initial mass during natural incubation.

survey covered the eggs of some 65 species of birds, ranging in mass from 1.5 to 500 grams and in incubation time from 11 to 70 days. The results showed a remarkably consistent trend: regardless of mass or incubation time, a typical egg will lose 15 percent of its initial mass during natural incubation. This loss gives rise to the air-cell volume, whose functional importance to the embryo we have already discussed.

The gas spaces within the egg are essentially saturated with water vapor, so that at the average incubation temperature for most species (35.6 degrees Celsius) the vapor pressure within the egg is 44 torr. For the egg to lose the requisite amount of water the vapor pressure in the microclimate of the typical bird's nest must be maintained at about 15 torr, equivalent to a relative humidity of 45 percent. That humidity level can be maintained only by periodically ventilating the nest with drier atmospheric air. It is not known how the parent bird senses the humidity of the nest, but through its behavior it is able to regulate the passage of water vapor from the nest into the drier ambient air. The parent therefore has two major functions during incubation: it not only warms the

eggs to an optimal temperature but also maintains the humidity of the nest air within close tolerances.

The length of embryonic development, or incubation time, is probably determined by genetic factors, but the metabolic rate of the embryo must be tuned to this incubation time so that by the end of the period—long or short—the embryo is mature enough to hatch and survive. One might therefore predict the intriguing possibility that the exact geometry of the eggshell's pores (and hence the shell's oxygen conductance) is calibrated both to the egg's mass and to its incubation time.

It seems clear that the eggshell and its associated membranes are closely adapted to the respiratory needs of the embryo, although certain compromises have been made in the course of evolution to ensure the mechanical stability of the egg and the fluid and acid-base balances of the embryo. Our studies have also demonstrated that the bird egg provides an ideal model for studying the diffusion of gases, which may eventually help in understanding the more complicated diffusion processes in the airways and air sacs of the human lung.

Duet-Singing Birds

22

W. H. Thorpe
August 1973

*The male and female of certain tropical species join
each other in remarkably precise song. The primary
function of this behavior is to maintain close
communication between the birds in dense foliage*

Newcomers to East Africa soon become familiar with a striking birdsong, heard sometimes in large gardens or parks but more frequently in open forest and bushy savanna country. The song is brief, about a couple of seconds in duration, but it is often repeated with great regularity over long periods. What makes the song particularly outstanding is that its few notes possess a flutelike or bell-like quality, exceedingly pleasant to the ear, that strikes almost every listener as being in some curious sense "musical." The singing bird is a shrike (*Laniarius aethiopicus*), known in some parts of its range as the bellbird or bell shrike. Obvious and conspicuous though its song is, many quite observant people have lived in East Africa for years without realizing that the performance comes from two singers rather than one. Not until the listener happens to get between the two birds does he realize that the first few notes of the song come from one direction and the rest from another, yet with an almost incredible precision of timing.

It is usual to speak of such a performance, with one member of a pair starting the song and the other completing it, as antiphonal song. Antiphonal song, however, is only one particular kind of what may in general be called duetting, a term that also includes polyphonic performances, when the two birds sing at the same time, each coordinating its individual song pattern with the other. Occasionally each bird may sing exactly the same pattern of notes at the same moment, that is, in unison. Alternatively, the two contributions may be different in pattern but overlap each other, again with precise coordination [*see bottom illustration on page 220*].

Shrikes of the genus *Laniarius*, which are found only in Africa, provide the most striking examples of duetting. It appears that all 15 species of the genus, ranging throughout tropical Africa, exhibit the behavior. This mode of mutual singing between a paired male and female is not, however, confined to shrikes. It is well developed in eight or nine other families of birds in different parts of the world, nearly all of them tropical in range. Such behavior seems in fact to be most characteristic of species that live in very dense tropical vegetation, where it must be difficult for the two members of the pair to keep in sight of each other. In such a setting the birds would find a vocal pair bond useful, if not essential. Duetting also appears to be characteristic of species in which the male and female are of identical appearance, remain paired for life and maintain their territories for the greater part of the year, perhaps for their entire lives.

My colleagues and I first studied duetting in the field in Kenya and Uganda during the years from 1962 to 1967. We were able to extend the work greatly with studies of captive birds in large tropical aviaries in England from 1964 to 1970. In our field studies we concentrated on three populations of bell shrikes in widely separated areas: on the shores of Lake Nakuru in Kenya, in southwestern Uganda about 400 miles to the west of the lake, and near Kapenguria in Kenya, 150 miles northwest of the lake. Our aim was to record as far as possible all the main duet patterns in the area, to plot territories where possible, and again where possible to identify individual birds by marking them with colored rings.

In the Lake Nakuru area we recorded 102 different duet patterns, in the Uganda area we had 22 examples and in the Kapenguria region 24. The tape recordings were analyzed by sound spectrograph, but because of the very pure tonal quality of the bell shrike's notes we found it much more satisfactory to represent the songs by simple musical notation rather than by sound spectrograms. The songs can be almost completely specified by the pitch of the notes, by the intervals (the difference in pitch between any two notes), by whether the sounds come in harmonic intervals (simultaneously) or in melodic intervals (successively) and by the duration of the notes, their timing and their overall pattern.

Both absolute and relative pitch are of great importance in the recognition of the duets, and these features can only be roughly assumed from sound-spectrographic analyses. Fortunately standard musical notation has been developed over the centuries for the specific purpose of communicating details of pitch and time. It is an elegant and foolproof method for the purpose. On the other hand, sound-spectrographic and other electronic methods of analysis give much information about acoustic structure (tonal quality), relative intensity (loudness) and the minutiae of timing (which are particularly needed in assessing response times). Hence for these purposes vocalizations are better portrayed by such methods.

In the Lake Nakuru and Uganda field areas the vegetation was so dense that it was often extremely difficult, if not impossible, to map the paired birds' territorial boundaries. Birds in the Kapenguria area were living under more open conditions, so that here the mapping of the territories was much easier. In one of the Kapenguria areas four pairs of birds were holding territories, and characteristic song patterns were recorded for each [*see illustration on page 223*]. It will be seen that certain series of notes and certain patterns are fairly general to the species. Indeed, one quickly repeated series of low notes (either G or G-sharp)

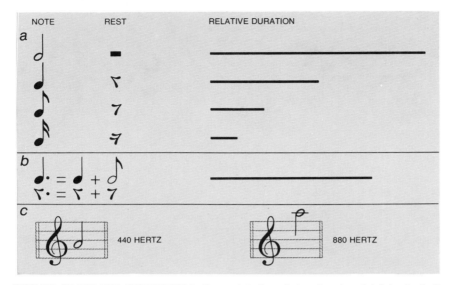

KEY TO STANDARD NOTATION indicates (a) the relative duration (right) of a half note and half rest compared with successively briefer intervals of sound or silence: quarter, eighth and 16th notes and rests respectively. The presence of a dot after either a note or a rest (b) increases the value of the symbol by one-half. Two staffs with G clefs are shown (c). The note on the staff at the left is a "tuning" A (440 hertz). The note on the staff at the right is one octave higher (880 hertz). The birdsongs are written one octave below true pitch.

VARIETIES OF SONG include duets (top) that may be antiphonal (a) or polyphonic. The notes and rests of one singer appear in black and those of the other singer in color. Polyphonic duets (b through d) can include phrases sung in unison (c) or phrases that overlap (d). Not all bell shrike songs are duets. Shown here is a trio (middle) recorded at Lake Nakuru in Kenya and a quartet (bottom) by captive shrikes at the University of Cambridge.

has a mellow sound that has given rise to another common name for the bell shrike: the tropical boubou shrike. Another clearly characteristic feature of the species is its tendency to produce intervals between successive notes of about an octave, either an octave below or an octave above. The species can be recognized by these features wherever it is found throughout the thousands of square miles of its range. Yet the more individual pairs are studied, the clearer it becomes that each pair of bell shrikes works out its own particular repertoire of duet patterns, so that the repertoire tends to be unique to that pair. Once one knows it well enough, it provides a means for individual identification.

Quite early in our studies we came on examples of trio singing and sometimes even quartet and quintet singing. One way that trio singing arises is through the intervention of one bird of a pair in a neighboring territory. (We were seldom able to determine whether it was the male or the female.) The "outside" singer would interpose its notes between those of the pair in "home" territory in an ordered manner and with extremely precise timing. The home pair in turn would sometimes minutely adjust the pattern and timing of its own duet to allow the neighbor to participate [see bottom illustration at left]. On one or two occasions the mate of the outside bird was seen standing by but not taking part. Trios, and perhaps quartets, can also be formed when one or two grown offspring of a pair, still residing within the parental territory or on its margins, join in with their parents' songs.

Apart from certain snarling or buzzing sounds used as alarm notes, vocalizations by bell shrikes in the wild under normal conditions consist of antiphonal singing between the members of a mated pair. The male bird is usually, but not necessarily, the leader. When the female starts the duet, she usually does so with a particular snarling note that may then be incorporated into the overall pattern of musical notes. In other species of shrike (and in bell shrikes in captivity) it may be much more usual for the female to start the duet. We have good evidence that the vocal repertoire is worked out and developed between the two members of a mated pair. Indeed, we have noted that when a bird is isolated by some mischance in the wild (as in a Nairobi garden where one bell shrike was kept under observation for nearly six months), it appears unable to produce any complex pattern of vocalization.

In this connection we found that

DUET SINGERS, a paired male and female bell shrike, are shown in an untypically open environment. Also known as the bellbird, the bell shrike is an African species belonging to the genus *Laniarius*. The paintings on this page were made by David Bygott.

POLYPHONIC SINGER that also maintains contact with its mate by singing duets, the white-browed robin chat (*Cossypha heuglini*) is found in the thick forest undergrowth and scrub of East Africa.

UNMUSICAL SINGER, the black-headed gonolek is another bird of the genus *Laniarius*. Of the 15 African shrike species in the genus few are as musical as the bell shrike, but they all sing duets.

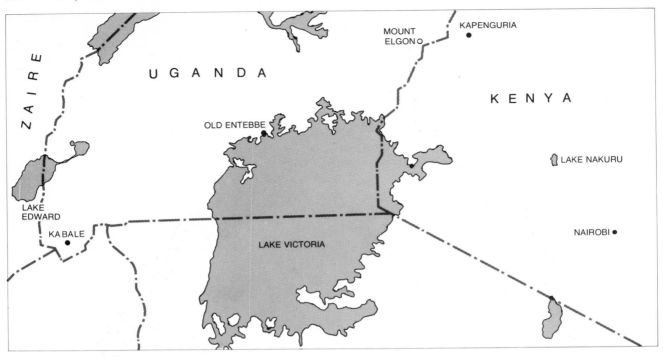

FIELD STUDIES of duetting birds were conducted at two areas in Kenya: Lake Nakuru, northwest of Nairobi, and Kapenguria, east of Mount Elgon. The third area was near Kabale, southeast of Lake Edward in Uganda. In all 148 different duet patterns were recorded.

where the birds seemed to be crowded in the wild the song patterns tend to be more elaborate than in areas where the birds have more space. This field observation was confirmed by studies of birds in captivity. When such birds, on arrival at our aviaries at the University of Cambridge, were all in cages in one room but were unable to see one another, trios and quartets of remarkable elaboration would quickly be built up, would be sung for a few hours or a day or two and then would be abandoned. When the birds were put out as pairs in the aviaries and therefore were no longer in close contact with other pairs, the duet patterns usually regressed to rather simple forms.

On the basis of both the field data and our aviary studies we can list the function of duetting under four headings in decreasing order of importance. The most important is the singer's recognition of, location of and maintenance of contact with its mate. The next is mutual stimulation between the two birds that form a pair, as a part of (or a substitute for) the ordinary methods of visual display. The third is an aggressive maintenance of the pair's territorial integrity. Last and least is mutual reassurance after some disturbance.

With respect to the first two functions it is important to realize that in the earth's temperate zones seasonal changes in the length of the day provide the most

important of the cues that initiate the secretion of birds' sex hormones and so bring potential pairs into the breeding condition. In the Tropics the day-length cue is very slight, if not completely absent. Moreover, other possible "seasonal" cues (such as variations in humidity, rainfall, degree of cloud cover and the like) tend to be unpredictable and to give little advance warning. It follows that if birds in the Tropics are to take full advantage of the time when breeding conditions are at an optimum, paired males and females must be in constant contact so that their behavior and their reproductive cycles are fully coordinated.

Our aviary experiments yielded many interesting facts about duetting. To mention a few, studies in the aviaries confirmed our field observation that, if one member of a pair is absent, the bird remaining in the territory tends to sing the whole duet pattern by itself: both its own contribution and its mate's. When the mate returns, however, a period of unison singing is not uncommon. The duet in unison will last for a few seconds; thereafter the pair resumes its antiphonal song as before. These shrike studies evidently confirm an argument put forward by Konrad Lorenz to the effect that "whole duet" vocalization in a partner's absence may be intended to secure the partner's return. It is almost as if one bird were using the charac-

teristic vocal performance of the other as a "name" that might serve as a recall.

A series of separation experiments in the aviaries yielded these conclusions. First, separation leads to an increase in the amount of vocalization by the deserted bird. In contrast, a bird that is moved to a new "territory" tends to decrease its vocalization. Second, if the bird remaining in the territory is a male, he employs all his usual vocalizations and in addition some of those of his missing partner. Third, if two members of a pair are separated for a long period, there is sooner or later a tendency to show a regression of vocalizations that can reduce the performance to what amounts to a juvenile condition.

If an isolated male hears a playback of his mate's voice, he will reply with the appropriate item in his own repertoire. The male is much less likely to respond to a playback of his own voice, however, and does so only by repeating the song that has just been played. This finding during our aviary studies confirmed still another conclusion based on fieldwork: even though notes of the bell shrike are very uniform in acoustic structure, they may be sufficiently different to be recognized on the basis of their vocal quality as well as by the pattern they form.

Our aviary experiments provided further evidence of this kind of recognizability. We found that a female bell shrike in the aviary will answer such notes of her own male as she may be able to hear but will not answer the notes of any neighboring pairs. In one set of experiments an extra male was kept in association with a duetting pair. The outside male was never heard to vocalize until the resident male was removed. When the removal took place, however, it became clear that the outside male had at least in part learned not only his rival male's repertoire but also that of the female. The resident female would respond to the educated outside male's song although she would not respond to the songs of strangers.

A remarkable result emerged from our difficulty in identifying the sex of captive birds. Because the male and female are exactly alike in appearance we made occasional mistakes in our caging, inadvertently constructing male-male and female-female "pairs." It sometimes happened that for weeks or months our mistakes had surprisingly little effect on the birds' behavior and vocalization. And so it became clear to us that two bell shrikes of the same sex, either male or female, can behave in a way that is indistinguishable from the behavior of a true pair. They may engage in mutual duetting, picking up and carrying nesting material, mutual preening, begging and even some forms of display.

The precision in timing in the bell shrike's duets is excellent. It was easier to study this, however, in another species of the same genus: the black-headed gonolek (*Laniarius erythrogaster*). The general build and pattern of the gonolek is very similar to the bell shrike's except that its underparts, instead of being white suffused with pink, are a brilliant crimson [*see bottom illustration at right on page 221*]. Throughout its range the gonolek is a bird of the thickest bush and undergrowth. We studied it both in Kenya and Uganda and in captivity. Its duet is unmusical and extremely simple. The initiating bird, in this species almost always a male, has a "yoick"-like note. This note is immediately followed by a tearing hiss, sometimes suggesting the ripping of cloth and sometimes being more like a sharp sneeze, from the female. Here, as with the bell shrike, the timing is so perfect as to make the duet sound like the song of one bird.

The timing of the gonolek is easy to investigate because the onset of the second bird's note is extremely sharp, giving the investigator an exact point of measurement. We recorded a consecutive series of eight duets of a pair of these birds at Old Entebbe in Uganda. The second bird, which was completely out of sight of the first, took its time cue

with extraordinary precision from the start of the first bird's note. The mean response time of the female in this series of duets was little more than 144 milliseconds, with a standard deviation of 12.6 milliseconds [*see illustration on page 224*]. In another series of seven consecutive duets the response time was much longer (425 milliseconds) but the standard deviation was even less (4.9 milliseconds). It is obvious that the species must have an extremely precise time sense; the accuracy does not decrease even if the response time is extended by a factor of four. I am not aware of any auditory reaction time in humans that has a standard deviation of less than 20 milliseconds.

Even more unusual is the performance of another African duetting species, a member of the genus *Cisticola* (the grass warblers) known as Chubb's cisticola (*Cisticola chubbi*). Chubb's cisticola is a small streaky-brown bird that inhabits long grass in bush-clad clearings at altitudes of between 5,000 and 8,000 feet. A series of six consecutive duets that I recorded, the two birds in this instance being in sight of each other, had a mean response time of 396 milliseconds and the remarkably small standard deviation of 2.9 milliseconds. That is about an eighth of the error a man would make under similar circumstances.

Is there any scientific basis for the impression of "musicality" the duets of the bell shrike so strongly suggest? The main investigator of this topic is Joan Hall-Craggs. As she has stated, it is useful to begin any such inquiry with the reasonable assumption that, since a bird's ear is similar to the human ear in its essential structure, it displays many of the same characteristics. At the same time we should remember that the perception of pitch probably begins at higher frequencies among most birds than among humans. The shortest time for the identification of pitch by man is approximately .05 second, assuming a signal in the middle range of frequency, but for birds it is quite likely that this time may be much reduced. It has also been calculated that the pitch of a tone is detectable when 70 percent of the energy in the spectrum lies within ±5 percent of the principal frequency. Such energy concentration is clearly discernible in the sound spectrograms of bell shrike songs, and most of the notes are of sufficient duration and concentration of sound energy to enable us to assess their pitch by ear.

Musical form, at its simplest, consists

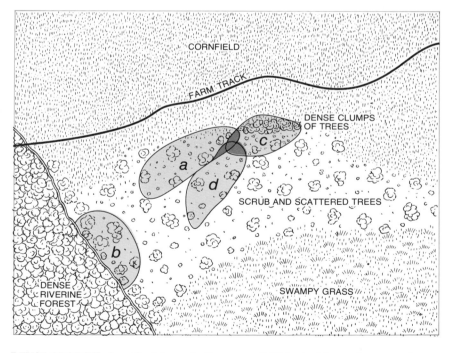

DENSE GROWTH along the fringe of a Kenya cornfield, backed by scrub, scattered trees and a thickly forested stream, contained four bell shrike breeding territories, three of them overlapping (*solid color*). Territories *a* and *b* contained paired adults only; the adult pairs in *c* and *d* shared the territory with juvenile birds. Both the territory overlap and the number of birds that were present led to frequent singing in trios, quartets and even quintets.

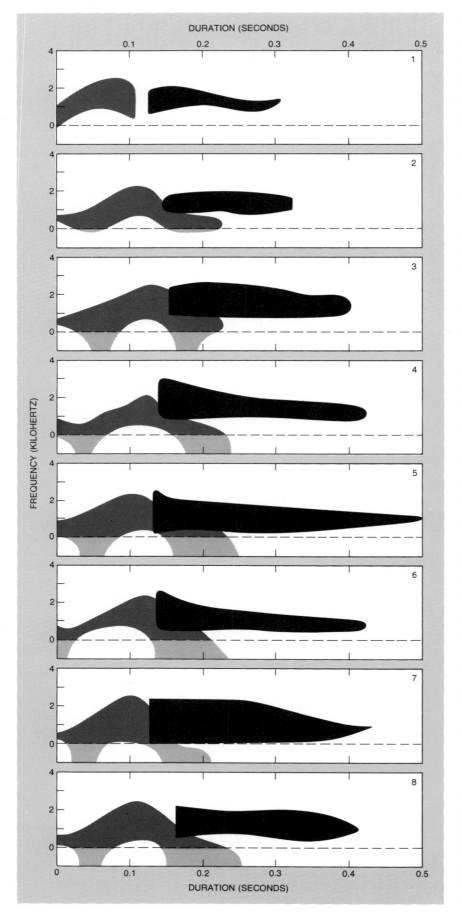

DURATION (SECONDS)

FREQUENCY (KILOHERTZ)

DURATION (SECONDS)

in the grouping together of units of sound energy in repeatable and consequently recognizable patterns of time and pitch. As Hermann von Helmholtz put it more than a century ago: "Melodic motion is change of pitch in time." It is obvious at a glance that the shrike songs epitomize melodic motion and therefore have musical form. To analyze that form one must first describe the intervals: the difference in pitch between any two tones.

We undertook such a study, using the duets of 10 pairs of one population of bell shrikes. The tones and intervals of the duets were subjected to physical analysis by taking single sounds from the field tapes and recording them on a sound spectrograph, which was then set to play the sound repeatedly at 2.5-second intervals. That signal was then matched, initially by ear, to a pure tone from a signal generator. The two tones were next matched precisely on a cathode ray oscilloscope by tuning the generated tone until a clear Lissajous figure with a ratio of 1:1 appeared repeatedly on the screen. (More recently we have employed a new instrument for this work. It is the "Melograph," designed and built at the University of Uppsala.) A frequency counter then gave a reading in hertz (cycles per second).

The absolute frequencies, as distinct from the intervals between them, were measured. It was found that the duets of all these birds fell within the range of 656 to 2,064 hertz. That is about one octave plus a sixth. The range of an individual pair varied from as little as a minor seventh (787 to 1,405 hertz) to a little less than a perfect 11th, that is, an octave plus a perfect fourth (798 to 2,064 hertz). The paired birds normally use only portions of the available frequency spectrum. In pairs where this uniformity is most marked a low band of sung frequencies is centered around 800 hertz, a middle band around 1,000 hertz and a smaller high band just below 1,200 to 1,220 hertz.

It was clear in almost every instance that the gaps of unused frequencies span

RAPID RESPONSE of female black-headed gonolek in eight successive duets is shown in the series of sound spectrograms at left. The song of the male is shown in gray; the female's response is in black. The series of duets was completed in some 30 seconds; the average response delay was .144 second. The apparent subzero frequencies are due to distortion and interference below 50 hertz.

FOUR DUETS recorded in the Lake Nakuru area exhibit distinctly different patterns. In instances when the observer could not tell which notes were sung by which bird the notes and rests appear in black only. Otherwise the second singer's part is shown in color.

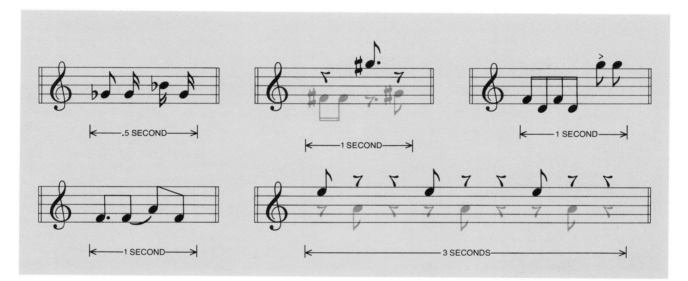

FIVE DUETS recorded in the Uganda study area provide a further example of differing bell shrike song patterns. In the third song, where the individual singers' contributions are unknown, an accent over the first G indicates that the singer put stress on the note.

TWO TRIOS were recorded in the Kapenguria study area shown on the facing page, where such singing was a frequent event. The notes of the first two singers appear in black and in color respectively; the notes of z, the third singer, are outlined in white.

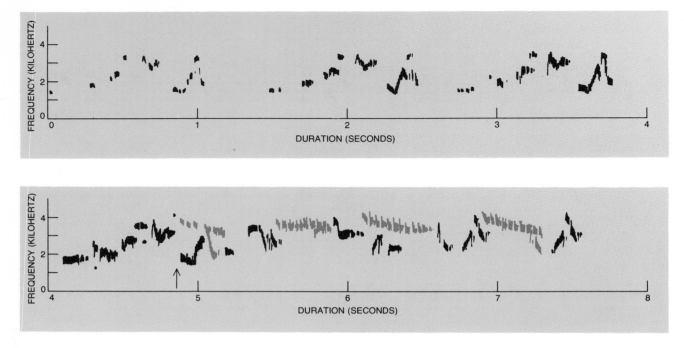

CRESCENDO DUET of the white-browed robin chat, some 7.5 seconds in duration, is seen in a sound spectrogram. During the first part of the duet the male utters four five-syllable phrases that progressively increase in amplitude. The female joins in (*arrow*), continuing the crescendo, whereupon the male mutes his higher notes but continues to accompany the female in a low-pitched song.

wider ranges in the available spectrum than the bands of sung notes do, giving the impression that the birds are using a series of notes resembling a gapped scale. There is not sufficient consistency, however, to postulate such a scale, nor is there good reason to suppose that the birds are unable to sing notes in the unused section of the spectrum. The distribution of the used frequencies suggests that the syrinx, the sound-producing organ of the bird, may be such that these notes are produced more easily and/or to greater effect than such notes as might have been expected to be present in the bands of unused frequency. The tendency in most pairs of birds for the notes to cluster around 800, 1,000 and 1,200 hertz, however, suggests that the birds are producing most readily the fourth, fifth and sixth harmonics of a fundamental at about 200 hertz. These tones, derived from the lower reaches of the harmonic series, give rise to the ordinary major triad approximately on G in octaves five to six. If indeed the birds are utilizing the harmonics in this manner, it goes part of the way toward explaining their decided proclivity for singing duets that incorporate, or are based on, a major or minor triad.

In music if two tones or frequencies are adjacent, then the interval is described as "melodic." When, as often happens in bell shrike duets, two sounds occur synchronously, or when one tone is sustained while another tone is sounded above or below it, the interval is termed harmonic. All 15 species of the genus *Laniarius* sing antiphonally, but the bell shrike and one other species I shall not discuss here appear to be unique among them in singing melodic lines that are sometimes antiphonal and sometimes polyphonic and sometimes even sung in unison.

According to musical theory, the sounding together of two notes may lead to a predominant use of consonant intervals in two-part or multipart singing. Helmholtz, who investigated the properties of consonance and dissonance from the physical point of view in the 1860's, showed that the "roughness" of dissonance that we (and presumably birds as well) experience is based on a physical phenomenon, namely "beats": periodic variations in the amplitude of the sound pressure due to the interference of two sound waves of different frequencies. According to Helmholtz, beats are maximally disturbing to man at about 33 per second. It might be expected, however, that with birds this critical figure would be substantially increased because of their faster identification of pitch.

Now, the original physiological explanation of beats was that two tones sounding together forced into vibration overlapping regions of the basilar membrane of the ear. This explanation, which was once much in doubt, has now been largely rehabilitated, although no completely satisfactory physiological description of the phenomenon has yet been devised. This does not, however, affect the reality of the phenomena of dissonance and beats. Helmholtz drew a curve illustrating the degree of consonance and dissonance of intervals within the octave. If we draw this curve to the same scale as a curve that shows the incidence of these intervals as they are used by the bell shrikes, we find close agreement between them.

The shrikes' predisposition to sing consonant intervals is fully demonstrated by both aural and physical analyses. But since there are dissonant intervals as well, although in much smaller numbers, it cannot be argued that these birds are compelled by the structure of their syrinx to sing consonant intervals. It may be, however, that once such intervals are learned they are found to be functionally the best. It can also be argued that good, steady consonances might well assist in the effectiveness of the duets as a contact-maintenance system, particularly if it is important for the distance to be judged accurately.

Hence we can conclude the topic of bell shrike aesthetics by saying that the apparent musicality of the songs of these species depends primarily on the birds' having a hearing apparatus that responds in the same way to the roughness of dissonance as our own does. To quote Joan Hall-Craggs: "To the musical listener these songs may seem overharmonious; nevertheless, it is the kind of harmony to which man aspired and which probably reached its peak in Mozart. No musical listener could call the songs 'unmusical' or 'displeasing'; their only fault from our point of view rests in their brevity and simplicity."

Two other examples of antiphonal singing among East African birds are particularly interesting when they are compared with the songs of the shrikes

because they illustrate still other aspects of duetting. One of the birds is a member of the genus *Cossypha* (family Turdidae): the white-browed robin chat *Cossypha heuglini*. It is the sole known duettist among the 15 species of the genus.

Here again the sexes look alike. The birds are found in dense vegetation, in riverine forest and secondary scrub whether in farmland or garden, and from the East African coast up to an altitude of 6,000 feet. They are excessively shy, spending most of the time hidden in the undergrowth, feeding on the ground and usually singing at dawn and dusk from a perch in a low bush. The song is a long one, lasting five seconds or more, and starts with male solo phrases showing a

gradual crescendo. When the loudness reaches a critical level, it provides the signal for the female to join in. The birds then proceed together, continuing the crescendo and with the pitch steadily rising, although after the female takes part the male tends to cut out his higher notes, giving a lower-pitched accompaniment of the female's downward glissandos [see illustration on page 226].

The grass warblers (genus *Cisticola*) are a huge assemblage: 40 species and 153 races. Of these it seems likely that only four species are duettists, yet they are duettists of the highest precision. As I have mentioned, I have recorded the duets of Chubb's cisticola. One other species, *Cisticola nigriloris,* which is found in the highlands of northern Malawi and southern Tanzania, is a singer of special distinction. It is a persistent duettist, and the pair's usual theme is a very high-pitched four-note whistle: G (at 3,240 hertz), E-flat (near 2,568), E-flat again (but at 5,000) and B (at 4,064), all with a continuous squeaking or croaking accompaniment. In two separate recordings of this species, made in areas of Tanzania more than 100 miles apart, the entire four-note phrase is suddenly transposed to another key after the first half-dozen or so bouts. This suggests the interesting possibility that the musical transposition of the song is a species-specific character! If that is true, it is, as far as I am aware, unique.

To sum up, we can say that duetting clearly plays a very important part in the signal system between male and female in a large number of bird species, in particular species that inhabit tropical regions. These elaborate song patterns show many interesting features, of which only a few have been discussed here. Perhaps the most interesting result of our investigations of duetting is the light cast on the heretofore little appreciated precision and synthesizing power of avian aural perception, the great precision of response time and the equally great exactness of control of the vocal organs. The use of these vocal powers for individual recognition is in line with observations made over the past decade by Beat Tschanz of the University of Bern, by C. G. Beer of Rutgers University and by other investigators. Their work has shown that in many colonial nesting birds (for example auks, terns, gulls, gannets and penguins) brief calls of a half-second duration or less can have enough acoustic detail not only to serve as labels identifying the calling species but also to label the individual caller.

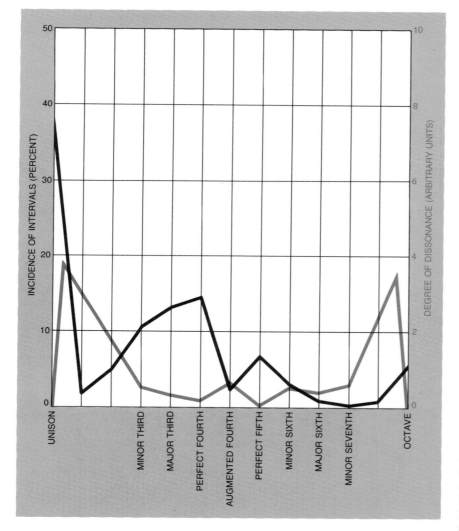

CONSONANT INTERVALS are characteristic of the bell shrike's songs. The black line indicates the intervals most frequently sung among selected semitones within the octave, expressed as percentages of the total number of intervals in the sample. The colored line is a modification of Hermann von Helmholtz' curve of consonance and dissonance between a note of fixed frequency and another note that changes smoothly from the same frequency to a frequency one octave higher. The closer the curve is to the base line, the greater the consonance is. Most of the intervals in the songs coincide with minimally dissonant frequencies.

23 How Birds Sing

Crawford H. Greenewalt
November 1969

The mechanism of bird song has traditionally been compared to either a wind musical instrument or the human vocal apparatus. The analysis of the bird songs themselves points toward an entirely different system

Some years ago I read a book in which, among other things, the author summarized the theories that had been advanced to explain the physiological processes employed by a singing bird. These theories, it seemed to me, were totally unacceptable, and I determined, perhaps with more rashness than wisdom, to see if I could find an explanation that did no violence to either the anatomical findings or the laws of physics.

The theories to which I took exception compared the singing bird either to a musical instrument—the clarinet, the oboe or the trumpet—or alternatively to the human voice (that is, a bird was believed to employ the same devices we do when we speak or sing). In a clarinet, for example, pitch and timbre are controlled by the effective length of the barrel of the instrument; the vibrating reed is in effect driven by and so forced to conform to the harmonic spectrum of the resonator. If a bird sang in this fashion, pitch could be varied only by extension and retraction of the neck. For a song sparrow, with its two-octave range, the neck would have to be extended by a factor of four—clearly a physical impossibility. Furthermore, birds sing many phrases in which the wave form is sinusoidal (a train of pure sine waves), without an associated harmonic spectrum. Resonators such as the barrel of a clarinet must by definition produce harmonics and cannot generate a sinusoidal wave form.

As for the human-voice theory, when we speak we produce at the glottis a series of puffs of air mathematically equivalent to a harmonic spectrum with an infinity of components, and with a fundamental frequency corresponding to the interval between puffs. The resulting acoustical disturbance is then modulated in our oral passages to produce the spoken word. This mechanism does not (and cannot) produce a purely sinusoidal wave form; every speech sound is associated with a harmonic spectrum of considerable complexity.

Negatives such as these are neither satisfying nor sporting, and to remedy both potential criticisms I undertook to develop a physiological and acoustical model that would describe a singing bird. The approach was to study in detail the bird songs themselves, and to develop from their constituent parts some notion of the associated acoustical processes. It seemed useless to employ an anatomical approach because the many excellent anatomical studies in the scientific literature have produced no useful conclusions, and because the acoustical analysis of human speech has been so strikingly successful in elucidating our own vocal performance.

I might pause here to note that I have written a book—*Bird Song: Acoustics and Physiology* (Smithsonian Institution Press, 1968). In it much detail is given on the state of the literature, the instrumentation my associates and I have developed for the analysis of bird song, and

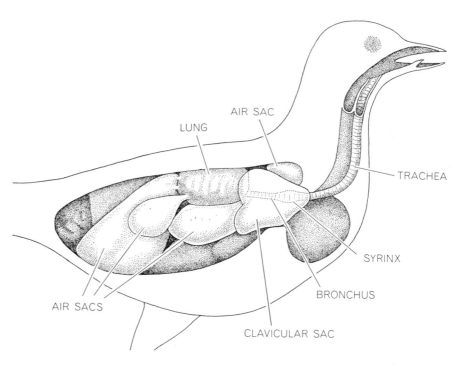

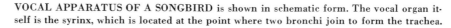

VOCAL APPARATUS OF A SONGBIRD is shown in schematic form. The vocal organ itself is the syrinx, which is located at the point where two bronchi join to form the trachea.

the proofs, mathematical and otherwise, for the findings I am about to describe. This article is in effect a summary of that book, and if the reader should wish more detail he will find it there.

The vocal organ of birds is called the syrinx. It is located deep in the thoracic cavity, at the point where the two bronchi join to form the trachea [*see illustrations below*]. It is difficult to decide from the detailed anatomy of the syrinx exactly what parts are important in vocalization, and precisely how sound is produced. At one time or another almost every anatomical element in the syrinx has been assigned a role in vocalization; unhappily there is an overabundance of possibilities.

I have proposed the relatively simple functional structure depicted in the top illustration on page 234. The elements are the tympanic membranes and their associated musculature, the external labia and the system of internal air sacs (not shown in the illustration) that force air through the bronchial passage and bulge the membrane into the bronchial lumen, or passageway. The illustration depicts the highly evolved syrinx of a songbird. At successively earlier stages of avian evolution the syrinx loses the external labia, then the syringeal muscles and ends up as a simple tube with

a membrane on its periphery and contained within an air sac.

It should be kept in mind that the functional elements of the syrinx are doubled, that is, there is a set for each bronchus. Since each bronchial passage has its own membrane, musculature and nervous system, it is evident that birds can control each passage independently of the other; they can sing what might be called an internal duet.

The system operates as follows: When a bird undertakes to sing, it in effect closes a valve between the lung and the syrinx. Then it compresses (with its chest muscles) the air in a system of sacs. Pressure in the clavicular sac, which surrounds the syrinx, forces the exceedingly thin tympanic membrane into the bronchial passage, closing it momentarily. Tension is then applied to the syringeal muscles, which, acting in opposition to the sac pressure, withdraw the bulged membrane from the opposite bronchial wall, thus creating a passage through the bronchial tube. Air streaming through the passage past the tensed membrane stimulates it to vibrate, and song is produced. If only one of the two voices is to be used, no tension is applied to the other membrane, and the corresponding bronchial passage remains closed. When a duet is sung, both membranes are under tension; there are

two airstreams and hence two vibrating membranes and two simultaneous sounds.

The illustrations on the next two pages show three complex songs analyzed in terms of amplitude and frequency. The songs embrace almost every vocal gymnastic of which birds are capable. Note, for example, the extremely rapid amplitude modulations, the wide range in the shape and extent of the amplitude envelopes and the relatively large frequency intervals: from just over two to just under seven kilocycles per second. The amplitude displays are precise and require no qualification. In the frequency displays there are a time delay and an integration of frequencies over small time intervals that introduce ambiguities for precise analysis.

The question of whether or not a bird can use its two acoustical sources independently is vital to the elucidation of the mechanics of bird song. If, for instance, the bird's trachea behaved like the barrel of a clarinet, both sources, that is, both vibrating membranes, would be forced to conform to the resonances of the trachea. The two sources would then merely reinforce each other, increasing the amplitude, or loudness, of the sound. If, on the other hand, the bird's trachea behaved like human oral cavities, and the vibrating membranes were analo-

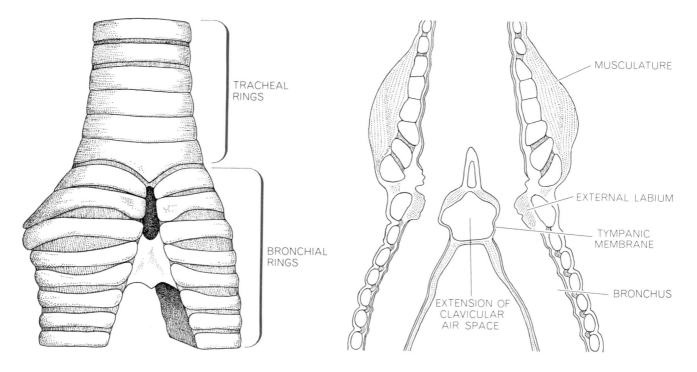

TRACHEAL RINGS

BRONCHIAL RINGS

MUSCULATURE

EXTERNAL LABIUM

TYMPANIC MEMBRANE

BRONCHUS

EXTENSION OF CLAVICULAR AIR SPACE

ANATOMY OF THE SYRINX sheds little light on its function. At left is the skeleton of the syrinx in the magpie; at right, a section through the syrinx of the European blackbird. Both drawings are based on studies published by the anatomist V. Häcker in 1900.

gous to the human glottis, the resulting wave form should be equivalent to a harmonic spectrum of great complexity involving three fundamental frequencies, one for each source and one for the first resonance of the trachea.

The fact that the two sources can produce two harmonically unrelated sinusoidal wave forms was first shown by Ralph K. Potter, George A. Kopp and H. C. Green of the Bell Telephone Lab-

oratories, for a fragment of the song of a brown thrasher. Since the phenomenon is an important one, I have searched for and found many similar examples in species representative of most families of birds. One example is provided by a relatively long phrase from the song of a mockingbird [*see illustration on page 232*]. In the displays the two voices were separated with sharply discriminating acoustical filters; frequency was determined by measuring time intervals for

10 successive sine waves. The two voices are harmonically unrelated and overlap on the time axis. We must conclude that neither the musical-instrument theory nor the human-voice theory is operative.

Other evidence may be found in phrases that cover a large frequency range. If such a "glissando" traverses a tracheal resonance or antiresonance, there should be a marked increase or decrease in amplitude at the appropriate frequencies. An example is a glissando

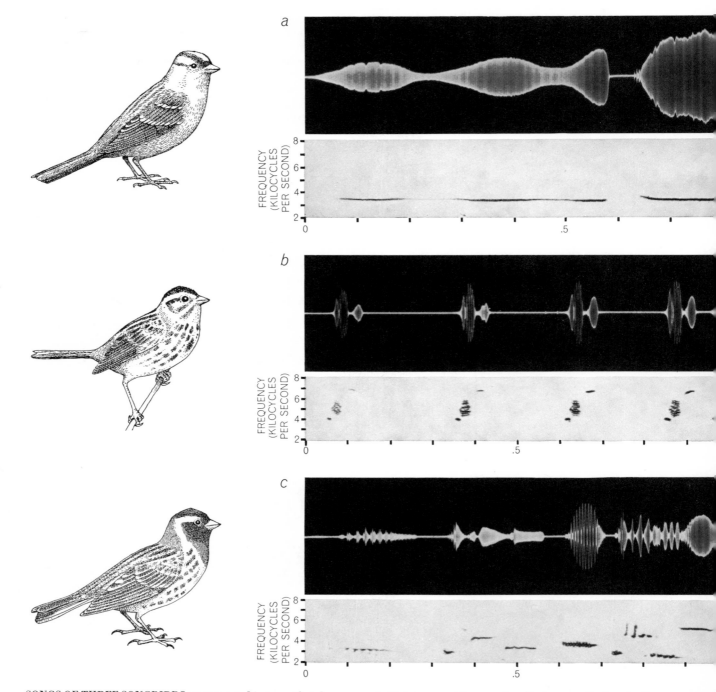

SONGS OF THREE SONGBIRDS are presented in traces that show amplitude and frequency as a function of time. The top record for each bird is an oscillogram that displays amplitude; the bottom record is a sound spectrogram that displays frequency. At *a* is the

sung by a yellow warbler that embraces a full octave [*see illustration on page 233*]. There are changes in amplitude in the glissando, but in an acoustical sense they are very small (less than three decibels), and it is most unlikely that they are associated with tracheal resonances. The two minima at 90 and 130 milliseconds appear at frequencies of 4.8 and 6.5 kilocycles per second. One of these could correspond to a resonance; both of them could not.

Although the evidence seems quite conclusive that the primary vibrations produced in the syrinx traverse the trachea without attenuation, amplification or change of any sort, we must offer a valid explanation for this rather surprising acoustical inertness of the trachea. The trachea is a tube. A tube, if its acoustical losses are small, exhibits resonances, and one would expect it to be an effective modulator, even with its relatively soft walls. A possible explana-

tion—indeed, the only likely explanation —is that the impedance of the source (the vibrating membrane in its constricted passage) closely matches the impedance of the trachea. Calculations based on reasonable assumptions indicate that this condition will obtain where the mean cross-sectional area of the trachea is about 10 times that of the syrinx. The curve relating this area ratio to attenuation is fairly flat and shows that the ratio can be substantially higher or lower than

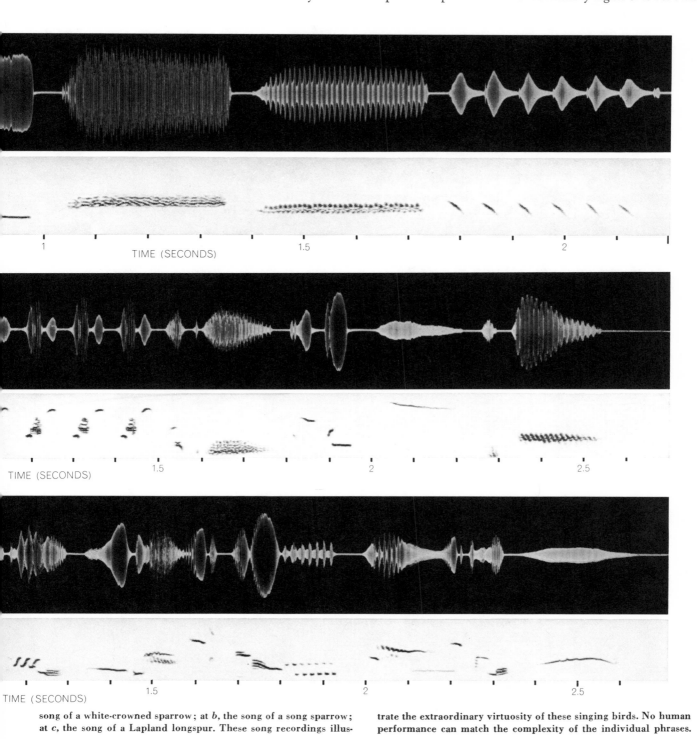

TIME (SECONDS)

TIME (SECONDS)

TIME (SECONDS)

song of a white-crowned sparrow; at *b*, the song of a song sparrow; at *c*, the song of a Lapland longspur. These song recordings illus-**trate the extraordinary virtuosity of these singing birds. No human performance can match the complexity of the individual phrases.**

10 before tracheal attenuation becomes important.

There is another way of expressing the effect of variation in the relative cross sections of source and resonator that may be easier to comprehend. If we take a tube closed at one end and open at the other, the resonances will occur at multiples 1, 3, 5, 7 and so on of the fundamental frequency. If the tube is open at both ends, the resonances will occur at multiples 0, 2, 4, 6 and so on of the fundamental frequency. If now we begin with a tube open at both ends and gradually close off one end, we will in due course arrive at a twilight zone within which the tube shows no resonant effects. This presumably is the zone in which birds sing.

Perhaps this is another example of Nature's ingenuity in dealing with the needs of her diverse creatures. The necks of birds (which contain and limit the trachea) have many functions, for instance feeding, preening and nest-building. It would be odd if such functions operated to restrict freedom in an activity as important as song.

So far I have undertaken to show that bird song has its origin in the syrinx,

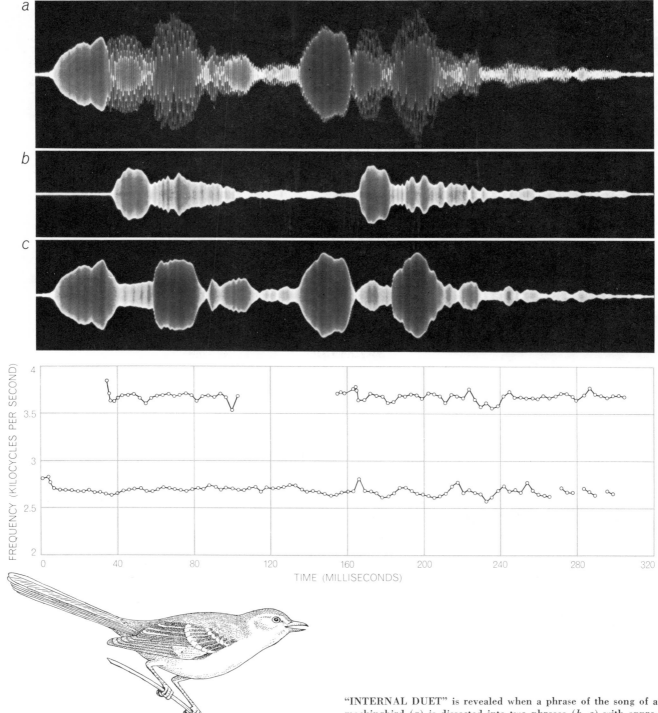

"INTERNAL DUET" is revealed when a phrase of the song of a mockingbird (a) is dissected into two phrases (b, c) with appropriate filters. The plots at bottom show the frequencies in b and c.

that the syrinx contains two acoustical sources which can be independently controlled to produce an internal duet, and that the sounds which originate in the syrinx pass through the trachea to the ear of the listener without further modulation. I must now show precisely how the sources in the syrinx operate and how the extraordinarily rapid and complex modulations so common in bird song are produced.

I have noted that pressure in the clavicular sac forces the internal tympanic membranes into the bronchial lumen against tension applied to the membrane by the muscles of the syrinx. Air streaming past the resulting constriction in the bronchial passage stimulates the membrane to vibrate. If this postulate is correct, it follows that in any rapid modulation amplitude and frequency must be coupled; an increase in frequency can be produced only by increasing the tension in the syringeal muscles. At a given pressure in the clavicular sac this tension will increase the cross section of the bronchial passage, which, as we shall see, must produce either an increase or a decrease in the acoustical amplitude.

The direct coupling of frequency and amplitude, that is, amplitude increasing with increasing frequency, appears in curves for Townsend's solitaire in which frequency and amplitude are simultaneously plotted against time [*see upper illustration on page 235*]. The reverse process, with amplitude falling as frequency rises, appears in similar curves for the red-winged blackbird [*see lower illustration on page 235*]. In curves for the song sparrow one can see both types of coupling within the modulating period: amplitude rises with increasing frequency up to 6.8 kilocycles and falls above that frequency.

These phenomena can best be explained by referring again to the simplified model of the syrinx shown on the next page. If we start with just sufficient tension (T) on the tympanic membranes to balance the pressure P, the distance across the passage (D) will be zero and no air will flow. A small increase in tension will open the passage and allow the membrane to vibrate at a frequency corresponding to the tension, but the amplitude of vibration will be restricted to low values by the small distance across the passage. As the tension increases, frequency and amplitude will increase together, as a larger distance across the passage permits greater vibrational amplitude in the membranes. With a further increase in membrane tension, and a correspondingly larger distance across

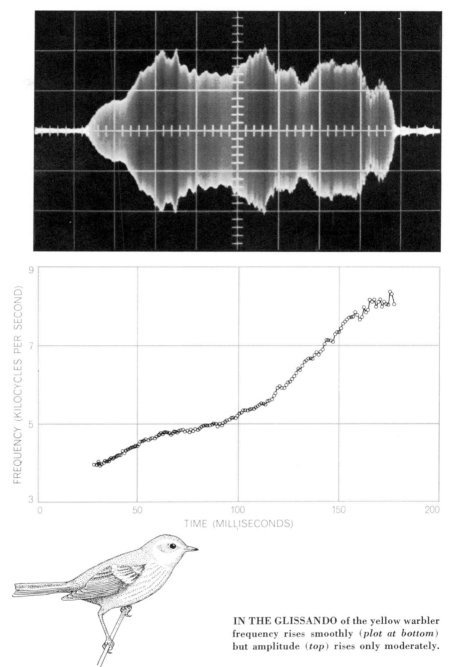

IN THE GLISSANDO of the yellow warbler frequency rises smoothly (*plot at bottom*) but amplitude (*top*) rises only moderately.

the passage, we arrive at a point where the airflow through the syringeal constriction can no longer stimulate the membrane to vibrate through the allowable distance D, and the amplitude will decrease. At the limit—a tension sufficiently large to open the passage fully—the amplitude will be zero, and the airflow from the bird's lungs will escape through the trachea without sound production. It should be understood that airflow is used here in an acoustical sense; it is a time-varying flow that is controlled by the vibration of the tympanic membrane. Air could well leak past the syringeal constriction, but this

airflow would be continuous and would produce no sound.

Amplitude-frequency coupling always accompanies rapid modulation, but it is not necessarily present when the period of the modulation is long. Consider a song sparrow phrase about 50 milliseconds long [*see top illustration on page 236*]. The modulating frequency remains constant at about 300 cycles per second, as does the frequency excursion. There is, however, a gradual rise and fall in amplitude from the beginning of the phrase to the end. Such comparatively long-term changes in amplitude without

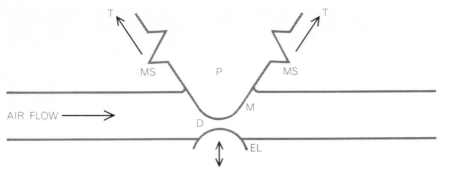

SIMPLIFIED MODEL OF THE SYRINX indicates how it functions. Air flows from the lungs at left into the trachea at right. The pressure of air in the clavicular sac (P) forces the tympanic membrane (M) into the bronchial lumen, or passage. Tension (T) is produced in the membrane by the syringeal muscles (MS). The resultant of the two forces P and T determines the distance across the lumen (D) and also the vibrating frequency. EL is external labium, which can regulate distance across bronchial lumen without affecting frequency.

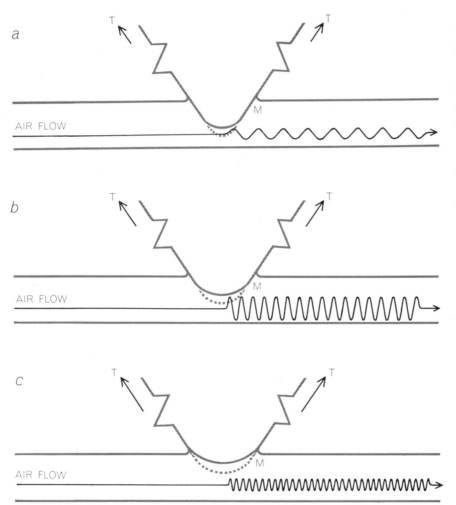

AMPLITUDE AND FREQUENCY ARE COUPLED when changes in either are rapid. In a a tone of a given amplitude is produced when the airflow causes the tensed tympanic membrane (M) to vibrate. In b the tension (T) is increased, causing the membrane to vibrate faster. Increased tension also retracts membrane, further opening the passage. The membrane can therefore vibrate through a larger distance, increasing amplitude of song. This is termed positive coupling. In c tension on the membrane has increased beyond a threshold; the tension is so great that the membrane can no longer vibrate across the entire passage. Beyond this threshold amplitude decreases with frequency, that is, the coupling is negative.

an accompanying change in frequency are relatively common. We find the necessary control mechanism in the external labium ["EL" in the bottom illustration on page 236], whose movement into and out of the bronchial lumen provides a simple device for changing amplitude without affecting muscle tension and hence without changing the frequencies produced in the tympanic membrane.

I must confess that this role for the external labium rests on a somewhat shaky anatomical base. Many anatomists report the presence of this member, particularly in the songbird syrinx; it is a pillow-like structure erected on the bronchial half-ring directly opposite the tympanic membrane. Only one anatomist, however, describes muscular attachments that could move the labium into and out of the bronchial lumen. I trust that some interested anatomist will note this opportunity for a definitive publication.

The bird could, of course, change the air pressure in its sac system, but this would have two effects whose resultant is at best ambiguous. Increasing the sac pressure would drive the membrane farther into the bronchial lumen, thereby decreasing its cross section; at the same time it would increase muscle tension. The increased pressure drop across the constricted bronchial passage would increase flow and hence would compensate for the reduction in cross section. I am not rash enough to predict the resultant of these phenomena, but it seems clear that they could not produce the overall rise and fall in amplitude exhibited in the song sparrow phrase on page 230. For that we need the external labium or some other anatomical feature that affects amplitude alone.

In any event, these rapid and highly variable modulations are so common as to be a prime characteristic in the songs of most birds. They can be repetitive, that is, there is a modulating frequency that continues for 50 to 500 milliseconds, or they can be nonrepetitive, that is, they may vary rapidly and randomly in amplitude, in frequency or in both.

Many phrases sung by the song sparrow comprise modulations that are repetitive. The modulating frequency averages 300 cycles per second, and amplitude ranges much more widely within a modulating period than frequency. In the songs of other species the modulating frequency ranges from about 100 cycles per second to something over 400. We are dealing here with two oscillating systems superimposed on each other. The first is the tympanic membrane vibrating

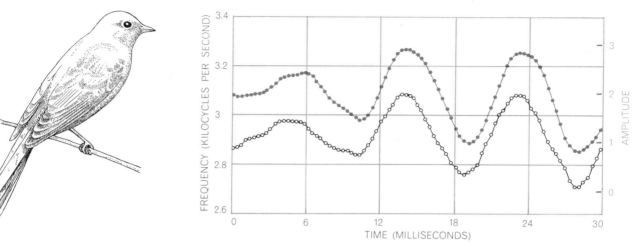

POSITIVE COUPLING of amplitude and frequency is shown in this analysis of a phrase sung by Townsend's solitaire. The colored curve traces the amplitude of the phrase; the black curve traces the frequency. The curves rise and fall together over the time period.

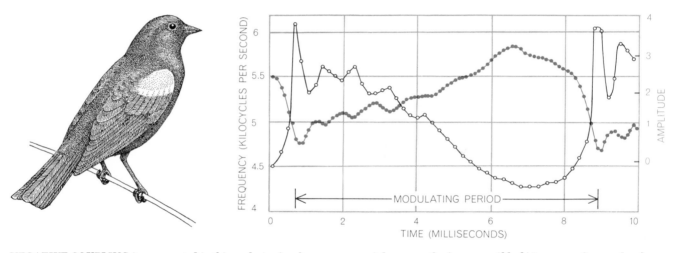

NEGATIVE COUPLING is represented in this analysis of a phrase sung by a red-winged blackbird. Here when the amplitude (*colored curve*) decreases, the frequency (*black*) increases. Curves also show the characteristic modulating period of this phrase in the song.

at its natural, or "carrier," frequency. The second includes the syringeal muscles, whose vibration would produce a periodic change in tension and hence a change in both frequency and amplitude. The mass and elasticity of the muscle system presumably limits its natural frequency of vibration to relatively low values—up to, say, 500 cycles per second. The much lower mass of the tympanic membrane allows vibration up to 10 kilocycles per second.

Nonrepetitive modulations can be seen in the courtship song of the brown-headed cowbird [*see illustration on page 237*]. This bird of unprepossessing appearance and habits is the undisputed winner in the decathlon of avian vocalization. Roger Tory Peterson characterizes the first phrase in the illustration as "glug" and the second phrase as "gleeee." Consider the following features: The fre-

quency range in the two phrases is, by a large margin, wider than it is in any other bird song. It extends from .75 to 10.7 kilocycles per second—nearly four octaves! The maximum frequency at 10.7 kilocycles per second is higher than what we have found for any other bird, just nosing out the 10.5 kilocycles per second at the top of the blackpoll-warbler song. Both voices are used in the second subphrase of the "glug," and the frequency spread between the two voices (two full octaves) is exceeded only by that of the American bittern.

The first note in the "gleeee" is the shortest I have encountered. It lasts a bit less than two milliseconds and comprises a packet of 12 sine waves at 6.4 kilocycles per second. The glissando at 50 milliseconds in the "gleeee" is one of the most rapid, covering the range from five to eight kilocycles per second in four milliseconds and 23 sine waves, an aver-

age of 130 cycles per wave. The modulating frequency of the high voice in the second subphrase of the "glug" is about 700 cycles per second, higher by a large margin than any other. These performances are truly remarkable. What purpose is served by a "glug" comprising five widely different subphrases, together with a "gleeee" including a note of negligible duration, two rapid glissandi and a peak frequency of 10.7 kilocycles per second, only Madame Cowbird will know.

There is not much point in comparing the impressions bird songs make on human and on avian ears. The difference is moot; birds do not sing to us but to their own kind—to seduce a willing female, for example, or to warn off a potential male competitor. We are inclined to put everything we see or hear into our own standard of reference, and we wax lyrical over the song of a nightingale or a

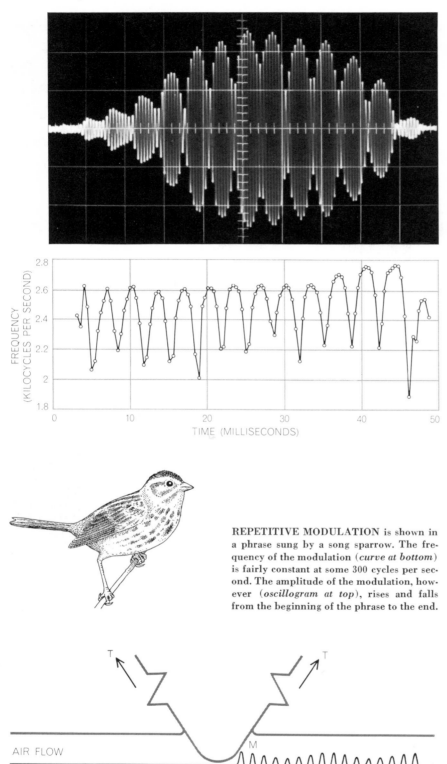

REPETITIVE MODULATION is shown in a phrase sung by a song sparrow. The frequency of the modulation (*curve at bottom*) is fairly constant at some 300 cycles per second. The amplitude of the modulation, however (*oscillogram at top*), rises and falls from the beginning of the phrase to the end.

EXTERNAL LABIUM (*EL*), which is located in the bronchial wall opposite the tympanic membrane (*M*), may be the structure that enables the song sparrow and other birds to modulate amplitude without increasing or decreasing frequency. Normally a change in one alters the other, when both are controlled by tension on the tympanic membrane. If, however, the bird can diminish the distance across the bronchial lumen by extending the labium into it, it would be able to lower amplitude without affecting frequency, since this means of changing distance across the passage would not affect tension on the tympanic membrane.

thrush simply because they happen to sing within the ambit of our own musical experience. The fact is that the rapid modulations we have been discussing cannot be perceived as such by human ears. They are smeared, as it were, to produce what to us seems like a note of a different quality, or timbre, and one that on the whole we find unpleasant. It is easy for us to resolve a trill or a tremolo if its frequency is 30 cycles per second or less, but when the frequency rises to 100 cycles per second or more we hear a note of a rather unpleasant buzzy quality. Hence the beautiful complexity of the Lapland longspur song is completely lost in our ears, whereas it seems more than likely that Madame Longspur finds it delightful and enticing.

I have examined experimentally frequency perception and time perception for the avian ear. I conclude that its frequency discrimination, as expressed in the relation $\Delta f / f \times 10^{-3}$ (f is of course frequency), lies between 2 and 5. Time discrimination appears to be no greater than .5 millisecond. For human ears frequency discrimination is about the same, but time discrimination is perhaps 50 to 100 times worse for humans than it is for birds. There is then the strong presumption that birds hear *as such* the rapid modulations so characteristic of their songs, and that the information content even in relatively simple songs must be enormous. One readily understands how birds of the same species can recognize individuals from subtleties in their songs that are imperceptible to a human listener.

So far I have discussed only those phrases in bird song for which the basic wave form is sinusoidal without significant harmonic content. As we shall now see, harmonics do occur in bird song, but there is no broad generalization relating to the presence or absence of harmonics in the songs of the several bird families. One might say with some confidence that songs of the Passeriformes in which harmonics appear are relatively rare, whereas in the songs and calls of birds in other families phrases with substantial harmonic content are comparatively common. Each statement will, however, have numerous exceptions.

It can nonetheless be said with considerable assurance that for any given species there is a threshold frequency below which harmonics occur and above which one hears a phrase without significant harmonic content. This threshold varies widely for different species, from a value near 4,000 cycles per second for

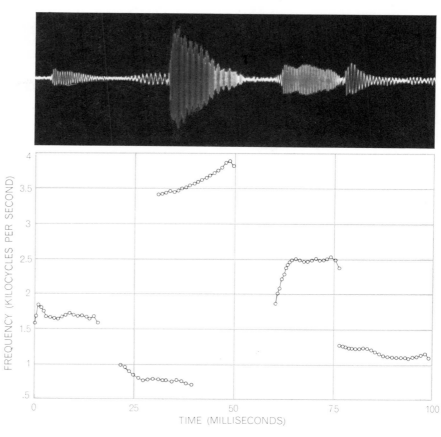

the blue-gray gnatcatcher to below 500 cycles per second for the barred owl. Such threshold frequencies can be determined only when a bird sings over a range of frequencies that embrace the threshold. This circumstance is uncommon, because the majority of the Passeriformes sing only in the frequency range giving rise to phrases free of harmonics, and birds of other families sing only in the range giving rise to harmonic phrases. Indeed, whether or not a bird passes through the harmonic threshold in its songs or calls appears to be a matter of choice; there is no physiological reason that would prevent a crow from singing a harmonic-free phrase, or a wood warbler, by way of contrast, from singing a phrase with substantial harmonic content.

As an example of the development of harmonic spectra as the fundamental descends below the threshold frequency, I offer a glissando sung by a smooth-billed ani that embraces nearly three octaves (from 485 to 3,500 cycles per second). As the frequency rises dominance shifts from the fourth harmonic through the third and second harmonics to the fundamental frequency. The transition frequencies (the frequency at which the relative amplitudes of adjacent harmonics are equal) are 1,600 cycles per second for the fundamental and the second harmonic, 950 cycles per second for the second and third harmonics and 560 cycles per second for the third and fourth harmonics. In all the many cases I have examined in which the fundamental passes through the threshold, curves of relative amplitude plotted against frequency show a small frequency interval embracing each transition between

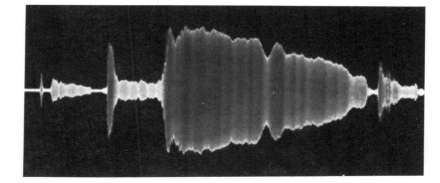

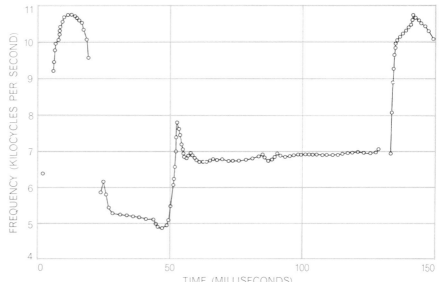

NONREPETITIVE MODULATION is seen in the courtship song of the brown-headed cowbird. In the oscillogram and frequency analysis at top is the phrase described as "glug"; in the corresponding records at bottom is the phrase "gleeee." Both of the phrases cover a large range of frequencies.

harmonics and a larger interval during which a particular harmonic contains a relatively large fraction of the acoustical energy. I have found no glissandi for which the dominant harmonic is higher than the fourth, but there are many calls in which the fundamental is constant, and in which the associated harmonic

spectra show similar characteristics, that is, a dominant harmonic with adjacent harmonics falling off rapidly in relative amplitude.

To understand how harmonic spectra with these characteristics can be generated in the syrinx, let us return once again to my simplified model of the organ. Imagine the tension in the tympanic membrane gradually being reduced, with the membrane at its vibrational peak approaching the opposing bronchial wall (or the external labium) more and more closely. The point will come when the bronchial wall will *constrain* the membrane, forcing it to depart from a pure sinusoidal vibration. At this point the second harmonic will become evident, increasing in amplitude as membrane tension falls and the constraint of the opposing bronchial wall influences

an increasing percentage of the period of vibration (the period of the fundamental). As the process continues, the amplitude of the fundamental will fall as the amplitude of the second harmonic rises. As membrane tension decreases still further, the second harmonic will become constrained and the third harmonic will become dominant. At this point the membrane can be visualized as being in a state of *rippling* vibration, with a fundamental fixed by membrane tension and the associated harmonic spectrum dictated by the constraints imposed by the passage within which the membrane is vibrating.

Among the ducks and geese harmonic spectra are found with many terms and with amplitudes showing no particular pattern. Such spectra must be associated with a form of membrane vibration re-

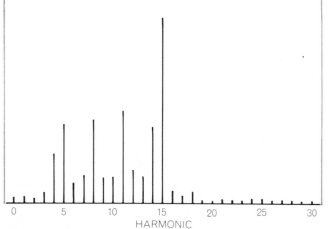

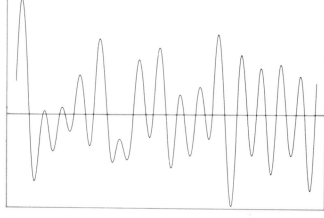

INDIAN HILL MYNA SAYS "AH" as in "Charlie." At left is the harmonic spectrum of the sound. At right is the wave form of the sound, which does not decay in amplitude as it would if it were generated by a resonant system such as the human vocal apparatus.

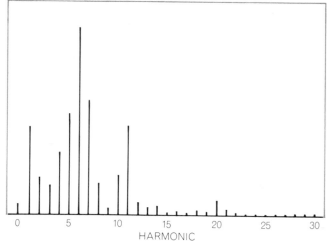

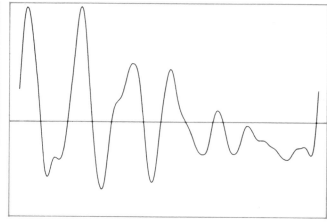

AUTHOR SAYS "AH" as in "Charlie." The wave form shows a decay in amplitude. The two "ahs" sound alike, but one is generated by a nonresonant mechanism and the other by a resonant one. This is a fundamental difference between the vocal apparatus of birds and the vocal apparatus of men. The vertical lines in the harmonic spectra represent the relative intensity of sound at each harmonic.

sembling the pulses produced in the human glottis, that is, a high-amplitude pulse followed by a series of less violent ripples of variable period.

Throughout the harmonic domain, whatever the species and whatever the wave form or harmonic spectrum may be, the evidence shows quite clearly that there is no tracheal modulation; the call is produced in the syrinx and passes unchanged through the trachea.

We come now to those birds that produce a more or less convincing imitation of the human voice. The question is whether such birds bring into play some completely new physiological or acoustical mechanism, or whether they achieve their imitations using the same mechanisms that produce their normal songs. I have selected the Indian hill myna as the standard of reference because its imitation of the human voice is excellent; it might well deceive the listener into thinking a person is speaking. A phrase was selected from the myna repertoire and was examined in detail in comparison with the same phrase spoken by me.

The reader will recall that the human voice originates as a series of puffs of air emanating from the glottis, the period between puffs corresponding to the fundamental frequency (80 to 180 puffs per second for the male voice). This acoustical disturbance is modulated in passing through our oral cavities so as to reinforce certain frequencies and attenuate others. Areas of reinforcement are called "formants" and are characteristic of particular vowel sounds. The wave form and the corresponding harmonic spectrum for the vowel "a" as enunciated by the myna and by me are shown in the illustrations below. The sound was unmistakably "ah" for both of us, but the associated wave forms are entirely different.

When the acoustical disturbance originating at the glottis stimulates a resonator (the oral cavities) to vibrate at a natural frequency, the generated wave form will have the frequency of the resonator, and the amplitude of the wave will decay exponentially over a period corresponding to that of the fundamental. One can readily isolate the formants for the myna and me corresponding to the vowel "a" and see if the resulting wave form fits these criteria. We find that the amplitude for my formants does indeed decay exponentially within the fundamental period; for the myna there is no decay and only random change in amplitude. This is the most convincing evidence we can offer that resonators are not involved in the myna "imitation."

How, then, is the imitation produced? It is important first to realize that the myna need not reproduce the human wave form at all. Since the human ear is not sensitive to phase, the myna need produce only an approximation of the amplitudes of the several harmonics, and this can be done with literally an infinity of wave forms. The ability to produce a separate harmonic spectrum with each of the two acoustical sources should be adequate to produce a reasonably good imitation, particularly since it has been shown that much of the human voice spectrum is redundant even if the criterion is recognition of the speech of a particular individual.

Let me summarize. The physiology and acoustics of bird vocalization are unique in the animal kingdom. Sound is produced at the syrinx in an air stream modulated by an elastic membrane vibrating in a restricted passage bounded by the walls of the bronchus. This source-generated acoustical disturbance appears not to be modified in its passage through the trachea. The syrinx contains two independently controllable sources, one in each bronchus, enabling the bird to produce two notes or phrases simultaneously. Harmonics arise below a threshold frequency by mechanical constraints on the vibrating membrane, forcing a departure from a purely sinusoidal wave form. The source-generated sounds can be modulated in frequency or in amplitude or (more usually) in both with extraordinary rapidity, so rapidly that human ears cannot perceive the modulators as such, receiving instead impressions of notes of varying quality or timbre.

I end this account by pointing out that it has been in effect a scientific detective story, with conclusions reached by analyzing the evidence in the bird songs themselves. The criminal did not confess in the last chapter, and the evidence must remain circumstantial, without direct proof. Had I the deductive powers of an Albert Campion, a Gideon Fell or any of the other erudite detectives of fiction, coupled with the persuasiveness of Perry Mason, I might have done better. In any event I have developed a model, highly convincing to me, and I shall patiently await experimental evidence that will raise my spirits if the answer is yes but will not be too devastating if it should be no.

VII

BIRDS AND PEOPLE

VII · BIRDS AND PEOPLE

INTRODUCTION

The lives of birds and humans have been intertwined for a long time. Man has hunted, tamed, and worshipped birds for millenia. Before the rise of the ancient civilizations, humans were few, other animals were many, and the world was ringed round with mystery. The comings and goings of birds, harbingers of the seasons, must have touched the imagination of Paleolithic peoples just as they do those of us living today. Beliefs linking "Easter eggs" and fertility, owls and wisdom, crows and ill-tidings have their origins before the dawn of history.

Although it is unlikely that they were ever a major food item, wild birds were welcome sources of eggs and extra meat for preagricultural tribes. Birds tamed by Stone Age peoples include geese in Europe, chickens in Southeast Asia, and turkeys in the Americas. Primitive humans hunted for food whether they enjoyed it or not. Today, most people hunt for pleasure, returning for a short time to fields and streams, to a facsimile of the life of yesteryear. Ten million hunters spend over a billion dollars a year in the United States. Hunts by professionals and amateurs wreaked havoc in the last century, causing the extinction or near extinction of such sea and shore birds as the Great Auk and Eskimo Curlew and such land birds as the Passenger Pigeon.

Shooting birds for market, an important industry of the last century, has been replaced by a mammoth poultry industry. Backyard flocks of poultry that were once advertised as a business suitable for retired couples have given way to mechanized ranches with hundreds of thousands to millions of birds each. The plentiful supplies of inexpensive poultry meat and eggs enjoyed by consumers in the United States and other developed nations are the products of at least three generations of agricultural research and discoveries. Nutritionists provided detailed information on the energy, amino acid, fatty acid, mineral, and vitamin requirements of poultry; geneticists selected for rapidly growing animals with particular meat and egg properties; veterinarians perfected vaccines for a number of avian diseases; embryologists worked out the procedures needed for incubation of the eggs; and physiologists devised the lighting and management protocols to maximize growth and egg production. The status of the poultry industry is reviewed by environmental physiologist Wilbor O. Wilson in the first article in this section ("Poultry Production").

The human population has had an enormous impact upon the ecology of the Earth since the Industrial Revolution. Many people consider that birds and their responses to the effects of civilization are important indicators of ecological change and the quality of the environment. They are like the canaries once kept in coal mines; the death of one of these birds warned the miners of the presence of deadly gases. David B. Peakall focuses on one example, DDT, in his article ("Pesticides and the Reproduction of Birds").

Not so very long ago, DDT was one of the prime examples of how chemistry would give people victory in their struggle for freedom from disease and starvation (see Fig. 1). Since its introduction in 1942, so much of this long-lasting chemical has been used to eradicate insects that carry human diseases and destroy crops that significant amounts of it have found their way as far as the Antarctic. DDT seemed virtually nontoxic to vertebrates, including man. But it wasn't. It kills birds, fish, and other animals. Like many other long-lived fat-soluble chemicals, DDT becomes more and more concentrated as it moves up a food chain, accumulating in the fat stores of the animals that inadvertently consume it. As early as 1952, scientists found that American Robins and other birds in the Midwest died from DDT applied to control the beetles that carry Dutch Elm disease. The concentration of DDT rose to 140 ppm (parts per million) in earthworms and to 440 ppm in American Robins from an initial concentration of 10 ppm in the soil. When 7,300 elms were sprayed with DDT in 1963 in New England, 70 percent of the American Robins died, and there was high mortality of other species, including chickadees, nuthatches, creepers, and woodpeckers. Ironically, DDT was not effective in controlling Dutch Elm disease.

One of the best examples of how DDT and its analogues become concentrated is the case of the Western Grebes of Clear Lake, a shallow California lake north of San Francisco. DDD, an analogue of DDT, was applied to the waters of the lake in 1949, 1954, and 1957 in concentrations of less than 0.05 ppm to kill larvae of the Clear Lake gnat, a tiny midge insect that was a great nuisance to the inhabitants and tourists of the region. As early as 1954, R. L. Rudd of the University of California at Davis and his students recorded the deaths of over 100 Western Grebes, loss of a breeding colony of approximately

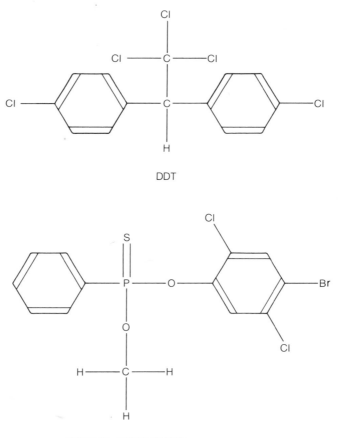

DDT

PHOSVEL (LEPTOPHOS)

Figure 1. Structures of DDT and Phosvel.

1,000 breeding pairs, and lack of reproduction of the few pairs that remained. Analyses showed that DDD had been concentrated 80,000-fold in the visceral fat of largemouth bass and Western Grebes.

The Western Grebes and the largemouth bass are on the top of a food chain; they eat the blackfish and bluegills that eat the plankton that first concentrated the DDD from the lake water. Each step in the chain is accompanied by an increase in the concentration of DDD stored in fat (see Table 1). It was

TABLE 1.   BUILDUP OF DDD IN THE FOOD CHAIN OF CLEAR LAKE, CALIFORNIA.

Sample	Concentration (ppm)
Water[1]	0.02
Plankton	5
Bluegill[2]	125–254
Largemouth bass	1550–1700
Western Grebe	1600

Source: From R. L. Rudd, *Pesticides and the Living Landscape*, University of Wisconsin Press, 1966.

[1]Estimated initial concentration.

[2]Values in visceral fat.

not until 1967 (10 years after application of the pesticide ceased) that the reproduction of the birds was successful enough to maintain the population.

DDT and its analogues hit the front pages again the the mid-1960s, when egg shells of the Brown Pelican thinned and reproduction of the species ceased on Anacapa Island off the California coast. Environmentalists insisted the problem was due to DDT contaminating the waters of the Los Angeles Basin from a chemical plant that manufactured it. The evidence was not airtight, but the reproduction of the birds began to improve when the plant shut down.

The use of DDT and related chemicals was banned for most situations in the United States by the Environmental Protection Agency in 1972. But the problems with pesticides have not gone away. Interdiction of long-lived chlorinated hydrocarbons has led to increased use of other, more short-lived agents, some of which are highly toxic to both humans and birds. One example is the insidious effect known as "delayed neurotoxicity," in which some organophosphate agents cause progressive nerve damage that may not appear until weeks after exposure. People and chickens are particularly susceptible. So is the water buffalo. Death of a number of water buffalo in Egypt several years ago led M. B. Abou-Donia, a young toxicologist, to conduct experiments with chickens and establish that a commonly used pesticide, Leptophos, also known as Phosvel (see Fig. 1), was responsible for the deaths. Data like his, and reports of neurological problems of workers in the plant manufacturing it, were instrumental in preventing its registration for commercial use in the United States.

The land abides, but for how long and for what purposes? In 1750, there were 750 acres per person of forest in the United States. The number had fallen to 67 in 1900 and to 5 in 1965. A governor of California once jocularly suggested that once you had seen one tree, you had seen them all; someday one forest may be all there will be to see.

The increasing destruction of habitat and the pollution of what remains by urbanization and agriculture has eroded the traditional apolitical posture of the wildlife biologist to the point that Olin S. Pettingill, Jr., a distinguished avian biologist, asks every ornithologist to be a "militant conservationist." On the other hand, there are those who feel that scientists compromise their usefulness to society when they become advocates, and that they should let the facts speak for themselves.

Aldo Leopold, a pioneer in wildlife management, in his book *A Sand County Almanac*, argued that the issues were moral, not merely scientific. He advocated that we enlarge our conception of a social ethic from humans to land. First, he said, people felt loyalty to a tribe, then to a city-state, next to a nation. The next step is to extend our social consciousness to the planet itself. "When we see land as a community to which we belong," said Leopold, "we may begin to use it with love and respect. There is no other way for land to survive the impact of mechanized man, nor for us to reap from it that esthetic harvest it is capable, under science, of contributing to culture. That land is a community is the basic concept of ecology, but that land is to be loved and respected is an extension of ethics."

The 1960s witnessed what was said to be a conflict between generations in terms of attitudes and life styles. The "generation gap" with regard to the land is a different one; the issues lie between the living, the dead, and the unborn. Each generation feels the Earth is theirs; each knows that they are the most modern, progressive, and important of people. They see themselves as heirs to the ages, entitled to the riches of the Earth. And then they die, passing on what is left to their children. The ethic of conservation is one of common sense; it says we are caretakers, holding the land in trust for future generations, with an obligation to pass it on to our children in a little better shape than it was when we inherited it.

On dedicating a monument to the Passenger Pigeon in 1947, Aldo Leopold said "We have erected a monument to commemorate the funeral of a species. . . . We grieve because no living man will see again the onrushing phalanx of victorious birds, sweeping a path for spring across the March skies, chasing the defeated winter from all the woods and prairies of Wisconsin. . . . For one species to mourn the death of another is a new thing under the sun."

With knowledge comes power—with power, responsibility. But it has been difficult to convince members of industrial societies that they are stewards and not conquerors of the planet. Antoine de Saint Exupery, philosopher, poet, and pioneer flier, reached some perspective on the matter: "What are the hundred years of the history of the machine compared with the two hundred thousand years of the history of man? It was only yesterday that we began to pitch our camp in this country of laboratories and power stations . . . the life of the past seems to us nearer our true natures . . . every step on the road of progress takes us farther from habits . . . we had recently begun to acquire. We are in truth emigrants who have not yet found our homeland."

REFERENCES

Abou-Donia, M. B., and D. G. Graham. "Delayed Neurotoxicity from Long-term Low-level Topical Administration of Leptophos to the Comb of Hens." *Toxicology and Applied Pharmacology* 46:199–213, 1978.

Leopold, A. *A Sand County Almanac and Sketches from Here and There*. Oxford Univ. Press, New York, 1949.

Poultry Production

Poultry Production

24

Wilbor O. Wilson
July 1966

*The per capita consumption of poultry in the U.S. has
more than doubled during the past 30 years. To meet
the demand, automatic factories today convert tons of
feed into tons of meat and eggs*

The term "chicken feed" used to be a synonym for insignificance. Biologically and agriculturally the domestic fowl were not a major factor in American life. Over the past 30 years, however, their status has changed remarkably. Today the production of poultry is no longer a trivial or small-scale business. A few figures will illustrate the dimensions of the change. In 1935 the annual consumption of poultry in the U.S. amounted to 13.1 pounds of chicken and 1.5 pounds of turkey per capita; in 1965 the consumption per person had risen to 33.3 pounds of chicken and 7.4 pounds of turkey. Thirty years ago comparatively few commercial egg farmers kept more than 2,500 hens; nowadays ranches consisting of 30,000 laying hens are not uncommon, and the average annual production of eggs has been increased from 121 per hen in 1930 to 217 per hen today.

Paradoxically, although the poultry industry has grown greatly in size, it has almost disappeared from sight on the American scene. A generation ago nine out of 10 farms in the U.S. kept chickens or other poultry; today in much of the countryside the chicken yard is becoming a rarity. Poultry production is now conducted mainly in establishments that are best described as factories. A technological revolution has transformed this field of agriculture, and in so doing it has raised poultry to a position of new importance in man's economy.

Origins of Poultry Production

The cultivation of poultry as a food source is actually a rather recent development. Chickens were domesticated early in man's history (witness the cock's crow mentioned in the Bible and the painting of a cock on a potsherd found in the Egyptian tomb of Tutankhamen), but it appears that these animals at first were used primarily for the sport of cockfighting. Until the 20th century the chicken was prized more as a showpiece than as an item for the table. Beautiful breeds of chickens were raised for exhibition, and more than 200 varieties of them, bearing names such as the Golden Laced Wyandotte and the Speckled Sussex, were measured by a "Standard of Perfection" in appearance that was established by the American Poultry Association in 1874. It was not until about 1910 that the raising of hens for egg-laying became a more important enterprise in the U.S. than the breeding of fancy poultry for exhibition.

Nonetheless, the domestic fowl have historically contributed to man's material welfare and his culture in a multitude of ways. The Declaration of Independence was written with a quill pen made from a goose feather. Painters since early times have used egg yolk as a durable vehicle for pigments. In California today geese are employed to weed the cotton fields: they eat the grassy weeds and leave the cotton plants alone. Another useful fowl, developed in our laboratory at the University of California at Davis, is the Japanese quail: requiring very little cage space and laying more than 300 eggs a year, this bird has proved to be an excellent subject for the testing of antifertility drugs.

Our debt to the chicken in science and medicine is profound. It was the ill effects of a diet of polished rice on a flock of chickens, first investigated by the Dutch physician Christiaan Eijkman in 1896, that led to the discovery of vitamins and their dietary importance. The chicken was one of the chief early instruments for studies of the sex hormones, because of its conspicuous manifestations of their effects, particularly on the cock's comb. Louis Pasteur's development of the first vaccine for a bacterial disease (anthrax of cattle) originated from his investigation of fowl cholera. Later the chick embryo—that is, the fertilized chick egg—was found to be an ideal medium for culturing microorganisms, including viruses, and this led to the conquest of many infectious diseases. Today a stubborn disease of poultry—fowl leukosis—serves as one of the most useful experimental tools in the investigation of cancer.

Modern Poultry Production

This article is concerned with the production of poultry as food. In the U.S. this essentially means the production of chickens and turkeys. Other birds—guinea fowl, ducks, geese, swans, pigeons, peafowl and quail—are important contributors to the food supply elsewhere in the world and may become so in the U.S. in the future, but they are not a large factor here at the present time. The chicken, of course, is universal. The turkey is indigenous to America and was raised by the Indians long before the Europeans arrived; according to the archaeological evidence, Indians in New Mexico domesticated the bird thousands of years ago.

Until recent years the practicable size of poultry flocks was rigorously limited by technical difficulties. Diseases and other factors that attacked the birds under crowded conditions made it impossible to handle and sustain large flocks economically. Elaborate forms of management were tried but all failed. In the 1930's, however, intensive research promoted by the Poultry Science Association and carried out by investigators at agricultural experiment stations in the U.S. began to yield solutions to the problems. The advances fall under four headings: improved breeding, improved feeding, control of disease and improved management, including mechanization.

The breeding of chickens has gone through an evolution of drastic change in objectives. Originally and up to fairly recent times the breeders selected chickens primarily for their fighting ability. Then, in the exhibition era, the animals were bred for fancy feathers, combs, colors and shapes. Today the breeders' objectives are utilitarian and twofold: maximum meat production and maximum egg production.

As it happens, these goals are difficult to attain in one bird. Large birds tend to have low egg production, and good egg-layers tend to be small—about half the size of the meat breeds. Chickens such as the Plymouth Rock, the Wyandotte and the Rhode Island Red were developed in the latter half of the 19th century as a compromise. Produced by crossbreeding between the two types, they are of fairly good size and give fairly good egg production. In the present system of poultry production, however, specialization is the rule. Poultry farmers raise their birds either for meat or for egg production, and they select their breeds for high performance in one or the other.

The pioneer of modern fowl breeding was the British biologist William Bateson, who even before Gregor Mendel's genetic experiments with plants were generally known had discovered the same basic principles of inheritance in experiments with chickens. These principles, involving the action of single genes, apply with particular fidelity to feather color and comb type. Rate of growth—the ability to gain weight rapidly in the first few weeks of life—is under the control of a number of genes that act additively. This too is a highly heritable characteristic.

One instance of selection concerns the work of British breeders. They developed a tightly feathered, well-muscled chicken called the Cornish. It laid few eggs and had low fertility, and for many years it was used only for exhibition. The Cornish, however, eventually was found to be an excellent stock for meat birds, and most of the modern strains of fryers or broilers are descended from that stock on one side of the family tree.

Breeding for egg production turned

POULTRY STRAINS that lead in popularity today often have some distant European and Asiatic ancestors in common, but they are fundamentally the product of selective breeding programs in which many new varieties and strains have been developed during the past 20 years. A strain-cross involving two strains of the single-comb White Leghorn variety (*a*) yields a superior producer of white eggs. A variety-cross of the Rhode Island Red with the

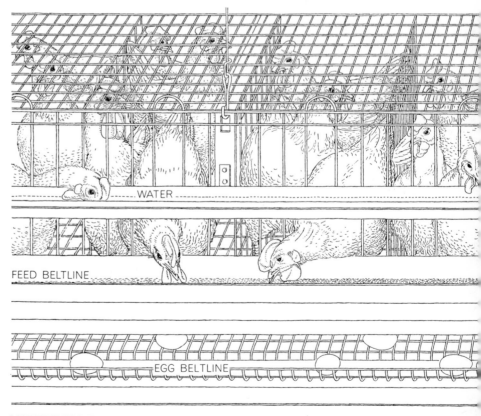

MODERN EGG FACTORY automatically handles the nutrient demands and the egg output of large numbers of virtually immobilized laying hens. Feed reaches the birds on a moving

Barred Plymouth Rock (*b*) yields chicks with a sex-linked gene affecting feather color. The cockerels are readily culled 24 hours after hatching; the hens are superior producers of brown eggs. The meat fowl are larger than egg fowl and often have Cornish blood in their ancestry. One such rooster (*c*) and a White Plymouth Rock hen, when crossed, yield a hen whose offspring are prime broiler fowl. Because dark pinfeathers are objectionable, the Broad-Breasted Bronze turkey (*d*) is not often raised for market. Instead the Bronzes have been bred with white-feathered turkeys, such as the White Holland, to produce birds with the best features of both.

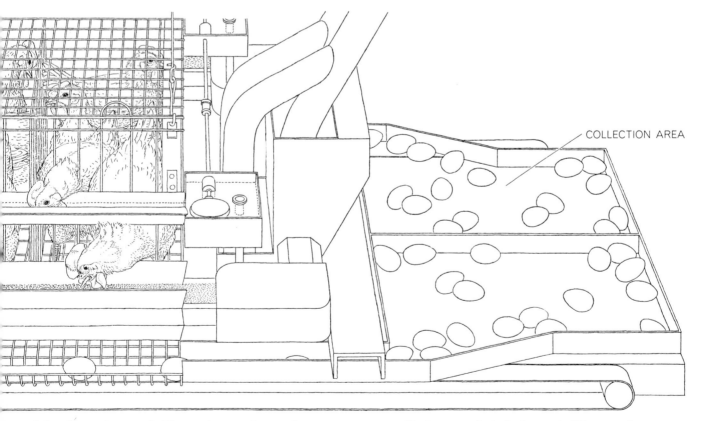

COLLECTION AREA

belt and water in a trough. The cage bottoms slope so that, as soon as a hen lays an egg, it rolls away to a moving belt and is carried to a collection area. A single factory building may house more than 50,000 hens, which produce an average 3,000 dozen eggs a day.

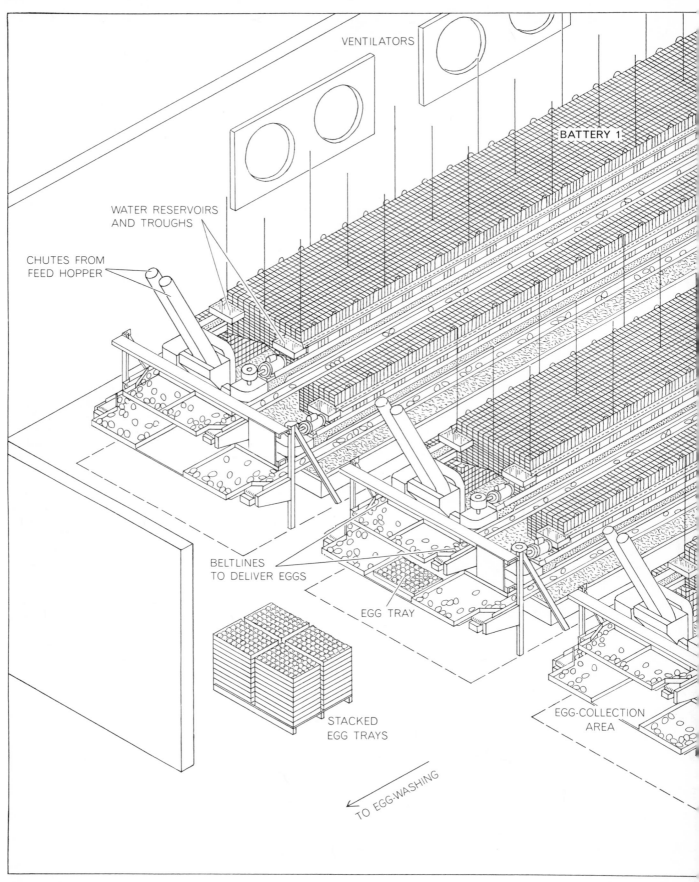

VENTILATORS

BATTERY 1

WATER RESERVOIRS
AND TROUGHS

CHUTES FROM
FEED HOPPER

BELTLINES
TO DELIVER EGGS

EGG TRAY

STACKED
EGG TRAYS

EGG-COLLECTION
AREA

TO EGG-WASHING

TWO-TIERED BATTERIES are suspended from the roof of the egg-production unit illustrated. In cross section the four rows of cages in each battery form two "stairsteps" back to back. Each cage contains two or three hens. Suspension from above facilitates me-

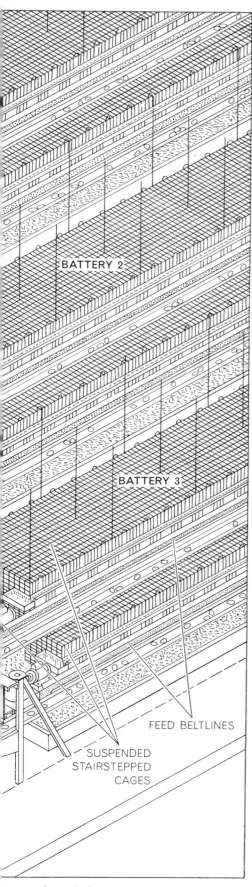

BATTERY 2

BATTERY 3

FEED BELTLINES

SUSPENDED
STAIRSTEPPED
CAGES

chanical cleaning; a 20,000-bird flock produces more than a ton of droppings a day.

out to be more difficult. This capacity seems to be less accurately controlled by a bird's genes than body weight or feather color is. Moreover, egg production is greatly influenced by diet and by environmental circumstances, making it difficult to assess the fowl's inherent laying capacity. Finally, an egg farmer is interested not only in the number of eggs a hen produces but also in the size, color and quality of the eggs, and these properties are not under a single genetic control. Scientific testing in recent years has shown, however, that heredity is an important factor in the improvement of laying breeds. Different strains of hens, reared under basically the same conditions, have been found to vary in production by as many as 45 eggs a year.

A bird, unlike a plant, is not altogether at the mercy of its environment. It maintains its own internal stability (homeostasis) and thus can tolerate considerable variation in the weather. Furthermore, in poultry husbandry today conditions such as temperature and light are carefully controlled; diet can be accurately suited to the bird; resistance to disease can be supplied by vaccination. All of this helps to simplify the breeding of chickens and turkeys for productive capacity; the breeder does not need to be so concerned, as in plant-crop breeding, with genetic adaptation to local climates or specific diseases. Indeed, today's breeders have developed birds that are raised the world around.

Since 1932 the Poultry Husbandry Department of the University of California at Berkeley has been breeding a population of hens for improvement in egg production. The feeding, housing and management of the birds have been kept more or less uniform; no outside genetic material has been introduced since 1941, and the only important variable has been the progressive selection of the best layers in the flock for reproduction. The experiment has produced a steady rise in the annual production of eggs per hen [see bottom illustration on page 252], even though inbreeding, such as this flock has experienced, usually reduces egg-laying capacity. Hybridization by the crossing of inbred strains could have increased the gain, and the use of hybrid chickens is now common practice in commercial husbandry.

Of the nearly 200 varieties of chickens that used to be raised in the U.S., only four or five are commercially important today. The meat breeds, as I have mentioned, can all trace their ancestry in part to the Cornish breed. Practically all the important egg-laying

strains are derived from the Leghorn breed. The popular present strains of turkeys (featuring white feathers and a plump breast) can also be traced back to a single superior stock: a breed called the Broad-Breasted Bronze that was developed in England and introduced in the U.S. in the 1930's.

Chicken Feed

Turning now to the feeding of poultry, we must observe that the modern fowl thrives on a diet almost totally foreign to any food it ever found in nature. Its feed is a product of the laboratory. The nutrition of the chicken has been investigated more thoroughly than that of most other animals, including man. It was by experiments on chickens that investigators determined the needs of animals for vitamin D (the sunshine, or cod-liver-oil, vitamin), the antihemorrhagic vitamin K, the vitamin-B complex, vitamin G (riboflavin) and various essential minerals. Fowl are primarily grain eaters, but research has established that they cannot live by grain alone. Their requirements of protein, minerals, vitamins and energy-suppliers have been established in much detail, and ways have been found to enhance the efficiency of their diet by artificial supplements such as antibiotics. Since cost is a prime factor in successful poultry husbandry, the computer has been enlisted to calculate the correct proportions of various available ingredients that differ in price in order to achieve a ration of fixed dietary value at minimum expense.

The barnyard fowl used to live on scraps from the farmer's table and what insects and grain it could find in the field. Later it was promoted to a standard feed consisting of a mixture of four grains and meat and bone scraps, supplemented with milk and greens. In the present poultry factories the ration is one omnibus mixture containing all the necessary ingredients, presented in the form of a mash or in pellets. The ration varies, of course, with the bird: a growing pullet, for example, needs more vitamins and protein than a mature, laying hen does.

The efficiency of a fowl's conversion of feed into meat or eggs, under favorable conditions, is impressive. In a 1964 egg-laying test in California the average production of the hens entered was better than a pound of eggs for each three pounds of feed consumed by the bird. Young fryers marketed at the age of eight weeks weigh about four pounds and generally yield about a pound of

WASHING EGGS is one of the final steps en route to market. After leaving the washing machine eggs often receive light coating of oil to reduce evaporation before consumption.

CANDLING MACHINE moves 30 dozen eggs a minute past two inspectors who keep watch not only for eggs that are not clean or have cracked shells but also for any internal defects.

body weight for each two pounds of feed they have eaten. The turkey does even better: up to the age of six weeks it converts each pound of food into nearly a pound of tissue. From the sixth to the 26th week turkeys gain weight at the rate of more than a pound a week. As chickens and turkeys grow larger and older, the efficiency of their conversion of feed into meat declines.

Along with the advances in nutrition, considerable progress has been made in the control of poultry diseases. By improved sanitary practices, the use of medicated feeds and vaccination poultrymen in the U.S. have eradicated fowl plague and greatly reduced the toll from formerly catastrophic diseases such as coccidiosis, pullorum disease, bronchitis, laryngotracheitis, Newcastle disease (a viral invasion of the nervous system), fowl pox, fowl cholera and fowl typhoid. In spite of these gains, however, the overall disease mortality among chickens has been reduced only moderately: from about 20 percent 25 years ago to 15 percent today. The chief reason for the persisting high rate is leukosis, the cancer-like disease of the blood. In chickens and turkeys, as in man, this leukemic disorder still frustrates the search for prevention or cure.

Mechanization

Undoubtedly the most striking change that has taken place in the poultry industry is in the scale of its operations and the standardization, or mechanization, of nearly all its processes. Once the hen has delivered its offspring in the form of eggs, the hatching and rearing of the young can be taken over entirely by artificial devices. In present practice the procedure is so highly mechanized that from the hatching of the egg to the delivery of the final product in the supermarket (a dozen boxed eggs or a neatly packaged fryer) almost no human handling is involved.

There are highly efficient poultry factories today that integrate all the operations under one management: hatching, production of feed, rearing both egg-layers and meat chickens and marketing the products. For the most part, however, poultrymen still obtain their raw materials from special processors: chicks from hatcheries and feed from dealers in that commodity. The feed is delivered not in the cotton sacks that once provided material for the farmer's wife's dresses but by the ton in bulk. In the egg-producing branch of the industry there are specialists who rear the chicks through the pullet stage and then deliver them to the egg rancher. The pullet rancher receives only female chicks; the crowing of the chanticleer is never heard on his ranch. The supplying hatchery determines the sex of its chicks when they are a day old. The supplier then kills the males and ships the females.

The term "ranch" in this industry is now in a sense a misnomer, as the "ranches" consist of roofed buildings. In the comparatively mild climate of California these are generally open to the air. Many modern poultry houses, however, are entirely enclosed (some even have no windows) so that the light, temperature, humidity and ventilation can be controlled with precision. It has been found that the control of light during the rearing of pullets can increase their later egg production as laying hens and even influence the size of their eggs; it can also improve the growth of meat chickens and turkeys and reduce cannibalism and other vices of poultry. Control of temperature and humidity is also important, particularly during the early weeks of growth. After the first few weeks of brooding, during which the young fowl must be kept warm, the control is designed to maintain a cool, even temperature: poultry produce best at a temperature between 50 and 70 degrees Fahrenheit.

The chicken's or turkey's home today is generally a small cage, whose dimensions have been reduced as mechanization has proceeded. The laying hen used to be allowed an individual cage about 16 inches high, 12 inches wide and 18 inches deep—affording a total floor space of 1.5 square feet. Many poultrymen now keep three hens in a cage of this size, and it has been found feasible to maintain two hens in a cage only eight inches wide. The feeding of caged poultry has been thoroughly mechanized. Commonly the feed is sluiced mechanically into a trough outside the wire front of the cage, and the food delivery is regulated by a time clock. Other systems employ an electrically driven feed hopper or a large hopper in which the birds receive bulk rations that last for several days. "Chicken feed" today is measured in tons: for a flock of 60,000 hens, although each bird eats only about a quarter of a pound a day, the daily ration amounts to seven and a half tons.

The cleaning of the poultry house, the most unpleasant chore of the old-fashioned chicken farm, is now handled by skip-loading tractors or small powered cleaners of various types. The

AUTOMATIC FEEDING of turkeys is accomplished by a weekly filling of hoppers that hold 500 pounds of feed at the Ephrata Turkey Farm in Ephrata, Pa. Up to the age of six weeks turkeys eat only a little more than a pound of feed for each pound that they gain.

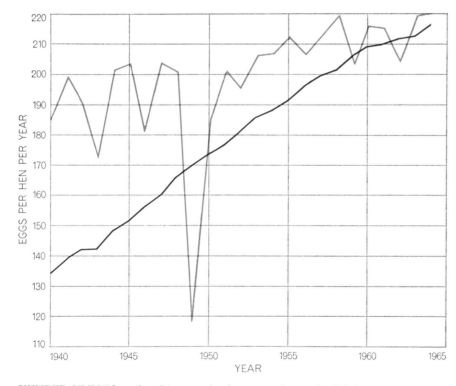

NUMBER OF EGGS produced in a year by the average hen in the U.S. has risen more than 40 percent in the past 25 years (black curve). Although part of the gain is due to improved feeding and shelter, selective breeding has been the predominant factor. One example is the 15 percent increase within a genetically closed flock at the University of California at Berkeley (colored curve); each generation's best layers mothered the next generation. The large production dip in 1949 reflects an outbreak of Newcastle disease during that year. The chart is based on the work of Hans Abplanalp and I. M. Lerner of the University of California.

gathering of eggs, formerly the most pleasant aspect of keeping chickens, also is now fully mechanized. The hen's cage or nest is usually designed with a sloping floor so that the egg rolls gently out of the cage as soon as it is laid. (As far as can be determined, the disappearance of the egg does not make the hen neurotic.) A moving belt catches and carries off the eggs to a collection area, where they are picked up and packed by pneumatic "fingers." Before they are packed they are washed, dried and sometimes sprayed lightly with oil to protect them against evaporation and loss in quality on the way to the consumer.

The Turkey

Turkeys are raised by mass-production methods similar to those used for chickens destined for the meat market. In the turkey's case, however, the breeding of the birds for large size has markedly reduced their fertility. Consequently a large proportion of the turkeys produced today (about 90 percent of those in California) are bred by artificial insemination.

The composite result of the improvements in poultry-raising technology is a spectacular increase in the birds' health and productivity. Turkeys are marketed at 18 weeks (for females) or 22 weeks (for males) instead of at 30 to 35 weeks, and the amount of feed required to raise them to market weight has been nearly halved.

Similar improvements have been achieved with chickens. Twenty years ago it took 14 weeks and 12 pounds of feed to produce a three-pound fryer chicken; today it takes only six to seven weeks and five or six pounds of feed. Hens in well-run egg factories now produce considerably more than 240 eggs a year (the minimum required for commercial success in a modern establishment).

The mechanization of the industry naturally has reduced drastically the amount of human labor required. Studies by the University of California Agricultural Extension Service over the years show that, whereas in 1935 the labor requirement on a commercial egg farm averaged two man-hours per hen per year, in 1964 it averaged only three-tenths of a man-hour per year. The present price of eggs (and of chicken and turkey) of course reflects the improvements in production and the savings in labor. The real price of eggs, allowing for the depreciated dollar, is lower today than it was before World War II, and the price of poultry meat is considerably lower. The year-round availability of eggs and poultry has also been improved. The laying season, formerly concentrated in the months of February, March, April and May, has been extended over the entire year, and it is now uncommon to find cold-storage eggs in the market. Freshly killed turkeys, once marketed only at Thanksgiving and Christmas, are now available throughout the year. The same is true of fryer chickens, which used to be known as "spring" chickens.

Economics

The new poultry technology has radically altered both the economics of the industry and the position its products occupy in the American diet. It has made poultry production a large-scale business and yet in a sense a shrinking enterprise from the standpoint of the number of people engaged in it. As in other branches of agriculture, the pressures of price competition and advancing technology in the poultry industry compel an ever increasing enlargement of the unit of production. The small poultry farm cannot compete in efficiency with a modern mechanized ranch. Moreover, this field of agriculture receives no governmental protection in the form of price supports or production quotas. The result has been a rapid decimation of the number of poultry farmers. Even the specialized units, while growing in size, have been reduced in number. The number of chick hatcheries in California, for example, decreased from 371 in 1947 to 81 in 1964, and the number of hatcheries for turkeys from 142 to 74—this in spite of the great increase in consumption of poultry during that period. Of course, the shrinkage in the number of producing units has been more than made up for by the expansion of the size of the surviving establishments. The poultry industry today requires large capital, high technical skill, business acumen and fewer and fewer workers.

The new role of poultry in the U.S. diet represents no less pronounced a change than the position of poultry in agriculture. Turkey or chicken was once a special item reserved for Sunday dinner or holiday feasts; today it is an everyday staple. Poultry has become competitive in price with red meat and fish and is offered in inviting new forms. The aged, noble hen that used to require several hours of boiling to be made edible has been relegated to canned dog food and is replaced in the market by young fryers or broilers or by the chicken "TV dinner" and turkey roll that need only warming up. Chickens and turkeys now come with a stamp of guaranteed quality; about 85 percent of the dressed poultry sold in the U.S. is Government-inspected.

As we have noted, the annual consumption of poultry meat in the U.S. has more than doubled in the past 30 years—from 14.6 pounds per capita to 40.7 pounds. This is still considerably less than the 167 pounds of red meat the average American ate in 1965, but it seems likely that poultry will continue to gain a larger share of the meat diet.

Eggs too have been gaining steadily in favor. An egg contains only about 70 to 75 calories (thereby qualifying as a friend of the dieter), yet it is a rich source of vitamins, unsaturated fats, protein and other essential nutrients. Indeed, it would be a completely balanced food if one ate the shell! The shell's contribution (calcium) can easily be obtained from a supplement such as milk or a vegetable. Other aspects that promise a bright future for the egg as food are the extreme simplicity with which it can be prepared (notably as the boiled breakfast food) and its versatility. The egg's culinary possibilities, still only partly explored, cover a wide range, from the conversion of egg white into meringue and candies to the use of the yolk's emulsifying property to make mayonnaise or its yellow color to lend attractiveness to other dishes.

Research, particularly in the land-grant colleges and universities of the U.S., has been primarily responsible for the extraordinary development of the efficient new poultry technology and its products as a growing contribution to the U.S. food supply. It seems fair to say that continuation of the research will yield increasing benefits as time goes on.

Pesticides and the Reproduction of Birds

by David B. Peakall
April 1970

High concentrations of chlorinated hydrocarbon residues accumulate in such flesh-eaters as hawks and pelicans. Among the results are upsets in normal breeding behavior and eggs too fragile to survive.

The birds of prey have had an uneasy coexistence with man. Apart from the training of certain hawks for falconry and the veneration of the eagle as a symbol of fortitude, the predatory birds have been preyed on by the human species. In many parts of the world farmers, hunters and bird-lovers have waged unceasing warfare on the rapacious birds as pests, and egg collectors have further threatened their survival by raiding their nests for the beautifully pigmented eggs. Nevertheless, over the centuries the birds of prey on the whole survived well. The peregrine falcon, for example, is known to have maintained a remarkably stable population; records of aeries that have been occupied more or less continuously by peregrines go back in some cases to the Middle Ages.

About two decades ago, however, the peregrines in Europe and in North America suddenly suffered a crash in population. The peregrine is now rapidly vanishing in settled areas of the world, and in some places, particularly the eastern U.S., it is already extinct [*see illustration, page 256*]. The abrupt population fall of the peregrine (known in the U.S. as the duck hawk) has been paralleled by sharp declines of the bald eagle, the osprey and Cooper's hawk in the U.S. and of the golden eagle and the kestrel, or sparrow hawk, in Europe. The osprey, or fish hawk, has nearly disappeared from its haunts in southern New England and on Long Island; along the Connecticut River, where 150 pairs nested in 1952, only five pairs nested in 1969.

The population declines of all these raptorial birds are traceable not to the killing of adults but to a drastic drop in reproduction. It has been found that the reproduction failures follow much the same pattern among the various species: delayed breeding or failure to lay eggs altogether, a remarkable thinning of the shells and much breakage of the eggs that are laid, eating of broken eggs by the parents, failure to produce more eggs after earlier clutches were lost, and high mortality of the embryos and among fledglings.

Examination of the geographic patterns suggests a cause for the birds' reproductive failure. The regions of population decline coincide with areas where persistent pesticides—the chlorinated hydrocarbons such as DDT and dieldrin—are widely applied. Attrition of the predatory birds has been most severe in the eastern U.S. and in western Europe, where these pesticides first came into heavy use two decades ago. Analysis confirmed the suspicions about the pesticides: the birds were found to contain high levels of the chlorinated hydrocarbons. In areas such as northern Canada, Alaska and Spain, where the use of these chemicals has been comparatively light, the peregrine populations have remained normal or nearly normal. Recent studies show, however, that even in the relatively isolated North American arctic region the peregrines now have fairly high levels of chlorinated hydrocarbons and their populations apparently are beginning to decline.

The birds of prey are particularly vulnerable to the effects of a persistent pesticide such as DDT because they are the top of a food chain. As George M. Woodwell of the Brookhaven National Laboratory has shown, DDT accumulates to an increasingly high concentration in passing up a chain from predator to predator, and at the top of the chain it may be concentrated a thousandfold or more over the content in the original source [see "Toxic Substances and Ecological Cycles," by George M. Woodwell; SCIENTIFIC AMERICAN, March,

1967]. The predatory birds, as carnivores, feed on birds that have fed in turn on insects and plants. Hence the birds of prey accumulate a higher dose of the persistent pesticides and are more likely to suffer the toxic effects than other birds.

The idea that the predatory birds' decline is due to an internal toxic effect, rather than to a change in their behavior or their habitat, has been verified by many experiments. One of the most interesting was a field test made by Paul Spitzer, now at Cornell University, working in cooperation with the Patuxent Wildlife Research Center in Maryland. He transferred eggs from nests of the failing osprey population in New England to nests of a successful population in the Chesapeake Bay area and placed the Chesapeake eggs in the New England nests. The Chesapeake eggs hatched as successfully in the New England nests as they would have at home with their own parents, whereas the New England eggs transferred to Chesapeake nests produced as few viable young as would have been expected if they had been incubated in their original nests in New England. The experiment thus indicated that the fate of the eggs was determined by an intrinsic factor in the egg itself.

The first clue to what was happening to the predatory birds' reproduction system came in the early 1960's when Derek Ratcliffe of the British Nature Conservancy, puzzled by the extraordinary number of broken eggs he found in peregrine nests, examined the shells of peregrine eggs that had been collected over a period of many years. He found that the eggs collected since the late 1940's show a sharp drop in thickness of the shell, averaging 19 percent. Similar findings were subsequently made on peregrine eggs in North America and on the eggs of other species of predatory birds whose populations were decreasing. It became apparent that something must be wrong with the birds' calcium metabolism and that the effects of the suspected pesticides would bear looking into.

Experiments were started in several laboratories. At the Patuxent Wildlife Research Center, Richard D. Porter and Stanley N. Wiemeyer, working with kestrels, found that a mixture of DDT and dieldrin in doses measured in a few parts per million brought about a significant decrease in the shell thickness of the birds' eggs. Robert G. Heath of the Patuxent center tested the effects of

DDE, the principal metabolic product of DDT, on mallard ducks. DDE is now a ubiquitous feature of the earth's environment; it is estimated that there are a billion pounds of the substance in the world ecosystem, and traces of it have been found in animals everywhere, from polar bears in the Arctic to seals in the Antarctic. Heath found that DDE caused the failure of mallard eggs in two ways: by increasing the fragility of the eggs, leading to increased breakage soon after laying, and by the death of the embryos in intact eggs toward the end of the period of incubation. James H. Enderson of Colorado College and his associate Daniel D. Berger, studying the eggs of prairie falcons in the Southwest

desert, established that the amount of thinning of the shells and the mortality rate for the embryos were related to the quantity of DDE in the egg. Enderson and Berger also found that when they fed starlings loaded with dieldrin to falcons, the falcons' eggs showed similar thinning.

The ultimate in thinness of birds' eggshells was discovered recently in colonies of the brown pelican off the California coast. The DDE content in the eggs of this wild population (as measured by Robert Risebrough of the University of California at Berkeley) ranged as high as 2,500 parts per million, and the eggshells were so thin that the eggs could not be picked up without denting the

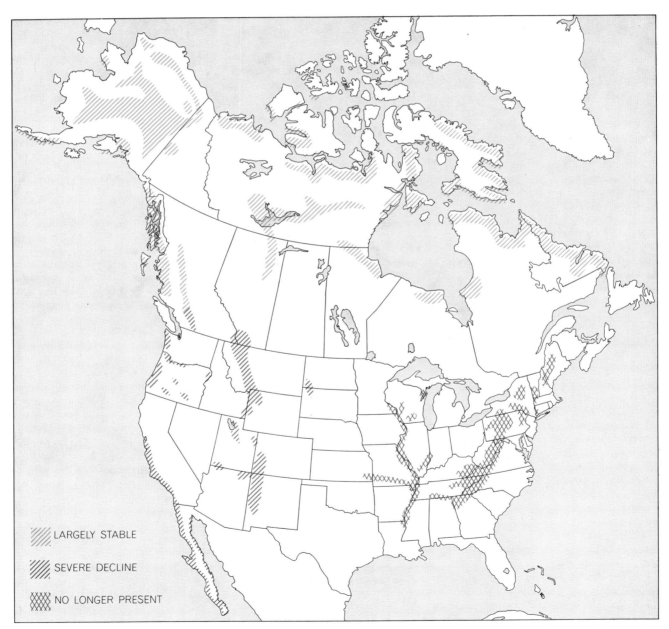

LARGELY STABLE

SEVERE DECLINE

NO LONGER PRESENT

NESTING AREAS of the peregrine falcon, or duck hawk, in the Northern Hemisphere of the New World are shown on this map. Shades of color show the extent of interference with normal reproduction resulting from ingestion of pesticides by the birds.

shells [*see illustration, page 258*]. In a colony on the Anacapa Islands off the coast it was found that the 300 pairs of nesting pelicans had not produced a single viable egg. Their nests, visited shortly after the eggs were laid, contained many broken eggs.

Field studies and laboratory experiments suggest that the thinning of eggshells does not increase in direct proportion to the DDE dose. In fact, small doses can produce dramatic effects. A content of only 75 parts per million in the egg reduces the shell thickness by more than 20 percent; beyond that, as the dose increases the decrease in shell thickness is more gradual [*see illustration at right*]. In the case of the brown pelican very heavy doses may thin the shell to a mere film.

Studies of white pelicans and cormorants have implicated the polychlorinated biphenyls (PCB's), now widely used as plasticizers, as another threat to birds of prey. These compounds cause thinning of the eggshells, although not as effectively as DDT and its metabolites do. Preliminary laboratory studies show that PCB's are particularly effective, however, in delaying the onset of breeding. The PCB's are given off when plastic materials are burned, and they are widely distributed over the earth. They resemble DDT in molecular structure and produce similar physiological actions in animals.

Much interest has focused on the question of how the chlorinated pesticides produce their destructive effects in the predatory birds—a question that is of no small concern to man, who also is the top of a food chain. Oddly enough, the beginning of light on this question came about through an accidental discovery involving an animal totally unrelated to the birds: the laboratory rat. Larry G. Hart and James R. Fouts of the University of Iowa College of Medicine were investigating the effects of food deprivation on the metabolism of drugs in rats. The drug they were using was hexobarbital, and in one experiment they were startled to find that the rats' sleeping time after receiving a standard dose of the barbiturate was much shorter than it had been in previous tests. Reexamining the conditions of the experiment, they found that the only unusual factor was that the cages had been sprayed with chlordane to control bedbugs. Pursuit of this clue led to the finding that chlordane induced rat liver cells to synthesize enzymes that speeded up the metabolism of hexobarbital. The enzymes brought about hydroxylation of the barbiturate, thereby making it more soluble

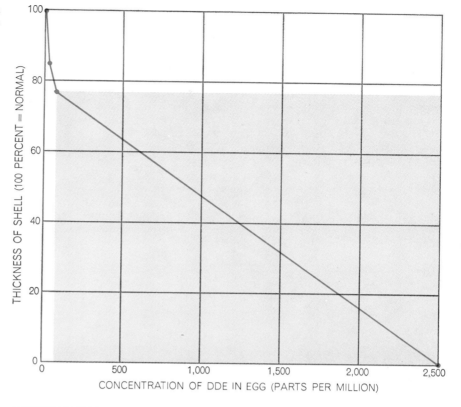

SEVERE EFFECT of the concentration of relatively small amounts of the persistent chlorinated hydrocarbon pesticides is evident in this graph. When the parent's concentration is enough to add as few as 25 parts per million of pesticide to the egg, the shell becomes 15 percent thinner than normal. Soon after the shells become more than 20 percent thinner than normal (*area of light color*) eggs are usually not found in nests because of breakage.

in water and hastening its excretion. Further experiments showed that these enzymes could hydroxylate a wide variety of substances, including the sex hormones: estrogen, testosterone and progesterone.

Because the investigators were interested primarily in drug research and their reports were published mainly in pharmacological journals, these discoveries did not come to the attention of workers studying the effects of pesticides on wildlife until several years later. I myself came on the published findings only incidentally in the course of preparing lectures for medical students. The fact that chlordane could change the balance of sex hormones in animals immediately suggested a possible explanation of the mechanism whereby the chlorinated pesticides inhibit reproduction in birds. It was capable of explaining their reproductive failure in general and the alteration of the calcium balance in the egg in particular.

My colleagues and I at Cornell University launched on a program of experiments designed to explore the interesting questions suggested by this

new aspect of the problem. To explain them I must briefly outline the complex chain of physiological events that characterizes breeding by birds. The cycle is initiated by a seasonal or climatic stimulus: the lengthening of daylight in spring in the northern Temperate Zone or rainfall in the arid and tropical regions. These signals cause an increase in the production of hormones in the nerve cells of the medial eminence of the bird's brain. The bloodstream carries these hormones to the anterior pituitary gland, which in turn dispatches to the gonads (the testes or ovaries) hormones that stimulate these organs to produce the sex hormones. The sex hormones not only generate physical changes in the reproductive organs and evoke breeding behavior but also promote the storage of a supply of calcium for the eggs.

Let us look first into the question of how a pesticide may affect the calcium supply. We carried out our experiments on the rather small Asian pigeon known as the ringdove, so that I shall describe the situation in this bird. The female forms the shell of the egg in the uterus within a period of 20 hours, and she needs 240 milligrams of calcium to pro-

CRUSHED EGG in the nest of a brown pelican off the California coast had such a thin shell that the weight of the nesting parent's body destroyed it. The concentration of DDE in the eggs of this 300-pair colony reached 2,500 parts per million; no eggs hatched.

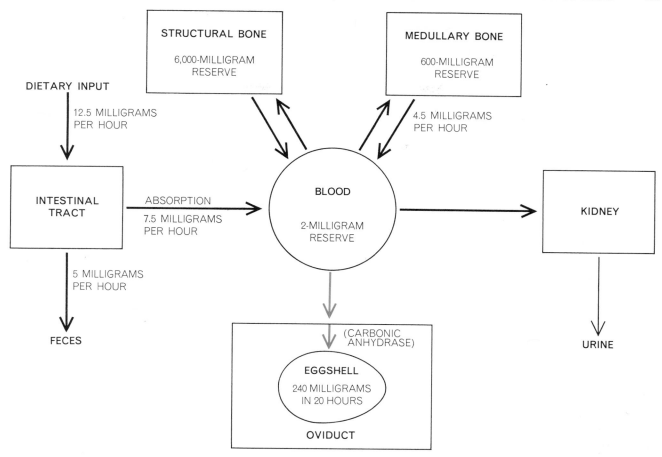

CALCIUM FOR EGGSHELL, which is formed around each egg in the last 20 hours before laying, is drawn in part from the bird's food supply and in part from calcium reserves in the bird's bones. The key to shell formation, however, is the enzyme carbonic an- hydrase, which makes the supply of calcium carried in the ring- dove's bloodstream available to the bird's oviduct at a rate of 12 milligrams per hour. When laying ringdoves are injected with DDE, the action of the enzyme is severely inhibited, causing thin shells.

duce a shell of normal thickness. Since the calcium content of the circulating blood, even at the time of ovulation, is only two milligrams (barely a 10-minute supply), the bird must draw on other sources to meet the demand. About 60 percent of the demand is supplied by the bird's food intake; the rest is provided by a store of calcium in the marrow of the bones [see "How an Eggshell Is Made," by T. G. Taylor; beginning on page 208]. This calcium reserve is laid down in the bone cavities early in the breeding cycle, and the amount of the deposit is controlled by the levels of estrogen in the blood and tissues. Obviously, therefore, a deficiency of estrogen will reduce the bird's calcium reserve. It seemed unlikely, however, that the reduction of this reserve alone could account for the drastic shell-thinning observed in eggs loaded with pesticides. If the *supply* of calcium were the sole problem, the birds could augment the supply by drawing on the calcium embodied in the skeleton; furthermore, birds on a very low calcium diet have

been found to cease egg-laying rather than laying eggs with abnormally thin shells. Was it possible, then, that the thinness of the eggshells was due less to the deficiency in supply than to a failure in delivery of calcium to the shell?

In our experiments we bred pairs of ringdoves in cages and delayed feeding the birds a pesticide until after they had completed at least one successful breeding cycle, thereby demonstrating their natural capability. For the experiment we separated the members of each pair, isolated them in individual cages where they had an eight-hour day instead of their normal 16-hour day and fed them a standard dose of DDT in their food. After three weeks we gave each bird an oral dose of radioactive calcium and returned the birds to cages with their original partners for pairing under long-day conditions. A number of days later we examined the birds, some before they laid eggs, others immediately after they finished laying their clutch. In both cases the birds showed a consid-

erable rise of enzyme activity in the liver. A substantially lower level of estrogen was found in the bloodstream of the birds that had not yet laid eggs. After the eggs had been laid, low estrogen levels were found in both experimental and control birds; this was to be expected because the level of estrogen falls at the time of egg-laying. We found that less labeled calcium was stored in the bone marrow of the experimental birds than in the marrow of control birds that had not been fed the pesticide.

Eggs laid by the pesticide-treated birds were notably thin-shelled, as was to be expected. We proceeded to experiments designed to determine whether this was due simply to the shortage of stored calcium or to something that prevented calcium from reaching the shell. In order to resolve this question we resorted to the tactic of injecting pesticides into females within a period of hours before they laid their eggs. In that short interval there would not be time for any significant change in the supply of calcium by way of an alteration of the

260

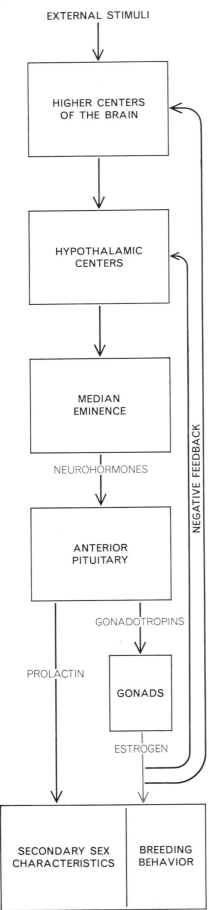

EXTERNAL STIMULI

HIGHER CENTERS
OF THE BRAIN

HYPOTHALAMIC
CENTERS

MEDIAN
EMINENCE

NEUROHORMONES

NEGATIVE FEEDBACK

ANTERIOR
PITUITARY

GONADOTROPINS

PROLACTIN

GONADS

ESTROGEN

SECONDARY SEX
CHARACTERISTICS

BREEDING
BEHAVIOR

estrogen levels through the activity of liver enzymes; consequently if the pesticide produced an effect, it would be not on the stored supply but on the delivery of calcium to the eggshell, which as we have noted is laid down within 20 hours of the laying of the egg. And with regard to delivery it was known that an enzyme, carbonic anhydrase, plays an important role in making calcium available to the eggshell in the oviduct. One could therefore look for a possible effect on the activity of this enzyme.

We tried two chlorinated hydrocarbons: dieldrin and DDE. Dieldrin, when injected into a ringdove shortly before it laid its egg, did not produce any significant thinning of the eggshell or inhibit the activity of carbonic anhydrase in the oviduct. DDE, on the other hand, severely depressed the activity of the enzyme and brought about a marked decrease in the thickness of the eggshell.

Our experiments with ringdoves also showed that the chlorinated hydrocarbons cause a significant delay in breeding by birds. Females that were fed pesticides did not lay eggs until 21.5 days (on the average) and sometimes as long as 25 days after pairing, whereas the normal interval, as indicated by the control birds, is 16.5 days on the average. The delay evidently was caused by the depression of the estrogen level resulting from the induction of liver enzymes by the pesticide. It turned out that dieldrin and the polychlorinated biphenyls were more powerful inducers of these enzymes than DDT was.

Delayed breeding is another factor in the predatory birds' population decline. Most birds do their breeding in the season when food is most plentiful, thus giving their young an optimal chance for survival. An artificial delay in their breeding consequently reduces the chances for reproductive success, and it is most serious for large birds, with their long egg-incubation period and the slower growth of the fledglings to maturity. It was found that the now extinct peregrine colonies along the Hudson River, the declining cormorant

BREEDING SUCCESS in birds involves the five sequential responses to external stimuli shown in the illustration at left. Breeding failures, due to late breeding or an inability to lay more eggs after earlier clutches are destroyed, result from the action of pesticides on the fifth response. They stimulate the activity of enzymes in the breeding bird's liver; the enzymes cut the amount of estrogen in the system below the level that is needed for normal sexual behavior.

rookery at Lake DuBay in Wisconsin and the failing pelican colonies in California were all notably late in breeding.

From this point of view it appears that dieldrin and the PCB's are greater threats to the predatory birds than DDT. Certain field and laboratory studies tend to bear out that deduction. Derek Ratcliffe and J. D. Lockie, in long-term observation of the nests of golden eagles in Scotland, found that although abnormal eggshell breakage began in 1952, about the time that DDT was introduced, marked decline in the breeding success of these birds did not begin until 1960, after the introduction of dieldrin. In laboratory experiments on the bobwhite quail James B. DeWitt and John L. George of the U.S. Fish and Wildlife Service found that one part per million of dieldrin was effective in reducing the success in hatching and survival of chicks, whereas it took 200 parts per million of DDT to produce the same effect. Robert Heath found in his studies of mallard ducks, however, that DDE severely impaired reproductive success at doses as low as 10 parts per million. Thus there appears to be a considerable difference in the effect of DDT and its metabolites on different species of birds.

We come to the following conclusions concerning the physiological mechanisms responsible for the various harmful effects on bird breeding that are brought about by the persistent insecticides. Abnormally late breeding and the failure of birds to lay eggs after their early clutches have been lost can be explained in terms of the induction of liver enzymes that lower the estrogen levels in the birds. The failure, or apparent failure, of birds to lay any eggs at all may be due either to depression of the estrogen level or to the circumstance that the eggs were broken and eaten by the parents shortly after they were laid, so that observers found no eggs in the nest on visiting them. The reduction in clutch size may also be accounted for by early breakage and eating of some of the eggs, as this has been noted mainly in cases where the nests were not checked frequently. The thinning of eggshells and breakage of the eggs evidently is due largely to the inhibition of carbonic anhydrase by DDT and its metabolites. We are left with some phenomena that are still unexplained. Why does a low dose of pesticide produce relatively more thinning of the eggshell than larger doses do? What is the mechanism that kills embryos in the shell? These questions need further investigation.

The effect of the pesticides in disturbing the calcium balance of birds probably is not of direct concern to man, because birds are a special case in their high calcium requirement at breeding time. It seems, however, that we should be concerned about the pesticides' effects on the hormone balance and on other physiological systems. The induction by pesticides of liver enzymes that lower the estrogen levels has been found in a wide variety of vertebrates, including a primate, the squirrel monkey. There is little doubt that this effect applies to man as well. Moreover, the chlorinated hydrocarbons are known to alter the glucose metabolism and inhibit an enzyme (adenosine triphosphatase, or ATPase) that plays a vital role in the energy economy of the human body.

The recent finding by investigators at the National Cancer Institute that a dose of 46 milligrams of DDT per kilogram of body weight can produce a fourfold increase in tumors of the liver, lungs and lymphoid organs of animals indicates that DDT should be banned for that reason alone. Human cancer victims have been found to have two to two and a half times more DDT in their fat than occurs in the normal population. Investigators in the U.S.S.R. recently reported that DDD, another metabolite of DDT, reduces the islets of Langerhans, the site of insulin synthesis.

The peregrine population crash has prompted two international conferences of concerned investigators, in 1965 and again in 1969. It is encouraging to note that in Britain, where severe restrictions were imposed in 1964 on the use of chlorinated hydrocarbon pesticides, the peregrine population has increased in the past two years. The Canadian government recently announced licensing restrictions that are expected to reduce the use of these pesticides by 90 percent, and many states in the U.S. are also instituting or considering such restrictions. Environmental problems do not respect political boundaries, and in the long run it will do little good if restrictions on the use of these hazardous toxins are applied only to certain regions or parts of the globe.

The long-term effects of the chlorinated hydrocarbons in the environment on human beings are admittedly much more difficult to detect or assess than the spectacular effects that have been seen in the predatory birds. Still, the story told by the birds is alarming enough. It seems obvious that agents capable of causing profound metabolic changes in such small doses should not be broadcast through the ecosystem on a billion-pound scale.

BIBLIOGRAPHIES

I DIVERSITY OF BIRDS

1. Birds as Flying Machines

THE BIOLOGY OF BIRDS. J. A. Thomson. The Macmillan Company, 1923.

THE BIRD: ITS FORM AND FUNCTION. C. W. Beebe. Henry Holt and Company, 1906.

FUNCTIONAL ANATOMY OF THE VERTEBRATES. D. P. Quiring. McGraw-Hill Book Company, Inc., 1950.

A HISTORY OF BIRDS. W. P. Pycraft. Methuen & Co., 1910.

2. The Geography of Birds

THE GEOGRAPHIC DISTRIBUTION OF ANIMALS. A. R. Wallace. Macmillan and Co., 1876.

SYSTEMATICS AND THE ORIGIN OF SPECIES. Ernst Mayr. Columbia University Press, 1942.

II FLIGHT

3. Bird Aerodynamics

THE FLIGHT OF BIRDS: ANALYZED THROUGH SLOW-MOTION PHOTOGRAPHY. John H. Storer. Cranbrook Institute of Science, Bulletin No. 28; 1948.

4. The Soaring Flight of Vultures

COMPETITION FOR FOOD BETWEEN VULTURES IN EAST AFRICA. Hans Kruuk in Ardea, Vol. 55, No. 3–4, pages 171–193; December, 1967.

NEW SOARING PILOT. A. Welch, L. Welch and F. Irving. John Murray [Publishers] Ltd., 1968.

SOARING BEHAVIOUR AND PERFORMANCE OF SOME EAST AFRICAN BIRDS, OBSERVED FROM A MOTOR-GLIDER. C. J. Pennycuick in Ibis, Vol 114, No. 2, pages 178–218; April, 1972.

5. The Energetics of Bird Flight

THE USE OF D_2O^{18} FOR MEASURING ENERGY METABOLISM IN COLUMBA LIVIA AT REST AND IN FLIGHT. Eugene A. LeFebvre in The Auk, Vol. 81, No. 3, pages 403–416; July, 1964.

RESPIRATORY EXCHANGE AND EVAPORATIVE WATER LOSS IN THE FLYING BUDGERIGAR. Vance A. Tucker in Journal of Experimental Biology, Vol. 48, No. 1, pages 67–87; February, 1968.

III   MIGRATION AND NAVIGATION

6. An Oceanic Mass Migration of Land Birds

BIRD MIGRATION. Donald R. Griffin. Natural History Press. 1964.

RADAR ORNITHOLOGY. Eric Eastwood. Methuen and Co., 1967.

AUTUMNAL BIRD MIGRATION OVER THE NORTHWESTERN ATLANTIC OCEAN. Timothy C. Williams, Janet M. Williams, Leonard C. Ireland and John M. Teal in *American Birds*, Vol. 31, No. 3, pages 251–267; May, 1977.

7. The Stellar-Orientation System of a Migratory Bird

DIE STERNENORIENTIERUNG NACHTLICH ZIEHENDER GRASMUCKEN. E. G. Franz Sauer in *Zeitschrift für Tierpsychologie*, Vol. 14, pages 29–70; 1957.

BOBOLINK MIGRATORY PATHWAYS AND THEIR EXPERIMENTAL ANALYSIS UNDER NIGHT SKIES. William J. Hamilton III in *The Auk*, Vol. 79, pages 208–233; 1962.

MIGRATORY ORIENTATION IN THE INDIGO BUNTING, PASSERINA CYANEA. PART II: MECHANISM OF CELESTIAL ORIENTATION. Stephen T. Emlen in *The Auk*, Vol. 84, pages 463–489; 1967.

BIRD MIGRATION: INFLUENCE OF PHYSIOLOGICAL STATE UPON CELESTIAL ORIENTATION. Stephen T. Emlen in *Science*, Vol. 165, No. 3894, pages 716–718; August 15, 1969.

CELESTIAL ROTATION: ITS IMPORTANCE IN THE DEVELOPMENT OF MIGRATORY ORIENTATION. Stephen T. Emlen in *Science*, Vol. 170, No. 3963, pages 1198–1201; December 11, 1970.

BIRD MIGRATION. Donald R. Griffin. Dover Publications, Inc., 1974.

8. The Mystery of Pigeon Homing

ORIENTATION BY PIGEONS: IS THE SUN NECESSARY? William T. Keeten in *Science*, Vol. 165, pages 922–928; 1969.

MAGNETS INTERFERE WITH PIGEON HOMING. William T. Keeton in *Proceedings of the National Academy of Sciences of the United States of America*, Vol. 68, No. 1, pages 102–106; January, 1971.

HOMING IN PIGEONS WITH IMPAIRED VISION. K. Schmidt-Koenig and H. J. Schlichte in *Proceedings of the National Academy of Sciences of the United States of America*, Vol. 69, No. 9, pages 2446–2447; September, 1972.

RELEASE-SITE BIAS AS A POSSIBLE GUIDE TO THE "MAP" COMPONENT IN PIGEON HOMING. William T. Keeton in *Journal of Comparative Physiology*, Vol. 86, pages 1–16; 1973.

ORIENTATION OF HOMING PIGEONS ALTERED BY A CHANGE IN THE DIRECTION OF AN APPLIED MAGNETIC FIELD. Charles Walcott and Robert P. Green in *Science*, Vol. 184, No. 4133, pages 180–182; 1974.

THE ORIENTATIONAL AND NAVIGATIONAL BASIS OF HOMING IN BIRDS. William T. Keeton in *Advances in the Study of Behavior: Vol. 5*, edited by D. S. Lehrman, R. Hindle and E. Shaw. Academic Press, 1974.

IV   EVOLUTION

9. Darwin's Finches

DARWIN'S FINCHES. David Lack. Cambridge University Press, 1947.

SYSTEMATICS AND THE ORIGIN OF SPECIES. Ernst Mayr. Columbia University Press, 1942.

10. Visual Isolation in Gulls

ANIMAL SPECIES AND EVOLUTION. Ernst Mayr. Harvard University Press, 1963.

THE EVOLUTION OF BEHAVIOR IN GULLS. N. Tinbergen in *Scientific American*, Vol. 203, No. 6, pages 118–130; December, 1960.

THE STUDY OF INSTINCT. Nikolaas Tinbergen. Oxford University Press, 1950.

11. A Study in the Evolution of Birds

CHANGE IN STATUS OF THE BRIDLED GUILLEMOT AFTER TEN YEARS. H. N. Southern in *Proceedings of the Zoological Society of London*, Vol. 121, pages 657–671; 1951.

THE GENETICAL THEORY OF NATURAL SELECTION. R. A. Fisher. Oxford University Press, 1930.

GENETICS AND THE ORIGIN OF SPECIES. Theodosius Dobzhansky. Third edition. Columbia University Press, 1951.

MORPHISM AND EVOLUTION. Julian Huxley in *Heredity*, Vol. 9, Part 1, pages 1–52; April, 1955.

POLYMORPHISM. E. B. Ford in *Biological Reviews of the Cambridge Philosophical Society*, Vol. 20, No. 2, pages 73–88; April, 1945.

THE THEORY OF ADAPTIVE POLYMORPHISM. A. J. Cain and P. M. Sheppard in *The American Naturalist*, Vol. 88, No. 842, pages 321–326; 1954.

V BEHAVIOR

12. How an Instinct Is Learned

On the Stimulus Situation Releasing the Begging Response in the Newly Hatched Herring Gull Chick (Larus argentatus argentatus Pont). N. Tinbergen and A. C. Perdeck in Behaviour, Vol. 3, pages 1–39; 1950.

A Critique of Konrad Lorenz's Theory of Instinctive Behavior. Daniel S. Lehrman in The Quarterly Review of Biology, Vol. 28, No. 4, pages 337–363; December, 1953.

An Introduction to Animal Behavior; Ethology's First Century. Peter H. Klopfer and Jack P. Hailman. Prentice-Hall, Inc., 1967.

The Ontogeny of an Instinct: The Pecking Response in Chicks of the Laughing Gull (Larus atricilla L.) and Related Species. Jack P. Hailman in Behaviour, Supplement 15; 1967.

13. Mimicry in Parasitic Birds

Character Displacement. W. L. Brown, Jr., and E. O. Wilson in Systematic Zoology, Vol. 5, pages 49–64; 1956.

Homage to Santa Rosalia, or Why Are There so Many Kinds of Animals? G. E. Hutchinson in The American Naturalist, Vol. 93, No. 870, pages 145–159; May–June, 1959.

Evolution in Changing Environments. Richard Levins. Princeton University Press, 1968.

On the Methods of Resource Division in Grassland Bird Communities. Martin L. Cody in The American Naturalist, Vol. 102, No. 924, pages 107–147; March–April, 1968.

14. Incubator Birds

Breeding Habits in the Family Megapopiidae. H. J. Frith in The Ibis, Vol. 98, No. 4, pages 620–638; October, 1956.

Nesting Habits of the Brush-Turkey. D. H. Fleay in The Emu, Vol. 36, Part 3, pages 153–163; January, 1937.

Temperature Regulation in the Nesting Mounds of the Mallee-Fowl, Leipoa Ocellata Gould. H. J. Frith in C.S.I.R.O. Wildlife Research, Vol. 1, No. 2, pages 80–95; December, 1956.

15. "Imprinting" in a Natural Laboratory

"Imprinting" in Animals. Eckhard H. Hess in Scientific American, Vol. 198, No. 3, pages 81–90; March, 1958.

Imprinting in Birds. Eckhard H. Hess in Science, Vol. 146, No. 3648, pages 1128–1139; November 27, 1964.

Innate Factors in Imprinting. Eckhard H. Hess and Dorle B. Hess in Psychonomic Science, Vol. 14, No. 3, pages 129–130; February 10, 1969.

Development of Species Identification in Birds: An Inquiry into the Prenatal Determinants of Perception. Gilbert Gottlieb. University of Chicago Press, 1971.

Natural History of Imprinting. Eckhard H. Hess in Integrative Events in Life Processes: Annals of the New York Academy of Sciences, Vol. 193, page 124; 1979.

16. The Lek Mating System of the Sage Grouse

On the Evolution of Mating Systems in Birds and Mammals. Gordon H. Orians in The American Naturalist, Vol. 103, No. 934, pages 589–603; November–December, 1969.

The Strut Display of Male Sage Grouse: A "Fixed" Action Pattern. R. Haven Wiley in Behaviour, Vol. 47, Nos. 1 and 2, pages 129–152; 1973.

Evolution of Social Organization and Life-History Patterns among Grouse. R. Haven Wiley in Quarterly Review of Biology, Vol. 49, No. 3, pages 201–227; September, 1974.

17. Ecological Chemistry

Plant Poisons in a Terrestrial Food Chain. Lincoln P. Brower, Jane Van Zandt Brower and Joseph M. Corvino in Proceedings of the National Academy of Sciences, Vol. 57, No. 4, pages 893–898; April 15, 1967.

Ecological Chemistry and the Palatability Spectrum. Lincoln P. Brower, William N. Ryerson, Lorna L. Coppinger and Susan C. Glazier in Science, Vol. 161, No. 3848, pages 1349–1350; September 27, 1968.

VI PHYSIOLOGY AND SONG

18. Salt Glands

THE SALT GLAND OF THE HERRING GULL. Ragnar Fänge, Knut Schmidt-Nielsen and Humio Osaki in *Biological Bulletin*, Vol. 115, pages 162–171; October, 1958.

SALT GLANDS IN MARINE REPTILES. Knut Schmidt-Nielsen and Ragnar Fänge in *Nature*, Vol. 182, No. 783–785; September 20, 1958.

19. The Brain of Birds

BRAIN LESIONS IN BIRDS: EFFECTS ON DISCRIMINATION ACQUISITION AND REVERSAL. Laurence J. Stettner and William J. Schultz in *Science*, Vol. 155, No. 3770, pages 1689–1692; March 31, 1967.

EFFECTS OF ENDBRAIN LESIONS UPON VISUAL DISCRIMINATION LEARNING IN PIGEONS. H. P. Zeigler in *The Journal of Comparative Neurology*, Vol. 120, No. 2, pages 161–194; April, 1963.

OBSERVATIONS ON THE COMPARATIVE ANATOMY OF THE AVIAN BRAIN. Stanley Cobb in *Perspectives in Biology and Medicine*, Vol. 3, No. 3, Spring, 1960.

20. How an Eggshell Is Made

CALCIFICATION AND OSSIFICATION. MEDULLARY BONE CHANGES IN THE REPRODUCTIVE CYCLE OF FEMALE PIGEONS. William Bloom, Margaret A. Bloom and Franklin C. McLean in *The Anatomical Record*, Vol. 81, No. 4, pages 443–475; December 26, 1941.

CALCIUM METABOLISM AND AVIAN REPRODUCTION. K. Simkiss in *Biological Reviews*, Vol. 36, No. 3, pages 321–367; August, 1961.

THE EFFECT OF PITUITARY HORMONES ON OVULATION IN CALCIUM-DEFICIENT PULLETS. T. G. Taylor, T. R. Morris and F. Hertelendy in *The Veterinary Record*, Vol. 74, No. 4, pages 123–125; January 27, 1962.

EGGSHELL FORMATION AND SKELETAL METABOLISM. T. G. Taylor and D. A. Stringer in *Avian Physiology*, edited by Paul D. Sturkie. Comstock Publishing Associates, 1965.

21. How Bird Eggs Breathe

DIFFUSION OF GASES ACROSS THE SHELL OF THE HEN'S EGG. O. Douglas Wangensteen, Donald Wilson and Hermann Rahn in *Respiration Physiology*, Vol. 11, pages 16–30; 1970–71.

RESPIRATORY GAS EXCHANGE BY THE AVIAN EMBRYO. O. Douglas Wangensteen and Hermann Rahn in *Respiration Physiology*, Vol. 11, pages 31–45; 1970–71.

RESPIRATORY PROPERTIES OF CHICKEN EMBRYONIC BLOOD DURING DEVELOPMENT. Hiroshi Tazawa, Tomohisa Mikami and Chiyoshi Yoshimoto in *Respiration Physiology*, Vol. 13, pages 160–170; 1971.

THE AVIAN EGG: AIR-CELL GAS TENSION, METABOLISM AND INCUBATION TIME. H. Rahn, C. V. Paganelli and A. Ar in *Respiration Physiology*, Vol. 22, pages 297–309; 1974.

THE AVIAN EGG: INCUBATION TIME AND WATER LOSS. H. Rahn and A. Ar in *The Condor*, Vol. 76, No. 2, pages 147–152; 1974.

22. Duet-Singing Birds

DUETTING AND ANTIPHONAL SONG IN BIRDS: ITS EXTENT AND SIGNIFICANCE. W. H. Thorpe in collaboration with J. Hall-Craggs, B. Hooker, T. Hooker and R. Hutchison in *Behaviour: Monograph Supplement XVIII*. E. J. Brill, The Netherlands, 1972.

NON-VERBAL COMMUNICATION. Edited by R. A. Hinde. Cambridge University Press, 1972.

23. How Birds Sing

BIRD SONG: ACOUSTICS AND PHYSIOLOGY. Crawford H. Greenewalt. Smithsonian Institution Press, 1968.

VII BIRDS AND PEOPLE

24. Poultry Production

THE AMERICAN STANDARD OF PERFECTION. American Poultry Association, Inc., 1966.

A HISTORY OF DOMESTICATED ANIMALS. F. E. Zeuner. Hutchinson of London, 1963.

SELECTION FOR EGG NUMBER WITH X-RAY-INDUCED VARIATION. H. Abplanalp, Dorothy C. Lowry, I. M. Lerner and E. R. Dempster in *Genetics*, Vol. 50, pages 1083–1100; November, Part 2, 1964.

THE SIGNIFICANT ADVANCES OF THE PAST FIFTY YEARS IN POULTRY NUTRITION. L. C. Norris in *Poultry Science*, Vol. 37, No. 2, pages 256–274; March, 1958.

25. Pesticides and the Reproduction of Birds

PESTICIDES AND THE LIVING LANDSCAPE. Robert L. Rudd. The University of Wisconsin Press, 1964.

PESTICIDE-INDUCED ENZYME BREAKDOWN OF STEROIDS IN BIRDS. D. B. Peakall in *Nature*, Vol. 216, No. 5114, pages 505–506; November 4, 1967.

PEREGRINE FALCON POPULATIONS: THEIR BIOLOGY AND DECLINE. Edited by Joseph J. Hickey. The University of Wisconsin Press, 1969.

MARKED DDE IMPAIRMENT OF MALLARD REPRODUCTION IN CONTROLLED STUDIES. Robert G. Heath, James W. Spann and J. F. Kreitzer in *Nature*, Vol. 224, No. 5214, pages 47–48; October 4, 1969.

FOR FURTHER READING

Bull, J., and J. Farrand, Jr. *The Audubon Field Guide to North American Birds: Eastern Region.* Knopf, New York, 1977.

Bruun, B. *The Larousse Guide to the Birds of Britain and Europe.* Larousse & Co., Inc., New York, 1978.

De Schaunsee, R. M. *The Birds of Colombia and Adjacent Areas of South and Cental America.* Livingston Publishing Co. Wynnewood, Pennsylvania, 1964.

Falla, R. A., R. B. Sibson, and E. G. Turbott. *Field Guide to the Birds of New Zealand and Outlying Islands.* Houghton Mifflin, Boston, 1967.

Farner, D. S., and J. R. King (editors). *Avian Biology* (4 vols.). Academic Press, New York, 1971–1974.

Ffrench, R. *A Guide to the Birds of Trinidad and Tobago* (rev. ed.). Harrowood Books, Newtown Square, Pennsylvania, 1976.

Fisher, J., and R. T. Peterson. *The World of Birds.* Doubleday, New York, 1964.

Glenister, A. G. *Birds of the Malay Peninsula, Singapore and Penang.* Oxford University Press, New York, 1951.

Hyde, G. E. *Birds: A Primer of Ornithology.* The English Universities Press, Ltd., London, 1962.

Lanyon, W. E. *Biology of Birds,* Natural History Press, Garden City, 1963.

Lockley, R. M. *Animal Navigation.* Hart Publishing Company, New York, 1967.

Pasquier, R. F. *An Introduction to Ornithology.* Houghton Mifflin, Boston, 1977.

Penny, Malcolm. *Birds of the Seychelles and the Outlying Islands.* Taplinger Publishing Co., New York, 1974.

Peterson, R. T. *A Field Guide to the Birds.* Houghton Mifflin, Boston, 1947.

Peterson, R. T. *A Field Guide to Western Birds.* Houghton Mifflin, Boston, 1961.

Peterson, R. T. *The Birds.* Time, Inc., New York, 1968.

Peterson, R. T., and E. L. Chalif. *A Field Guide to Mexican Birds.* Houghton Mifflin, Boston, 1973.

Peterson, R. T., G. Mountfort, and P. A. D. Hollom. *A Field Guide to the Birds of Britain and Europe* (2nd ed.). Houghton Mifflin, Boston, 1966.

Pettingill, O. S., Jr. *Ornithology in Laboratory and Field.* Burgess, Minneapolis, 1970.

Robbins, C. S., B. Bruun, and H. S. Zim. *Birds of North America.* Golden Press, New York, 1966.

Scott, P. *The World Atlas of Birds.* Random House, New York, 1974.

Udvardy, M. D. F. *The Audubon Society Field Guide to North American Birds: Western Region.* Knopf, New York, 1977.

Van Tyne, J., and A. J. Berger. *Fundamentals of Ornithology* (2nd ed.). Wiley, New York, 1976.

Welty, J. C. *The Life of Birds.* Saunders, Philadelphia, 1975.

Williams, J. G. *Field Guide to the Birds of East and Central Africa.* Houghton Mifflin, Boston, 1964.

Witherby, H. F., F. C. R. Jourdain, N. F. Ticehurst, and B. W. Tucker. *The Handbook of British Birds.* H. F. and G. Witherby, Ltd., London, 1943.

American and British Ornithological Journals

American Birds. National Audubon Society. 950 Third Avenue, New York, NY 10022.

The Auk. American Ornithologists' Union. Museum of Natural History, Smithsonian Institution, Washington, DC 20560.

Bird Study. British Trust for Ornithology. Beech Grove, Tring, Hertfordshire, England.

British Birds. 10 Meton Road, Bedford, England.

Bulletin of the British Ornithologist' Club. University Museum, Department of Zoology, Downing Street, Cambridge, England.

The Condor. Cooper Ornithological Society. Department of Biology, University of California, Los Angeles, CA 90024.

The Wilson Bulletin. Wilson Ornithological Society. The Museum of Zoology, University of Michigan, Ann Arbor, MI 48104.

Scientific American articles about birds, not included in this book

The Navigation of Birds. Donald R. Griffin. December 1948.

Bird Sonar. Donald R. Griffin. April 1952.

The Social Order of Chickens. A. M. Guhl. February 1956 (Offprint No. 471).

The Language of Birds. W. H. Thorpe. October 1956.

Penguins. William J. L. Sladen. December 1957.

Celestial Navigation by Birds. E. G. F. Sauer. August 1958.

The Language of Crows. Hubert and Mabel Frings. November 1959.

The Evolution of Behavior in Gulls. N. Tinbergen. December 1960 (Offprint No. 456).

The Behavior of Lovebirds. William C. Dilger. January 1962.

Red-Feather Money. William Davenport. March 1962.

The Soaring Flight of Birds. Clarence D. Cone. April 1962.

The Evolution of Bowerbirds. E. Thomas Gilliard. August 1963 (Offprint No. 1098).

The Antarctic Skua. Carl R. Eklund. February 1964.

The Reproductive Behavior of Ring Doves. Daniel S. Lehrman. November 1964 (Offprint No. 488).

The Navigation of Penguins. John T. Emlen and Richard L. Penny, October 1966.

The Phalarope. E. Otto Hohn. June 1969 (Offprint No. 1146).

How an Instinct Is Learned. Jack P. Hailman. December 1969 (Offprint No. 1165).

The Great Albatrosses. W. L. N. Tickell. November 1970 (Offprint No. 1204).

The Social Order of Turkeys. C. Robert Watts and Allen W. Stokes. June 1971.

How Birds Breathe. Knut Schmidt-Nielsen. December 1971.

INDEX

Geographic dispersal (*continued*)
  influence of barriers and routes in, 16
  man and, 22
  migration and, 20
  ocean currents and, 16–18
  predators and, 22
  winds and, 16
  young versus old herring gulls and, 19
Geographic distribution, 14–15, 17–22
  adaptations and, 19
  climate and food and, 16–18
  changing climate and, 15
  changing environment and, 15, 18
  evolution of species and, 15–16
  families and, 16–17
George, J. L., 260
Gilbert, J., 145
Gizzard, 181
Gliding, 24, 26, 32–33, 37
Glycosides, cardiac
  chemical structure of, 175
  effect on birds, 169, 171–176
  effect on insects, 169
Gnatcatcher, Blue-gray, threshold
    frequency of song, 236–237
Godwit, Hudsonian, migration of, 62
Goldcrests, number of eggs laid per year,
    135
Gonads, 107–108, 137, 138, 257
  See also Ovary; Testicles
Gonolek, Black-headed, 221
  duet song of, 223, 224
Goose
  Bar-headed, flight altitude of, 58
  Canada
    flight speed of, 36
    wing area and weight of, 26, 28
  Ross', migration of, 56
  Sea Brant, food supply and survival,
      18–19
Goshawk, Australian Gray, color phases
    of, 115
Gossage, H., 31
Gossette, R., 194–195
Gottlieb, G., 152
Gould, J., 99
Grebe
  Pied-billed, wing area and weight of,
      26, 28
  Western, effect of pesticides on,
      243–244
Green, H. C., 230
Green, R., 82–83
Greenewalt, C. H., 228
Grosbeaks
  bill of, 4
  migration of, 20
Goshawk, color phases of, 115
Gross, A., 20
Grouse
  blood supply to breast muscle, 13
  innate behavior, 123
  Palla's Sand, food and dispersal of, 19
  Sage
    number of eggs laid, 158
    food of, 158
    feathers of male, 160, 164
    lek mating system of, 158–167
    mortality rate in male, 164
    shelter for, 158

strutting sequence of, 162–163
weight of, 158
wing and flight of, 37
Guano birds, food and survival of, 17
Guillemot
  Brunnich's, displacement by, 117
  Common, 96–97
    color polymorphism and evolution,
        113–119
    distribution, 116
    egg and nest of, 6
    nesting sites of, 116–119
    population turnover of, 119
    size of, 116
Gull
  Black-backed, salt gland of, 191
  Glaucous
    breeding range of, 104–105
    eye color of, 103, 106, 110
    hybridization of, 96
    visual isolation of, 103–111
    wing-tip pattern of, 107
  Herring
    banding of, 20–21
    breeding range of, 101–105
    displacement by, 21
    egg air cell oxygen pressure and
        atmosphere, 216
    eye color of, 106
    instinct and learning, 130–133
    migration distance and dispersal of,
        19
    salt gland of, 191
    visual isolation of, 103–111
    wing anatomy, 36
    wing-tip pattern of, 106
    wing area and weight of, 26, 28
  Kelp, food of, 19
  Kumlien's
    breeding range of, 104–105
    eye color of, 103, 106, 110
    wing-tip pattern of, 107
    visual isolation of, 103–111
  Laughing
    displacement by, 21
    flight in wind tunnel, 46–47
    instinct and learning, 126–131
  Ring-billed
    gliding and wing of, 33
    learning by, 130
    migration and magnetic orientation,
        83
  Thayer's
    breeding range of, 104–105
    eye color of, 103, 106, 110
    feather pattern of, 107
    visual isolation of, 103–111
  Western, hybridization of, 96

Hall-Craggs, J., 223, 227
Hankin, E. H., 38
Harlow, H. F., 194
Hart, L. G., 257
Hartzler, J., 162
Hatching
  effects of pesticides, 255–261
  field versus incubator, 152
  incubator birds and, 142, 144, 148
  oxygen needed during, 210, 217

of parasitic young, 135
role in feeding instinct, 127
synchronization of, 151, 154–55
Hawk(s)
  Coopers, decline of, 255
  distribution of, 14
  eggshell pore area and egg mass, 215
  flight speed of, 58
  migration of, 56
  ovaries of, 178
  Sharp-shinned, flight speed 36
  wing of, 26
Hearing
  frequency and time perception, 236
  song perception, 227
Heart rate and weight, 12–13
Heath, R. G., 256, 260
Helmholtz coil, 82
Helmholtz H. von, 226
Heron(s)
  feet of, 6
  Great Blue
    flight speed of, 36
    wing area and weight of, 26, 28
  Little Blue, salt gland of, 191
  Louisiana, salt gland of, 191
  soaring of, 27
  wings of, 37
  territory of, 124
Hesperornis, 92, 94
Hoffman, K., 80
Hoffman, W., 96
Homeostasis, 9
Honeycreeper, Hawaiian, bills of, 94–95
Honeyguides, parasitism of, 135
Howard, H. E., 124
Hoyt, D. F., 216
Hummingbird(s)
  Allen's, metabolism and flight of, 13
  Ecuadorian, range of, 15
  egg weight, 213
  eggshell pores of, 214
  flight of, 27, 36, 53
  food of, 18
  heart weight and rate, 13
  number of species in South America,
      15
  Ruby-throated, flight speed of, 36
  wing area and weight of, 26, 28
Huxley, J., 116
Huxley, T. H., 178

Ichthyornis, 92
Imprinting, 149–157
  age after hatching and, 152
  associative learning process,
      laboratory study of, 149–157
  auditory, 149, 154–157
  electric shock, effect on, 156
  field versus laboratory method of
      study, 151–157
  Gottlieb, Gilbert, studies of, 152
  inheritance of, 155–156
  Lorenz, Konrad Z., studies of, 149
  of parasitic birds, 141
  visual, in gull, 111
Incubation
  air cell formation during, 210
  development of chicken embryo
      during, 209–212, 216–217